Ethical AI and Data Management Strategies in Marketing

Shefali Saluja
Chitkara University, India

Varun Nayyar
Chitkara University, India

Kuldeep Rojhe
Chitkara University, India

Sandhir Sharma
Chitkara University, India

A volume in the Advances in Marketing, Customer Relationship Management, and E-Services (AMCRMES) Book Series

Published in the United States of America by
IGI Global
Business Science Reference (an imprint of IGI Global)
701 E. Chocolate Avenue
Hershey PA, USA 17033
Tel: 717-533-8845
Fax: 717-533-8661
E-mail: cust@igi-global.com
Web site: http://www.igi-global.com

Copyright © 2024 by IGI Global. All rights reserved. No part of this publication may be reproduced, stored or distributed in any form or by any means, electronic or mechanical, including photocopying, without written permission from the publisher. Product or company names used in this set are for identification purposes only. Inclusion of the names of the products or companies does not indicate a claim of ownership by IGI Global of the trademark or registered trademark.

Library of Congress Cataloging-in-Publication Data

CIP Pending

Ethical AI and Data Management Strategies in Marketing
Shefali Saluja, Varun Nayyar, Kuldeep Rojhe, Sandhir Sharma
2024 Business Science Reference

ISBN: 979-8-3693-6660-8
eISBN: 979-8-3693-6662-2

British Cataloguing in Publication Data
A Cataloguing in Publication record for this book is available from the British Library.

The views expressed in this book are those of the authors, but not necessarily of the publisher.

For electronic access to this publication, please contact: eresources@igi-global.com.

Advances in Marketing, Customer Relationship Management, and E-Services (AMCRMES) Book Series

Eldon Y. Li
National Chengchi University, Taiwan & California Polytechnic State University, USA

ISSN:2327-5502
EISSN:2327-5529

Mission

Business processes, services, and communications are important factors in the management of good customer relationship, which is the foundation of any well organized business. Technology continues to play a vital role in the organization and automation of business processes for marketing, sales, and customer service. These features aid in the attraction of new clients and maintaining existing relationships.

The Advances in Marketing, Customer Relationship Management, and E-Services (AMCRMES) Book Series addresses success factors for customer relationship management, marketing, and electronic services and its performance outcomes. This collection of reference source covers aspects of consumer behavior and marketing business strategies aiming towards researchers, scholars, and practitioners in the fields of marketing management.

Coverage

- Online Community Management and Behavior
- Telemarketing
- Mobile Services
- Legal Considerations in E-Marketing
- Customer Retention
- Text Mining and Marketing
- Data mining and marketing
- B2B Marketing
- Ethical Considerations in E-Marketing
- Database marketing

IGI Global is currently accepting manuscripts for publication within this series. To submit a proposal for a volume in this series, please contact our Acquisition Editors at Acquisitions@igi-global.com or visit: http://www.igi-global.com/publish/.

The Advances in Marketing, Customer Relationship Management, and E-Services (AMCRMES) Book Series (ISSN 2327-5502) is published by IGI Global, 701 E. Chocolate Avenue, Hershey, PA 17033-1240, USA, www.igi-global.com. This series is composed of titles available for purchase individually; each title is edited to be contextually exclusive from any other title within the series. For pricing and ordering information please visit http://www.igi-global.com/book-series/advances-marketing-customer-relationship-management/37150. Postmaster: Send all address changes to above address. Copyright © 2024 IGI Global. All rights, including translation in other languages reserved by the publisher. No part of this series may be reproduced or used in any form or by any means – graphics, electronic, or mechanical, including photocopying, recording, taping, or information and retrieval systems – without written permission from the publisher, except for non commercial, educational use, including classroom teaching purposes. The views expressed in this series are those of the authors, but not necessarily of IGI Global.

Titles in this Series

For a list of additional titles in this series, please visit: www.igi-global.com/book-series

Driving Green Marketing in Fashion and Retail
Theodore K. Tarnanidis (International Hellenic University, Greece) Evridiki Papachristou (International Hellenic University, Greece) Michail Karypidis (International Hellenic University, Greece) and Vasileios Ismyrlis (Hellenic Statistical Authority, Greece)
Business Science Reference • copyright 2024 • 312pp • H/C (ISBN: 9798369330494) • US $295.00 (cur price)

Global Perspectives on Social Media Influencers and Strategic Business Communication
Nicky Chang Bi (University of Nebraska at Omaha, USA) and Ruonan Zhang (Rollins College, USA)
Business Science Reference • copyright 2024 • 430pp • H/C (ISBN: 9798369309124) • US $300.00 (our price)

Future of Customer Engagement Through Marketing Intelligence
Mudita Sinha (Christ University, India) Arabinda Bhandari (Presidency University, India) Samant Shant Priya (Lal Bahadur Shastri Institute of Management, India) and Sajal Kabiraj (Häme University of Applied Sciences, Finland)
Business Science Reference • copyright 2024 • 286pp • H/C (ISBN: 9798369323670) • US $355.00 (our price)

New Trends in Marketing and Consumer Science
Theodore K. Tarnanidis (University of Macedonia, Greece) and Nikolaos Sklavounos (International Hellenic University, Greece)
Business Science Reference • copyright 2024 • 516pp • H/C (ISBN: 9798369327548) • US $365.00 (our price)

AI Innovation in Services Marketing
Ricardo Correia (Instituto Politécnico de Bragança, Portugal & CiTUR, Portugal) and Dominyka Venciute (ISM University of Management and Economics, Lithuania)
Business Science Reference • copyright 2024 • 299pp • H/C (ISBN: 9798369321539) • US $285.00 (our price)

Ethical Marketing Through Data Governance Standards and Effective Technology
Shefali Saluja (Chitkara Business School, Chitkara University, India) Varun Nayyar (Chitkara University, India) Kuldeep Rojhe (Chitkara University, India) and Sandhir Sharma (Chitkara Business School, Chitkara University, India)
Business Science Reference • copyright 2024 • 328pp • H/C (ISBN: 9798369322154) • US $285.00 (our price)

701 East Chocolate Avenue, Hershey, PA 17033, USA
Tel: 717-533-8845 x100 • Fax: 717-533-8661
E-Mail: cust@igi-global.com • www.igi-global.com

Table of Contents

Preface xvi

Chapter 1
A Preliminary Study on Ethics and Sustainability in Hospitality Employer Branding 1
    Vasco Ribeiro Santos, ISLA Santarém, Portugal & GOVCOPP, Portugal
    Patrícia Simão, ISLA Santarém, Portugal
    Filipa Martinho, ISLA Santarém, Portugal
    Bruno Sousa, Polytechnic Institute of Cávado and Ave, Portugal & CiTUR, Portugal
    Isabel Reis, ISLA Santarém, Portugal & CEFAGE, Portugal
    Marta Sampaio, ISLA Santarém, Portugal & CEFAGE, Portugal

Chapter 2
AI in Marketing: AI-Powered Chatbot 11
    Chander Prabha, Chitkara University Institute of Engineering and Technology, Chitkara University, Punjab, India
    Shalini Kumari, Chitkara University Institute of Engineering and Technology, Chitkara University, Punjab, India

Chapter 3
Analyzing Demarketing Through Bibliometric Methods 26
    Kavya Shabu, Dayananda Sagar University, India
    Pragathi Prakash, Dayananda Sagar University, India
    Truptha Shankar, Dayananda Sagar University, India

Chapter 4
Blockchain and Its Derived Technologies: Shaping the Future Generation of Digital Businesses With a Focus on Decentralized Finance and the Metaverse 41
    Gurwinder Kaur Dua, Post Graduate Government College, Chandigarh, India

Chapter 5
Consumer Policy: The Relationship Between AI and Data Privacy 56
    Chander Prabha, Chitkara University Institute of Engineering and Technology, Chitkara University, Punjab, India
    Shefali Saluja, ChItkara University, Punjab, India

Chapter 6
Digital Transformation of Marketing Processes, Customer Privacy, Data Security, and Emerging Challenges in Fostering Sustainable Digital Marketing 71
    Hina Gull, Imam Abdulrahman Bin Faisal University, Dammam, Saudi Arabia
    Saqib Saeed, Imam Abdulrahman Bin Faisal University, Dammam, Saudi Arabia
    Hamzah A. K. Alaied, Imam Abdulrahman Bin Faisal University, Dammam, Saudi Arabia
    Ali N. A. Alajmi, Imam Abdulrahman Bin Faisal University, Dammam, Saudi Arabia
    Madeeha Saqib, Imam Abdulrahman Bin Faisal University, Dammam, Saudi Arabia
    Sardar Zafar Iqbal, Imam Abdulrahman Bin Faisal University, Dammam, Saudi Arabia
    Abdullah M. Almuhaideb, Imam Abdulrahman Bin Faisal University, Dammam, Saudi Arabia

Chapter 7
Global Ambitions, Local Realities: Uber Eats' Marketing Strategy in India and Its Demise 89
    Gurloveleen Kaur, Chitkara University, India
    Megha Goyal, Chitkara University, India

Chapter 8
Impact of e-WOM on the Brand Image and Purchase Intention of the Consumer: An Empirical Study 108
    Namita Kochhar, GNA University, Phagwara, India
    Nidhi Bhagat, Lovely Professional University, India

Chapter 9
Revolutionizing Marketing by Utilizing the Power of Artificial Intelligence 125
    Priya Jindal, Chitkara Business School, Chitkara University, Punjab India
    Anju Rohilla, Panipat Institiute of Engineering and Technology, India

Chapter 10
Leveraging Artificial Intelligence in Education: Enhancing Learning Experience 140
    Sargunpreet Kaur, Lovely Professional University, India
    Komal Budhraja, Fortune Institute of International Business, India
    Anurag Pahuja, Lovely Professional University, India
    Varun Nayyar, Chitkara University, India
    Shefali Saluja, Chitkara University, India

Chapter 11
Science Mapping of "Artificial Intelligence in Education" Literature Landscape: A Bibliometric and Content Analysis Discourse 156
    Ajay Chandel, Lovely Professional University, India
    Anjali Sharma, Mittal School of Business, Lovely Professional University, India
    Abbineni Praveen Chowdary, Lovely Professional University, India
    Shefali Saluja, Chitkara University, India

Chapter 12
Role of Artificial Intelligence in Strategic Debt Sustainability Planning 177
    Shveta Gupta, Chitkara University, India
    Gurwinder Singh Badal, Chitkara University, India
    Dhiresh Kulshrestha, Chitkara University, India

Chapter 13
Rise of Artificial Intelligence in Marketing: Strategies for Ethical Implementation 186
    Jaswinder Pal Singh, Chitkara University, Punjab, India
    Neha Mishra, Chitkara University, Punjab, India

Chapter 14
Unveiling the Transformative Landscape: A Bibliometric Exploration of AI Integration in
Healthcare 205
    Ajay Chandel, Lovely Professional University, India
    Krishan Gopal, Lovely Professional University, India
    Anurag Pahuja, Lovely Professional University, India
    Varun Nayyar, Chitkara University, India

Chapter 15
Examining the Impact of AI on Education: Ethical, Psychological, and Pedagogical Perspectives .. 223
    Anurag Pahuja, Lovely Professional University, India
    Sargunpreet Kaur, Lovely Professional University, India
    Komal Budhraja, Fortune Institute of International Business, India
    Sakshi Kathuria, Fortune Institute of International Business, India

Chapter 16
Addressing Ethical Concerns in Digital Marketing: Challenges, Strategies, and Industry
Participation 241
    Gurloveleen Kaur Maan, Chitkara University, India
    Navleen Kaur, Sri Guru Granth Sahib World University, India

Compilation of References 256

About the Contributors 288

Index 292

Detailed Table of Contents

Preface xvi

Chapter 1
A Preliminary Study on Ethics and Sustainability in Hospitality Employer Branding 1
    Vasco Ribeiro Santos, ISLA Santarém, Portugal & GOVCOPP, Portugal
    Patrícia Simão, ISLA Santarém, Portugal
    Filipa Martinho, ISLA Santarém, Portugal
    Bruno Sousa, Polytechnic Institute of Cávado and Ave, Portugal & CiTUR, Portugal
    Isabel Reis, ISLA Santarém, Portugal & CEFAGE, Portugal
    Marta Sampaio, ISLA Santarém, Portugal & CEFAGE, Portugal

Tourism is currently one of the main sectors of profit for the worldwide economy. The new segments of ethical and sustainable tourists increasingly seek to obtain unique and sustainable experiences during their trip and stay, thus creating a greater connection with the destination, acquiring cultural and personal enrichment, and thus having a greener consumption. This pre-liminary research aims to explore ethics and sustainability in employer branding applied in the hotel industry, in which it is intended to correlate these very current and little explored themes. From an interdisciplinary perspective, the chapter presents insights for tourism marketing and organizational management (i.e. ethics and employer branding). Findings and practical implications for management are presented.

Chapter 2
AI in Marketing: AI-Powered Chatbot 11
    Chander Prabha, Chitkara University Institute of Engineering and Technology, Chitkara
        University, Punjab, India
    Shalini Kumari, Chitkara University Institute of Engineering and Technology, Chitkara
        University, Punjab, India

Chatbots in marketing employ artificial intelligence (AI) and natural language processing (NLP) to quickly and accurately answer client questions. Chatbots may learn and forecast consumer needs without human intervention, enhancing service and satisfaction. Digital marketing AI chatbots identify relevant online data points and optimize activities for clients and businesses. The scripted, rule-based, and AI-powered chatbots are leading AI chatbots that learn from previous interactions, personalize depending on customer profiles and preferences, and use predictive intelligence and analytics. Chatbots minimize support and live operator utilization, saving businesses money and time by automating user experience and transactional functions. AI in marketing and chatbots for customer care, sales, shopping, and marketing are covered in this chapter. However, chatbots can't handle complex requests or recognize human traits. Chatbots should not replace human connection and should boost customer pleasure and help through AI marketing.

Chapter 3
Analyzing Demarketing Through Bibliometric Methods 26
    Kavya Shabu, Dayananda Sagar University, India
    Pragathi Prakash, Dayananda Sagar University, India
    Truptha Shankar, Dayananda Sagar University, India

Marketing is the game changing strategic tool used to influence and nudge consumer behaviour towards a product. Demarketing is an inverse marketing strategy which would help shape the demand and behaviour of the consumer. This chapter intends to bring forward the prominent papers and research made along with the leading authors in this area, identification of research areas yet to be explored, the thematic perception of research through which the topic of demarketing has been approached. Through this chapter it found that more stress is given to demarketing in the field of health concerns and sustainable tourism, while identifying some of the core source papers in this area and prominent papers by Philip Kotler acting as a base in this area.

Chapter 4
Blockchain and Its Derived Technologies: Shaping the Future Generation of Digital Businesses
With a Focus on Decentralized Finance and the Metaverse 41
    Gurwinder Kaur Dua, Post Graduate Government College, Chandigarh, India

Indeed, blockchain played a pivotal role in the Industrial Revolution and is considered as one of the most valuable technological developments that evolved from the past years. Decentralized finance (DeFi) and the metaverse have roots in blockchain which has brought a fundamental transition in people's lives. These evolving technologies have a major effect on the future landscape of digital platforms. This study delved into the development of digital trades in the coming future, with a special focus on the aforementioned fundamental technologies. Initially, this study scrutinized DeFi-based technologies, encompassing GameFi, SciFi, SocialFi, and other foundational elements crucial for upcoming job roles and businesses. Subsequently, the authors explored metaverse-based occupations, including metaverse-based educational institutions and markets anticipated to emerge as widely adopted enterprises.

Chapter 5
Consumer Policy: The Relationship Between AI and Data Privacy.. 56
    Chander Prabha, Chitkara University Institute of Engineering and Technology, Chitkara
        University, Punjab, India
    Shefali Saluja, ChItkara University, Punjab, India

Consumer policy is designed to protect welfare and rights of consumers. The recent advancements in artificial intelligence (AI) and its integration with the privacy aspects of consumer information need potential attention due to illegal activities in terms of fraud. The rapid progress of AI represents significant risks to safeguarding consumer privacy and ensuring data security. The integration of AI inside several industries, such as e-commerce platforms, and financial technology, has become prevalent. This leads to emphasizing the significance of developing comprehensive legal and regulatory frameworks to address effectively the challenges related to consent, data minimization, accuracy, discrimination, and bias. The chapter explores the concept of AI and its public and private use in consumer policies. The key components are highlighted in making consumer policy along with the relationship between AI and data privacy aspects. Finally, it presents the challenges faced by consumers in accessing vital information, that lead to imbalances between companies and customers.

Chapter 6
Digital Transformation of Marketing Processes, Customer Privacy, Data Security, and Emerging
Challenges in Fostering Sustainable Digital Marketing 71
    Hina Gull, Imam Abdulrahman Bin Faisal University, Dammam, Saudi Arabia
    Saqib Saeed, Imam Abdulrahman Bin Faisal University, Dammam, Saudi Arabia
    Hamzah A. K. Alaied, Imam Abdulrahman Bin Faisal University, Dammam, Saudi Arabia
    Ali N. A. Alajmi, Imam Abdulrahman Bin Faisal University, Dammam, Saudi Arabia
    Madeeha Saqib, Imam Abdulrahman Bin Faisal University, Dammam, Saudi Arabia
    Sardar Zafar Iqbal, Imam Abdulrahman Bin Faisal University, Dammam, Saudi Arabia
    Abdullah M. Almuhaideb, Imam Abdulrahman Bin Faisal University, Dammam, Saudi Arabia

Marketing is a core business function to communicate the value of a product to its customers. Digital technologies have transformed this business function into digital marketing, which is the core focus of the digital transformation drive of business organizations. Digital marketing relies on modern technologies to reach out to prospective customers, and other stakeholders in the community. However, this technological transformation has brought data security and privacy challenges for organizations as well. In this chapter, the authors have conducted a systematic literature review to understand these challenges and presented a framework for organizations to respond to these challenges in an agile manner. This framework outlined four key enablers and associated strategies to better achieve these enablers to foster a sustainable digital marketing process in business organizations. This framework benefits business organizations and policymakers to improve the digital marketing effectiveness of their organizations to maximize the benefits of digital transformation.

Chapter 7
Global Ambitions, Local Realities: Uber Eats' Marketing Strategy in India and Its Demise 89
    Gurloveleen Kaur, Chitkara University, India
    Megha Goyal, Chitkara University, India

This case examines Uber Eats' journey since its inception in 2014, focusing on its challenges in India. It showcases how Uber Eats adapted to serve customers globally, handling rapid growth, technological advancements, and partnerships. Despite facing hurdles like operational efficiency and the COVID-19 pandemic, Uber Eats emphasized innovation to stay ahead. The case also looks at Zomato's acquisition of Uber Eats in India, highlighting its impact on the food delivery industry and competition with Swiggy. It aims to offer insights into Uber Eats' performance, partnerships, and competition, providing valuable lessons for industry players. The case concludes with discussion questions to deepen understanding of strategic initiatives and industry trends.

Chapter 8
Impact of e-WOM on the Brand Image and Purchase Intention of the Consumer: An Empirical Study 108
    Namita Kochhar, GNA University, Phagwara, India
    Nidhi Bhagat, Lovely Professional University, India

In this digital age, any information is just a click away, whether it is relating to business news or the fashion world. Consumers today do not rely on print media for any news; rather, they resort to online platforms for exploring the details with regard to the any product or services before making any buying decisions. In this chapter, the researcher has tried to explore how e-WOM has influenced the brand image and shaped consumers' perception towards product purchase decisions. The population of the study are the customers who use online platforms for purchasing or making purchase decisions. A structured questionnaire has been filled in by 341 respondents so as to analyse the impact of factors on the consumer's perception of purchase. The statistical technique used is SEM. The findings indicate that electronic word of mouth (e-WOM) significantly affects brand image and also has a substantial impact on purchase intentions. Further, brand image of a product also influences the consumer buying decisions.

Chapter 9
Revolutionizing Marketing by Utilizing the Power of Artificial Intelligence 125
    Priya Jindal, Chitkara Business School, Chitkara University, Punjab India
    Anju Rohilla, Panipat Institiute of Engineering and Technology, India

Industrial 4.0 redesigned the way the business manufactures and distributes their product among customers. Artificial intelligence occupies its place in almost every type of business and its operation. The chapter aims to explore the ways how the artificial intelligence is integrated into marketing domain and helps the marketers in making sound strategies. In order to understand the use of artificial intelligence in marketing and identifying its implication on marketing industry, the review of the available literature is conducted. The study shows that the employment of artificial intelligence in marketing operations aids the firm in identifying the target market, offering the highly personalized services, achieving the time and cost efficiency through automation, effectively engage the customers and enhances connectivity with customer across the multiple platforms. The study also reveals the various AI tools used by the firm to stimulate their marketing operations and to stay competitive in this digital era.

Chapter 10
Leveraging Artificial Intelligence in Education: Enhancing Learning Experience............................ 140
    Sargunpreet Kaur, Lovely Professional University, India
    Komal Budhraja, Fortune Institute of International Business, India
    Anurag Pahuja, Lovely Professional University, India
    Varun Nayyar, Chitkara University, India
    Shefali Saluja, Chitkara University, India

The integration of artificial intelligence (AI) technologies into education has emerged as a promising avenue to revolutionize the learning experience. With the use of AI tools and methodologies, teachers can tailor educational pathways to suit their students' individual needs, respond to differences in teaching style and provide prompt feedback so that they are more engaged and comprehended. Various applications of artificial intelligence in the field of education such as intelligent tutoring systems, adaptive learning platforms, and natural language processing tools are examined to highlight their effectiveness for dealing with educational challenges and supporting student success. This chapter looks at the potential of artificial intelligence for improving education practices, with a focus on increasing learning processes and optimising student results. It highlights the importance of responsible use of AI to reduce biases and ensure equal opportunities for all in order to address concerns about ethics and possible problems related to integration of AI into education.

Chapter 11
Science Mapping of "Artificial Intelligence in Education" Literature Landscape: A Bibliometric and Content Analysis Discourse 156
    Ajay Chandel, Lovely Professional University, India
    Anjali Sharma, Mittal School of Business, Lovely Professional University, India
    Abbineni Praveen Chowdary, Lovely Professional University, India
    Shefali Saluja, Chitkara University, India

Educational methods are being transformed by AI-powered systems that enable independent study, tailored instruction, and the gaining of varied disciplines. On the other hand, AI's use in education has also sparked a global debate on areas related to ethics in classroom education. The objective of this work is to present a thorough examination of academic literature about the application and challenges of artificial intelligence (AI) in educational settings. Through the use of sophisticated bibliometric methods such as co-citation analysis, bibliographic coupling, and keyword co-occurrence analysis, the of this work is to map out the ongoing debate on use of artificial intelligence in education and identify the underlying patterns, connections, and new developments in this area. The chapter proposes future routes for research and innovation in this quickly developing field in addition to providing insights on the historical evolution and current status of AI in education.

Chapter 12
Role of Artificial Intelligence in Strategic Debt Sustainability Planning 177
    Shveta Gupta, Chitkara University, India
    Gurwinder Singh Badal, Chitkara University, India
    Dhiresh Kulshrestha, Chitkara University, India

Artificial intelligence is being utilised to discover fiscal hazards, shady tendencies and patterns, and dangerous entities in revenue creation. Previously, public debt was regarded as a vital tool for temporarily increasing revenue or purchasing power in exchange for the government's commitment to repay the main sum borrowed and, in most cases, interest on that principal. However, it has now become a permanent feature. The purpose of the government borrowing is to fill up the gap between the government revenue and proposed spending for the fiscal year. The objective of the study is to examine the significance of artificial intelligence in estimating the public debt on fiscal deficit of the government's, and to examine the trends in the revenue and fiscal deficits, with the view to identify the factors responsible for the same. The secondary data has been collected from Union Government's budget documents of various years. Further economic surveys and various other publications of Government of India, RBI, and other regulatory bodies has also been used to collect data and other relevant information. To analyse the collected data, statistical techniques such as solow model, trend regression analysis, and ratio analysis etc., has been used. The analysis results found that liabilities and debt in relation to GSDP have been increasing, and this has been particularly noticeable throughout the UDAY scheme's execution era and efficiency can be achieved with the use of AI in the field. However, the debt-to-GDP ratio is significantly below the 25% target set by the fourteenth finance commission.

Chapter 13
Rise of Artificial Intelligence in Marketing: Strategies for Ethical Implementation......................... 186
    Jaswinder Pal Singh, Chitkara University, Punjab, India
    Neha Mishra, Chitkara University, Punjab, India

The chapter provides an overview of the wide-ranging impact of artificial intelligence (AI) on commercial opportunities, emphasizing its various applications and ethical considerations. It discusses AI's role in enhancing industry efficiency, banking transactions, marketing, and beyond, while also addressing concerns such as bias, discrimination, and data protection. The chapter underscores the importance of AI ethics and the need for responsible development and usage, as highlighted by the implementation of AI codes of ethics by tech companies. It further explores major ethical issues related to autonomous AI systems, including machine bias, privacy concerns, and job displacement, particularly in the marketing industry. Additionally, it mentions the European Commission's efforts to establish ethical principles for trustworthy AI and the legal implications of AI marketing, such as data privacy and consumer protection laws. Finally, it suggests the role of government and regulators in setting AI marketing technology laws to ensure fair competition and market practices.

Chapter 14

Unveiling the Transformative Landscape: A Bibliometric Exploration of AI Integration in Healthcare 205

    Ajay Chandel, Lovely Professional University, India
    Krishan Gopal, Lovely Professional University, India
    Anurag Pahuja, Lovely Professional University, India
    Varun Nayyar, Chitkara University, India

This study uses bibliometric analysis to investigate the methods, thematic insights, and revolutionary possibilities of AI integration in healthcare. It provides insights into the evolution of AI in healthcare through topic mapping, keyword co-occurrence, co-citation, and bibliographic coupling. Keyword co-occurrence highlights important themes like federated learning, digital healthcare, and the internet of things, while co-citation analysis identifies emerging subjects like federated machine learning. The relationships between different research streams and the effects of explainable AI and machine learning on healthcare IT are made clear by the bibliographic coupling. Thematic mapping offers a graphic synopsis of several subjects, from systemic modifications to technical innovations. By educating stakeholders, this study helps them make decisions and sets the stage for future research. It directs efforts to maximize AI's potential for bettering patient outcomes and providing healthcare to practitioners, policymakers, and researchers.

Chapter 15

Examining the Impact of AI on Education: Ethical, Psychological, and Pedagogical Perspectives .. 223

    Anurag Pahuja, Lovely Professional University, India
    Sargunpreet Kaur, Lovely Professional University, India
    Komal Budhraja, Fortune Institute of International Business, India
    Sakshi Kathuria, Fortune Institute of International Business, India

Education is a fundamental aspect of human development, crucial for both individuals and societies. This chapter provides a comprehensive exploration of education, its significance, and its multifaceted nature. Education encompasses the acquisition of knowledge, skills, values, and attitudes through formal and informal means. It empowers individuals to understand their environment, make informed decisions, and contribute to society's betterment. However, the integration of artificial intelligence (AI) in education raises ethical, psychological, and pedagogical concerns. AI's capability to generate coherent responses may compromise academic integrity and undermine critical thinking. Furthermore, excessive dependence on AI may diminish students' motivation and self-efficacy, leading to passive learning and eroding trust in the educational system. Pedagogically, AI cannot replace the nuanced guidance and personalized feedback offered by teachers, potentially disrupting the traditional teacher-student dynamic.

Chapter 16
Addressing Ethical Concerns in Digital Marketing: Challenges, Strategies, and Industry Participation 241
    Gurloveleen Kaur Maan, Chitkara University, India
    Navleen Kaur, Sri Guru Granth Sahib World University, India

The study comprises social and cultural issues pertaining to buying and selling on the digital platform. Ethics in marketing plays a vital role in building sustainable goals. The aim of writing the chapter is to throw light on the psychological influences of the customers while ethically imparting the product information through the marketers. The varied marketing strategies like remarketing, pay per click, demographic targeting, emotional and social bond connectivity, etc., are discussed with real cases of Abbot shoes, Surf excel, Red Label, Patagonia, and others. Market research, data collection, truthful branding, ethical digital advertising, regulatory compliances, and others are a few challenges observed in the proper execution of digital marketing. It is not just a mere saying by companies that we are following the right practices; they need to follow the same in their day-to-day operations. Tata Steel, Wipro, Just Water, Ocado, Hello Fresh, People Tree's and others are few renowned organizations using the sources of digital marketing in the right direction.

Compilation of References 256

About the Contributors 288

Index 292

Preface

INTRODUCTION

In order to achieve the one source of information that marketers strive for, an effective data governance strategy should aim to eliminate silos and establish regulations for data classification, storage, and processing. As we know, AI marketing also refers to the application of artificial intelligence by marketers to learn more about their target audience and create more effective content. So marketing for firms these days, especially on digital platforms, requires critical thinking on data management systems, machine learning methods, and attributes like customer trust, societal ethics, and managing consumer feedback with the utmost utilisation of technology in different ways. Considering the fierce rivalry in the industry and the accessibility of vast, diverse, and intricate information, it is still debatable how businesses might use big data to their advantage at various analytical levels and create effective marketing strategies. Moreover, as technology evolves further, a greater stream of digitalized data will be produced, necessitating the integration of people and processes and making corporates to utilize this data for competitive edge, advancements, and information management to add value to their existing businesses. It also seems that ethical concerns such as protecting data privacy and security when using sensitive consumer information should be addressed by ethical businesses where prior consent is required while accessing personal information and guaranteeing the integrity of big data usage as well as the equitable treatment of stakeholders.

Data management with ethical standards would entail analyzing the data generated digitally on several digital platforms and then trying to understand these users' data in relation to their consumption behaviour, monitoring applications that manage the traffic of networks, and finally building eco-enterprise models that can enable economic and social values with effective ethical standards. No doubt, it is a predefined notion that the value of big data analytics is an upheld task to be taken care of by all tech experts, but meanwhile, it is also questionable about the morality of its use and its final implementation to create ease of technology adaptation while keeping into consideration data governance standards. Other than this, studying the advertising standards and challenges on online platforms with the adoption of technology, where virtual assistance in the form of avatars is serving companies while handling consumer psychological mindsets with their database management, is again a big challenge to work on. Finally, learning database governance strategy as a whole is vital for corporates to manage their online marketing operations in the best manner possible with the adoption of ethical standards for carrying out operations that ultimately benefit consumers on different web or social media platforms.

RELEVANCE OF ETHICAL AI AND DATA MANAGEMENT STRATEGIES IN MARKETING

Due to the rapid changes in the field of technology, it has become crucial and important aspects of current research to touch on the relevant data governance standards to help marketers follow ethical ways of using the digital data of online consumers in today's global economy. Companies will need to go beyond privacy and security of data to guarantee that data is handled ethically both inside and outside the company in order to maintain customer confidence. Similar to the effects of climate change, information misuse is spreading over the world and necessitating significant response. In light of the ever-evolving behavior of consumers, the study of ethical data governance and its application in the current world of marketing has assumed a lot of significance to provide a safe and secure journey for online consumers. The level of data breaches in current times requires vast data governance strategies to create high-end value for all concerned and preserve and implement sustainable practices as per industry standards. In the coming times, strict implementation of data governance standards is going to pick up pace to create ease in providing better consumer privacy in their data being used by companies for higher promotions of products and services. Companies are now highly calibrated to work on data governance standards so that their future is safe and they are at ease when they come across the competitive standards being set up by corporates. It provides guidelines for the proper use of data in the public sector, highlighting the significance to moral frameworks and community norms. These frameworks act as recommendations for comprehending the ethical and practical ramifications of technology, data processing, and data dissemination. An ethically motivated strategy for data governance promotes good data literacy, adherence to privacy regulations, and responsible utilization of the technologies used to create, process, and disseminate data. With such development, a new era of opportunity seems to be prevailing, which leads to sustainable development for people, government, and corporate stakeholders, enriching the end experience of consumers and providing high-end protection for their daily needs.

Target Audience

It has been projected that the book would benefit a broader range of various industries, embracing businesses, authorities, academia, and the public at large. In the global economy of today, this study is beneficial in touching on pertinent data governance principles to assist marketers in leveraging online consumer digital information in an ethical manner. Here, the companies who think that safeguarding client trust is their prime task, this work makes companies look beyond the protection of data and privacy and make sure that data is treated wisely within as well as outside the organization. The book empowers how ethical marketing through data governance standards and the effective usage of modern technology can set new standards for emerging markets to be captured by organizations by setting up new strategies and even exceeding them to achieve global presence with high-end convenience, which can be termed extremely advantageous, leading to a highly efficient environment. Enterprises are now keen to work on data governance standards with the aim to secure the future of their company and appear at ease when they confront company norms that are set competitively. The authors evaluated the benefits and relevant effects of accepting learning database governance plan as a whole, which is equally essential for companies to run their online marketing operations as efficiently as possible. This book is suitable for customers, students, and businesses who are eager to learn about security standards.

CHAPTER CONTRIBUTION

Chapter 1: A Preliminary Study on Ethics and Sustainability in Hospitality Employer Branding

This chapter addresses the intersection of growing consumer expectations and corporate identity initiatives when special contributions are considered in the hospitality industry. The results section of the current research clearly demonstrates this.

Chapter 2: AI in Marketing: AI Powered Chatbot

The chapter focuses into the methods by which these chatbots accumulate knowledge and forecast the demands of buyers, which enhances the quality of customer service and overall satisfaction. However, the authors also underline the limitations of chatbots and stress on the importance of human interaction in conjunction with AI-powered customer care, delivering vital perspectives for marketers managing the ever-changing arena of AI technology.

Chapter 3: Analyzing Demarketing through Bibliometric Methods

The authors employ bibliometric analysis to methodically assess and map noteworthy studies in the field of the demarketing. This technique allows them to recognize and illustrate major issues and fields where additional investigation is needed.

Chapter 4: Blockchain and Its Derived Technologies Shaping the Future Generation of Digital Businesses with a Focus on Decentralized Finance and the Metaverse

The article examines the possibility of blockchain technology to significantly affect the trajectory of future digital firms. Additionally, it discusses the core significance of blockchain in these establishing fields.

Chapter 5: Consumer Policy: The Relationship Between AI and Data Privacy

The chapter investigates the difficulties and advantages of AI for consumer policy, underlining the necessity of comprehensive legal frameworks that sufficiently tackle issues across data privacy.

Chapter 6: Digital Transformation of Marketing Processes, Customer Privacy, Data Security and Emerging Challenges in Fostering Sustainable Digital Marketing

The chapter gives a organized methodology for companies to efficaciously tackle challenges while establishing an efficient digital marketing plan.

Chapter 7: Global Ambitions, Local Realities: Uber Eats' Marketing Strategy in India and its Demise

This case here completely divulges one of the major standpoints reflecting the dynamism in the field of food delivery work and side by side looking at the different strategic exertions, alliances, and finally the competitive challenges.

Chapter 8: Impact of e-WOM on the Brand Image and Purchase Intention of the Consumer: An Empirical Study

The contributors utilize qualitative research and statistical analysis to demonstrate the substantial impact of electronic word-of-mouth (e-WOM) on customer attitudes and purchasing choices.

Chapter 9: Revolutionizing Marketing by Utilizing the Power of Artificial Intelligence

The study explored the impact of AI on various promotional strategies, precisely concentrating the inbuilt capacity it can offer to boost tailored assistances, affordability, and purchaser gratification, while conducting a survey for the existing studies.

Chapter 10: Leveraging Artificial Intelligence in Education Enhancing Learning Experience: Leveraging Artificial Intelligence in Education

The chapter has ponder upon the dynamism and potential benefits of AI technologies, like Intelligent Tutoring Systems as well as Adaptive Learning Platforms, while catering different educational hindrances and even improvements leading to enhanced student achievements.

Chapter 11: Science Mapping of 'Artificial Intelligence in Education' Literature Landscape: A Bibliometric and Content Analysis Discourse

The initiative of research has uplifted the academic debates about AI in instructive settings, where highlighted areas pinpointing important subjects in education were explored with better insights and such evolution in the present situation of artificial intelligence (AI) was even configured while have such learning.

Chapter 12: Role of Artificial Intelligence in Strategic Debt Sustainability Planning: Sustainable Debt Strategic Plan

For better prediction and assessment of fiscal risk, the use of AI as a technology provides better insight related to sustainable debt ingenuities. The research also provided in-depth insights into the impact of fiscal planning through AI.

Chapter 13: Rise of Artificial Intelligence in Marketing: Strategies for Ethical Implementation

In this research, the authors have conducted evaluations and discovered the importance of focusing on moral research and inaccuracies when using AI, which has led to a conscious approach to its deployment and promotion.

Chapter 14: Unveiling the Transformative Landscape: A Bibliometric Exploration of AI Integration in Healthcare

This current research highlighted the actual advancement in the field of artificial intelligence catering the discipline of healthcare, emphasizing the modern scenario in this field of research. The researchers even analyzed how this discussion can be triggered in academia for its better learning and implementation.

Chapter 15: Examining Impact of AI on Education: Ethical, Psychological, and Pedagogical Perspectives

The chapter additionally addresses issues such as integrity in academia, student motivation, and the significance of instructors in education fueled by artificial intelligence. The authors investigate every facet of these complex concerns, presenting an in-depth analysis of AI's impact on education and highlighting the importance for suitable integration of AI.

Chapter 16: Addressing Ethical Concerns in Digital Marketing: Challenges, Strategies, and Industry Participation

The chapter emphasises the value of ethical marketing practices through examination of the cultural and social difficulties in online purchasing and selling. The authors share useful knowledge into successfully dealing with ethical challenges in digital advertising and advocating the widespread implementation of moral methods through the utilization of case studies and advertising approach evaluations.

CONCLUSION

The book on Ethical Marketing through Data Governance Standards and Effective Technology is anticipated to be extremely advantageous for all those involved in corporate ecosystems, embracing all kinds of goods and services. This work also provides significant inferences in the world of technology, where a wide range of audiences residing in different areas of the world are likely to get theoretical and practical input related to data governance standards related to their day-to-day use of technology. The topics covered are so diverse in nature that it gives unique competences by espousing a universal approach. This book is also an eye-opener for diverse stakeholders who are tech-savvy, leading to new opportunities related to their existing businesses and portfolios. Not limiting its impact, this work will provide significant information to policymakers, which makes the administrations create new frameworks keeping into consideration data governance standards related to technological inception by people as well as corporate houses in their routine work. Also, the title embraces learning database governance strategy as a whole, which again is vital for corporates to manage their online marketing operations in the best manner possible with the adoption of ethical standards for carrying out operations that ultimately benefit consumers on different web or social media platforms.

Chapter 1
A Preliminary Study on Ethics and Sustainability in Hospitality Employer Branding

Vasco Ribeiro Santos
https://orcid.org/0000-0002-3535-9377
ISLA Santarém, Portugal & GOVCOPP, Portugal

Patrícia Simão
ISLA Santarém, Portugal

Filipa Martinho
ISLA Santarém, Portugal

Bruno Sousa
https://orcid.org/0000-0002-8588-2422
Polytechnic Institute of Cávado and Ave, Portugal & CiTUR, Portugal

Isabel Reis
https://orcid.org/0000-0002-2008-9124
ISLA Santarém, Portugal & CEFAGE, Portugal

Marta Sampaio
https://orcid.org/0000-0003-0004-601X
ISLA Santarém, Portugal & CEFAGE, Portugal

ABSTRACT

Tourism is currently one of the main sectors of profit for the worldwide economy. The new segments of ethical and sustainable tourists increasingly seek to obtain unique and sustainable experiences during their trip and stay, thus creating a greater connection with the destination, acquiring cultural and personal enrichment, and thus having a greener consumption. This pre-liminary research aims to explore ethics and sustainability in employer branding applied in the hotel industry, in which it is intended to correlate these very current and little explored themes. From an interdisciplinary perspective, the chapter presents insights for tourism marketing and organizational management (i.e. ethics and employer branding). Findings and practical implications for management are presented.

INTRODUCTION

The hospitality sector faces global challenges in attracting and retaining talent, for several reasons, such as: unskilled labour; high turnover rate; excessive working hours; high competition and low pay (Santos, Sousa, Costa & Au-Yong-Oliveira, 2021; Santos et al., 2023). Therefore, it is very important

DOI: 10.4018/979-8-3693-6660-8.ch001

not only to attract the right talent, but to be able to motivate and involve current employees, so that they have no interest in leaving the organisation, for this reason, it is necessary to find tools that can solve these problems in the hotel sector as high difficulty in hiring (Baum & Hai, 2019). The new segments of ethical and sustainable tourists increasingly seek to obtain unique and sustainable experiences during their trip and stay, thus creating a greater connection with the destination (Laitamaki, Hechavarría, Tada, Liu, Setyady, Vatcharasoontorn & Zheng, 2016), acquiring cultural and personal enrichment, and thus having a greener consumption (Fennell, & Bowyer, 2019). Ethical and sustainable tourists travel in a more ecological way, love to discover destinations and their identities, know, and respect their cultures, customs, and local communities, use the resources available by the environment without compromising future generations, preserving local traditions and natural resources (Veloso, Walter, Sousa, Au-Yong-Oliveira, Santos & Valeri, 2021). Therefore, hotel organisations have begun to think about reviewing their strategies, so that they can meet the needs and demands of new market segments and contribute to more sustainable tourism, through more sustainable and responsible management with Green Human Resources Management (GHRM) policies (Ribeiro & Gavronski, 2021), obtaining an employer brand with a more positive and sustained image, thus attracting and winning the most talented (Sullivan, 2009), with sustainability being a relevant factor in organisational strategic planning (Cvelbar & Dwyer, 2013).

The aim of this chapter is to understand the relationship between ethics and corporate social responsibility and EB strategy communication in retaining and attracting talent in the hospitality industry. More specifically, this research intends to explore the role of HRM practices in conjunction with the EB strategy in terms of attraction and retention being implemented by the hotel industry, to inform hospitality industry organisations about what advantages they can achieve by improving their reputation and image, by getting a good EB strategy and by being socially and environmentally responsible, and finally to confirm the existence of a link between business ethics and environmental sustainability.

THEORETICAL BACKGROUND

Regarding the theme of ethics and sustainability in employer branding applied in the hotel industry, we intend to analyse the main definitions of the following concepts of employer branding, ethics, and sustainability, according to their evolution over time and based on the hotel industry, to understand the complexity of each of the concepts. Due to globalisation and the fact that the world is constantly evolving, consumers in the tourism and hospitality sector, are increasingly demanding, and this quickly results in gradually shortening product and service life cycles and processes, it is necessary to obtain more innovative and creative strategies to exceed consumer expectations and desires (Lansing & Vries, 2007; Wang, 2014; Molina-Collado, Santos-Vijande, Gómez-Rico & Madera, 2022; Santos et al., 2023). The concept of employer branding consists of a tool capable of making employees aware of the advantages of belonging to the organization, fostering a sense of pride, and supporting talent retention. Continuous promotion of a strong employer brand attracts, motivates, and retains the best talents, ensuring an elevated level of continuous performance (Patra, Mukhopadhyay, Dash, 2019; Santos et al., 2023). It is important that the image and reputation, through the organization's employer branding, attract employees with high potential, offering a set of distinct benefits within the workplace (Pittz, Benson, Intindola, Kalargiros, 2017). It is easier to maintain good human resources practices by complementing them with employer branding strategy, thus continuing to implement new initiatives that create value and foster strong engagement between employees and the brand. This engagement will extend to all stakeholders and increase employee productivity, improve recruitment, retention, and motivation (Barrow & Mosley, 2005; Fernandes et al., 2023). Ethics and corporate social responsibility (CSR) have been gaining prominence in the current context we live in, from various perspectives and dimensions (Dias et al., 2020; Santos et al., 2023). Not only in the present but even more so in the future, sustainability will undoubtedly be considered a driving theme for the tourism and hospitality sector to position itself in the increasingly competitive market. In this sense, business innovation gains emphasis as it directly contributes to sustainability, considering that modern-day tourists prefer more innovative and sustainable products and services (Triantafillidou & Tsiaras, 2018).

Both tourism operators and tourists need to be aware of and consider this topic to reduce negative impacts on tourist hotspots and to bring benefits to the local community and themselves (Santos et al., 2021). Only through tourists' feedback can businesses reach new markets, build customer loyalty, and improve the promotion of tourism services. For this reason, the image of the employer brand is crucial to stay in the minds of current and potential consumers. However, the product or service is interconnected with the dynamics of supply and demand. Therefore, due to the new paradigm of tourism offerings, considering the diversification of products and services that stand out from competitors, creating competitive advantages and excellent business opportunities (Santos et al., 2023; Troise & Tani,2021).

Ethics play a fundamental role in an organization's innovation and employer branding strategies; otherwise, advertisements, novelties, and changes may contradict the common good, as many of these efforts focus on selling products or services and attracting tourists without respecting ethical principles (Islam, 2020). Another relevant factor is the diversity and inclusion of employees from various backgrounds, as it promotes coexistence, improvement, learning, and ensures company appreciation and competitive advantage. The allocation of compensations or benefits is another essential factor, which should be based on the evaluation of competencies, performance, and ethical behaviour in line with the organization's code of ethics. Therefore, this reorganization should be in tune with the company's cultural identity, with the purpose of promoting a good work environment, harmony, and integrity (Bharadwaj, Khan & Yameen, 2022; Azhar, Rehman, Majeed & Bano, 2024).

The hospitality sector will have to focus on SHRM for talent attraction and retention, as it is an area with specific and unique characteristics and competencies, requiring measures to address these specificities (Fernandes et al., 2023). However, the future of employment in the hotel industry falls short of expectations, being limited and restricted, with immense difficulties in recruitment. In this sense, it is essential to review and implement the employer branding strategy to address these specificities, with the aim of improving employee satisfaction in this industry and attracting potential candidates, resulting in beneficial organizational outcomes, and achieving organizational success (Wach, Wehner, Weißenberger & Kabst, 2020). Several authors have highlighted the challenges to be addressed in this industry, including: (1) Unskilled Workforce: The hospitality sector faces a problem of having a high proportion of unskilled individuals, making it difficult to recruit and select motivated and qualified professionals, especially for positions that involve significant customer interaction. The lack of adequate knowledge reflects on career development opportunities, leading to difficulties in retaining potential employees and projecting a negative image of the industry's concern for its employees' qualifications (Santos et al., 2023); (2) High Employee Turnover: The extreme seasonality of the industry, particularly during the low season when there is reduced demand [25], contributes to a high turnover rate. During this period, hotels try to retain their employees, but there are barriers to retention due to the temporary nature of employment contracts, with many employees being young and working on seasonal contracts; (3) Excessive Working Hours:

The seasonal nature of the industry, with a focus on the high season (Jiménez-Barreto, Loureiro, Braun, Sthapit & Zenker, 2021), means that employees often work long hours, including nights, holidays, and weekends. This lack of time for family and rest results in emotional and physical strain, causing stress and emotional exhaustion; (4) Low Salaries: Employees in this industry often face low salaries, leading some to hold multiple jobs simultaneously to make ends meet (Jiménez-Barreto, Loureiro, Braun, Sthapit & Zenker, 2021). The reluctance to pay overtime further contributes to the perception of hospitality as a temporary career option while seeking better opportunities (Santos et al., 2023).

In conclusion, organizations in the hospitality industry have been more focused on customers than on the operational aspect, i.e., the human capital, which is crucial for delivering excellent service and exceeding customer expectations (Malik & Khera, 2014). This has resulted in the neglect of employees' desires, needs, and expectations, leading to low wages, lack of professional recognition, and an unpleasant work environment, which in turn affects their personal lives, causing burnout. Therefore, it is essential not only to attract the right talents but also to promote offers and working conditions that improve the hospitality sector and motivate employees, resulting in favourable behaviours and increased job satisfaction, so that they have no interest in leaving the organization (Santos et al., 2023). This includes creating a positive work environment, achieving work-life balance, providing flexible working hours, investing in employee training and career development, effective leadership, personalized rewards systems, and a corporate culture that promotes talent attraction and growth (Santos et al., 2023). The primary focus of an employer branding strategy is to have a positive impact on employee retention and satisfaction, thus contributing to the overall success of the organization, key factor in talent attraction and retention. If there is an organizational culture that promotes talent growth, this strategy becomes well-developed and positive, leading to higher productivity and organizational commitment, achieving better outcomes through a strong, differentiated, and attractive brand image, with a correct positioning, gaining competitive advantages, and being more easily chosen in the decision-making process by potential candidates due to its distinction from the competition. Implementing performance evaluation strategies that help employees develop their knowledge and maximize their potential, creativity, and innovation within an organization that offers learning and employee development enhances the organization's employer branding (Potgieter & Doubell, 2020; Ahmad et al., 2020), as it fosters innovative products and a strong culture of innovation, increasing the organization's attractiveness in the market and attracting more potential candidates.

These practices are critical success factors because if an organization has a strong and successful brand and a compelling value proposition that showcases its unique selling points, it can achieve competitive advantages and meet talent management objectives (Santos et al., 2023). By fostering motivation, performance, and commitment, the organization enhances talent retention and attracts the right talents that aim to improve and develop the organization, resulting in lower turnover rates. Based on continuous feedback, word-of-mouth referrals, and shared experiences, ethical, moral, and socially responsible conduct, transparency, consistency, and differentiation from competitors are essential for successful employer branding. This leads to effective human resource management, always considering human capital as one of the most valuable assets of organizations, as its characteristics, skills, values, and experiences contribute to the competitive differentiation that influences organizational success/failure (Liu et al., 2021).

METHODOLOGY

Regarding the methodological approach, this study will adopt a qualitative methodology, and the chosen qualitative method is the Delphi method. The Delphi method is considered a powerful research technique as it gathers opinions and ideas from various experts, geographically separated, to obtain a diverse range of results related to the research problem. It enables a better understanding of the phenomenon under investigation, based on the current reality and context. Usually, the Delphi method involves three rounds, whether conducted online, in-person, or simultaneously, to gather as much information as possible about the research problem. The participants' responses may complement or contradict each other, considering they are different individuals, leading to convergent or divergent opinions, as they are thought and provided by different people. Based on this research question, the overall objective of this study is to understand the relationship between ethics and corporate social responsibility (CSR) and the communication of EB strategy in talent retention and attraction in the hotel sector. Specifically, this research intends to understand the importance of EB and environmental sustainability for decision makers and managers in the hospitality industry, explore the role of HRM practices in conjunction with EB strategy in terms of attraction and retention that are being implemented by hotels, inform organisations in the hospitality industry of the advantages they can achieve by improving their reputation and image, by achieving a good EB strategy and by being socially and environmentally responsible, and finally confirm the existence of a link between business ethics and environmental sustainability. In a second phase, the methodology translated into the Delphi method for data collection, as it is recognized as one of the most suitable techniques for conducting data collection in qualitative research, particularly in a comprehensive area like the tourism and hospitality sector. The application of this data collection technique offers numerous advantages, particularly because it is carried out in three stages and allows for an extensive exploration of ideas and perspectives of the participants.

The selection criteria for the participants focused on professionals who are competent and decision-makers in the marketing area, as they aim to improve and develop the field. The three rounds of the Delphi method will be conducted online, as it has proven to be the most beneficial approach to gather responses from all participants across the three stages, ensuring the smooth progression of the research. The questionnaire for the Delphi method, based on the review of relevant literature, was structured into three sections. The first section addresses Human Resources Management (HRM) practices in conjunction with the Employer Branding (EB) strategy concerning talent retention and attraction. This part involves identifying the instruments being implemented in the hotel establishments in Portugal and gauging the participants' opinions on their relevance for the effective functioning of this sector. The second section primarily focuses on factors related to the importance of business ethics and environmental sustainability. It aims to understand whether the executives responsible for these domains in each of the associations believe that these principles are being actively practiced in the various hotel units across Portugal. Finally, the third section delves into the advantages that hotel establishments can achieve by implementing an Employer Branding strategy and demonstrating social and environmental responsibility. These pieces of information are essential for the analysis of the collected results by the researcher, addressing both the research question and objectives. The Delphi method consists of rounds involving specific questions on a particular topic or theme. This process aims to obtain results relevant to the research and to better support the study. It leads to a better understanding of the presented questions and the responses provided by the participants, thereby facilitating the presentation of different opinions.

PRELIMINARY RESULTS

It was found that there is a link between dimensions, and it's becoming evident that the success of organizations depends on their commitment to ethics and social responsibility. Companies need to foster a strong organizational culture that embodies ethical and sustainable values, practices, actions, and behaviours. This not only promotes loyalty and trust among all stakeholders but also creates a positive work environment. Such factors, both internally and externally, contribute to improved organizational performance while upholding socially responsible conduct. Moreover, the organizational success in the current landscape relies heavily on ethics and social responsibility. Organizations must invest in sustainability policies and establish Green Human Resources Management (GHRM) practices, which integrate Environmental Management with Human Resources Management. These practices are directly and positively related to improved environmental performance, which can enhance organizational reputation, service quality, cooperation, attractiveness, and the ability to attract and retain high-quality candidates. By adopting such approaches, organizations can position themselves competitively and sustainably in the global market.

The EB strategy is related to the concept of a "great place to work." When hotel organizations adopt this strategy, they can achieve elevated levels of competitiveness through new, flexible, innovative, and creative work structures, thereby enhancing organizational development. This approach is based on a more creative, innovative, and eco-friendly organizational culture, primarily driven by knowledge. Knowledge has become a key factor in recruitment strategy (talent attraction and retention) as it is essential to enhance the knowledge of current employees, involving them in organizational strategies and appealing to more talented and qualified potential candidates. This leads to competitive advantages over competitors and enables quicker responses to market demands in this gradually digital landscape. Maintaining open, transparent, truthful, and consistent communication, giving employees more autonomy in organizational strategies, and encouraging individual initiative in decision-making demonstrate appreciation for employees. This fosters more creativity and innovation in the development of products and services, with the goal of guiding and advancing their careers, as it generates greater commitment and dedication, resulting in positive outcomes and organizational success.

In summary, there is a strong connection between the three dimensions mentioned earlier, as socially responsible organizations ensure organizational success, create value both for the organization and its workforce, and foster brand loyalty. They achieve a more positive image in the market by showcasing their organizational culture and what they offer to their employees, thereby increasing attractiveness to attract and retain high-potential talents and reduce turnover rates. It is crucial for organizations to maintain a differentiated, attractive, and appealing brand, particularly through green innovation, offering products and services that provide unique and authentic experiences to meet the demands of the current market. Such organizations tend to be more innovative and sophisticated, operating dynamic and flexible businesses with a focus on sustainable entrepreneurship. This involves the development of various dimensions, such as knowledge, skills, capabilities, attitudes, and green behaviours, fostering environmental awareness that encourages all stakeholders to take actions in favour of the environment, promoting sustainable environmental development that respects the limits of the planet.

FINAL CONSIDERATIONS

From an organizational perspective, it is crucial to improve working conditions as employees are valued more than ever, leading to increased loyalty, commitment, and performance among current employees. One key challenge for organizations is the ability to retain and attract talent. In this regard, organizations must invest in employer branding policies to understand what attracts potential and current employees to an organization. It is essential to stay updated on the latest trends in the recruitment market, as organizational competitiveness and competition for the best talents have increased.

Considering the practices of HRM and EB in the hotel industry, one notable aspect is the focus on ethics and social responsibility, aiming to ensure a more sustainable and innovative tourism sector by adopting sustainable practices among all stakeholders. By adopting more sustainable strategies, hotel organizations can position themselves competitively in the global market, gaining reputation and prestige compared to their competitors. This enhances the employer brand, making it innovative, distinctive, attractive, and stronger, leading to advantages in the market. The interplay between HRM practices and EB strategy in terms of attraction and retention in the hotel sector is crucial. Investing in a positive, innovative, and creative organizational culture, as well as social responsibility strategies that benefit employees, such as career progression, work-life balance, and continuous training to develop knowledge and skills contributes to motivation, commitment, talent retention, well-being, and consequently, lower turnover rates.

Environmental sustainability is a key aspect of business ethics, as it fosters transparent, integrous, assertive, truthful, and ethical organizational communication, contributing to organizational success. Lastly, the advantages that hotel units can achieve by implementing EB strategy and being socially responsible in environmental matters are critical success factors. A strong and successful brand, coupled with an appealing value proposition showcasing differentiating points, such as attractive compensation and benefits packages and open communication, leads to competitive advantages and achievement of talent management objectives. Although HR managers in this sector acknowledge the contributions of this strategy combined with HR practices in valuing employee well-being as a current priority, retaining professionals within organizations contributes to their reputation and image. As suggestions for future research, it may be interesting to conduct a quantitative study. This study has strengthened knowledge on the topics addressed in the academic and scientific communities, particularly regarding the contribution of HRM practices combined with EB strategy in attraction and retention in the hotel sector, as well as the importance of ethics and social responsibility applied to environmental sustainability in the organizational strategic plan and building a stronger and more positive reputation. Additionally, this chapter has shed light on the realities of hotel organizations, their methods of attracting and retaining talent in HR management, and how they are revising their strategies to achieve more sustainable management and greater profitability and organizational success, thereby enhancing existing practices and performance.

ACKNOWLEDGMENT

This work was financially supported by the Research Unit on Governance, Competitiveness and Public Policies (UIDB/04058/2020) + (UIDP/04058/2020), funded by national funds through FCT-Fundação para a Ciência e a Tecnologia

REFERENCES

Ahmad, A., Khan, M. N., & Haque, M. A. (2020). Employer branding aids in enhancing employee attraction and retention. *Journal of Asia-Pacific Business*, 21(1), 27–38. 10.1080/10599231.2020.1708231

Azhar, A., Rehman, N., Majeed, N., & Bano, S. (2024). Employer branding: A strategy to enhance organizational performance. *International Journal of Hospitality Management*, 116, 103618. 10.1016/j.ijhm.2023.103618

Barrow, S., & Mosley, R. (2005). *The employer brand: Bringing the best of brand management to people at work*. John Wiley and Sons, Ltd.

Baum, T., & Hai, N. T. T. (2019). Applying sustainable employment principles in the tourism industry: Righting human rights wrongs? *Tourism Recreation Research*, 44(3), 371–381. 10.1080/02508281.2019.1624407

Bharadwaj, S., Khan, N. A., & Yameen, M. (2022). Unbundling employer branding, job satisfaction, organizational identification and employee retention: A sequential mediation analysis. *Asia-Pacific Journal of Business Administration*, 14(3), 309–334. 10.1108/APJBA-08-2020-0279

Brien, A. (2014). Do I want a job in hospitality? Only Till I get a Real Job. In *Proceedings of the New Zealand Tourism and Hospitality Research Conference* (pp. 35–42). Victoria University of Wellington.

Cvelbar, L. K., & Dwyer, L. (2013). An importance–performance analysis of sustainability factors for long-term strategy planning in Slovenian hotels. *Journal of Sustainable Tourism*, 21(3), 487–504. 10.1080/09669582.2012.713965

Dias, A., Silva, G. M., Patuleia, M., & González-Rodríguez, M. R. (2020). Developing sustainable business models: Local knowledge acquisition and tourism lifestyle entrepreneurship. *Journal of Sustainable Tourism*, 1–20.

El Zoghbi, E., & Aoun, K. (2016). Employer branding and social media strategies. In *Information and Communication Technologies in Organizations and Society: Past, Present and Future Issues* (pp. 277-283). Springer International Publishing. 10.1007/978-3-319-28907-6_18

Eser, H. (2022, May). Big Data, Social Media and Employer Branding: An exploratory study from the hospitality industry. In *International Conference on Tourism Research* (Vol. 15, No. 1, pp. 110-116). 10.34190/ictr.15.1.273

Fennell, D. A., & Bowyer, E. (2019). Tourism and Sustainable transformation: A discussion and application to tourism food consumption. *Tourism Recreation Research*, 45(1), 119–131. 10.1080/02508281.2019.1694757

Fernandes, P. M., Sousa, B. B., Veloso, C. M., & Valeri, M. (2023). The role of endomarketing in human capital management: A study applied to the Minho Urban Quadrilateral. *EuroMed Journal of Business*. 10.1108/EMJB-12-2022-0212

Fernandes, R., Sousa, B. B., Fonseca, M., & Oliveira, J. (2023). Assessing the Impacts of Internal Communication: Employer Branding and Human Resources. *Administrative Sciences*, 13(6), 155. 10.3390/admsci13060155

Hein, A. Z., Elving, W. J., Koster, S., & Edzes, A. (2024). Is your employer branding strategy effective? The role of employee predisposition in achieving employer attractiveness. *Corporate Communications*, 29(7), 1–20. 10.1108/CCIJ-07-2022-0070

Islam, G. (2020). Psychology and business ethics: A multi-level research agenda. *Journal of Business Ethics*, 165(1), 1–13. 10.1007/s10551-019-04107-w

Jiménez-Barreto, J., Loureiro, S., Braun, E., Sthapit, E., & Zenker, S. (2021). Use numbers not words! Communicating hotels' cleaning programs for COVID-19 from the brand perspective. *International Journal of Hospitality Management*, 94, 102872. 10.1016/j.ijhm.2021.10287233897084

Kargas, A., & Tsokos, A. (2020). Employer branding implementation and human resource management in Greek telecommunication industry. *Administrative Sciences*, 10(1), 17. 10.3390/admsci10010017

Kaur, P., Sharma, S., Kaur, J., & Sharma, S. K. (2015). Using social media for employer branding and talent management: An experiential study. *IUP Journal of Brand Management*, 12(2), 7.

Kim, Y., & Legendre, T. S. (2023). The effects of employer branding on value congruence and brand love. *Journal of Hospitality & Tourism Research (Washington, D.C.)*, 47(6), 962–987. 10.1177/10963480211062779

Kimpakorn, N., & Dimmitt, N. (2007). Employer branding: The perspective of hotel management in the Thai luxury hotel industry. *Australasian Marketing Journal*, 15(3), 49.

Laitamaki, J., Hechavarría, L. T., Tada, M., Liu, S., Setyady, N., Vatcharasoontorn, N., & Zheng, F. (2016). Sustainable tourism development frameworks and best practices: Implications for the Cuban tourism industry. *Managing Global Transitions*, 14(1), 7.

Lansing, P., & Vries, P. D. (2007). Sustainable tourism: Ethical alternative or marketing ploy? *Journal of Business Ethics*, 72(1), 77–85. 10.1007/s10551-006-9157-7

Liu, Y., Vrontis, D., Visser, M., Stokes, P., Smith, S., Moore, N., Thrassou, A., & Ashta, A. (2021). Talent management and the HR function in cross-cultural mergers and acquisitions: The role and impact of bi-cultural identity. *Human Resource Management Review*, 31(3), 100744. 10.1016/j.hrmr.2020.100744

Malik, S., & Khera, S. N. (2014). New generation–great expectations: Exploring the work attributes of Gen Y. *Global Journal of Finance and Management*, 6(5), 433–438.

Molina-Collado, A., Santos-Vijande, M. L., Gómez-Rico, M., & Madera, J. M. (2022). Sustainability in hospitality and tourism: A review of key research topics from 1994 to 2020. *International Journal of Contemporary Hospitality Management*, 34(8), 3029–3064. 10.1108/IJCHM-10-2021-1305

Patra, G., Mukhopadhyay, I., & Dash, C. K. (2019). Digital employer branding for enabling gen Y in the ITeS sector in eastern India. *Prabandhan Indian J. Manag.*, 12(3), 38–49. 10.17010/pijom/2019/v12i3/142339

Pittz, T. G., Benson, P. G., Intindola, M., & Kalargiros, M. (2017). Opportunity or Opportunism? In advance: An Examination of International Recruitment via Employer and Nation Branding Strategies. *Business & Professional Ethics Journal*, 36(2), 157–176. 10.5840/bpej201742655

Potgieter, A., & Doubell, M. (2020). The Influence of Employer branding and Employees' personal branding on Corporate Branding and Corporate Reputation. *African Journal of Business & Economic Research*, 15(2), 109–135. 10.31920/1750-4562/2020/v15n2a6

Ribeiro, R. P., & Gavronski, I. (2021). Sustainable Management of Human Resources and Stakeholder Theory: A Review. *Revista De Gestão Social E Ambiental, 15*, e02729. 10.24857/rgsa.v15.2729

Santos, V., Simão, P., Reis, I., Sampaio, M. C., Martinho, F., & Sousa, B. (2023). Ethics and Sustainability in Hospitality Employer Branding. *Administrative Sciences*, 13(9), 202. 10.3390/admsci13090202

Santos, V., Sousa, M. J., Costa, C., & Au-Yong-Oliveira, M. (2021). Tourism towards sustainability and innovation: A systematic literature review. *Sustainability (Basel)*, 13(20), 11440. 10.3390/su132011440

Santos, V., Sousa, M. J., Costa, C., & Aun-Yong-Oliveira, M. (2021). Tourism towards Sustainability and Innovation: A Systematic Literature Review. *Sustainability (Basel)*, 13(20), 11440. 10.3390/su132011440

Silva, V., & Reis, F. (2018). *Capital Humano - Temas para uma boa gestão das organizações*. Edições Sílabo.

Taweewattanakunanon, R., & Darawong, C. (2022). The influence of employer branding in luxury hotels in Thailand and its effect on employee job satisfaction, loyalty, and intention to recommend. *Journal of Human Resources in Hospitality & Tourism*, 21(4), 501–523. 10.1080/15332845.2022.2106612

Triantafillidou, E., & Tsiaras, S. (2018). Exploring entrepreneurship, innovation and tourism development from a sustainable perspective: Evidence from Greece. *J. Int. Bus. Ent. Dev.*, 11(1), 53–64. 10.1504/JIBED.2018.090020

Troise, C., & Tani, M. (2021). Exploring entrepreneurial characteristics, motivations and behaviours in equity crowdfunding: Some evidence from Italy. *Management Decision*, 59(5), 995–1024. 10.1108/MD-10-2019-1431

Veloso, C. M., Walter, C. E., Sousa, B., Au-Yong-Oliveira, M., Santos, V., & Valeri, M. (2021). Academic tourism and transport services: Student perceptions from a social responsibility perspective. *Sustainability (Basel)*, 13(16), 8794. 10.3390/su13168794

Wach, B. A., Wehner, M. C., Weißenberger, B. E., & Kabst, R. (2020). United we stand : HR and line managers ' shared views on HR strategic integration. *European Management Journal*. 10.1016/j.emj.2020.09.012

Wang, C. J. (2014). Do ethical and sustainable practices matter? Effects of corporate citizenship on business performance in the hospitality industry. *International Journal of Contemporary Hospitality Management*, 26(6), 930–947. 10.1108/IJCHM-01-2013-0001

Chapter 2
AI in Marketing:
AI-Powered Chatbot

Chander Prabha
https://orcid.org/0000-0002-2322-7289
Chitkara University Institute of Engineering and Technology, Chitkara University, Punjab, India

Shalini Kumari
Chitkara University Institute of Engineering and Technology, Chitkara University, Punjab, India

ABSTRACT

Chatbots in marketing employ artificial intelligence (AI) and natural language processing (NLP) to quickly and accurately answer client questions. Chatbots may learn and forecast consumer needs without human intervention, enhancing service and satisfaction. Digital marketing AI chatbots identify relevant online data points and optimize activities for clients and businesses. The scripted, rule-based, and AI-powered chatbots are leading AI chatbots that learn from previous interactions, personalize depending on customer profiles and preferences, and use predictive intelligence and analytics. Chatbots minimize support and live operator utilization, saving businesses money and time by automating user experience and transactional functions. AI in marketing and chatbots for customer care, sales, shopping, and marketing are covered in this chapter. However, chatbots can't handle complex requests or recognize human traits. Chatbots should not replace human connection and should boost customer pleasure and help through AI marketing.

INTRODUCTION

AI-powered chatbots use AI and NLP to answer common inquiries in messenger interactions. These message, text, or speech discussions assist customers and companies. The AI Chatbot first analyses the question's intent and then gives the most relevant answer based on the data. AI-driven chatbots can learn and predict client wants without human involvement, which is their main benefit. First, businesses teach AI-powered bots to recognize and react to FAQs, related articles, and different variations of the same question. Then they can detect the most common questions and respond instantly, improving customer assistance. They learn from each discussion, comprehend the question context, and train to give more appropriate answers. Each conversation increases AI chatbots' ability to answer more questions and

DOI: 10.4018/979-8-3693-6660-8.ch002

Copyright © 2024, IGI Global. Copying or distributing in print or electronic forms without written permission of IGI Global is prohibited.

improve their accuracy. While the customer types their question, powerful AI bots can make real-time suggestions.

AI applications in digital marketing identify relevant information from billions of internet data points for business purposes. It would tell, what pricing converts best, when to post, what subject line works best, etc. Smart marketers follow all trends. It simplifies tasks and encourages innovation. Benefiting clients get value in the marketing industry AI changes (Priyanka, et al., 2023).

Further, AI chatbot software may understand language other than pre-programmed commands and respond based on data. Visitors can speak their minds and lead the conversation. AI chatbots learn from their talks and may adapt to new patterns and situations. This allows them to be used for many purposes, such as evaluating consumer emotions or predicting site visitors' preferences. Chatbots and AI have transformed digital marketing and customer engagement. In digital marketing, chatbots enable seamless, fast, and 24/7 customer engagements. They improve user experiences by streamlining communication, providing quick help, answering questions, and guiding transactions. This timeliness and accessibility boosts consumer satisfaction, conversions, and brand loyalty (Feng, 2023).

ROLE OF ARTIFICIAL INTELLIGENCE IN MARKETING

AI teaches computers to understand and behave like humans. Based on data, AI has produced a new intelligent machine that thinks, responds, and works like people. AI can do complex tasks like robotics, speech and image recognition, natural language processing, and problem-solving. AI includes numerous technologies that can do human-like activities. With typical commercial processes, these technologies can learn, behave, and perform like humans. Machines that mimic human intelligence save time and money in business dealings. AI aims to create human-like machines. It offers great prospects to many businesses. AI frightens or fascinates every industry mentioned. AI makes technology and devices think and act like humans. Technology is called the "next step" in the industrial revolution. Most of today's problems may be solved by AI and ML (De Mauro, et al., 2022).

Moreover, AI may foresee future issues. Create new technologies, industries, and surroundings with AI. AI replicates human intelligence in robots. Knowledge, logic, and, most crucially, self-correction are examples. AI understands, analyses, and decides that market and user behavior forecasts are made using existing user data. Companies globally use data forecasts to improve their sales and marketing strategies. Most marketing AI applications use ML, from personalizing product ideas to finding the best promotion channels, calculating churn rate or customer lifetime value, and constructing better customer groups.

Need for Artificial Intelligence in Marketing

AI is a fascinating and cutting-edge technology that enhances content strategy. This technology includes NLP, ML, deep learning, computer vision, and others. ML analyses data and provides analytical tools, which impact digital marketing. It aids marketing teams in needs-based analysis. Companies that employ AI save time by focusing on other digital marketing functions. AI is a huge, emerging technology with significant implications. Figure 1 shows several segments of AI applications in the marketing domain. It deals with pricing, product, promotion, strategy, and planning management.

AI in Marketing

Figure 1. Several segments for AI applications in the marketing domain

In the future, AI should be used in digital marketing to boost creativity and productivity. AI can help marketers categorize and move clients along their path for the optimal experience. Understanding customer data and what they want can help marketers boost ROI without wasting time. They can avoid time-wasting, client-annoying mind-numbing advertising. AI will customize marketing in many ways. Many companies use AI to personalize their websites, emails, social media postings, videos, and other materials to meet client needs. A major goal of AI is to automate jobs that require intelligence (Wang, *et al.*, 2022). This reduction in labor resources needed to complete a project or time spent on routine tasks boosts efficiency. Table 1 shows detailed AI applications in different segments.

Table 1. AI applications in different marketing segments

Marketing Segments	AI Applications in the Marketing domain
Customer	ML models and Clustering algorithms help analyze preferences and customer behavior, allowing marketers to create personalized and targeted campaigns for particular customer segments.
Personalized Content Recommendations	AI-powered recommendation engines analyze customer information to provide personalized content suggestions, like product recommendations, posts, or videos, to increase engagement among users.
Chatbots and Virtual Assistants	Chatbots and automated assistants driven by the use of NLP and ML allow for instantaneous communication with customers. They support inquiries, offer details, and improve user skills.
Lead scoring via Predictive Analytics	Forecasting models assist with lead scoring by analyzing past data and discovering trends that suggest the probability of conversion. This enables advertising professionals to concentrate on leads with the highest converting customer potential.
Email Marketing Optimization	Algorithms using AI optimize email advertising campaigns by analyzing user behavior, choices, and involvement patterns to customize the content, send emails at perfect times, and boost in general the campaign's success
Programmatic Advertising	Programmed marketing uses AI algorithms to automate the purchase of inventory for ads in real-time. AI analyses user behavior and competing patterns to provide more relevant and effective commercials.
Sentiment Analysis and Social Media Listening	AI tools track social networking sites to evaluate feedback from consumers and gain knowledge. Analysis of sentiment enables salespeople to comprehend how their business looks to consumers and change tactics as needed
Content Optimization and SEO	AI-driven instruments help to optimise material for engines like Google through analysing search trends, determining keywords that are pertinent, and suggesting content enhancements to boost rankings on search engines.
Visual Search	Visual searching uses algorithms for image recognition to allow consumers to conduct searches for goods and data through images. This is especially helpful for platforms that sell goods online.
Customer Journey Mapping	AI assists in mapping the consumer's journey by analyzing interactions and conversations across multiple channels. This data helps advertisers comprehend the customer's journey to conversion and optimize their advertising approaches as needed
Optimization and A/B Testing	AI algorithms make A/B testing easier by analysing various versions of an advertisement to identify their most operational components. This enables advertisers to optimize initiatives for better results.
Price Dynamics	AI is used to develop flexible pricing plans based on market dynamics, rivals' costing, and consumer behaviour. This allows companies to modify costs in the moment to maximize profits.
Customer Churn Prediction	ML models forecast client turnover by analyzing historical information and recognizing trends that suggest prospective turnover. This enables advertisers to employ proactive steps for retaining clientele.
Optimizing Voice Search	As voice-driven search grows more commonplace, AI is being used to optimize web pages for voice-based inquiries by analyzing organic speech and dialogue patterns.

AI applications mentioned in Table 1, do not solely increase productivity, additionally, they allow advertisers to provide more personalized and pertinent experiences that appeal to their intended consumers. The ongoing development of AI technologies is expected to further evolve and enhance advertising tactics through a variety of sectors.

AI'S ROLE IN DIGITAL MARKETING

In digital marketing, organizations work with customers and partners to create, convey, deliver, and sustain value for all stakeholders using technology. Technology-enabled artificial intelligence (AI) evaluates real-time service scenarios using data from digital and/or physical sources to provide personalized recommendations, alternatives, and solutions to customers' inquiries or problems, even complex ones.

Digital marketing companies use AI to optimize activities. AI support benefits to both customers and enterprises. AI-powered products aid clients in decision-making, purchasing, and company communication. However, the latter offers greater client behavior monitoring and analysis, leading to improved management. This enhances the effectiveness and efficiency of acts by both sides (Ahmed, 2024).

Companies are still in the early stages of implementing AI-enriched technologies and digital transformation, despite their proven success in business and marketing tasks. AI in marketing creates practical and ethical challenges, as with most high-potential technology. Although ethical concerns remain, artificial intelligence can help marketers cut costs by automating data-driven repetitive chores, boost sales, and improve large-scale prediction. Traditional marketing technology uses algorithms to program machines. The machine may define its algorithms, chart new courses, and uncover the boundless potential of marketing transformation thanks to AI.

AI-based marketing has led to rapid digital transformation in firms like Amazon, Facebook, Google, Microsoft, Apple, and Netflix. These companies use AI: "machine learning, deep learning, computer vision, speech and image recognition, natural language processing and natural language generation". Marketing experts employing AI-powered products can get a permanent competitive advantage due to their many benefits.

CONCEPT OF CHATBOT

Software chatbots simulate human conversation using text, voice, or both. Chatbots automate user requests and give real-time information. By scaling conversational self-service, a chatbot can fulfill internal and external communication demands. WhatsApp, Messenger, Instagram, eCommerce apps like Amazon, and websites can be integrated with it (Arsenijevic & Jovic 2019).

Types of Chatbots

There are three types of broadly categorized chatbots based on technical aspects. Figure 2 shows the types of chatbots.

Figure 2. Types of chatbots

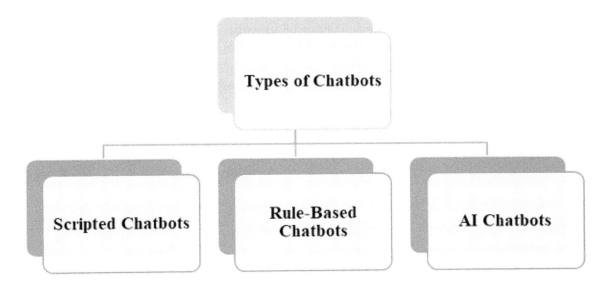

Scripted Chatbots

The scripted chatbot (Figure 3), answers user queries using pre-written keywords in a conversation flow. It accepts only text. Common inquiries can be answered by scripted chatbots. Scripted bots excel at handling frequently asked questions (FAQs). A programmed chatbot can automate the most common questions to encourage self-service and reduce customer support calls and expenditures.

Figure 3. Scripted chatbot example

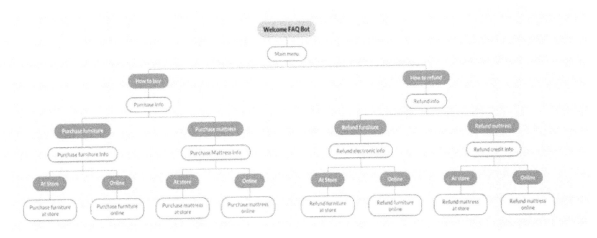

Rule-Based Chatbots

Rule-based chatbots (Figure 4) explain information by asking follow-up questions and answering them using a decision tree flow. Keywords, interaction structure, and follow-up questions and responses are predefined. Rule-based chatbots behave like flowcharts to anticipate and answer user questions. They're the next-generation scripted chatbot and can integrate with legacy systems. Companies utilize them to assist customers in finding products, arranging agent appointments, ordering pizza, checking flight status, etc.

Figure 4. Rule-Based chatbot

AI Chatbots

AI chatbots are presently the most advanced. AI-powered chatbots identify words, emotions, and sentences and respond intelligently or take action in real time. NLP, AI, and ML are used. AI-powered chatbots are context-aware and learn from previous interactions, unlike scripted or rule-based ones. They personalize interactions based on customer profiles and preferences obtained from past behavior using predictive intelligence and analytics. Bots get smarter with more interactions. An effective AI-powered chatbot can be laborious to design, train, and deploy, especially if you're building your solution. Accuracy can be difficult. To gain the significant benefits of your AI-powered chatbot, one need the proper partner to design and deploy it. AI-powered bots are great for human-like conversations (Furukawa, 2024).

AI Chatbot Working: The AI chatbot will be fed a lot of data that matches users' searches and produces appropriate results. Visitors to a website can ask the chatbot for clarification. An AI chatbot will analyze the question's intent, keywords, tone, sentiment, and other criteria to provide the best solution. If it cannot solve the problem, it will post follow-up questions to resolve it. The coder teaches an AI chatbot to interpret users' phrases during training. This allows the AI chatbot to naturally and conversationally answer complicated questions.

At its core, an AI chatbot evaluates input data and produces meaningful output. If a site visitor asks a question, the AI chatbot will analyze their purpose, tone, and sentiment to provide the best answer. The AI chatbot needs plenty of conversational data for this. Programmers educate AI chatbots on how to recognize word context. This comprehension lets the chatbot answer complicated questions naturally using conversation. Figure 5 shows the AI Chatbot's Inner working. It takes input from the user, analyzes the user's request, in turn, identifies the intent and entities of the request, and finally composes a reply.

Figure 5. Chatbot inner-working

Chatbots automate user experience and transactional features in many enterprises. Reduced support and live operator use have led to cost savings and efficiency gains for organizations. Chatbots replicate and analyze human speech and writing, allowing humans to talk to gadgets like live agents. Simple chatbots can answer to a single instance, whereas complex virtual assistants can learn and develop as they collect and process data to give better customization.

Many of our daily workflows incorporate chatbots. If someone shopping on an e-commerce site on a computer, a window may inquire if they need help. A person can also use voice input to order a beverage from a local retailer and receive an alert when it will be ready and how much it will cost. The following customer experience scenarios may involve a chatbot. Recent chatbot growth is due to the rapid digital revolution. Businesses increasingly use digital channels to engage and trade with customers. Chatbots are a top AI used in business to improve customer-facing functions. Chatbots and conversational platforms will be used every day by 70% of white-collar workers by 2022, according to Gartner. Personal robotic advisors like Google Assistant and Amazon Alexa and chatbots in Facebook Messenger and WeChat are examples (Sari, 2023; Saluja, 2024).

Chatbots boost performance, save money, and provide extra services to internal workers, clients, and partners. They help firms resolve stakeholder issues swiftly and without human intervention. Chatbots can grow, personalize, and be proactive for companies in the digital age. A human-powered firm can only serve a specific number of people at once, limiting capacity and growth. To be cost-effective, manual-effort-intensive companies must use rigid models, limiting their proactive and tailored outreach. Personalized chatbots allow firms to communicate with potentially unlimited clients and scale up or down based on current needs. Even with millions of consumers, a chatbot can give a personalized, nearly "humanlike" service (*AIContentfy*, 2023).

Table 2. Areas and factors concerning AI for marketing

Applications	Description
Digital Marketing (DM)	AI affects digital marketing considerably. Marketing can investigate consumer behavior and indicators with AI. They can then swiftly and successfully approach the relevant person. AI can process social media, email, and Web data quickly for marketers. Together with marketing automation, it can turn data into choices, meaningful interactions, and organizational benefits. AI marketing gathers data, analyses consumer behavior, predicts trends, and automates marketing decisions.
Decreased Human Errors	AI reduces human errors, especially in key areas. This technology can also create and optimize pleasant, relevant email content. AI exists to eliminate human error by preventing human involvement. Many companies worry about their employees' ability to protect customers and other critical data due to regular data security issues. AI can learn, adapt, and respond to an organization's cybersecurity needs to help solve problems. AI can reduce the slash-and-burn resources necessary to plan and implement marketing strategies.
Connect Business Processes.	Artificial intelligence connects corporate operations and provides a flawless experience using information technology. Businesses with AI-enabled marketers produce excellent results. Marketers may build and deploy more personalized and human-centered marketing strategies with AI. These tactics delight customers and turn them into brand loyalists. Technology like AI that controls customer micro-moments may improve interaction designs. AI helps firms elevate marketing.
Analyse Extensive Market Data	AI can evaluate enormous market data and forecast user behavior. It understands billions of searches and helps users decide to buy. AI helps identify issues and take action. AI and ML have far-reaching effects beyond simple tools. It profoundly changes our company processes. It virtually triples corporate efficiency.
Better Marketing Automation Tool	AI in marketing automation solutions lets marketers quickly discover eligible leads, improve nurturing, and create relevant content. The best dynamic content emails, especially one-on-one ones, leverage contextual emails to energize the brand and target subscribers' interests. Emails are relevant to subscribers based on geolocation, psychographics, behavioral data, and insights with dynamic content strategies.
Speeds up Data Processing	Artificial intelligence speeds up data processing, ensures accuracy and security, and lets the team focus on strategic goals to produce effective AI-powered campaigns. Real-time tactical data from AI lets marketers make decisions without waiting for campaigns to end. They may make better, more objective decisions based on data-driven reporting. AI helps with tiresome tasks.
Make Customer-Centered Choices	AI insights help companies understand customers and make customer-focused decisions. AI analyses massive social media, blogs, and other internet content to provide external market intelligence. AI systems' billions of data points let marketers create consumer identities quickly. On-site interactions, regional offers, purchase habits, past communications, referral sources, and others are considerations.
Enhanced Client Happiness and Income.	AI has several uses in marketing. Each application provides benefits like reduced risk, speed, customer satisfaction, revenue, etc. AI platforms may quickly allocate media spending to keep clients engaged and maximize campaign value. Customers can receive tailored messages at the proper time with AI. This technology may also assist marketers in detecting at-risk clients and offering incentives to return. AI-powered dashboards provide detailed data on what works, enabling channel replication and funding.
Development of a Predictive Model	AI-powered solutions may help collect data, construct a prediction model, and validate it on real clients. Every consumer receives personalized emails thanks to AI. Machine-learning algorithms may help detect alienated consumer groups about to leave for a competitor. AI-powered churn prediction analyses omnichannel events and identifies waning consumer involvement. It can engage people with relevant offers, push notifications, and emails. AI-powered churn prediction and personalized content increase customer engagement, lifetime value, and income.
Make Better Decisions	AI helps humans make better judgments by analysing quantitative and qualitative data. Google Ads AI lets account managers and marketers focus on campaign plans. Deep learning is more advanced ML. It involves processing massive amounts of data, particularly abstract and scattered data, to find complicated patterns and correlations that can be utilized to understand customer engagement and improve targeted ads and ROI. As AI becomes more accessible, agencies can analyze data, forecast trends, and improve brand quality.
Target Audience	Companies must understand and meet customer expectations. AI marketing helps companies identify their target demographic for more personalized client experiences. AI strengthens conversion management solutions. For complex strategic concerns, marketers may now compare smart inbound communication against traditional analytics. The e-commerce, retail, and enterprise sectors are increasingly interested in creating highly customized and efficient experiences as consumer expectations change with technology.

continued on following page

Table 2. Continued

Applications	Description
Assist Businesses	AI helps organizations understand client wants and provide a tailored user experience. Collection of purchase history and social media data helps companies reach customers more efficiently. Ad performance optimization relies on AI. Social media uses AI to drive automated marketing, advise best practices, highlight performance preferences, historical patterns, and the general environment, and acquire knowledge.
Deliver Valuable Information	AI technology simplifies data analysis and provides tailored information to clients based on their preferences. Consider it a tool to guide marketing initiatives towards higher-level goals. AI can help marketers use technology and human intelligence to personalize and respond to modern customers with relevant and timely messages. Successful algorithms analyze site visitor activity to display personalized ads promptly. Continuously gather and use data to inform future ad content changes. Using personal and behavioral data, AI can help merchants prioritize objectives and assist clients. Psychographics will offer deeper insights on aim, desire, and purchase habits that influence customers' product or service choices utilizing AI.
Enable Convenient Customer Support	With AI, we can provide clients with intelligent, straightforward, and convenient customer care throughout their journey. Providing a seamless and optimal consumer experience is crucial. Automation in marketing involves automating repetitive tasks and procedures. AI applications are crucial for marketing automation. AI uses ML to analyze and apply client data in real-time on a large scale. AI streamlines data separation, sorting, and prioritization. New AI-powered solutions are transforming marketing automation strategies. New platforms aim to improve marketing techniques by meeting changing client needs, such as personalized solutions.
Better Marketing Automation Tool	Using AI in marketing automation solutions enables faster lead identification, improved nurturing methods, and relevant content creation. The most effective emails are dynamic content, especially one-on-one ones, as they leverage contextual emails to energize brand messages and target subscribers' interests. Dynamic content strategies allow emails to be relevant to subscribers based on their geo-location, psychographics, behavioral data, and insights.
Ease Workload	Despite excelling at collecting insights from large amounts of data, we often squander time obtaining relevant information from difficult data. AI may help by reducing workload and saving time. AI in marketing, such as predictive analysis, can significantly impact all marketing activities. Predictive analysis using AI can extract significant value from existing data. AI-backed AI-based predictive lead scoring is a popular marketing application. This method is unique for sorting and rating leads. Predictive algorithm-based lead scoring will remain popular among marketers.
Improve Stock Control	AI can improve stock control during high demand, avoiding overbuying and maximizing business revenue. Each organization has unique dynamic pricing and demand forecasting needs. A customized solution from a team or vendor may be the best choice for achieving goals, depending on the tasks and clients served.
Digital Advertising	AI is widely utilized in digital advertising to maximize success, including on platforms like Facebook, Google, and Instagram, to provide professional expertise. User data, including gender, age, interests, and other criteria, is used to determine appropriate advertising. AI technology can help marketers identify and predict microtrends. This will enable them to make strategic decisions. By reducing digital advertising waste, companies may maximize their investment returns. AI impacts the future of digital marketing by utilizing IoT and connected gadgets.

CHATBOT IN MARKETING

Chatbot marketing uses computer programs to automate conversations with prospects and consumers on your website or app to boost sales. Chatbots allow firms to qualify and engage leads 24/7, regardless of whether their marketing and sales teams are online. Marketing chatbots can answer support queries, but they can also start discussions with website visitors, qualify, and upsell clients. One person builds messenger chatbots. Based on your rules, they deliver leads and potential consumers the messages you desire. You can limit your bot's appearance to unsigned website users. You can also show it to unsigned visitors who have been on your pricing page for more than 30 seconds. Chatbot marketing uses conversational automation to generate leads, qualify them, convert them, engage customers, and provide support. Marketers can use chatbots on the web, Facebook Messenger, WhatsApp, or native brand apps. You can use them in organic or paid promotions (Azad, 2024; Saluja, *et al.*, 2023).

Marketing Chatbot Benefits

Chatbots' continual operation is great. When team members are unavailable, they'll keep your marketing engine running and save them time. The main digital marketing channel automation chatbots can include. The conversational technique has various advantages over other marketing methods, including,

- Real-time responsiveness and reactions
- On-the-Spot Customer Experience Personalization
- Interactive Engagement
- Instant Data Collection and Processing

One example of chatbot marketing benefits is a conversational landing page campaign that engages potential buyers from the start. Using questions, the bot can rapidly determine client profiles, interests, and qualifications. Using chatbot preferences, unqualified leads can be nurtured. Schedule a demo for qualified leads. Hot ones can interact with human agents directly via the bot. There are various methods to use chatbots in digital marketing (Haleem, *et al.*, 2022). Bots may automate tasks, handle client questions, and even sales. Table 3 shows chatbot usage in different areas.

Table 3. Usage of chatbots in different areas

Usage	Description
Chatbots for Customer Service	Bots can be helpful if your business receives a lot of Messenger customer care queries or wants to start using Facebook Messenger. Create a chatbot that helps clients categorize their customer support issues before guiding them to the relevant person or answer.
Chatbots for Sales	Chatbots can guide prospects to your sales pipeline. A customer journey can start with it, whether you use it to schedule consultations or collect newsletter emails. Many clients don't want to call, so making online communication easy can be helpful.
Chatbots for Shopping	Facebook Messenger chatbots let your business offer in-app shopping. You can customize it to let customers browse and buy things in the chatbot.
Chatbots for Marketing	There are several chatbot marketing strategies. You may follow up with leads using it. After someone chats with your chatbot, you may send them useful and informative messages to encourage them to buy or sign up. This direct one-on-one communication might be even more powerful than email marketing in your digital marketing toolbox.

Limitations of Chatbots in AI Marketing

Chatbots are popular in AI marketing, but they have limitations. These include human emotionlessness, empathy, and intuition. Chatbot responses are pre-programmed and confined to their purpose. Another drawback is the inability to handle complex requests or issues that demand a deep understanding of the customer's issue. Some consumers prefer to speak to a human, especially with sensitive or difficult issues. Chatbots also fail to recognize human characteristics like slang and irony, which can lead to poor customer service. Failure of chatbots to recognize these distinctions can cause confusion and poor customer experiences. Chatbots may become overused, making organizations disregard human engagement and tailored communication (Verma, et al., 2021). Marketers should use chatbots to improve customer satisfaction and assistance. AI marketing using chatbots should not replace human interaction.

Future of AI Marketing in Chatbots

- AI marketing chatbots have a bright future. They offer many benefits that businesses value. The following are some prospective chatbot developments:
- Improved Natural Language Processing: chatbots are comprehending human language better. This will enable personalized responses and genuine client engagement.
- Voice Assistant Integration: chatbots will integrate with Alexa and Siri, allowing customers to communicate with businesses via voice commands.
- More Data: chatbots will have more data to understand user preferences, forecast behavior, and provide a more personalized experience.
- Integration with Augmented Reality (AR) and Virtual Reality (VR): chatbots can be combined with AR and VR to give clients a more immersive experience.
- New Platforms: chatbots will be available on additional platforms and devices, making it easier for businesses to customize consumer communication (Murthy, et al., 2024).
- Better Analytics: chatbots will log customer interactions, giving organizations important data on customer preferences, behavior, and satisfaction.

Challenges

Ethical concerns: AI in marketing creates ethical issues. This may involve privacy, data security, and responsible AI use. Chatbots may struggle to recognize language, irony, and emotions, which can lead to bad customer service (Hermann, 2022).

Failure to handle complex requests: Chatbots may struggle to handle complex requests or issues that demand a deep understanding of the customer's condition. Some clients prefer human interaction, especially for sensitive or difficult topics (*AIContentfy*, 2023).

Chatbot overuse: Organizations may ignore human involvement and individualized communication due to chatbot overuse. Marketers should combine chatbots with human connection to improve customer satisfaction and help (Sidlauskiene, *et al.*, 2023).

CONCLUSION

AI-powered chatbots have transformed marketing by answering customer questions quickly and accurately. These chatbots learn and predict client demands using AI and NLP, enhancing customer service and satisfaction. They optimize digital marketing by detecting relevant online data. Businesses can save money and resources by automating customer experience and transactions with chatbots. One must acknowledge chatbots' limits. They cannot understand sophisticated requests or slang and irony. Poor customer service might emerge from pre-programmed chatbot responses that lack empathy and intuition. Instead, then replacing human connection, chatbots should enhance it to improve customer

AI in Marketing

service. AI marketing in chatbots has huge potential for business growth. Improved natural language processing will enable personalized chatbot responses and actual client involvement. Chatbots can interact with Alexa and Siri to let customers talk to businesses. To give clients a more immersive experience, chatbots can be coupled with AR and VR. More data will help chatbots comprehend user preferences, predict behavior, and personalize experiences. This will improve analytics and log consumer interactions, giving organizations important data on customer preferences, behavior, and satisfaction. Chatbots can follow up on leads and communicate with customers based on marketing plans. Personalization can outperform email marketing.

REFERENCES

Ahmed, A. M. A. A. (n.d.). *The impact of artificial intelligence in digital marketing*. Diva-portal.org. https://www.diva-portal.org/smash/get/diva2:1663148/FULLTEXT01.pdf

Arsenijevic, U., & Jovic, M. (2019). Artificial Intelligence Marketing: Chatbots. *2019 International Conference on Artificial Intelligence: Applications and Innovations (IC-AIAI)*, (pp. 19–193). Research Gate.

Azad, A. (n.d.). *Marketing chatbots: The ultimate solution for 2023 and beyond*. Engati. https://www.engati.com/blog/chatbots-for-marketing

De Mauro, A., Sestino, A., & Bacconi, A. (2022). Machine learning and artificial intelligence use in marketing: A general taxonomy. *Italian Journal of Marketing*, 2022(4), 439–457. 10.1007/s43039-022-00057-w

Feng, H. (2023, August 2). *How AI-powered chatbots are transforming marketing and sales operations*. IBM Blog. https://www.ibm.com/blog/how-ai-powered-chatbots-are-transforming-marketing-and-sales-operations/

From chatbots to predictive analytics: Using AI marketing tools to enhance customer experience. (2023, June 30). AIContentfy. https://aicontentfy.com/en/blog/from-chatbots-to-predictive-analytics-using-ai-marketing-tools-to-enhance-customer-experience

Furukawa, G. (n.d.). *Revolutionizing marketing strategy: The power of AI chatbots*. Marketerhire.com. https://marketerhire.com/blog/marketing-chatbots

Haleem, A., Javaid, M., Asim Qadri, M., Pratap Singh, R., & Suman, R. (2022). Artificial intelligence (AI) applications for marketing: A literature-based study. *International Journal of Intelligent Networks*, 3, 119–132. 10.1016/j.ijin.2022.08.005

Hermann, E. (2022). Leveraging artificial intelligence in marketing for social good—An ethical perspective. *Journal of Business Ethics*, 179(1), 43–61. 10.1007/s10551-021-04843-y34054170

How Chatbots are Changing the Landscape of AI Marketing. (2023, May 30). *AIContentfy*. https://aicontentfy.com/en/blog/how-chatbots-are-changing-landscape-of-ai-marketing

Murthy, A., Mamoria, P., Kumar, R., Shrivastava, S., & Thomas, S. K. (n.d.). *Artificial intelligence and machine learning in marketing: A review of recent advances and future trends*. Eurchembull.com. https://www.eurchembull.com/uploads/paper/13a7ffd5fb16e0a1329d76392bf913cf.pdf

Priyanka, A. L., Harihararao, M., Prasanna, M., & Deepika, Y. (2023). A Study on Artificial Intelligence in Marketing. *International Journal For Multidisciplinary Research*, 5(3), 3789. 10.36948/ijfmr.2023.v05i03.3789

Saluja, S. (2024). Identity theft fraud- major loophole for FinTech industry in India. *Journal of Financial Crime*, 31(1), 146–157. 10.1108/JFC-08-2022-0211

Saluja, S., Kulshrestha, D., Sharma, S. (2023). *Cases on the Resurgence of Emerging Businesses*.

Sari, A. E. (2023, June 25). *AI in marketing: How chatbots are revolutionizing customer interaction*. Linkedin.com. https://www.linkedin.com/pulse/ai-marketing-how-chatbots-revolutionizing-customer-interaction-sari

Sidlauskiene, J., Joye, Y., & Auruskeviciene, V. (2023). AI-based chatbots in conversational commerce and their effects on product and price perceptions. *Electronic Markets*, 33(1), 24. 10.1007/s12525-023-00633-837252674

Verma, S., Sharma, R., Deb, S., & Maitra, D. (2021). Artificial intelligence in marketing: Systematic review and future research direction. *International Journal of Information Management Data Insights*, 1(1), 100002. 10.1016/j.jjimei.2020.100002

Wang, X., Lin, X., & Shao, B. (2022). How does artificial intelligence create business agility? Evidence from chatbots. *International Journal of Information Management*, 66(102535), 102535. 10.1016/j.ijinfomgt.2022.102535

Chapter 3
Analyzing Demarketing Through Bibliometric Methods

Kavya Shabu
Dayananda Sagar University, India

Pragathi Prakash
Dayananda Sagar University, India

Truptha Shankar
Dayananda Sagar University, India

ABSTRACT

Marketing is the game changing strategic tool used to influence and nudge consumer behaviour towards a product. Demarketing is an inverse marketing strategy which would help shape the demand and behaviour of the consumer. This chapter intends to bring forward the prominent papers and research made along with the leading authors in this area, identification of research areas yet to be explored, the thematic perception of research through which the topic of demarketing has been approached. Through this chapter it found that more stress is given to demarketing in the field of health concerns and sustainable tourism, while identifying some of the core source papers in this area and prominent papers by Philip Kotler acting as a base in this area.

INTRODUCTION

Demarketing is a strategy of marketing that aims to reduce the demand for a product by not marketing about a particular product. Demarketing strategy is used by the companies when they want to reduce the supply of a particular product in the market. It also known as limit-demand strategy. The term 'demarketing was coined by Philip Kotler and Sidney levy in HBR article titled "Demarketing, yes demarketing" in 1971. "Marketing Management: Analysis, Planning, and Control." He describes demarketing as a strategy to reduce demand for certain products or services when necessary. Demarketing is considered as an integral part of the product life cycle. Usually, at the end stages of a product life cycle,

DOI: 10.4018/979-8-3693-6660-8.ch003

the demarketing strategies are used to confirm the decreased demand for the product. Maruthi Suzuki adopted demarketing strategy during the end stage of its life cycle.

The leading causes for demarketing are found to be Overcapacity; when a business has more production capacity than it can efficiently utilize, it may employ demarketing to reduce demand and avoid overproduction. Seasonal Demand; Companies with seasonal products or services may use demarketing during peak seasons to balance demand throughout the year. Regulatory Compliance; In industries subject to government regulations, demarketing may be necessary to ensure compliance with limitations on advertising or sales. Conservation Efforts; In cases where there is a need to conserve resources, such as water, electricity, or fuel, demarketing campaigns can encourage consumers to use these resources more sparingly. Public Health and Safety is another major factor wherein the government and legal bodies are seen to take actions. Demarketing can be used in situations where excessive consumption of a product or service may have negative health or safety implications, such as alcohol, tobacco, or sugary beverages.

Demarketing can be made in three different forms Active; used by the companies when they want to reduce the demand for their products. To do this, they usually raise prices, decrease advertising, change the message for target audience etc. Passive; used by the government to restrict the consumption of certain products. Ex- Cigarettes. Absolute; complete withdrawal of products from the market. Example- Samsung withdrew their explosive Galaxy Note smartphones. Demarketing is an extensive process which can be exercised within the 4Ps (Fig. 1) of the business cycle. This is a common practice of marketing technique adopted by any organization. The additional factor identified to this is the social dimension; wherein the aspects of societal concerns are given due importance in the case of demarketing.

This study is relevant to all industries and government focusing on bringing up demarketing strategies and also for further research purposes wherein the ideal focus areas on developing demarketing techniques could be identified and worked upon. This method of marketing is evident prominently in the field of tourism, artificial intelligence and national policies.

Figure 1. Strategies of demarketing

Source: 12manage.com

LITERATURE REVIEW

The concept of sustainability is changing the thought on green marketing and green demarketing strategies and its mediating effect on green reputation. SEM model is built with the data of 217 Taiwan companies finds that green reputation fully mediates green-marketing and partially with demarketing link of environment performance. (Wang, C. H., & Juo, W. J). A particular brand's reputation towards the environmental aspects influence the consumer's band habits. It shows a strong consumer motives and attribution towards the sustainable practices of the brands. Armstrong Soule, C. A., & Reich, B. J. (2015), the study approaches the demarketing strategies of 4p's against the overtourism. The demarketing strategy can mitigate efforts towards overtourism across the globe (Gülşen, U.,2021).

Green demarketing promotion has gained scholarly attention for green marketing activities. In-depth demarketing gives a broad spectrum of consumer responses on environmental concerns (Hesse, A., & Rünz, S., 2022). Consumer response towards green marketing and demarketing, the modern environmentalism calls for decreased consumption overall. Consumer attitude is more favourable towards green ads than green demarketing ads because of the genuine environment concern (Reich, B. J., & Soule, C.

A. A.,2016). Unsustainable wild meat and sea-turtle meat trade is a threat to the wildlife. Social norms were a predicator of this consumption in rural and urban residents at Gulf of Guinea. The structured approach towards audience research can guide the changes required (Veríssimo, D.,2020). Green demarketing ads focus on the on the sustainability, attitude and message by low processing fluency and increased skepticism. There is high positive and significant effect of green demarketing ad message on the attitudes towards a negative mediated processing fluency (Wache, C. et.al, 2021)

Demarketing is a unintentional marketing resulting in driving consumers away from revised text books, regionally adapted text and launch of inappropriate programs (Madichie, N. O.,2013). The greatest hindrance for the acceptance of demarketing is cynicism. There was a positive relation between energy price increase and conservation. The efforts were towards acceptance of the demarketing by the customers (Ahmed, S. A.,2015). Cigarettes demarketing investigation aimed at understanding the nature and elements involved in the process. Link between independent variable like product, price, and place was analysed on the dependent demarketing variable of cigarettes (Salem, M.,2022). The demarketing of breast milk substitutes products has a relationship with the dependent variable of product, price and place along with the independent variable of demarketing in Palestine (Salem, M. Z. Y., 2013).

Demarketing is also prominently seen in the field of tourism the popular destination tries to avoid the impact of overtourism through demarketing strategy developed by the stakeholders of the destination. This can be effectively achieved through destination planning and demarketing strategies (Kodaş, B., & Kodaş, D. 2021). The unintentional consequences are the threat to the structured, intentional social marketing. The evaluation confirms of interventions confirms the social marketing behaviours amongst the society (Peattie, K.,2016).

Research Questions

RQ1: What is the average production and citation per year in the field of demarketing.
RQ2: which sources have high ranks as per the Bradford's Law?
RQ3: Which are the highest globally cited papers?
RQ4: What are the different themes and cluster based on the author keywords?
RQ5: Which are the highest iterated keywords in the field of demarketing by the authors?
RQ6: Which are the most crucial keywords based on the relevance and development degree?
RQ7: What does the conceptual structure map of the keywords in this scenario indicate?

Research Methodology

Bibliometric Analysis is conducted for the purpose of making statistical inference on all published materials available. Bibitex file is exported from the data of SCOPUS. The search was made for publications having the keywords "demarketing", "counter marketing", "anti marketing", "contraction marketing" or "negative marketing" in the title and abstract. The data was collected from scopus database for the years 1975 to 2023 where data was sorted on the basis of relevance and 162 documents were found from this database. The other filters ensured were on the basis of source and discipline that they belong to the marketing and economy stream excluding all papers related to the field of science, environment and technology.

The data was further run through Biblioshiny, an extension available in R studio for a comprehensive science mapping analysis and application of tools like: average annual production, average citation per year, source cluttering using Bradford's law, source impact, thematic mapping, clustering network through network visualization and factorial analysis were conducted. Based on the data extracted the nature of the data in hand has been drawn down in Table 1. Through the table it is evident that a total of 162 documents were extracted from 111 sources. 330 authors were identified with 38 single authored papers. The documents comprise with the leading majority of 121 articles.

Table 1. Main information

Description	Results
Timespan	1975:2023
Sources (Journals, Books, etc)	111
Documents	162
Annual Growth Rate %	5.8
Document Average Age	12.1
Average citations per doc	23.14
References	1
DOCUMENT CONTENTS	
Keywords Plus (ID)	328
Author's Keywords (DE)	418
AUTHORS	
Authors	330
Authors of single-authored docs	38
AUTHORS COLLABORATION	
Single-authored docs	42
Co-Authors per Doc	2.37
International co-authorships %	0
DOCUMENT TYPES	
article	121
book	3
book chapter	25
conference paper	5
editorial	1
note	1
review	5
short survey	1

Source: Researchers' Compilation using Biblioshiny

RESULTS AND DISCUSSION

RQ1: What is the average production and average citation per year in the field of de-marketing.

Figure 2. Growth using Biblioshiny

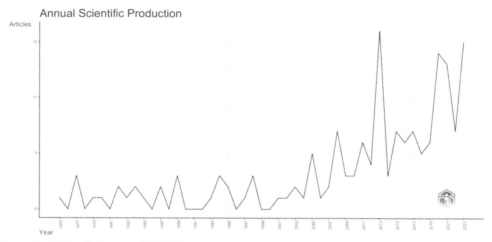

Source: Researchers' Compilation using Biblioshiny

The annual growth rate, scientific production and citations made helps understand the overview of the data extracted and its level of relevance. The average production is seen to have acquired a growth since 2003 and had the highest level of production on the basis of number of documents in the year 2013.

Figure 3.

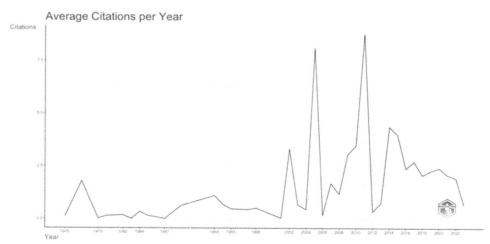

Source: Researchers' Compilation using Biblioshiny

Over the years the annual scientific production is seen to be in a rise for the search on "De-marketing" higher number of papers were produced in the year 2005 and 2011. A fall is seen in average publishing in the other years.

RQ2: Which sources have high ranks as per the Bradford's Law?

Figure 4.

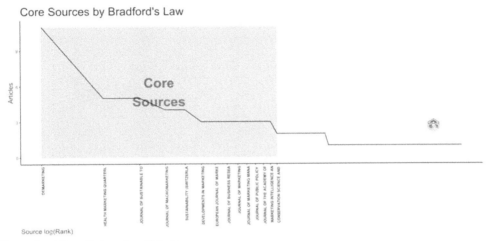

Source: Researchers' Compilation using Biblioshiny

As per the Bradford's law, the core sources has been identified as "Health Marketing Quarterly" (Comm, 1998; Majmundar et.al., 2019), "Journal of Sustainable Tourism" (Lu, & Nepal, 2009), "Journal of Macromarketing" (Drenten,&McManus,2016; Ekici,2021), "Sustainability" (Mura,2018).

RQ3: Which are the highest globally cited papers?

Figure 5.

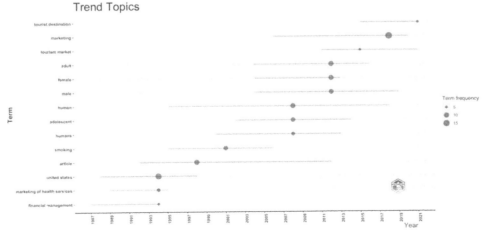

Source: Researchers' Compilation using Biblioshiny

Analyzing Demarketing Through Bibliometric Methods

The highest global citation is seen on the document of "Homburg C and Mark J, 2005" with the highest citation score of 685. The paper by Kotler and Mark J, 2011 is the second highest cited paper in the area of demarketing.

RQ4: What are the different themes and cluster based on the author keywords?

Network Visualization

Figure 6.

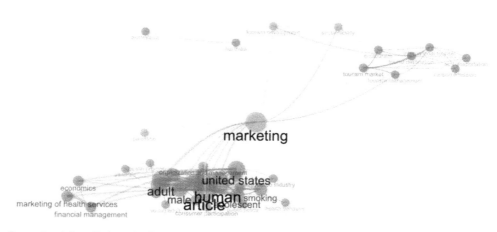

Source: Researchers' Compilation using Biblioshiny

The clusters are found to be closely linked with one another rather than well-defined sections classification. Clusters are clearly divided into five sets. The main word is "marketing" having a clear association with words like "human", "United states", "adult" etc. on the other hand is it connected to "Tourism market" (Çakar,2020), "carbon emission" (Gössling,2015), "eco-tourism" etc of the blue cluster. The violet cluster found here is of no connection but of the highest iterated words. The red cluster brings forward a tourism-oriented marketing research works while associating to demarketing topics which include the keywords apart from tourism as "air transportation", "carbon emission" (Gössling,2015), the keyword of "sustainability"(Hewitt, 2023) is also closely linked with the tourism aspect though his keyword has been set apart to the orange cluster. The economical aspects are highlighted in the brown cluster "economics", "marketing of health services" (Golden,1994) and "financial management" (Golden,1994) are the words and documents involved.

RQ6: Which are the highest iterated keywords in the field of demarketing by the authors?
Keyword -search analysis

Figure 7.

Source: Researchers' Compilation using Biblioshiny

The key words used in the articles selected for the studies is highlighted in the above image. The words like "marketing" "united states", "female", "smoking" etc looks like the highlighted ones and they have the association with each other as seen in the analysis.

RQ7: Which are the most crucial keywords based on the relevance and development degree?

Thematic Map

Figure 8.

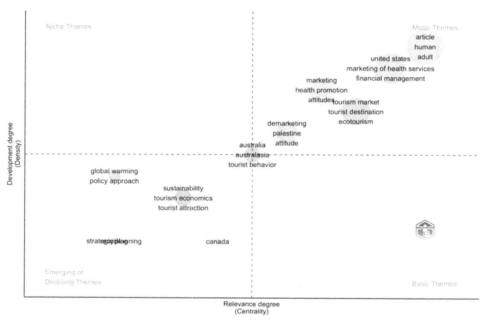

Source: Researchers' Compilation using Biblioshiny

This mode of analysis is used for further projection of higher relevant topics and areas with potential to be covered in upcoming studies. It could also project to research gap as not much studies are being made in these areas in the present and is of higher relevance.

It is visible from the above chart that, the keywords of "tourism market"(Cakar,2020), "tourism destination"(Gülşen,2021), "marketing of health services" (Golden,1994), "financial management" (Golden,1994), "eco-tourism", "health promotion"(Salem,2013), are the fields where more research could be made as if it is of high relevance and development degree.

RQ8: What does the conceptual structure map of the keywords in this scenario indicate?

Figure 9.

Source: Researchers' Compilation using Biblioshiny

The keywords' factorial analysis by applying the multiple correspondence analysis (MCA) has shown the whole of the keywords extracted from the abstract fall under one claustral formation itself as words are seen to have at least a minimal level of collinearity. "Practice attitudes", "health promotion" (Salem,2013), "health services"(Golden,1994), "attitude", "knowledge" and "information processing has similar research studies being processed. Another set of closely related research areas in the area of demarketing includes "smoking" (Salem,2022), "adolescence"(Yang,2013), "policy", "risk factors"(Guillou-Landreat,2020), "mass medium" (Guillou-Landreat,2020), "tobacco industry"(Lee,2004).

CONCLUSION

The data extracted from the Scopus database has enabled to bring out the different relevant articles in the context of demarketing. It is found that researches in this area age from the period of 1975. But the studies were relatively low based on the annual scientific production and average citation. The peak of publishing was seen in the year of 2013 and hence forward there is a growth in the production and exhaustive research in this field. The core sources identified were "Health Marketing Quarterly", "Journal of Sustainable Tourism", "Journal of Macro marketing", "Sustainability". Based on the clusters formed through the keyword analysis three core themes were identified; demarketing of health concerning products took the major cluster, but eventually the tourism and sustainable development is also seen to form another cluster addressing these keywords. The third cluster is of the financial management and economic aspects of demarketing. The thematic map analysis has also indicated the sustainability and demarketing as a crucial emerging theme which also includes tourism economics, tourist attraction, global warming, policy approach and strategic planning. Overall, all the keywords have shown one claustral formation with collinearity in the case f factorial analysis indicating all the papers extracted have closely related themes and keywords revolving around demarketing without a distinct separation.

REFERENCES

Ahmed, S. A. (2015). Correlates of Citizen Reaction to Demarketing Strategies. In *Proceedings of the 1985 Academy of Marketing Science (AMS) Annual Conference* (pp. 355-358). Cham: Springer International Publishing. 10.1007/978-3-319-16943-9_75

Armstrong Soule, C. A., & Reich, B. J. (2015). Less is more: Is a green demarketing strategy sustainable? *Journal of Marketing Management*, 31(13-14), 1403–1427. 10.1080/0267257X.2015.1059874

Budden, M. C., & Hossain, N. (1987). Tobacco demarketing campaigns and role model selection in developing countries: The case of Bangladesh. *Health Marketing Quarterly*, 4(2), 63–67. 10.1300/J026v04n02_0810282181

Çakar, K., & Uzut, İ. (2020). Exploring the stakeholder's role in sustainable degrowth within the context of tourist destination governance: The case of Istanbul, Turkey. *Journal of Travel & Tourism Marketing*, 37(8-9), 917–932. 10.1080/10548408.2020.1782307

Comm, C. L. (1998). Demarketing products which may pose health risks. *Health Marketing Quarterly*, 15(1), 95–102. 10.1300/J026v15n01_0610179066

Drenten, J., & McManus, K. (2016). Religion-related research in the Journal of Macromarketing, 1981-2014. *Journal of Macromarketing*, 36(4), 377–387. 10.1177/0276146715623051

Ekici, A., Genc, T. O., & Celik, H. (2021). The future of macromarketing: Recommendations based on a content analysis of the past twelve years of the Journal of Macromarketing. *Journal of Macromarketing*, 41(1), 25–47. 10.1177/0276146720966654

Golden, L. L., & Suder, A. J. (1994). Disease demarketing: The college AIDS challenge. *Health Marketing Quarterly*, 11(3-4), 105–124. 10.1300/J026v11n03_1010137011

Gössling, S., Scott, D., & Hall, C. M. (2015). Inter-market variability in CO2 emission-intensities in tourism: Implications for destination marketing and carbon management. *Tourism Management*, 46, 203–212. 10.1016/j.tourman.2014.06.021

Guillou-Landreat, M., Dany, A., Le Reste, J. Y., Le Goff, D., Benyamina, A., Grall-Bronnec, M., & Gallopel-Morvan, K. (2020). Impact of alcohol marketing on drinkers with Alcohol use disorders seeking treatment: A mixed-method study protocol. *BMC Public Health*, 20(1), 1–8. 10.1186/s12889-020-08543-632264848

Gülşen, U., Yolcu, H., Ataker, P., Erçakar, İ., & Acar, S. (2021). Counteracting Overtourism Using Demarketing Tools: A Logit Analysis Based on Existing Literature. *Sustainability (Basel)*, 13(19), 10592. 10.3390/su131910592

Happonen, M., Rasmusson, L., Elofsson, A., & Kamb, A. (2023). Aviation's climate impact allocated to inbound tourism: Decision-making insights for "climate-ambitious" destinations. *Journal of Sustainable Tourism*, 31(8), 1885–1901. 10.1080/09669582.2022.2080835

Hesse, A., & Rünz, S. (2022). 'Fly Responsibly': A case study on consumer perceptions of a green demarketing campaign. *Journal of Marketing Communications*, 28(3), 232–252. 10.1080/13527266.2020.1842483

Hewitt, J., Parker, L., McQuilten, G., & Khan, R. (2023). Sustainability Chic and the Future of Fashion Marketing. In *BEYOND THE DARK ARTS* (pp. 125–147). Advancing Marketing and Communication Theory and Practice. 10.1142/9789811276064_0007

Kodaş, B., & Kodaş, D. (2021). Demarketing as a potential solution to overtourism problems in tourism destinations. In *Overtourism as Destination Risk* (pp. 111–127). Emerald Publishing Limited. 10.1108/978-1-83909-706-520211009

Lee, D., Cutler, B. D., & Burns, J. (2004). The marketing and demarketing of tobacco products to low-income African-Americans. *Health Marketing Quarterly*, 22(2), 51–68. 10.1300/J026v22n02_0415914374

Lu, J., & Nepal, S. K. (2009). Sustainable tourism research: An analysis of papers published in the Journal of Sustainable Tourism. *Journal of Sustainable Tourism*, 17(1), 5–16. 10.1080/09669580802582480

Madichie, N. O. (2013). 13 "Unintentional Demarketing" In Higher Education. *Demarketing*, 45.

Majmundar, A., Cornelis, E., & Moran, M. B. (2019). Examining the vulnerability of ambivalent young adults to e-cigarette messages. *Health Marketing Quarterly*, 37(1), 73–88. 10.1080/07359683.2019.168011931880235

Mura, M., Longo, M., Micheli, P., & Bolzani, D. (2018). The evolution of sustainability measurement research. *International Journal of Management Reviews*, 20(3), 661–695. 10.1111/ijmr.12179

Peattie, K., Peattie, S., & Newcombe, R. (2016). Unintended consequences in demarketing antisocial behaviour: Project Bernie. *Journal of Marketing Management*, 32(17-18), 1588–1618. 10.1080/0267257X.2016.1244556

Reich, B. J., & Soule, C. A. A. (2016). Green demarketing in advertisements: Comparing "buy green" and "buy less" appeals in product and institutional advertising contexts. *Journal of Advertising*, 45(4), 441–458. 10.1080/00913367.2016.1214649

Salem, M., El-Agha, A., & Qasem, E. (2022, March). Demarketing of Cigarette Smoking in the West Bank, Palestine. In *International Conference on Business and Technology* (pp. 1095-1104). Cham: Springer International Publishing.

Salem, M. Z. Y. (2013). Factors affecting the demarketing of breastmilk substitutes in Palestine. *Breastfeeding Medicine*, 8(3), 302–311. 10.1089/bfm.2012.012023586626

Veríssimo, D., Vieira, S., Monteiro, D., Hancock, J., & Nuno, A. (2020). Audience research as a cornerstone of demand management interventions for illegal wildlife products: Demarketing sea turtle meat and eggs. *Conservation Science and Practice*, 2(3), e164. 10.1111/csp2.164

Wache, C., Möller, J., Mafael, A., Daumke, V., Fetahi, B., & Melcher, N. (2021, June). Do Not Buy our Product: Consumers' Responses towards Green-Demarketing Ad Messages: An Abstract. In *Academy of Marketing Science Annual Conference-World Marketing Congress* (pp. 111-112). Cham: Springer International Publishing.

Wang, C. H., & Juo, W. J. Sustainable environmental performance: The mediating role of green reputation in the choice of green marketing or green demarketing. *Corporate Social Responsibility and Environmental Management*.

Yang, Z., Schaninger, C. M., & Laroche, M. (2013). Demarketing teen tobacco and alcohol use: Negative peer influence and longitudinal roles of parenting and self-esteem. *Journal of Business Research*, 66(4), 559–567. 10.1016/j.jbusres.2012.01.004

Chapter 4
Blockchain and Its Derived Technologies:
Shaping the Future Generation of Digital Businesses With a Focus on Decentralized Finance and the Metaverse

Gurwinder Kaur Dua
Post Graduate Government College, Chandigarh, India

ABSTRACT

Indeed, blockchain played a pivotal role in the Industrial Revolution and is considered as one of the most valuable technological developments that evolved from the past years. Decentralized finance (DeFi) and the metaverse have roots in blockchain which has brought a fundamental transition in people's lives. These evolving technologies have a major effect on the future landscape of digital platforms. This study delved into the development of digital trades in the coming future, with a special focus on the aforementioned fundamental technologies. Initially, this study scrutinized DeFi-based technologies, encompassing GameFi, SciFi, SocialFi, and other foundational elements crucial for upcoming job roles and businesses. Subsequently, the authors explored metaverse-based occupations, including metaverse-based educational institutions and markets anticipated to emerge as widely adopted enterprises.

INTRODUCTION

The extensive adoption of the Internet has foundationally transformed traditional businesses, leading to the fall off of some while propelling the growth of others. As the Internet becomes extremely famous, business owners wants to offer services remotely to enhance their revenue streams while maintaining physical offices. Illustrations of such businesses consists of banks, supermarkets, jewellery stores, and automobile spare parts stores (Kreutzer, 2018; Zhou et al., 2007). In contrast, certain businesses specifically provide online offers without fulfilling to in-person customers, such as Google and Amazon (Hadi

DOI: 10.4018/979-8-3693-6660-8.ch004

Copyright ©2024, IGI Global. Copying or distributing in print or electronic forms without written permission of IGI Global is prohibited.

Kiapour et al., 2015). Overall, the Internet has instigated significant transition in the landscape of different professions which give rise to various innovative business models that have gained global traction.

The digital based economy is shaped by the development of the Internet along with cyberspace, which lead to the development of numerous technologies like financial technology (FinTech) (Gai et al., 2018) and insurance technology (InsurTech) (Stoeckli et al., 2018). These evolving technologies form the fundamentals for different services falling under the umbrella of centralized finance (CeFi) (Allen et al., 2002; Hoxby, 1996) which further support applications like shopping, tax, accounting, insurance, customer relationship management (CRM) applications, and other trading platforms. Moreover, they pave the way for the introduction of various web-based services, such as web-based taxi services, food ordering applications and ticket-issuing web pages which all are become integral parts of people's lives.

If technology and artificial intelligence (AI) have significantly assists individuals, businesses, and industries, they have led to the displacement of certain traditional kind of jobs as well (Akerkar, 2019; Canhoto and Clear, 2020; Di Vaio et al., 2020). So, business owners and employees working as per conventional practices must stay abreast of the new technological advancements to the digital era to sustain their businesses.

All kinds of businesses, whether traditional or modern, work on a centralized infrastructure and are covered by relevant laws. Nevertheless, small businesses have individual based policies and governed by stringent regulations over which they have no control (Chen, 2019). In consequence, they have to bear the brunt of these policies, having conflicts of interest (Ismail et al., 2017; Rangaswamy et al., 2020). On Contrary, big corporations can engage with the government to custom regulations as per their businesses. Negotiating regulatory changes with governments can be convoluted and demanding. Nevertheless, businesses can consider effective strategies including comprehending the regulatory process, conducting research, and fostering relationship and engaging with stakeholders. Successful illustrations of such negotiations consist of the Affordable Care Act (ACA) in the United States, The Paris Agreement on Climate Change and the European Union's General Data Protection Regulation (GDPR). Consequently, the need for a democracy based domain that enables all participants such as small businesses, retail markets, and big companies, to devour in significant decisions is crucial to ensure satisfaction among business owners.

Nakamoto (2008) introduced distributed bitcoin ledger as a practical implementation of blockchain technology. Bitcoin is considered as one of the most groundbreaking evolutions of the 21st century and blockchain development has gained significant attention from a different array of researchers, developers, and academics (Osgood, 2016; Qi et al., 2017). As explained in Section 2.1, the inherent features of blockchain technology assist a consensus-based approach among users who determine whether to record content on the blockchain. Consequently, blockchain technology can contribute as an infrastructure for democratic digital systems.

DeFi

By considering the potential attributes of blockchain technology, various evolving technologies have been invented. Among these, DeFi and the Metaverse highlighted as two significant innovations put forward approximately five years ago and are still considered cutting-edge technologies. Specifically DeFi technology presents a financial technology that leverages blockchain to hail various finance related issues (Chen and Bellavitis, 2019; Zetzsche et al., 2020).

Metaverse

While every developing job or business needs these cutting-edge technologies, with special focus on DeFi technology (Bernhard et al., 2021; Teng et al., 2022).

Metaverse based jobs offer a flawless digital environment involvement (Gu et al., 2023; Yawised et al., 2022). Like DeFi-based businesses, the roles in this sector need a wide range of fundamental technologies. Nonetheless, there is no need for understanding the background technologies for consumers as businesses are virtually presented in the application.

The paper is structured as follows: Section 2 discussed into blockchain technology as the foundational structure for future businesses and their derivative technologies. Section 3 categorizes the future generation of businesses into DeFi-based and Metaverse-based businesses in Subsections 3.1 and 3.2, respectively, with a detailed review of related studies. Section 4 briefly discusses the study and offers guidelines for future research. Finally, Section 5 wraps up the paper.

BLOCKCHAIN AND ITS DERIVED TECHNOLOGIES

Blockchain

The concept of blockchain was first operationalized as a distributed ledger technology by Bitcoin in 2008 so it is not a novel concept (Nakamoto, 2008). Anyone can have access to bitcoin as it is available publicly and anyone can their transactions. Another kind of blockchain is the consortium blockchain, which has limited access and is available for access solely to authorized individuals for transactions and information exchange. On the contrary, private blockchains are customised distributed ledgers technology for special organizations, with limited access for authorized personnel only (Andreev et al., 2018). To adhere to the need of this study, an explanation in detail of blockchain technology is provided.

Structure

The term "blockchain" is a blend of "block" and "chain." A "block" consist of data blocks having transactions such as data and its roots, timestamps, the hash of the previous block, and the nonce (Ferretti and D'Angelo, 2020; Nakamoto, 2008), while "chain" presents the chaining of blocks to previous ones until reaching the genesis block (the first mined block).

Following are certain technical terms related to blockchain

Main data, data root: Recorded data (transactions) in the block and their root calculated by the Merkle tree.

Prev_hash: Hash of the previous block.

Timestamp: Block generation time.

Nonce: Random number solving the mining puzzle.

Smart Contract

Szabo (1996) developed smart contracts which enable code execution without the interference of intermediary involvement. Nakamoto (2008) combined blockchain technology as the foundation for Bitcoin and assisting in smart contract implementation. Distributed ledger technology (DLT) can execute code in a predetermined programming language like Solidity for the Ethereum blockchain (Antonopoulos and Wood, 2018; Tikhomirov et al., 2018). Smart contracts, which are recorded on public blockchains, are implemented in a distributed manner under the blockchain nodes' supervision. Smart contracts necessitate five essential components: signers, commitments, conditions, oracle(s), and host platforms which further ensure its execution guarantees while upholding security, trust, efficiency, and beneficiary removal.

Features

Based on blockchain's structure and objectives, blockchain provides several key features, consisting of:
a) From origin it is considered as a crucial blockchain feature, anonymity, providing secure untraceability, has evolved due to regulatory requirements, now supporting conditional privacy.
b) Blockchain's state machine and smart contracts enable autonomous operation.
c) Blockchain nodes are distributed around the world, and all of them can be full nodes. Therefore, being distributed is one of the blockchain's features.
d) Linking each block to previous ones avoid change in old blocks since each change appears in the current/next block. Moreover, many full nodes worldwide cause record transactions in many places. These two factors provide immutability for blockchain technology.
e) All smart contracts block headers, and algorithms are recorded in the blockchain and are assigned serials e.g., block numbers. Hence, they all are open source for the public.
f) Public access to blockchain transactions brings transparency (Ferretti and D'Angelo, 2020; Muzammal et al., 2019; Nakamoto, 2008)

Cryptocurrency and Token Distinctions

- Cryptocurrency: Digital currencies developed on public blockchains, transacted on specialized blockchains and secured by cryptographic tools.
- Tokens: Developed on existing public blockchains, are used as rewards or payment-only assets with specific properties and tokens do not have specialized blockchains.

Decentralized Autonomous Organization (DAO)

A Decentralized Autonomous Organization (DAO) is a decentralized entity working as a Decentralized Application (DApp) with the help of smart contracts on a blockchain network. This arrangement enables members to participate in decentralized decision-making and management without the interference of central authority or intermediary. It is a community driven organization using blockchain technology so that it can function autonomously. Funds are transparently managed with the help of blockchain and members are able to propose and vote on decisions (Wang et al., 2019).

DAOs consist of a set of rules encoded on a blockchain that govern the behaviour and assist in asset distribution of its members. Members can propose and vote on various decisions through a consensus mechanism. The governance process is transparent and incorruptible due to the steadiness of the blockchain. Moreover, financial resources of DAO are securely stored and managed on the blockchain, making it resistant to external control and empowering members to directly control their assets on their own.

Aim of DAOs is to operate autonomously, their autonomous operations are currently limited to the AI algorithms and codes they consider. In practicality, DAOs are operated by their beneficiaries who are having a significant number of existing tokens, allowing for human control over DAO managing operations. Examples of DAOs include MakerDAO, Curve, Mantra DAO, LidoDAO, MetisDAO, and ClearDAO.

Metaverse

The Metaverse is a digital domain presenting a three-dimensional (3D) cyberspace where users can adhere to their daily lives needs remotely. It combines real and virtual worlds to create digital spaces where users can connect, collaborate, content creation, and other virtual activities. The Metaverse offers an immersive experience surpassing traditional digital media, accessible through various devices like computers and VR headsets (Lee et al., 2022; Wang et al., 2022).

By integrating blockchain technology into the Metaverse increases security and decentralization. It makes possible the creation of secure digital assets for the purpose of trading within the Metaverse and implements decentralized systems for transparent decision-making. Blockchain technology also assists in interoperability among various Metaverse domains, allowing users to exchange digital assets and create a connected virtual world (Lee et al., 2022).

The term Digital Twins (DT) consists of accurate simulations of physical entities supported by various technologies. DT is currently considered cutting-edge and continuously developing. DTs provide realistic behaviour for virtual entities in the Metaverse which make them necessary components for creating an authentic virtual reality. Hence, an ideal Metaverse replicates the physical world through a DT (Far and Rad, 2022).

The concept of Internet of Things (IoT) has become a necessary part of daily life, interconnecting different devices through the Internet. In the context of the Metaverse, IoT technology apart from the fact that increases digital experiences, similarly serves to the improvement of the Metaverse itself (Maksymyuk et al., 2022).

Simulation is a foundational aspect of digital environments and for the Metaverse, because they rely upon visual simulations for their existence. Web 3.0 technologies, rely and built on blockchain technology, contributes as the infrastructure for the Metaverse (Kshetri, 2022).

Extended Reality (XR), augmented reality (AR) and virtual reality (VR), serves as the user interface for the users in Metaverse. While different technologies support XR tools, they are entirely beyond the extent of this study and will not be further discussed.

With regard to applications, the Metaverse contributes for diverse opportunities for second lives, with different new applications under consideration for future implementation. Popular applications consist of education, entertainment, marketing, medicine, new job opportunities and businesses within the Metaverse (Park and Kim, 2022).

Digital Twins (DTs) as a Metaverse has been introduced in smart cities and they endeavoured to introduce with notable examples including Seoul and Dubai. The Metaverse has significantly supported these cities in various domains, like predicting future trends, forcasting risks in smart city operations, and attracting virtual tourists (Banaeian Far and Imani Rad, 2022).

FUTURE GENERATION OF DIGITAL BUSINESSES

In context of the future landscape of digital trades, this study delineates two key areas: DeFi-based technologies and Metaverse-based ventures.

DeFi Based Technologies

DeFi has the capability to revolutionize traditional financial practices and increase business operations in numerous ways. Its decentralized nature can remove intermediaries and related costs, leading to increased efficiency and cost-effectiveness. Specifically beneficial for small and medium-sized enterprises (SMEs), DeFi provides programmability to create customized financial instruments and smart contracts, thereby streamlining financial functions, decreasing operational expenses, and enhancing efficiency. The transparency of DeFi venture, enhance trust and credibility in businesses, with blockchain technology boosting secure and trustworthy financial transactions, specifically for organisations managing sensitive financial data or requiring high transparency levels.

Novel technologies within the DeFi venture are represented as potential assisting agent of prospective job opportunities (Bernhard et al., 2021; Teng et al., 2022). These technologies are considered as subgroups of DeFi but can be customised to meet specific business needs. The subsequent discourse delves into evolving DeFi-based concepts.

BusiFi

BusiFi, derived from "Business Finance," consists of various businesses, with FinTech playing a significant role in increasing accessibility and efficiency specifically for BusiFi's participants worldwide (Sun et al., 2021).

FanFi

FanFi technology emphasis on financial technology leverage by loyal individuals and fans of different entities.

GemeFi

GemeFi relate to blockchain-based gaming that allows players to earn rewards through gameplay, known as "play-to-earn" (Kiong, 2021).

These functionalities confirm users' earnings and intercept fraud activities in games with substantial revenues, such as casino games, which could direct to the loss of users' rewards in the game's regulations by the host. The term play-to-earn has evolved as a new approach to earning income, specifically appealing

Blockchain and Its Derived Technologies

to young individuals with limited financial management experience. In consequence, GameFi smooth users' financial management procedures, making them able to effortlessly retain their earnings. GameFi has extended beyond play-to-earn by adding additional features such as smart contracts for peer-to-peer gaming and blockchain technology to enhance security in the gaming sector. These innovations have the capability to transit the gaming industry and reshape how gamers engage with the gaming ecosystem. Nevertheless, the environmental affect of blockchain technology on gaming necessitates attention due to the substantial energy consumption and carbon emissions related with blockchain mining. GameFi domain should traverse eco-friendly technologies, like proof-of-stake consensus algorithms, to decrease their carbon footprint and serves to sustainable development within the gaming industry.

IndFi

IndFi, a part of BusiFi, was designed to fulfil to industrial applications by removing intermediaries and brokers from industrial contracts and projects, thereby smoothening industrial procedures. In the future, IndFi is anticipated to develop into a tool consisting of all facets of industrial operations, like managing contracts, worker rights, factory loans and supply chain management. Through the utilization of blockchain venture, IndFi can increase transparency in industrial processes, fostering enhanced trust and efficiency within the industry. Smart contracts can further mitigate fraud risks potentially revolutionizing the industrial sector by offering a secure and efficient domain for managing industrial operations.

MediaFi

MediaFi, a subset of DeFi, provides a solution for managing multimedia content creation by giving decentralized applications (DApps) to aid multimedia producers in overseeing their productions. To be practical and appealing to a broad audience, MediaFi should extend beyond financial tasks to support numerous activities such as tax payments, TV broadcasting rights management, intellectual property rights and multimedia production-related editing tools. The combination of blockchain technology in MediaFi can give numerous advantages, including increased transparency and trust in financial and production processes. Smart contracts can automate contract execution, reducing fraud risks and saving time. By utilizing the benefits of MediaFi, multimedia producers can emphasis on creating high-level of content without botheration about the financial and administrative aspects of production, fostering creativity and innovation in the multimedia industry. In conclusion, MediaFi has the capability to revolutionize the multimedia industry by giving a equitable system for managing financial and administrative tasks. Beyond financial management, MediaFi can increase the production process by providing services such as overseeing broadcasting rights and intellectual property, thereby contributing to the growth and advancement of the multimedia industry.

RegFi

RegFi, a specialized subdivision of DeFi and associated technologies, addresses the financial support required for implementing regulatory policies, specifically established by governments. By establishing strong bond between businesses and governments, RegFi promotes transparency in the regulatory process through blockchain technology. Smart contracts which relates to RegFi automate policy execution and ensure compliance, while decentralized governance models like DAOs facilitate community involvement in decision-making, creating a more inclusive system.

SciFi

SciFi aims to support researchers in different fields by offering fair and transparent financial assistance to increase the quality of their work. DApp-based technologies, such as the SciFi DApp, can help scientific teams with regard to managing finances and optimizing research processes. To ripe the benefits of SciFi, experts recommend combining complementary applications for budget management, project timelines, and payment services.

SocialFi

SocialFi addresses the developing needs of social media users by tokenizing different parts of social networks using NFTs or dNFTs. Future social media domain should be tokenized, include user-based controls, and feature a blockchain-based payment system to empower the financial aspects of next-generation social media platforms. While MediaFi and SocialFi offer similar services, SocialFi emphasis on user authentication protocols, scalability, DAO implementation, and the utilization of NFTs and dNFTs to meet the unique requirements of social media platforms.

Metaverse-Based Business Opportunities

The Metaverse represents a wealth of opportunities for innovative trades, spanning virtual real estate, fashion and gaming. Virtual real estate ventures offer users the capability to trade, purchase, and rent virtual properties with limitless customization choices. Similarly, virtual fashion enterprises empower users to design and sell digital apparel and accessories customised to individual tastes. Virtual event trade assist the hosting of virtual gatherings like concerts and exhibitions with unrestricted attendance. In addition to that, the Metaverse offers a domain for virtual gaming businesses to expand their market reach and revenue potential beyond traditional gaming domains.

The Metaverse provides as a virtual domain that enables global participation in various job roles and business ventures, giving access to a worldwide customer base (Gu et al., 2023; Yawised et al., 2022). This inclusive nature of the Metaverse emphasis the creation of diverse sub-groups and services, platform for plethora of opportunities for entrepreneurs. The following section outlines key Metaverse-based business prospects, including practical examples, relevant studies, and suggested future recommendations.

While Metaverse-based businesses have the capability to revolutionize work practices and commerce, challenges related to governance, trust, security, and privacy. However, the Metaverse represents an exciting landscape for entrepreneurs, business owners and innovators to traverse new business models and generate value in the digital platforms.

MetaAd: Revolutionizing Advertising in the Metaverse

Metaverse-based advertising presents a groundbreaking concept to promoting products and services, by removing the need for physical materials, traditional collaborations, and travel. By combining Web 3.0 and smart contracts, Metaverse advertising ensures a secure, transparent and efficient environment for advertising companies, new services, and upcoming products. The versatility of Metaverse advertising allows for diverse advertisement formats, including banners on virtual structures, logos on digital cards, and virtual company offices and conference halls, visible to a global audience (Hollensen et al., 2022; Kim, 2021). The evolution of Metaverse advertising agencies brings a new occupation that can work virtually within the Metaverse or physically in the real world, adhering to individuals seeking to advertise in this innovative space.

MetaAca: Transforming Education With Metaverse-based Academies

The rise of virus-induced pandemics like COVID-19 has increased the adoption of online and remote education by academic institutions. While virtual education formats have gained widespread acceptance, the leverage of Metaverse-based education remains limited. This study explores a future where Metaverse-based academies ("MateAca") revolutionize online education, encompassing academia, universities, schools, and skill-training centres. Utilising Metaverse technologies like DT, IoT, and XR, MateAca provides a more immersive educational experience, simulating real classrooms and authentic tools/devices for online students. The transforming of existing educational institutions to MateAca is anticipated to attract international students and raise the quality of education, with dedicated education centres within renowned metaverse.

MetaEx: Redefining Exhibitions in the Metaverse

Global exhibitions incur significant costs on yearly basis, such as setup expenses, equipment transfers, and international visits. Companies explore substantial resources in these events to show their products, engage with competitors, and connect with potential clients (Ando et al., 2013; Choi and Kim, 2017; Hawkins, 2022). Exhibitions are typically affected by the organizing team, officially established companies, and visitors who present the target market for the showcased products. These three elements face challenges due to the inefficiency of exhibition costs. Hence, a cost-effective solution that consists of all aspects of an outstanding exhibition would greatly benefit all involved parties.

MetaEx is an evolving exhibition domain and a novel business model that offers a 3D virtual environment for expos. While establishing a specialized exhibition domain in the Metaverse may involve substantial initial costs for businesses, there are no extra maintenance expenses. Once the MetaEx business is established, the host can create revenue by hosting multiple international exhibitions, charging admission fees to attendees, and renting out exhibition stands.

MetaFash: Redefining Fashion in the Metaverse

MetaFash emphasis on fashion events, such as small and specialized exhibitions showing the latest trends. Fashion enthusiasts are eager to attend these events globally and be the first to view novel collections, willing to pay significant amounts for the experience. MetaFash, a Metaverse-based domain, utilizes 3D scanning and printing technologies backed by AI to allow fashion companies to exhibit their products in various colors and sizes to a global audience. Visitors and companies can also engage in immediate virtual buying and selling while trying out items that match their preferences, sizes, and styles.

MetaMark: Transforming Marketplaces

MetaMark presents Metaverse-based marketplaces that provide retailers, marketers, and service providers a visual domain to sell products and introduce services to a global audience. These marketplaces, known as MetaMark in this study, enable individuals from around the globe to launch businesses and attract a different customer base, potentially enhance sales and generating substantial earnings.

MetaMed: Reforming Medical Services

MetaMed, on the contrary, represents as to a set of medical services evolved on a public blockchain and customised for Metaverse applications. It contributes as an AI-enhanced TeleVisit DApp powered by extended reality, with the involvement of a team of specialists in different fields to adhere to people and patients worldwide. MetaMed utilises blockchain combining in the Metaverse to assist remote medical services, ensuring secure health record maintenance and autonomous payment systems without intermediaries or additional fees.

MetaMeet: Transforming Social Networks

MetaMeet, a key subdivision of SocialFi technology in the Metaverse, provides Web 3.0-based social networks in Metaverse. This domain enables easy management of service providers and offers a user-friendly DApp for consumers, meeting the growing demand for independent and autonomous virtual meeting platforms in formal settings.

MetaTra: Transforming Travel Services

Lastly, MetaTra addresses the costly nature of travel by providing publicly available application based simulations of cities, allowing individuals to observe specific locations and landscapes from their homes, providing an enjoyable, exciting and accessible alternative to traditional travel experiences. Google Earth is a well-known exemplar of this technology, with other additional services available as well. However, a substantial limitation of these applications is the lack of accurate representations or detailed information on large-scale maps, as users are limiting to viewing the general structure of simulated cities.

DISCUSSION AND FUTURE DIRECTIONS

In latest years, Metaverse of different smart cities like Dubai, Seoul, and New York have been established or are planned for the near future. These Metaverse technologies include Digital Twins (DTs) with features that offer a more realistic experience, including natural senses, intricate city details, multiple simulations, and valid reactions to events. The main goals of these Metaverse are to enhance the quality and efficiency of citizens' daily lives activities and attract international tourists in a modern and cost-effective manner.

MetaTra, which stresses on Metaverse based travel, enables individuals to observe cost-effective and highly realistic international travel. An ideal MetaTra service would represent a fully mapped and DT-enabled representation of the world, possibly attracting a large user base and generating significant revenue, akin to Google Earth.

The combination of blockchain technology with other cutting-edge technologies has led to transformative ideas that increase people's daily lives and businesses. AI, a prominent technology, has brought substantial benefits to various sectors. Nonetheless, the practical implementation of AI has direct to the development or replacement of certain job roles into modern forms.

In addition to, the integration of AI and blockchain technology has substantial enhanced digital businesses. The practical application of these technologies in robotics and industrial automation has transformed product management systems and supply chains. The combination of AI-enabled blockchain technology is expected to usher in a new era of businesses and create exciting opportunities for interactions between individuals and companies.

While dealing with theoretical and practical challenges is critical when combining AI-enabled blockchain technology. Theoretical challenges consists the requirement for research to determine effective integration approaches and designing algorithms that can adjust the blockchain technology's unique features while utilizing AI capabilities. Practical challenges include implementation costs, availability of skilled personnel, and organizational culture changes.

To direct businesses in implementing practically AI-enabled blockchain ventures, a comprehensive framework is needed. This study offers a detailed review of various DeFi subdivisions expected to underpin Metaverse-based businesses, specifically when powered by AI. Guidelines and future directions are guided to deal with legal, regulatory, ethical, and technical challenges in combining DeFi technology into Metaverse-based businesses, ensuring the development of safe, reliable, and efficient ventures that maximize the potential of DeFi and AI technologies.

The rapid growth in AI technology has direct to the displacement of conventional job roles, having a major challenge for individuals lacking high-tech skills. To deal with this concern, it is compulsory for governments to regulate the advancement of AI within industries to ensure that its pace aligns with the development of the workforce. Such regulatory measures are necessary to prevent widespread unemployment which results from the adoption of AI-based technologies and to ensure equitable distribution of its benefits across society.

Implementing CeDeFi-Based Platforms: In 2020, Zhao launched the approach of Centralized Decentralized Finance (CeDeFi), which integrates elements of DeFi and CeFi technologies. Fundamentally, CeDeFi can be considered as an enhanced version of CeFi that includes blockchain and related technologies, providing a semi-distributed system. Through CeDeFi, users can access decentralized exchanges (DEX), distributed liquidity protocols and yield farming methods, although some services may need bank permissions. CeDeFi contributes as a distributed infrastructure that prioritizes users' asset security and accountability. Notable CeDeFi service providers include MakerDAO, Synthetix, Compound, and Midas investments. Hence, the Combination of CeDeFi-based technologies and businesses in the Metaverse can give secure platforms for retailers and companies while ensuring compliance with regulatory standards.

Adopting DeFi 2.0: Decentralized Finance 2.0 (DeFi 2.0) presents the latest iteration of DeFi, dealing different issues present in its predecessor, like scalability, smart contract vulnerabilities, liquidity pool challenges, oracle dependencies, and centralized control by third parties. DeFi 2.0 is expected to incorporate Know Your Customer (KYC) and Anti-Money Laundering (AML) mechanisms. Several DeFi 2.0 projects have been established, including Rari Capital, Convex Finance, Uquid, Synapse, and Tokemak, with additional projects like Abracadabra and Olympus expected for release in 2023. This study recommends the integration of DeFi 2.0 into future business models, specifically those related to Metaverse-based enterprises.

Enhancing Digital Twins (DTs): DTs portrays a significant role in shaping highly accurate metaverse, but their detailed design can be computationally intensive, requiring powerful computers and data centres. This constitutes a challenge for Web 3.0 concepts such as the Metaverse, which necessitate practical user-maintenance environments while exactly reflecting Metaverse-based objects.

Utilizing Cloud-Assisted Metaverse: The data-intensive nature of the Metaverse has directed the developers to leverage large-scale databases with rapid response capabilities. Nonetheless, this concept contradicts the distributed nature of blockchain systems. To reconcile these demands, a cloud-assisted Metaverse architecture has been proposed, storing crucial data on a public blockchain and large-volume components in the cloud. Implementing cloud-assisted data auditing protocols is significant for successful implementation and increasing the throughput of the Metaverse.

Ensuring Conditional Privacy: In the area of computer networks, user privacy is most important, but complete privacy may facilitate criminal activities. Balancing user privacy with the needs of security agencies is necessary in Metaverse-based businesses. Security protocols providing conditional privacy in distributed computer networks, specifically in Metaverse contexts, are recommended to deal with these concerns.

Increasing Background Technologies: The Metaverse consists of a wide range of technologies and ancillary components. Improving different aspects such as economic models, governance practices, computational methods, business security, trust in Metaverse-based enterprises, international sales, retailer authentication, and marketing strategies can significantly contribute to the advancement of DeFi technologies and Metaverse-based businesses.

This study proposed that developers and academics devise systems that strike a harmonious equilibrium between autonomy and governmental oversight. Specifically, creating a semi-autonomous and cohesive infrastructure for businesses that facilitates the tracking of fraud activities by government and security agencies will resonate with the public and garner endorsement from authorities as a legitimate domain.

CONCLUSION

This study initiated by representing an overview of blockchain technology and delved into different blockchain-derived innovations, like NFTs, DAOs, DeFi, and the Metaverse. Subsequently, we posited that these ventures could lay the groundwork for the forthcoming era of enterprises. Expanding on this premise, this study identified numerous DeFi-based ventures and examined their potential advantages for businesses operating in the Metaverse. Lastly, this study advised developers to strike a balance between autonomy and governmental oversight. Specifically, we recommended the creation of a mechanism that enables authorities to apprehend wrongdoers while safeguarding business confidentiality. This strategy offers middle grounds that fulfil the need of both individuals seeking privacy and governments aiming to uphold law and order.

REFERENCES

Akerkar, R. (2019). *Artificial Intelligence for Business*. Springer Cham. 10.1007/978-3-319-97436-1

Allen, F., McAndrews, J., & Strahan, P. (2002). E-finance: An introduction. *Journal of Financial Services Research*, 22(Aug), 5–27. 10.1023/A:1016007126394

Ando, Y., Thawonmas, R., & Rinaldo, F. 2013. Inference of viewed exhibits in a metaverse museum. In: *2013 International Conference on Culture and Computing*. IEEE. 10.1109/CultureComputing.2013.73

Andreev, R., Andreeva, P., Krotov, L., & Krotova, E. L. (2018). Review of blockchain technology: Types of blockchain and their application. *Intellekt. Sist. Proizv*, 16(1), 11–14. 10.22213/2410-9304-2018-1-11-14

Banaeian Far, S., & Imani Rad, A. (2022). What are the benefits and opportunities of launching a metaverse for neom city? *Security and Privacy*, 6(3), e282. 10.1002/spy2.282

Bernhard, M., Bracciali, A., & Gudgeon, L. (2021). Financial Cryptography and Data Security. In: *Proceedings of FC: 25th International Conference on Financial Cryptography and Data Security*. Springer, Berlin, Heidelberg.

Canhoto, A. I., & Clear, F. (2020). Artificial intelligence and machine learning as business tools: A framework for diagnosing value destruction potential. *Business Horizons*, 63(2), 183–193. 10.1016/j.bushor.2019.11.003

Chen, R. (2019). *Policy and regulatory issues with digital businesses*. World Bank Policy Research Working Paper. https://documents.worldbank.org/en/publi cation/documents-reports/documentdetail/675241563969185669/policy-and-regulatory-issues-with-digital-businesses.

Chen, Y., & Bellavitis, C. (2019). Decentralized finance: blockchain technology and the quest for an open financial system. In: *Stevens Institute of Technology School of Business Research Paper*. SIT. 10.2139/ssrn.3418557

Di Vaio, A., Palladino, R., Hassan, R., & Escobar, O. (2020). Artificial intelligence and business models in the sustainable development goals perspective: A systematic literature review. *Journal of Business Research*, 121(Dec), 283–314. 10.1016/j.jbusres.2020.08.019

Far, S. B., & Rad, A. I. (2022). Applying digital twins in metaverse: User interface, security and privacy challenges. *J. Metaverse*, 2(1), 8–15.

Ferretti, S., & D'Angelo, G. (2020). On the ethereum blockchain structure: A complex networks theory perspective. *Concurrency and Computation*, 32(12), e5493. 10.1002/cpe.5493

Gai, K., Qiu, M., & Sun, X. (2018). A survey on fintech. *Journal of Network and Computer Applications*, 103(Feb), 262–273. 10.1016/j.jnca.2017.10.011

Gu, J., Wang, J., Guo, X., Liu, G., Qin, S., & Bi, Z. (2023). A metaverse-based teaching building evacuation training system with deep reinforcement learning. *IEEE Transactions on Systems, Man, and Cybernetics. Systems*, 53(4), 2209–2219. 10.1109/TSMC.2022.3231299

Hadi Kiapour, M., Han, X., & Lazebnik, S. (2015). Where to buy it: matching street clothing photos in online shops. In: *Proceedings of the IEEE International Conference on Computer Vision*. IEEE.

Hawkins, M. (2022). Metaverse live shopping analytics: Retail data measurement tools, computer vision and deep learning algorithms, and decision intelligence and modeling. *J. Self Govern. Manag. Econ.*, 10(2), 22–36. 10.22381/jsme10220222

Hollensen, S., Kotler, P., & Opresnik, M. O. (2022). Metaverse–the new marketing universe. *The Journal of Business Strategy*, 44(3), 119–125. 10.1108/JBS-01-2022-0014

Hoxby, C. M. (1996). Are efficiency and equity in school finance substitutes or complements? *The Journal of Economic Perspectives*, 10(4), 51–72. 10.1257/jep.10.4.51

Ismail, M. H., Khater, M., & Zaki, M. (2017). Digital business transformation and strategy: What do we know so far. *Cambridge Service Alliance*, 10, 1–35.

Kim, J. (2021). Advertising in the metaverse: Research agenda. *Journal of Interactive Advertising*, 21(3), 141–144. 10.1080/15252019.2021.2001273

Kiong, L.V. (2021). *DeFi, NFT and GameFi made easy: a beginner's guide to understanding and investing in DeFi, NFT and GameFi projects*. Independently published.

Kreutzer, R. T. (2018). *Praxisorientiertes Online-Marketing*. Springer. 10.1007/978-3-658-17912-0

Kshetri, N. (2022). Web 3.0 and the metaverse shaping organizations' brand and product strategies. *IT Professional*, 24(2), 11–15. 10.1109/MITP.2022.3157206

Lee, H. K., Park, S., & Lee, Y. (2022). *A proposal of virtual museum metaverse content for the mz generation*.

Maksymyuk, T., Gazda, J., Bugar, G., Gazda, V., Liyanage, M., & Dohler, M. (2022). Blockchain-empowered service management for the decentralized metaverse of things. *IEEE Access : Practical Innovations, Open Solutions*, 10(Sep), 99025–99037. 10.1109/ACCESS.2022.3205739

Muzammal, M., Qu, Q., & Nasrulin, B. (2019). Renovating blockchain with distributed databases: An open source system. *Future Generation Computer Systems*, 90(Jan), 105–117. 10.1016/j.future.2018.07.042

Nakamoto, S. (2008). Bitcoin: a peer-to-peer electronic cash system. Bitcoin. htt ps://bitcoin.org/bitcoin.pdf.

Osgood, R. (2016). The future of democracy: blockchain voting. *COMP116: Inf. Secur*. Tufts. https://www.cs.tufts.edu/comp/116/archive/fall2016/rosgood.pdf

Park, S. M., & Kim, Y. G. (2022). A metaverse: Taxonomy, components, applications, and open challenges. *IEEE Access : Practical Innovations, Open Solutions*, 10, 4209–4251. 10.1109/ACCESS.2021.3140175

Qi, R., Feng, C., & Liu, Z. (2017). *Blockchain-powered internet of things, e-governance and e-democracy. E-Democracy for Smart Cities. Advances in 21st Century Human Settlements*. Springer.

Rangaswamy, A., Moch, N., Felten, C., van Bruggen, G., Wieringa, J. E., & Wirtz, J. (2020). The role of marketing in digital business platforms. *Journal of Interactive Marketing*, 51(Aug), 72–90. 10.1016/j.intmar.2020.04.006

Stoeckli, E., Dremel, C., & Uebernickel, F. (2018). Exploring characteristics and transformational capabilities of insurtech innovations to understand insurance value creation in a digital world. *Electronic Markets*, 28(3), 287–305. 10.1007/s12525-018-0304-7

Sun, X., Zhang, X., & Xia, Z. (2021). Artificial intelligence and security. In: *Proceedings of ICAIS: International Conference on Artificial Intelligence and Security*. Research Gate.

Teng, H., Tian, W., & Wang, H. (2022). Applications of the decentralized finance (DeFi) on the ethereum. In: *Proceedings of IEEE Asia-Pacific Conference on Image Processing, Electronics and Computers (IPEC)*. IEEE. 10.1109/IPEC54454.2022.9777543

Wang, F., Qin, R., Wang, X., & Hu, B. (2022). Metasocieties in metaverse: Metaeconomics and metamanagement for metaenterprises and metacities. *IEEE Transactions on Computational Social Systems*, 9(1), 2–7. 10.1109/TCSS.2022.3145165

Wang, S., Ding, W., Li, J., Yuan, Y., Ouyang, L., & Wang, F.-Y. (2019). Decentralized autonomous organizations: Concept, model, and applications. *IEEE Transactions on Computational Social Systems*, 6(5), 870–878. 10.1109/TCSS.2019.2938190

Yawised, K., Apasrawirote, D., & Boonparn, C. (2022). From traditional business shifted towards transformation: The emerging business opportunities and challenges in 'metaverse' era. *INCBAA*, 162, 175.

Zetzsche, D. A., Arner, D. W., & Buckley, R. P. (2020). Decentralized finance (DeFi). *J. Fin. Regul.*, 6(Sep), 172–203. 10.1093/jfr/fjaa010

Zhou, L., Dai, L., & Zhang, D. (2007). Online shopping acceptance model-a critical survey of consumer factors in online shopping. *Journal of Electronic Commerce Research*, 8(1), 1–41.

Chapter 5
Consumer Policy:
The Relationship Between AI and Data Privacy

Chander Prabha
https://orcid.org/0000-0002-2322-7289
Chitkara University Institute of Engineering and Technology, Chitkara University, Punjab, India

Shefali Saluja
https://orcid.org/0000-0002-8560-5150
ChItkara University, Punjab, India

ABSTRACT

Consumer policy is designed to protect welfare and rights of consumers. The recent advancements in artificial intelligence (AI) and its integration with the privacy aspects of consumer information need potential attention due to illegal activities in terms of fraud. The rapid progress of AI represents significant risks to safeguarding consumer privacy and ensuring data security. The integration of AI inside several industries, such as e-commerce platforms, and financial technology, has become prevalent. This leads to emphasizing the significance of developing comprehensive legal and regulatory frameworks to address effectively the challenges related to consent, data minimization, accuracy, discrimination, and bias. The chapter explores the concept of AI and its public and private use in consumer policies. The key components are highlighted in making consumer policy along with the relationship between AI and data privacy aspects. Finally, it presents the challenges faced by consumers in accessing vital information, that lead to imbalances between companies and customers.

INTRODUCTION

Consumers are an important aspect of the market. Without consumers, the existence of the market doesn't persist. The data privacy of consumers faces various challenges. During any purchase, while billing, the consumer has to enter their details. These details can be used for mischievous purposes by intruders. Governments, consumer organizations, and companies employ various measures such as prohibitions, legislation, advisory mechanisms, litigation, and self-regulatory standards to address these issues. The relationship between corporations and customers exhibits imbalance, as consumers are at a

DOI: 10.4018/979-8-3693-6660-8.ch005

Copyright ©2024, IGI Global. Copying or distributing in print or electronic forms without written permission of IGI Global is prohibited.

Consumer Policy

disadvantage due to their limited access to crucial information. Moreover, the field of behavioral economics uncovers notable biases, wherein habits, social norms, and irrational views influence individuals' daily buying patterns. The governance of consumer policy exhibits variations, which can be attributed to diverse concepts and ideologies, as evidenced by the field of comparative politics. The difficulties of consumer policy encompass complex digital markets, the service economy, and the goal of sustainable consumption (Ezechukwu, 2023, pp. 191–221).

The advancements in Artificial Intelligence (AI) and the application of Big Data in consumer policy have resulted in notable enhancements. Nevertheless, it is imperative to recognize that these advancements also present potential risks to customer privacy and data security. The utilization of AI in the evaluation of consumer credit throughout the underwriting process has been bolstered by the enforcement of credit data-sharing legislation and the presence of credit reporting organizations. The adoption of a hybrid credit data-sharing approach, which integrates a closely monitored nationwide database, possesses the potential to effectively manage risks while maintaining the benefits of underwriting powered by AI. The outbreak of the COVID-19 pandemic has led to a significant increase in the need for Electronic Commerce (E-Commerce). The use of AI holds the potential to offer benefits to both customers and E-Commerce platforms. However, the matter of privacy arises, prompting authorities to emphasize the improvement of surveillance to cultivate consumer confidence and protect privacy. The incorporation of financial technology, which includes AI and data-driven decision-making, has substantial implications for safeguarding consumer financial privacy. The necessity to update consumer financial privacy legislation arises in light of the challenges posed by AI and financial technology. The use of Big Data and Machine Learning (ML) techniques in decision-making processes has raised concerns regarding the protection of consumer rights and the maintenance of data privacy (Ruggeri, 2021). The next section discusses Artificial Intelligence and its private and public use in consumer policies.

ARTIFICIAL INTELLIGENCE (AI)

AI aims to develop computer programs capable of executing tasks often carried out by human beings (Lukitosari, et al., 2020). The tasks can be classified as intelligent, encompassing abilities like; visual and auditory perception, learning and adaptation, reasoning, pattern recognition, and decision-making (which plays an important role in consumer policies to maintain the congenial environment to safeguard users' data). The word 'AI' encompasses a range of interconnected methodologies and technologies, viz; machine learning, predictive analytics, natural language processing, and robotics (Figure 1). AI holds the potential to deliver a multitude of benefits, including enhanced operational efficiency and cost reduction, significant advancements in healthcare and research, improved safety measures in the automotive industry, and overall convenience (Hyde & Cartwright, 2023; Online, 2023). However, similar to the introduction of any novel technology, the utilization of AI presents a multitude of societal and legal difficulties.

Figure 1. Artificial intelligence

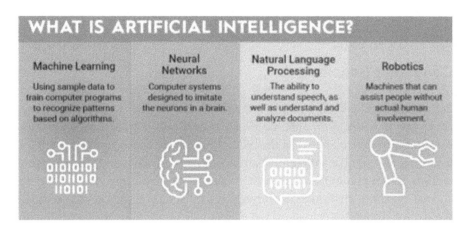

Most individuals see AI's impact on customer experiences (Figure 2) neutrally or positively across industries. AI was most well received in entertainment (54%), retail (51%), healthcare (48%), and advertising (44%). However, in customer service, the positive impact is 40%, neutral is 38%. The techniques and methods are in demand now to increase this positive impact of AI in customer service.

Figure 2. AI impact on customer experience

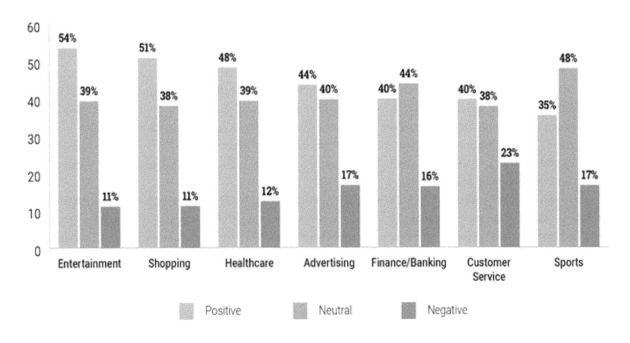

Consumer Policy

Exploration is also needed on how AI familiarity affects a person's everyday experience of AI. It has been found that 35% of respondents utilize AI-powered tools or services at work or in education. This group was more inclined to be enthusiastic about AI's impact on customer experiences in other areas of their lives (Onorato, 2022).

AI Role in Consumer Policies

AI serves an instrumental part in forming and affecting consumer policies in a variety of methods. Policymakers have begun to recognize the necessity for revised laws and regulations to deal with the difficulties and possibilities posed by AI in the realm of consumers as technology advances (Lagioia, et al., 2022). Below are a few significant elements of artificial intelligence's role in consumer regulations:

Data Protection and Privacy: AI frequently entails the gathering and examination of massive amounts of information about customers. Policymakers must enact stringent regulations that safeguard individuals' privacy and assure liable data usage. Consumer regulations might set the openness and endorsement needed for AI systems that handle private data, tackling concerns about ownership of data, availability, and control.

Algorithmic Fairness and Bias: AI systems can unintentionally reinforce prejudices in training information, resulting in prejudiced results. Consumer policies seek to tackle algorithmic prejudice in AI systems by encouraging equality, openness, and transparency. Policymakers might ask firms to inspect and evaluate their AI procedures for bias regularly, and to apply remedial measures to address any issues that are discovered.

Consumer autonomy and Rights: Consumer protection laws might contain regulations that allow users to comprehend, test, and choose out of AI-driven choices that impact them. Specific laws can help to ensure that consumers understand the way AI systems affect their liberties and provide ways to seek alternatives in an instance of damage or discontent.

Product Liability and Safety: Powered by AI, goods and services might cause liability issues in the case of issues or negative outcomes. Policymakers might be required to come up with structures to assess liability as well as responsibility in AI-related cases. Regulations about consumer protection might call for enterprises to check the reliability and security of AI goods, with penalties if they fail to do so.

Openness and Explainability: Companies may be required to deliver concise descriptions of how artificially intelligent machines arrive at choices that impact consumers under certain policies. This openness is critical for fostering user confidence as well as comprehension. In light of the consequences and possible hazards connected with various applications of artificial intelligence, rules might define the extent of openness needed.

Awareness Perspective of Education: The law-makers must initiate to consumers from the AI perspective, its use, that helps in making legible decisions and understanding the role of AI Technologies. The companies must provide approachable facts related to AI to their customers, to ensure transparency in the process of data usage and decision-making.

Anti-Monopoly Measures: AI has the capability to clout the dynamics of the market. Certain policies must be in place to control anti-monopoly practices. Anti-trust measures could be adopted to raise and address issues about the pre-eminence of various AI-powered services and platforms. AI technologies' role in consumer policies deeply includes:

- Addressing concerns related to privacy,

- empower consumers,
- maintain fairness,
- establish liability frameworks,
- promote transparency,
- and Adapting regulations to the dynamic landscape

Policymakers must strike a balance between the beneficial effects of AI breakthroughs and the necessity to safeguard customers' data while preserving a legitimate and equitable market.

Public and Private Uses of Artificial Intelligence in Consumer Policies

Significant advancements in the field of AI have resulted in the widespread utilization of AI technologies across both public and private domains. According to a recent AI study by the UK House of Lords (Parliament, 2024), AI is a tool that has already become extensively integrated into various aspects of our daily existence. AI serves as a computational tool that has the potential to boost decision-making processes across several domains. By leveraging AI, subject matter experts in different sectors can provide enhanced services and achieve groundbreaking advancements that were previously unattainable. AI technologies play a crucial role in enabling economic transactions and providing tailored services and products, meeting the growing demand of customers and citizens. Personalization is observed within the private sector through the implementation of travel management systems, shopper suggestion algorithms, and targeted advertising strategies. Additionally, personalization is also evident in social domains, such as medical diagnosis and treatment, individualized education approaches, and the optimization of resource utilization. AI is being vastly used in both private and public sectors to make and enforce consumer policies. Below are some facts that show the AI's role in consumer policies in these domains (CMP, 2024).

Public Use of AI in Consumer Policies

Regulatory Compliance and Enforcement: Governments use AI for monitoring and enforcing compliance with consumer protection regulations. Machine-automated systems are analyzing lots of data to detect and address violations in policies more effectively.

Fraud Detection and Prevention: AI is utilized by government agencies to identify and avert fraudulent activities, safeguarding customers from fraud and illegal activities. Algorithms based on AI may identify deviations in trade and patterns of anomalous behavior that reveal fraud.

Handling of Consumer Complaints: Government agencies use chatbots powered by AI and digital assistants to deal with customer queries and complaints. When necessary, these computerized systems can provide guidance, and information, and raise concerns to humans for assistance.

Market Surveillance: Artificial intelligence is used in the surveillance of markets to detect improper business practices, unlawful behavior, and price rigging. Market information and patterns can be analyzed by automated systems to guarantee a competitive and equitable marketplace for customers.

Policy Analysis and Development: Authorities use artificial intelligence to analyze the trends and data to create consumer policies. Comprehending novel problems, evaluating the effect of current policies, and tailoring guidelines to advances in technology are all part of this.

Accessibility and Inclusivity: Tools based on AI are used to guarantee that customer strategies are readily available to all citizens. It involves algorithms for Natural Language Processing (NLP) to improve the readability of policy documents while offering different formats for people with impairments.

Private Uses of AI in Consumer Policies

Customer Support and Engagement: AI-powered chatbots and AI-powered virtual assistants are used by private businesses to improve relations with clients and involvement. These resources assist customers in more efficiently navigating goods, amenities, and regulations.

Personalized Marketing and Recommendations: To offer customized recommendations for goods and targeted advertising, AI algorithms analyse buyer behaviours and choices. This data-driven strategy is used by privately owned businesses to customize their offerings to specific customer requirements.

Risk Assessment and Credit Scoring: Banking organizations and lending firms make use AI to evaluate consumer financial standing. Computerized systems use a variety of indicators to calculate ratings for credit and arrive at choices regarding loans.

Product Safety and Quality Assurance: This ensures compliance management, transparency in the supply chain, and predictive analysis for demand and supply.

- **Compliance Management:** Companies use artificial intelligence to handle affairs and make sure that they adhere to the protection of consumers' regulations and laws. Companies can use automated systems to monitor regulatory changes, evaluate their effect, and make the necessary modifications to stay in line.
- **Supply Chain Transparency:** AI serves to improve supply chain transparency, permitting customers to arrive at more informed decisions concerning ethical factors. The Bitcoin network and artificial intelligence (AI) can be paired to monitor the beginning and end points of goods.
- **Predictive Analytics for Demand and Supply:** Private companies use artificial intelligence to forecast demand from customers, boost levels of stock, and automate operations in the supply chain. It helps in the prevention of deficits, the reduction of waste, and the effective transfer of goods.

Both the private and public uses of artificial intelligence in customer regulations possess an opportunity to enhance effectiveness, openness, and in general satisfaction with customers. Yet it is critical to tackle moral issues such as confidentiality and prejudice to make sure that AI deployment is consistent with protecting customers' principles. Cooperation among both the private and public sectors is critical for striking the right equilibrium while developing a regulatory framework that promotes creativity all while protecting the rights of consumers.

LITERATURE REVIEW

The author (Pappalardo, 2022), focussed on defining and estimating customer damages via misleading or unlawful conduct, as well as strategies for estimating customer damage from confidentiality. The article presents in tandem different subsections from pertinent financial literature, resulting in an improved understanding of other methods of determining customer damages from a fiscal point of view. In addition, discussion was done on the controversy over the significance of psychological economics in consumer policy, wrapping up that the right instruments (AI Tool) based on the policy's goals; regulations suitable to change customer preferences in a specific direction might differ from guidelines useful to improve the user surroundings.

The authors (Chawla & Kumar, 2022) discussed two laws viz. the Consumer Protection Act, 2019 and the Consumer Protection (E-commerce) Rules, 2020 concerning consumer protection in India. With an effective legal structure and safeguards for customers in place, the future of e-commerce appears bright. The outcomes add to the body of expertise on e-commerce and protecting client rights by explicating the primary variables that influence loyalty and confidence in customers, as well as providing a stimulating viewpoint on e-consumer safety in India, which has wider repercussions. According to the findings, while the emphasis on customer confidentiality as well as rights security issues is overly broad, the regulatory framework's investigation has restricted its reach.

The act of buying, customer studies, and customer research are all vital components of modern society, and they are of curiosity not just to advertising professionals but also to lawmakers and scholars in other fields (MacInnis, et al., 2020). Consumers today communicate with AI in an abundance of capacities. Researchers in marketing recognize that AI has significant potential advantages for customers and their daily lives (Pitardi, et al., 2021; Pitardi et al., 2022). Yet, numerous innate tensions are raised with the usage of AI for customers, such as issues with privacy, dehumanization, and perhaps dependency (Lobschat, *et al.*, 2021; Pultoni, et al., 2021).

BACKGROUND AND KEY COMPONENTS FOR BUILDING CONSUMER POLICY IN THE AGE OF AI

This section presents some facts in background analysis and some key components in the age of AI for consumer policies.

Background

AI is predicted to affect most people shortly. Ernst & Young found that Belgium and Luxemburg invested over 100 million euros in AI during the past decade. Another PWC analysis found that 'AI might contribute up to $15.7 trillion to the global economy in 2030' (PwC, 2024). The Federal Public Service (FPS) Economy, SMEs, Middle Classes, and Energy commissioned a study on Belgians' impression of AI and found a market for AI-based goods and services. European Commission unveiled the 'Artificial Intelligence for Europe' agenda on 25 April 2018. It proposed AI ethical norms that would consider consumer protection. The Commission also highlighted that the widespread use of AI-enabled technologies in business-to-consumer transactions must be fair, transparent, and compliant with consumer laws and that customers should receive clear information about product use, features, and qualities. The European Commission established an Independent High-Level Expert Group on Artificial Intelligence in June 2018, which issued its final version of the 'Ethics Guidelines for Trustworthy AI' on 8 April 2019 (AI Guidelines) as an AI project assessment list. Respect for human autonomy, damage reduction, justice, and explainability are AI Guidelines and ethical imperatives. AI Guidelines suggest that 'different opportunities and difficulties come from AI systems applied in the context of business-to-consumer' without elaborating or mentioning consumer law's applicability to AI-based applications. The EU Parliament's Internal Market and Consumer Protection Committee approved a resolution on AI and automated decision-making technologies on January 21, 2020, recommending that the EU legal framework, including consumer law acquis, data protection legislation, product safety, and market surveillance legislation, be examined to ensure it can respond to AI and automated decision-making (Europa, n.d.). After that, the European Commission released its AI White Paper. The European Commission seems to focus on product safety and liability risks from AI-based applications. It mentions the General Data Protection Regulation, anti-discrimination laws, and consumer protection laws such as the Unfair Practises and Consumer Rights Directives. In the age of AI, European institutions are concerned with consumer policy, but its form is ambiguous.

However, in present 'consumer law' this paradigm is intimately tied to citizen market standing. Citizens are only consumers when they are presented with economic activity from a commercial entity, while they act (mostly) outside their profession to meet their consuming demands. It's tied to another prevailing paradigm. The information paradigm implies rational customer behavior with enough information. The weaker party is less informed. Information imbalance between consumers and businesses is a market failure, hence consumer law is justified to restore balance. Behavioral economists have shown that market failures are caused by cognitive biases that limit customers' autonomy, not only information differences, which can be remedied by supplying relevant information. Some consumers may be more susceptible to particular corporate practices.

Key Components

Establishing operational customer regulations in the era of AI necessitates an extensive and innovative approach (André, et al., 2018; Kaur, et al., 2021). Policymakers ought to think about the following key components (Figure 3):

Consent and Data Privacy: The policy requirement is to bolster the privacy of data protection and laws. The implementation is done by setting up rigorous standards for keeping records, collaborating, and confidentiality, as well as concise and informed authorization processes for the gathering and utilization of sensitive information.

Figure 3. Key components for building consumer policies

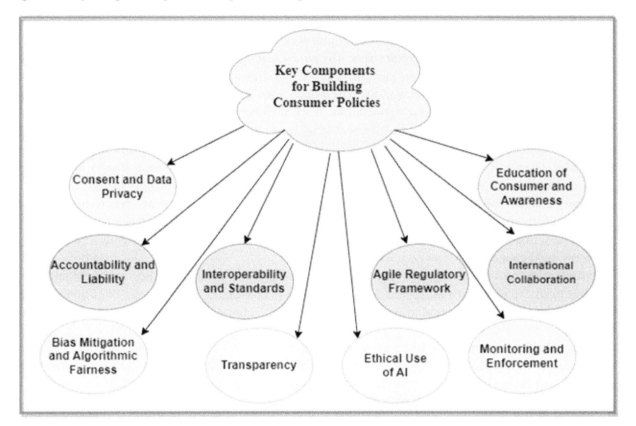

Transparency: The key policy requirement is to require openness in AI systems, requiring firms to offer detailed descriptions as to how their artificial intelligence techniques make consumer-impacting decisions. It is implemented by encouraging the creation of explainable models for AI and strategies that enable businesses to make clear the inner workings of their artificial intelligence (AI) systems in an accessible way.

Accountability and Liability: The policy requirement is to outline the regulatory structure to assess accountability in instances of AI-related damage or failure, determining accountability for businesses that set up AI systems. This is implemented by setting precise boundaries of accountability, promoting openness about AI system strengths and constraints, and putting in place strategies to address customer liability.

Bias Mitigation and Algorithmic Fairness: The policy requirement is to create regulations for tackling and minimizing prejudices in AI strategies to guarantee that every group of customers is treated fairly. This is implemented by encouraging companies to carry on bias audits regularly. It must provide and use tools for bias mitigation. At last, it must establish penalties for unfair results.

Consumer Policy

Interoperability and Standards: Promoting industry development standards and operational ability to ensure competition, transparency, and consumer choice is the policy requirement. It is implemented by encouraging collaboration between academia, industry, and Standards-setting regularities for establishing precise and common frameworks for the development of AI and its deployment.

Education of Consumer and Awareness: The policy requirement is to invest in outreach campaigns and educational initiatives to educate customers about artificial intelligence, its implications, and its entitlements. This is accomplished by working with stakeholders of industries to ensure that the consumers have reach to information related to applications of AI, their benefits, and potential risks.

Ethical Use of AI: The policy requirement is to create an ethics code for the utilization of AI in consumer-facing services that emphasizes accountable and moral AI practices. It is implemented by establishing committees and review boards for rigorous evaluation of the societal impact of the usage of AI framework and subsequently guiding firms in following ethical standards.

International Collaboration: Ensuring consistent standards related to AI usage in consumer policies and fostering international collaborations is the policy requirement. It is implemented via multilateral and bilateral discussion engagement, sharing best practices. It also deals with harmonizing across borders concerning AI-related customer policies.

Monitoring and Enforcement: The policy requirement is to enhance agency oversight and legal systems to ensure adherence to AI-related laws that protect consumers. Implementation is done by providing resources for audits regularly, monitoring, and legal actions to hold companies responsible for adhering to AI customer policies.

Agile Regulatory Framework: Setting up a regulatory framework capable of adapting to the constantly shifting surroundings of AI technologies is the policy requirement. It is implemented by continuously updating and reviewing policies to keep on track with emerging risks, technological advancements, emerging risks, and changing consumer expectations.

By incorporating these key components into customer policies, policymakers may establish an equitable regulatory framework that encourages creativity while protecting the rights of customers and psychological well-being in the age of AI. Cooperation with stakeholders from the industry, investigators, and coalitions of supporters on an ongoing basis is vital for promoting policies that are efficient and relevant as time goes by.

CHALLENGES FACED BY CONSUMERS

Consumers might encounter a variety of challenges when obtaining critical details regarding consumer policies. These obstacles can make it difficult for them to come up with sensible choices, comprehend their privileges, and get around the marketplace (Technology magazine, 2024; Victorian, 2021). Table 1 shows some of these challenges and their impact.

Table 1. Challenges encountered by consumers and their impact

Aspect	Challenge	Impact
Complexity and Legalese	Consumer policies tend to be expressed with intricate legal vocabulary, which makes the conditions and terms hard to comprehend for ordinary consumers.	Consumers might find it difficult to understand their legal rights and responsibilities, potentially resulting in disagreements and exploitative practices.
Information Overload	The plethora of data is accessible via internet and in multiple documents can be overwhelming for customers, making it difficult to narrow down and concentrate on the most pertinent information.	Consumers may overlook critical information or fail to recognize the importance of specific policy clauses.
Lack of Standardization	Consumer policies vary throughout manufacturing sectors and firms, making it difficult for customers to make comparisons among terms.	Clients may find it difficult to comprehend and navigate policy variations, particularly when interacting with various suppliers of services.
Hidden Fees and Terms	Some policies may have additional costs, conditions of use, or terms which are not clearly stated.	Individuals may be astonished by unforeseen expenses or become entangled by terms they were unaware of, resulting in discontent and conflicts.
Inaccessible Formats	Regulations may be given in formats that are inaccessible to all customers, even those who are visually impaired or who lack knowledge of digital technology.	A few groups representing consumers might have difficulties accessing and comprehending policy information, restricting their ability to arrive at well-informed choices.
Updates and Changes	Consumers may not be notified when policies are updated or changed.	Consumers might inadvertently breach up-to-date terms or fail to notice modifications which impact their rights as well as their duties.
Fragmented Information	Consumer policy information may be dispersed across numerous mediums, internet pages, and forms.	Consumers might be unable to find accurate and current data, resulting in disarray and potential policy non-compliance.
Limited Consumer Education	A lot of customers may be unaware of their entitlements and the validity of customers policies.	Consumers may not fully understand what they are entitled to, and businesses can take benefit of this ignorance.
Language Barriers	Consumer policies are frequently provided in a particular language, posing difficulties for individuals who cannot speak or devour the language fluently.	Consumers who have weak language skills may overlook crucial information, resulting in miscommunication and possible conflicts.
Lack of Redress Mechanisms	When consumers suspect their rights are being infringed they might encounter challenges when looking for a settlement or solution.	Without efficient resolution mechanisms, customers could feel helpless and dissuaded from going after complaints.

To address these obstacles, legislators, enterprises, and advocacy organizations must work together to increase openness, standardize data, simplify language acquisition, and guarantee that critical customer policy guidance is readily available to all customers. Enhancing consumer education and involvement is also critical for equipping people with the knowledge to make educated choices while safeguarding their rights.

RELATIONSHIP BETWEEN AI AND PRIVACY

In recent years, there have been significant advancements in technology and the integration of AI, driven by the growing digitization of consumer-centric applications, media, and commerce (Saluja et al,2022). Furthermore, it has been observed that not all AI utilize personal information. There exist numerous use cases within 5G networks that are designed to enhance the quality and dependability of infrastructure, without necessitating the provision of privacy-sensitive data to AI systems (Quach, et al., 2022; Schneider, et al., 2017). However, concerning AI and privacy, it is imperative to approach the

Consumer Policy

issue of privacy impact with due care. Say, AI systems possess the potential to discern and recognize an individual who may have been considered unidentifiable based on the perspective of the input dataset. The inadvertent occurrence of such identification can arise from the computational processes of the AI system. In this section, the emphasis is on devising the requisite procedures to guarantee a commendable degree of privacy during the development of AI systems.

The association between AI and confidentiality in customer policies is vital and intricate. As AI innovations become better and more commonplace, regulators and policymakers have to tackle several important factors to guarantee an appropriate equilibrium among the positive effects of AI and the preservation of people's privacy (Okazaki, et al., 2020; Kronemann, et al., 2023). Table 2 presents these important factors, their challenges, and the policy-making approach.

Table 2. Important factors in concern with AI and data privacy, challenges, and policy approach

Factors for Consideration	Challenge	Policy Approach
Data Collection and Use	• Large Dataset management as AI often relies on training and thus improving models. • May include sensitive personal information.	Consumer policies must establish concise and clear guidelines on: • types of Data Collection, • purpose of its use, • need to obtain informed consent from concerned personnel.
Informed Consent	• AI systems can arrive at intricate and automated based on data provided by users, making it difficult for individuals to comprehend the ramifications.	• Policies must mandate transparent disclosure of how AI systems process personal data • Ensure individuals about the consequences and provide meaningful consent.
Algorithmic Transparency	• The intricacy of AI algorithms might be opaque. • Makes difficult for individuals to understand decisions.	• By promote algorithmic transparency, the companies have to provide explanations for automated decisions • Allowing individuals to access and understand the logic behind those decisions.
Minimization of Data	• AI systems are often intended to gather any information as feasible, resulting in unnecessary invasions of people's privacy.	• Persuade data reduction principles, in which AI systems only gather and analyze the bare minimum of information required to accomplish their goals, reducing the possibility of privacy violations.
Protection of Biometric Data	• Issues have been raised regarding the gathering and utilization of personally identifiable information in AI applications, particularly in recognition of faces and biometric applications.	• Implementing particular guidelines for the utilization of biometric information, facilitating that its gathering and use are strictly regulated and that people are given additional safeguards.
Discrimination and Profiling	• The algorithms used by artificial intelligence may unintentionally sustain biases, causing adverse results for a particular category of people.	• Encourage anti-discrimination regulations and necessitate businesses to carry out periodic reviews of their AI systems to detect and correct bias. • Policies ought to develop repercussions for actions that are discriminatory.
Security of Data	• Because of the growing reliance on AI, an error in the integrity of AI systems could pose vital risk to privacy.	• Increase security of data prerequisites, facilitating that firms using AI take strong precautions to safeguard the integrity and security of client information.
Right to Explanation	• Persons may be unaware of the factors that influence AI-driven choices	• Create the right for people to ask for clarification for automated choices that have an important effect on them, as well as the ability to confront and appeal such choices.

continued on following page

Table 2. Continued

Factors for Consideration	Challenge	Policy Approach
Cross-Border Data Flow	• AI applications frequently require data transfers across borders, increasing questions regarding conformity with various privacy laws.	• Encourage international collaboration and the harmonization of standards for privacy to provide individuals with consistent security no matter where their personal information is dealt with.
Privacy by Design	• Privacy concerns may not be appropriately addressed in the creation of AI systems.	• Persuade a privacy-by-design strategy, in which concerns about privacy are incorporated into the AI application development lifecycle from the start.

The association between AI and confidentiality in customer policies is dynamic, requiring continual review and change (Routledge.com, n.d.). Policymakers must be forward-thinking when dealing with new obstacles and ensure that privacy safeguards are kept alongside AI advancements in technology. The success of a regulatory structure requires public-private collaboration, norms from the industry, and ongoing conversations (Saluja, 2024; Saluja, et al., 2023).

CONCLUSION

The concern of AI and data privacy in consumer policy shows how firms and individuals have incomplete information and purchase biases, which can cause market failures. Big data and AI could compromise customer privacy and data security. Need for appropriate legal and regulatory frameworks to address AI consent, data minimization, accuracy, discrimination, and bias. The methods based on evolutionary game theory can be proposed for protecting online shopping privacy with AI technologies including machine learning, deep learning, and computer vision. AI is expected to impact society and the global economy, with investments rising and economic contributions in the trillions. AI ethical guidelines that protect consumers have been proposed by the European Commission. It requires a balance between AI technology for convenience and efficiency and consumer rights and privacy. To do so, stakeholders must prioritize openness, accountability, and the creation of legislation that protects consumer privacy and promotes responsible AI use.

REFERENCES

André, Q., Carmon, Z., Wertenbroch, K., Crum, A., Frank, D., Goldstein, W., Huber, J., Boven, L., Weber, B., & Yang, H. (2018). Consumer choice and autonomy in the age of artificial intelligence and big data. *Customer Needs and Solutions*, 5(1), 28–37. 10.1007/s40547-017-0085-8

Artificial intelligence (AI) and data privacy for companies. (n.d.). Consent Management Platform (CMP) Usercentrics. https://usercentrics.com/knowledge-hub/data-privacy-artificial-intelligence/

Artificial Intelligence and Privacy - Issues and Challenges. (2021, April 13). Office of the Victorian Information Commissioner; Office of Victorian Information Commissioner. https://ovic.vic.gov.au/privacy/resources-for-organisations/artificial-intelligence-and-privacy-issues-and-challenges/

Chawla, N., & Kumar, B. (2022). E-commerce and consumer protection in India: The emerging trend. *Journal of Business Ethics*, 180(2), 581–604. 10.1007/s10551-021-04884-334257470

Ezechukwu, N. V. (2023). Consumer Protection and Trade Governance: A Critical Partnership? *Journal of Consumer Policy*, 46(2), 191–221. 10.1007/s10603-023-09538-7

Hyde, R., & Cartwright, P. (2023). Exploring Consumer Detriment in Immersive Gaming Technologies. *Journal of Consumer Policy*, 46(3), 335–361. 10.1007/s10603-023-09544-9

Kaur, H., & Singh, T. (2021). Book review: "consumer happiness: Multiple perspectives", by tanusree Dutta and Manas Kumar Mandal (eds.). *Journal of Consumer Policy, 44*(4), 585–591. 10.1007/s10603-021-09494-0

Kronemann, B., Kizgin, H., Rana, N., & K. Dwivedi, Y. (2023). How AI encourages consumers to share their secrets? The role of anthropomorphism, personalisation, and privacy concerns and avenues for future research. *Spanish Journal of Marketing-ESIC, 27*(1), 3–19. 10.1108/SJME-10-2022-0213

Lagioia, F., Jabłonowska, A., Liepina, R., & Drazewski, K. (2022). AI in search of unfairness in consumer contracts: The terms of service landscape. *Journal of Consumer Policy*, 45(3), 481–536. 10.1007/s10603-022-09520-9

Lobschat, L., Mueller, B., Eggers, F., Brandimarte, L., Diefenbach, S., Kroschke, M., & Wirtz, J. (2021). Corporate digital responsibility. *Journal of Business Research*, 122, 875–888. 10.1016/j.jbusres.2019.10.006

Lukitosari, V., Simanjuntak, T. F., & Utomo, D. B. (2020). A game-theoretic model of marketing strategy using consumer segmentation. *Journal of Physics: Conference Series*, 1490(1), 012026. 10.1088/1742-6596/1490/1/012026

MacInnis, D. J., Morwitz, V. G., Botti, S., Hoffman, D. L., Kozinets, R. V., Lehmann, D. R., Lynch, J. G.Jr, & Pechmann, C. (2020). Creating boundary-breaking, marketing-relevant consumer research. *Journal of Marketing*, 84(2), 1–23. 10.1177/0022242919889876

Okazaki, S., Eisend, M., Plangger, K., de Ruyter, K., & Grewal, D. (2020). Understanding the strategic consequences of customer privacy concerns: A meta-analytic review. *Journal of Retailing*, 96(4), 458–473. 10.1016/j.jretai.2020.05.007

Online, E. T. (2023, April 25). AI and Privacy: The privacy concerns surrounding AI, its potential impact on personal data. *Economic Times*. https://economictimes.indiatimes.com/news/how-to/ai-and-privacy-the-privacy-concerns-surrounding-ai-its-potential-impact-on-personal-data/articleshow/99738234.cms

Onorato, A. (2022, May 3). *Report: Consumers open to AI in marketing, but privacy concerns remain. Cdp.com - Leading CDP Industry Resource for Marketing & Sales - News, Analysis and Thought Leadership Content on the CDP Industry*. CDP. https://cdp.com/articles/report-consumers-open-to-ai-in-marketing-but-privacy-concerns-remain/

Pappalardo, J. K. (2022). Economics of consumer protection: Contributions and challenges in estimating consumer injury and evaluating consumer protection policy. *Journal of Consumer Policy*, 45(2), 201–238. 10.1007/s10603-021-09482-4

Pitardi, D., & Marriott, H. R. (2021). Alexa, she's not human but... Unveiling the drivers of consumers' trust in voice-based artificial intelligence. *Psychology and Marketing*, 38(4), 626–642. 10.1002/mar.21457

Pitardi, V., Wirtz, J., Paluch, S., & Kunz, W. H. (2022). Service robots, agency and embarrassing service encounters. *Journal of Service Management*, 33(2), 389–414. 10.1108/JOSM-12-2020-0435

PricewaterhouseCoopers. *Sizing the prize*. PwC. https://www.pwc.com/gx/en/issues/data-and-analytics/publications/artificial-intelligence-study.html

Puntoni, S., Reczek, R. W., Giesler, M., & Botti, S. (2021). Consumers and artificial intelligence: An experiential perspective. *Journal of Marketing*, 85(1), 131–151. 10.1177/0022242920953847

Quach, S., Thaichon, P., Martin, K. D., Weaven, S., & Palmatier, R. W. (2022). Digital technologies: Tensions in privacy and data. *Journal of the Academy of Marketing Science*, 50(6), 1299–1323. 10.1007/s11747-022-00845-y35281634

Ruggeri, F., Lagioia, F., Lippi, M., & Torroni, P. (2021). Detecting and explaining unfairness in consumer contracts through memory networks. *Artificial Intelligence and Law*, 30(1), 59–92. 10.1007/s10506-021-09288-2

Saluja, S. (2024). Identity theft fraud- major loophole for FinTech industry in India. *Journal of Financial Crime*, 31(1), 146–157. 10.1108/JFC-08-2022-0211

Saluja, S., Aggarwal, A., & Mittal, A. (2022). Understanding the fraud theories and advancing with integrity model. *Journal of Financial Crime*, 29(4), 1318–1328. 10.1108/JFC-07-2021-0163

Saluja, S., Kulshrestha, D., & Sharma, S. (2023). *Cases on the Resurgence of Emerging Businesses*. 1–316.

Schneider, M. J., Jagpal, S., Gupta, S., Li, S., & Yu, Y. (2017). Protecting customer privacy when marketing with second-party data. *International Journal of Research in Marketing*, 34(3), 593–603. 10.1016/j.ijresmar.2017.02.003

Chapter 6
Digital Transformation of Marketing Processes, Customer Privacy, Data Security, and Emerging Challenges in Fostering Sustainable Digital Marketing

Hina Gull
Imam Abdulrahman Bin Faisal University, Dammam, Saudi Arabia

Saqib Saeed
https://orcid.org/0000-0001-7136-3480
Imam Abdulrahman Bin Faisal University, Dammam, Saudi Arabia

Hamzah A. K. Alaied
Imam Abdulrahman Bin Faisal University, Dammam, Saudi Arabia

Ali N. A. Alajmi
Imam Abdulrahman Bin Faisal University, Dammam, Saudi Arabia

Madeeha Saqib
Imam Abdulrahman Bin Faisal University, Dammam, Saudi Arabia

Sardar Zafar Iqbal
Imam Abdulrahman Bin Faisal University, Dammam, Saudi Arabia

Abdullah M. Almuhaideb
https://orcid.org/0000-0002-2004-5324
Imam Abdulrahman Bin Faisal University, Dammam, Saudi Arabia

ABSTRACT

Marketing is a core business function to communicate the value of a product to its customers. Digital technologies have transformed this business function into digital marketing, which is the core focus of the digital transformation drive of business organizations. Digital marketing relies on modern technologies to reach out to prospective customers, and other stakeholders in the community. However, this technological transformation has brought data security and privacy challenges for organizations as well. In this chapter, the authors have conducted a systematic literature review to understand these challenges

DOI: 10.4018/979-8-3693-6660-8.ch006

Copyright ©2024, IGI Global. Copying or distributing in print or electronic forms without written permission of IGI Global is prohibited.

and presented a framework for organizations to respond to these challenges in an agile manner. This framework outlined four key enablers and associated strategies to better achieve these enablers to foster a sustainable digital marketing process in business organizations. This framework benefits business organizations and policymakers to improve the digital marketing effectiveness of their organizations to maximize the benefits of digital transformation.

INTRODUCTION

Marketing is the process of promoting and selling products or services to potential customers. It is AN essential business FUNCTION TO communicate value proposition to target audience and RESULTS IN increase sales (Saeed, 2019). As advancements in technologies have made the computation more efficient (Gull et al., 2021), the adoption of technologies in organizationAL processes has increased tremendously. However, to foster a successful usage of technologies usability of technological systems is critical (Saeed et al., 2013). With the digital transformation DRIVE of businesses, marketing departments also embraced information technologies and as a result, marketing has undergone a significant transformation (AlKhateb et al., 2023). Businesses are now able to reach their customers through various digital channels and this has resulted in the evolution of digital marketing (Saura et. al., 2023). Digital marketing has revolutionized the way businesses interact with their customers, providing them with a more personalized and immersive experience (Chaffey & Ellis-Chadwick, 2019). Despite the benefits of digital marketing, it has also introduced additional challenges FOR BUSINESS ORGANIZATIONS (Saeed et al., 2019). For instance, The use of customer data in digital marketing has raised concerns about the privacy of individuals and their right to control their personal information (Chiu & Ho, 2023). Businesses that collect, store, and use customer data are required to adopt ethical practices. Recently, the term sustainable digital marketing has been used IN LITERATURE, which advocates for adopting a sustainable digital marketing strategy focusing on community building and revenue generation using an ethical and moral approach ((Rauturier, 2023), (Zhang et al., 2023), (Hidayat et al., 2022)). Adopting such a strategy requires SIGNIFICANT refinement efforts to achieve the desired outcomes by business organizations (AMEEN ET AL., 2024).

Recently, the use of ARTIFICIAL INTELLIGENCE (AI) in digital marketing has made things more complicated regarding customer privacy and data safety ((AMEEN ET AL., 2021), ((Gull et al., 2022), (Gull et al., 2023), (NALBANT & AYDIN, 2023)). AI algorithms are designed to learn from customer data and provide businesses with insights that can improve their marketing strategies (Biswas et al., 2023). However, the use of AI in digital marketing raises questions about the potential misuse of customer data (Mazur, 2023). The introduction of regulatory guidelines has been crucial IN maintaining and controlling privacy and data safety in digital marketing. These regulations ensure that businesses comply with legal requirements, respect customers' privacy, and prevent the misuse of their personal information. Failure to comply with these regulations can lead to significant legal and financial consequences for businesses (Mandal, 2023).

While digital technologies are now critical for businesses, they impact marketing in several ways by improving analytics, channel management, value co-creation, and augmenting employee skills. However sustainable digital marketing implies marketing takes on a more strategic role with a systematic analysis in an ethical manner. Therefore, in this systematic literature review, we explore the challenges and implications for organizations in fostering sustainable digital marketing strategies. Risks and obstacles to

Digital Transformation of in Fostering Sustainable Digital Marketing

sustainable digital marketing are identified and recommendations focusing on cultural shifts to increase employee awareness, organizational solutions to fill competency gaps, and relational efforts to foster external collaboration are discussed.

The rest of the chapter is structured as follows: Section 2 presents the methodology adopted to conduct the literature review and Section 3 presents the main contributions of our literature review. Section 4 presents the discussion and is followed by a conclusion in Section 5.

MATERIAL AND METHODS

In this literature review, we have followed the PRISMA guidelines (Page et al., 2021) and included only the papers published between 2019 and 2023. We downloaded the papers from google scholar using the four key terms which include "sustainable digital marketing challenges", "digital marketing and privacy guidelines", "digital marketing and security guidelines", "digital marketing, artificial intelligence, ethics and security" and "regulations for artificial intelligence in digital marketing". After applying relevant filters, We found a total of 113 papers, among them there were five duplicate papers and a further 17 papers were excluded based on our inclusion criteria, which were as follows:

- The paper is published between 2019 and 2023.
- The paper is not a review paper or a book.
- The paper focuses on digital marketing and security/privacy aspects.

As shown in Figure 1, out of these 91 papers 66 papers were excluded based on title and content filtering and as a result, papers included in the final review were twenty-five. As shown in Figure 2, there were 3 papers published in 2019, 5 papers were from 2020 and 7 papers were published in 2021. There were three papers published in 2022 and seven were published in 2023.

Figure 1. Number of accepted articles in SLR

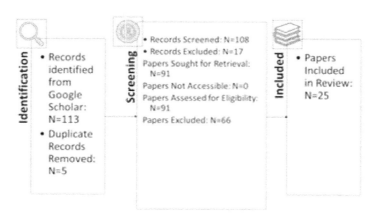

Figure 2. Annual distribution of research articles

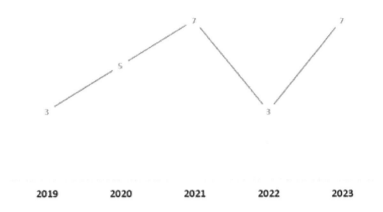

RESULTS

In this section based on our literature review, we present major security and privacy challenges for the sustainability of digital marketing.

SECURITY AND PRIVACY OF CONSUMER DATA

Data management and customer privacy are inherent responsibilities of corporations, which hold asymmetric power over customer's data. An important factor to consider is that "Do customers give importance on data privacy?". In a study (Winegar & Sunstein, 2019) authors investigated how much customers give importance to data privacy by surveying in America. According to a survey of 2,416 respondents, the average customer is ready to pay $5 each month to protect confidential information (within certain constraints) but would pay 80 dollars to gain access to private information. Furthermore, when knowing that information includes health-related data, people want considerably greater sums of money than when they know that such data contains geographic data. Data privacy has recently been a key concern because of sellers' recent exploitation of consumer data. Because of several obstacles, preserving privacy in today's Web 2.0 world is extremely challenging. People readily post their pictures, videos, hobbies, educational background, address, location, credit card information, and numerous other information across different internet platforms; nonetheless, they continue to be worried about their information and preserve that it plays a significant role in their decision-making process when making online shopping. The concern over the privacy of data and actual online behavior is creating the situation known as the privacy paradox. In another study, Kushwaha et al. (Kushwaha et al.,2021) examined the conflict between customer desires and conduct regarding data privacy and sharing of information. Their study's objective was to pinpoint the factors that affect consumers' positive behavior of data disclosure.

The investigators examined risk-benefit, nature of data, trust in the brand, and intent to disclose as crucial factors in defining a certain kind of disclosure behavior. Considering the first factor, a customer's behavioral intention is established based on beliefs, personal standards, and perceptual bias. Previous investigations have found a substantial association between intention and conduct, and intention can be used to predict behavior. The users frequently express their disclosure goal, but do not express their true disclosure intention. Even on trusted sites, customers' privacy concerns outweigh their desire to share information. It is possible that a person's stated desires do not reflect their actual behavior, due to other circumstances that influence both intention and behavior independently. The second factor identified is risk benefit analysis. Risk assessment is a crucial part of data privacy. It is the process of determining who, how much, how, and to what degree personal data should be shared. The risk benefit calculation is performed to increase benefits while decreasing the risk of information exposure. The third factor is the nature of data, the sensitive nature of the data requested by the organization defines the organization's desire to reveal personal information. Customers may utilize the type and amount of private information to determine their intentions on data sharing. The normal data, such as address, contact number, postal code, name, and so on, suffers fewer losses. When the perceived risk is low, this type of data is easily shared by customers. The next factor is the customer's trust in the brand. Consumer trust in the brand influences their willingness to provide information. If the business violates data privacy, customers' faith in the brand decreases, and customers may be hesitant to share their personal information with the company in the future. Customers may exhibit positive disclosure behavior if the company has a favorable trust image in the market regarding data privacy, and vice versa. In this research, a standardized questionnaire was used to conduct the survey in two rounds. Customers at shopping center outlets were among those who responded. In the initial stage, participants were questioned prior to their entry into the shopping centers. While the subsequent set of queries focused on disclosing behaviors, the initial set of queries addressed risk rewards, the type of data, confidence in the brand, and behavioral intent. 376 people were picked using convenient sampling approaches and questioned using a standardized survey. More than 300 samples were regarded as adequate for data analysis and model validation using structural equation modeling. The findings imply that customers weigh the risks of sharing data against the perceived advantages before deciding whether or not to share information. The choice or decision of the sellers to share certain details with the organization also depends on the type of requested data. When the damage is small, people might not think twice about disclosing and sharing routine data, but when the loss is significant, they might think again before acting negatively, when sharing such information. They usually object to disclosing this kind of information.

Bleier et. al. (Bleier et. al., 2020) analyzed whether contextual integrity may cause issues regarding privacy using a privacy viewpoint. They believe that small startups tend to be at a distinct disadvantage when compared with giant established companies. However, they emphasize that companies may employ a variety of methods to reduce issues related to privacy, as well as that in certain instances, issues related to privacy can have an advantageous effect on data-driven advertising by promoting privacy as well as offering a source of competitive advantage. Bandra et.al. (Bandra et.al.,2021) investigated the customer's privacy and their behavior in digital markets. An online survey was used to collect data from online shoppers. Based on the study they identified several factors; the first one is privacy empowerment. Having control over one's information is fundamental to privacy empowerment. Specifically, privacy empowerment is a psychological construct that refers to an individual's perception of how much control he or she has over how their personally identifiable information been shared and used. The second one is the customer's trust which is considered as the most challenging factor to investigate privacy over the years. The third one is organizational responsibility towards privacy. In this study, perceived organizational privacy responsibility represents customer beliefs of business commitments to preserve customer privacy. The next factor is regulatory protection which describes the process by which various government and industry bodies develop privacy rules to regulate and track the use of customer data. Based on these factors several hypotheses had been developed in this study. The findings of the study showed that inadequate organizational privacy obligations and regulatory protection may deplete customers of their personal empowerment and harm confidence in businesses, causing worries about privacy and consequent defensive behaviors.

While digital technologies give firms access to vast amounts of data, they also generate significant privacy tensions for consumers. The authors develop a conceptual framework that incorporates the viewpoints of companies, customers, and regulators to comprehend these tensions. Understanding how emerging technologies like AI threaten consumer privacy and how customers perceive different firm information strategies. Investigating actual consumer privacy behaviors and responses and the role of privacy-protecting technologies. Examining the effects of privacy regulations on firm performance, compliance, and actions that mold regulations over time. Assessing how privacy regulations impact firm networks and ecosystems while potentially restricting data benefits. In essence, though the authors' framework provides new insights, much work remains to empirically test the framework and comprehensively understand how digital technologies, data strategies, and privacy issues affect all relevant stakeholders. The authors propose a conceptual framework that integrates the viewpoints of companies, customers, and regulators to grasp privacy tensions from digital technologies and data strategies. However, they argue that further research is needed to better understand consumer privacy concerns, behaviors and responses, and the impacts of privacy regulations on firms and ecosystems. Empirically testing the framework could provide a fuller view of how digital technologies impact performance in contexts marked by growing privacy worries. The key takeaway is that all parties - firms, consumers, and regulators - must develop effective approaches that balance data opportunities while respecting consumer privacy in the digital age (Quach et al., 2022).

Brough et. al (Brough et al., 2021) examined the effects of the COVID-19 outbreak on customers' privacy and the implications for coming days' privacy and public policies. In COVID-19, they have determined a number of variables about client privacy. The first one was increased surveillance. For instance, "smart city" techniques to dealt with the congestion of traffic have been adapted to monitor adherence to social distance laws in the UK and India. Powerful spying tools have been used in Israel to collect mobile phone data from people, enabling the government to monitor their movements, interactions, and interpersonal connections to vigorously track and halt the outbreak of the virus. The second factor is new digital records; Because of government-imposed limitations, operations that used to take place offline have shifted online, increasing the number of digital records including sensitive information. Many people, for example, were obliged to give sensitive data while creating new internet accounts to shop for essential goods and services. Furthermore, private data that was previously not generally kept online may now be acquired and retained electronically. Concerningly, certain online customers might not have the expertise to fully comprehend their privacy risks, especially vulnerable populations who adopted electronic commerce lately, including seniors, the disabled, expatriates, and families with lower incomes. The third identified factor is more data sharing; Governments have released additional personal data without individuals' agreement as they have presented residents with details regarding possible exposure to viruses. For instance, the South Korean government openly shared confidential data regarding virus victims, particularly full demographics, jobs, travel histories, and social interaction, to alert those who may be vulnerable. As more workers switch to working from home, they have begun using and passing data over potentially vulnerable networks and channels. This raises the risk of disclosing sensitive data that could have been more secure. For instance, Zoom has serious privacy and security issues even though banks, colleges, medical facilities, and other organizations have adopted it widely since the outbreak.

Considering mounting concerns about the security and privacy of Internet of Things (IoT) devices, consumers often do not have access to this information when purchasing these devices. In a study (Emami-Naeini et al., 2019), respondents were questioned about the IoT gadgets they purchased. While the majority had not considered privacy and security before purchasing, people reported later growing concerns because of media reporting, opinions shared by friends, or unexpected gadget behavior. Those who looked for privacy and security information before making a purchase reported that finding it was difficult or impossible. They were also asked to rate the factors they would consider when purchasing IoT devices, privacy and security were ranked second only to features and price. Finally, the authors showed interviewees their prototypes with privacy and security labels. Almost everyone said it was simple and useful, and it urged them to think about privacy and security while making IoT purchases.

ETHICAL HANDLING OF CUSTOMER INFORMATION

Tackling the challenges faced by aging populations is a popular topic for businesses, lawmakers, and academics. However, there has been little study on how senior consumers adopt or reject the latest technological advances. Advertisers have to comprehend how older customers adopt technology and use digital channels in light of shifting financial influence and rising digital adoption rates. In a study, Nunan et al. (Nunan et al., 2019), investigated the behavior of the old population about digital marketing. Advertisers have to comprehend how older customers adopt technology and use digital channels in light of shifting financial influence and rising digital adoption rates. The marketing profession has to take into account the demands of all consumers to successfully concentrate on enhancing customers' quality of life. Furthermore, marketing cannot be separated from the primary challenges that shape societies.

Changes in the way browsers and mobile devices manage cookies from third parties and advertising are going to have a significant influence on the online marketing industry. A study (Thomas, 2021) investigated these modifications to the growth of the ad-tech and online media sectors, wrapping up that even though these changes may benefit consumers by securing them from intrusive third-party monitoring. At the same time, the changes allow for a more equitable connection between marketing and the material in which it displays.

Anshari et al., (Anshari et al., 2023) emphasized the significance of ethical compliance in the deployment of AI for collecting, managing, interpreting, and analyzing large datasets. It highlights the need for ethical considerations to address concerns related to user data privacy, consent, and discrimination in marketing. Responsible and ethical data usage is essential for the effective and efficient use of data. Awareness and control of data collection and usage can minimize ethical issues and public concerns. The ethical use of AI requires the active participation of all stakeholders, including organizations and individuals, who must uphold fairness, trust, and social responsibility to ensure successful implementation.

Social networking sites collect and exchange information about customers for research and sale to potential buyers, and it is widely utilized in advertising. They must get informed permission to gather, maintain, analyze, and trade this data. Yet, customers may agree to consent without understanding the consent details. Another study (Hanlon & Jones, 2023) looked at the complexities of privacy regulations and raised ethical concerns about users' capacity to understand their consent behaviors. The study examined the availability of terms of service from a major social media network using reading scores and comprehension measures. The results demonstrate that because of proficiency in reading and document size, it is doubtful that all users, especially children, will be able to authorize the consent activities, raising ethical difficulties. There are also practical ramifications for administrators and policymakers, and authorities to assess users' access to sites where they cannot fully understand the privacy regulations.

A study (Nuss et al., 2023), examined Australians' opinions through a survey about governmental attempts to safeguard children from online advertising of hazardous food and beverage goods. The majority of responders agreed that the government should protect children from harmful food and beverage marketing and promotion. There was significant backing for government efforts to avoid harmful food and drink advertising on online venues (e.g., internet sites) and for different methods of digital marketing (e.g., brand advertising on social media). The entire prohibition of this kind of marketing to children earned the most support. The majority of the participants believed that hazardous food and beverage companies should not be allowed to acquire private data about youngsters for promotional purposes.

SOCIAL MEDIA MARKETING AND PRIVACY IMPLICATIONS

New digital platforms have been widely adopted in recent years, enabling unprecedented levels of interaction, data sharing, and collaboration among billions of people. These novel settings provide a whole new, challenging environment for marketing and promotion. Choudhary et. al. (Choudhary et. al., 2020) investigated several marketing challenges and opportunities related to social media applications i.e., TikTok. Studies have also shown the effect of digital marketing on the online purchase intention of customers. Dastane (Dastane, 2020) conducted a study to investigate the effect of electronic advertising on online shopping customers in Malaysia. Tatlow-Golden et al., (Tatlow-Golden et al.,2020) investigated how digital marketing for unhealthy food items violates children's rights. They think that the rights of children to health and nutrition, privacy, and freedom against manipulation are all violated by contemporary digital advertising techniques of food items.

Rodrigues et al. (Rodrigues et al. 2020) elucidated how various electronic advertising techniques and instruments affect the success of hiring. Their main objective is to ascertain whether and to what extent the validity of the data origin, content advertising, and organizational image affect candidates' decisions to apply for positions in the market. According to their research, when evaluating a job application, people believe the organization's online advertising materials to be more relevant and trustworthy. It's generally accepted that LinkedIn is a more trustworthy source than Facebook for job postings. LinkedIn has a favorable impact on candidates' choices regarding content advertising as well as the standing of businesses.

Marketers are increasingly employing customized marketing that is customized to customers according to data about their tastes and habits obtained through the collection of private data. The study (Hayes, 2021) looked at the role of consumer-brand ties and social media platform circumstances in the success of targeted advertising. Consumers assess the benefits of personalized brand information against the privacy risks associated with disclosing personal information. They selected two famous brands to study privacy issues in social media. According to the findings, strong consumer-brand links raise the perceived value of information disclosure by increasing perceived benefits and decreasing perceived risks, even though perceived hazards dominated privacy calculation decisions.

DATA SCIENCE AND AI APPLICATION IN MARKETING AND PRIVACY CHALLENGES

Ensuring that artificial intelligence technologies maximize benefits while minimizing harm requires an ethical and sustainable approach. However, current proposals have limitations: most tend to emphasize potential risks without considering AI's benefits, if developed responsibly. Broad statements often lack the specificity needed to guide ethical AI development in concrete ways. Focusing solely on environmental sustainability overlooks the social and economic aspects of sustainability. Broader input from diverse stakeholders would strengthen ethical AI frameworks. Independent oversight is needed to implement sustainability principles in practice. Creating an optimal balance of innovation and risk mitigation is critical. Turning principles into implementable guidelines, standards, and best practices has yet to happen on a scale. Comprehensive policies across the AI lifecycle that promote sustainability are still lacking. Moving ethical and sustainable AI forward will require a holistic, action-oriented, and inclusive approach involving AI developers, businesses, policymakers, and the public to create technologies that truly maximize benefits and minimize harm to humanity. While any sustainability statement can begin the journey, significant work remains to operationalize ethical and sustainable AI in practice (Bogani et al., 2022).

Intelligence modeling in the AI era is one of the drivers of intelligent advertising that Rodgers & Nguyen (Rodgers & Nguyen, 2022) discussed. For example, intelligence modeling in the AI era is one of the drivers of intelligent advertising that Rodgers & Nguyen (2022) discussed. This study investigated AI stimuli and associated it with its neural network, deep learning, and machine learning subgroups in advertising.

Henz (Henz, 2021) emphasized the responsibility of humans in all aspects of AI creation, deployment, and usage. Adequate maintenance, diverse and inclusive programmer groups, and periodic auditing of algorithms are necessary to ensure the protection of AI systems. Though legal regulations are still lacking, governments and the European parliament recognize the ultimate responsibility of humans in decision-making processes involving AI. The creators and users of AI systems must act with moral responsibility, understand the potential risks and flawed decision-making, and work towards establishing efficient legal frameworks and regulatory guidelines to ensure the ethical and responsible use of AI as it continues to evolve.

Sundqvist et al. (Sundqvist et al., 2023) investigated the utilization of AI in digital marketing. The goal of this research is to look at how businesses employ artificial intelligence (AI) in their internet advertising and how this impacts their attempts to connect electronically. AI solutions, particularly text generators like ChatGPT, are becoming increasingly popular in online advertising among small and medium-sized companies. In the application of AI, larger firms consider ethical and regulatory considerations such as general data protection regulations (GDPR). A company's needs and resources determine the use and selection of AI technologies. While AI helps to boost margins, cut costs, and enhance effectiveness, it also introduces new difficulties such as potential talent gaps. Large organizations can invest more but struggle with implementation, but small and medium-sized organizations can adapt faster and accomplish development with AI. The study supports the financial viability of artificial intelligence in enterprises, notably in online advertising.

Mixed Reality (MR) is an idea that has been known for a long time, although it is just now gaining popularity. As technology has grown and become more generally available, the MR concept has evolved. The phrase was first used in the early 2000s to describe a variety of technologies, including augmented reality (AR), virtual reality (VR), and a combination of the two. Mixed reality (MR) is a revolutionary technological development that numerous firms have used to improve interaction with customers. Due to security and privacy concerns related to internet use, customers may not always be keen to communicate with businesses via the web. Mixed reality technology, on the other hand, blends the virtual and real worlds, allowing for improved contact with customers. Mixed reality technology enables more effective consumer interaction, better customer experiences, and more engagement. However, there are obstacles involved with the usage of mixed reality technology, such as cost, privacy, and security concerns; as a result, adoption of these technologies in industrialized countries is limited. It can be suggested that there is a need for businesses to invest in mixed-reality environments (Dube et al., 2023).

A study (Hutson, 2023) investigated the effects of innovations on online advertising such as Artificial Intelligence, Natural Language Processing, Virtual Reality, and Augmented Reality. It emphasizes the revolutionary nature of these advances in the areas of customization, online sales, and enhanced consumer experience. The study underlines that these advances in technology provide new ways for organizations to communicate with customers and optimize their advertising campaigns. It also acknowledges the enormous security and privacy risks posed by these breakthroughs, especially for data mining, customer data usage, and virtual environments.

The use and effectiveness of data sciences and digital marketing have both changed significantly since the turn of the twenty-first century. These days, data science's main focus is on expanding the company's data storage capacity, conducting customer and industry segmentation, and retrieving vital information regarding business difficulties (Saura, 2021). To examine the impact of growing company adoption of Data Science on Digital Marketing strategies, this study offered a thorough analysis of (i) techniques for investigation, (ii) applications and (iii) metrics of performance based on Data Science applied in the scientific literature to Digital Marketing strategies. The three mentioned elements are being investigated, described, and assessed through the eyes of a marketer instead of a data scientist's perspective. This research aims to help marketers and nontechnical investigators better comprehend the primary applications of Data Science to Digital Marketing and become more aware of the value of each such application by reviewing the main concepts of the Data Science framework applied to Digital Marketing. According to the study, the overarching purpose of Data Science is to extract information from data analysis to address specific research questions. DS approaches enable the extraction of patterns from databases to explain an issue or create hypotheses by studying the data. A basic assumption in DS is that the patterns found in data are (i) non-obvious and (ii) helpful to businesses. In this regard, it is crucial to highlight that people can identify a maximum of three traits, or features, of an item (product, service, community, etc.). These characteristics are also referred to as features or variables. Data Science patterns, on the other hand, have thousands of attributes. Based on the framework, the author designed several research questions, and the systematic literature review methodology is used to address these questions. The primary contributions of relevant studies were recognized and prioritized for the theoretical framework. The literature is rigorously studied in the second step to find commonalities and details of the Digital Marketing sector in Data Science. This process synthesizes earlier research and groups fundamental concepts and definitions. The third stage examines the important findings of the Data Science in Digital Marketing literature, focusing on the primary uses, applications, indicators, and techniques. Analysis of the results presents that data science provides a variety of perspectives and approaches to statistical data analysis such as descriptive statistics, linear regression, logistic regression etc. Moreover, a variety of performance metrics such as reliability, recall, and availability have also been identified that affect digital marketing.

DISCUSSION

Overcoming cultural and organizational obstacles is required by companies to fully leverage the opportunities of digital technologies through digital transformation (Saeed et. al., 2023, Tariq et al., 2022). Digital marketing is an important business function and in the previous section, we have documented different challenges and opportunities encountered in the digital marketing efforts of organizations (Pandey et al., 2022). Based on this, we have developed a framework to foster sustainable digital marketing for organizations. As shown in Figure 3, the first level describes four key aspects and lower levels present the recommended actions to achieve those objectives.

Figure 3. Framework for sustainable digital marketing

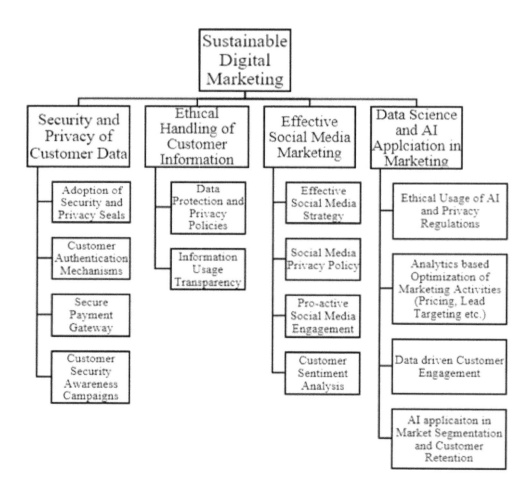

Security and privacy of customer data is a key challenge for organizations (Hutson et al., 2023), (Ogbuke et al., 2022), (Pires et al., 2022). Business organizations can use security and privacy seals on their websites to increase customer confidence that the websites are safe. The usage of secure IT infrastructure can minimize the probability and impact of security breaches. Modern technologies such as intrusion detection systems, encryption software, and secure data transfer protocols can be used to improve organizations' security agility. Furthermore, an agile cyber threat intelligence approach can help in robustly responding to cyber threat incidents (Schlette et al., 2021), (Naseer et al., 2023), (Saeed et al., 2023). Appropriate authentication mechanisms such as two-factor authentication can enhance the customer's confidence in the technological resources of the business organizations. Secure payment gateways can help in protecting the privacy of customer financial data (Oo, 2019). Additionally, organizations can use different campaigns to enhance the cybersecurity awareness of their customers and employees (Jibril et al., 2022), (Limna et al., 2023), (Saeed, 2023), (Saeed, 2023)).

Ethical handling of customer information is also critical to foster sustainable digital marketing. The establishment of data protection and privacy guidelines and making them public increases the customer's confidence (Andrew & Baker, 2021). Furthermore, data usage transparency also provides confidence to customers in the intended usage of their data. Furthermore, the establishment of regulatory frameworks such as GDPR, also helped customers increase their confidence in an organization (Zhang et al., 2020). Therefore, organizations must ensure to meet such relevant regulatory guidelines to improve their marketing processes.

Furthermore, social media has become a critical source for organizations to carry out marketing activities. To benefit from social media marketing departments of organizations need to develop an effective social media strategy. The security of social media data needs to be a core point of social media strategy (Wu et al., 2020). The provision of detailed, accurate, interesting, and up-to-date content on social media is key to keeping potential customers engaged. Furthermore, a proactive timely approach in reaching the queries and comments of social media users is also extremely critical to improving marketing efforts (Infante, & Mardikaningsih, 2022). Modern techniques could be employed for user sentiment analysis to understand the user response which will be used as input for the designing of appropriate marketing strategies (Capuano, 2021).

Recently, data science and AI have become a critical resource for organizations for data-driven monitoring of their business processes and AI has the potential to improve personalization, insights, and strategies in digital marketing by improving the forecasting process ((Saura, 2021), (Thomas, 2021), (Nunan & Di Domenico 2019)). But it also poses risks like privacy breaches, bias, and lack of transparency, therefore the ethical usage of AI and data science applications needs to be fostered in the marketing process (Anshari et al., 2023). Insights from diverse ethical traditions could help improve security regulations by considering stakeholder inclusion, cross-cultural insights, and international governance for developing and regulating AI responsibly. More work is needed to address these gaps to maximize the benefits of AI in the marketing processes of organizations. Therefore, the security of data becomes extremely critical to generate accurate analytics. A data-driven analysis approach can help to understand each organizational activity's effectiveness by providing feedback and lessons learned for future actions. In marketing activities, the effectiveness of marketing plans, equilibrium price analysis, demand and supply forecasts, and lead identification can benefit from data analytics applications to improve organizational operations. Furthermore, the customer engagement process can keep track of the number of returning customers and churn out analysis to design appropriate promotion strategies for different customer segments. We recommend to the researchers that the key findings highlight several potential avenues for future research aimed at maximizing the benefits of AI for marketing while minimizing its risks and impacts. An interdisciplinary research approach incorporating human-centric and application-specific perspectives could develop practical frameworks to guide ethical and responsible AI development and governance for marketing. While AI has great potential to improve digital marketing through personalized insights and strategies, risks like privacy breaches, bias, and lack of transparency must also be managed. Currently, companies lack practical guidance for implementing ethical AI due to limitations of existing ethical frameworks and insufficient input from underrepresented stakeholders, especially in fields like healthcare. Regulating AI holistically is challenging due to its diversity, so a risk-based approach focused on specific uses may be more practical. Insights from diverse ethical traditions could enable truly ethical AI that minimizes harm, but these perspectives remain underutilized. AI's unclear definition also hinders regulation and ethics efforts. Current AI ethics frameworks lack specifics and clear guidance. A multidimensional approach involving multiple stakeholders is needed to make them more actionable. There is a lack of practical methods and perspectives from underserved groups for ethical AI, especially in fields like healthcare. Insights from diverse ethical philosophies could contribute to truly ethical AI that minimizes harm, but they are underutilized. The definition of AI is unclear, complicating regulation and ethics frameworks. International cooperation based on shared values is seen as crucial but has yet to be fully realized. There are significant gaps in practical guidance, stakeholder inclusion, cross-cultural insights, and international governance to develop and regulate AI responsibly. More work is required to fill these gaps and maximize AI's benefits while minimizing risks. While the research highlights vital issues, practical tools, inclusive frameworks, global coordination, and actionable guidance are still needed to operationalize ethical and responsible AI. Addressing these gaps is essential for ensuring AI benefits society.

CONCLUSION

Adopting a sustainable digital marketing strategy is very crucial for business organizations to be competitive in the marketplace. Security and privacy of customer data is a critical challenge for organizations in their pursuit of this objective. In this chapter, we have conducted a systematic literature review and based on our findings we have proposed a framework to make the digital marketing efforts in an organization sustainable. We highlight the security and privacy of customer data, ethical handling of customer information, effective social media marketing, and data science and AI applications in marketing as key enablers. We further specify actions to optimally achieve these goals. In the future, organizations may adopt this framework and its results will be evaluated to evaluate its effectiveness.

REFERENCES

Alkhatib, S., Kecskés, P., & Keller, V. (2023). Green Marketing in the Digital Age: A Systematic Literature Review. *Sustainability*, 15(16), 12369.

Ameen, N., Tarba, S., Cheah, J. H., Xia, S., & Sharma, G. D. (2024). Coupling artificial intelligence capability and strategic agility for enhanced product and service creativity. *British Journal of Management*.

Ameen, N., Tarhini, A., Reppel, A., & Anand, A. (2021). Customer experiences in the age of artificial intelligence. *Computers in Human Behavior*, 114, 106548.32905175

Andrew, J., & Baker, M. (2021). The general data protection regulation in the age of surveillance capitalism. *Journal of Business Ethics*, 168, 565–578.

Anshari, M., Hamdan, M., Ahmad, N., Ali, E., & Haidi, H. (2023). COVID-19, artificial intelligence, ethical challenges and policy implications. *AI & Society*, 38(2), 707–720.35607368

Bandara, R., Fernando, M., & Akter, S. (2021). Managing consumer privacy concerns and defensive behaviours in the digital marketplace. *European Journal of Marketing*, 55(1), 219–246.

Biswas, B., Sanyal, M. K., & Mukherjee, T. (2023). AI-Based Sales Forecasting Model for Digital Marketing. [IJEBR]. *International Journal of E-Business Research*, 19(1), 1–14.

Bleier, A., Goldfarb, A., & Tucker, C. (2020). Consumer privacy and the future of data-based innovation and marketing. *International Journal of Research in Marketing*, 37(3), 466–480.

Bogani, R., Theodorou, A., Arnaboldi, L., & Wortham, R. H. (2022). Garbage in, toxic data out: A proposal for ethical artificial intelligence sustainability impact statements. *AI and Ethics*, •••, 1–8.36281314

Brough, A. R., & Martin, K. D. (2021). Consumer privacy during (and after) the COVID-19 pandemic. *Journal of Public Policy & Marketing*, 40(1), 108–110.

Capuano, N., Greco, L., Ritrovato, P., & Vento, M. (2021). Sentiment analysis for customer relationship management: An incremental learning approach. *Applied Intelligence*, 51, 3339–3352.

Chaffey, D., & Ellis-Chadwick, F. (2019). *Digital marketing*. Pearson uk.

Choudhary, N., Gautam, C., & Arya, V. (2020). Digital marketing challenge and opportunity with reference to tiktok-a new rising social media platform. *Editorial Board*, 9(10), 189–197.

Dastane, D. O. (2020). Impact of digital marketing on online purchase intention: Mediation effect of customer relationship management. *Journal of Asian Business Strategy*.

Dube, M., Musungwini, S., Mudzimba, E., & Watyoka, N. (2023). Mixed Reality in Confronting Consumer Security and Privacy Issues in Digital Marketing: Integrating the Best of Both Worlds for Better Interaction With Users. In *Confronting Security and Privacy Challenges in Digital Marketing* (pp. 252-266). IGI Global.

Emami-Naeini, P., Dixon, H., Agarwal, Y., & Cranor, L. F. (2019, May). Exploring how privacy and security factor into IoT device purchase behavior. In *Proceedings of the 2019 CHI Conference on Human Factors in Computing Systems* (pp. 1-12).

Gull, H., Alabbad, D. A., Saqib, M., Iqbal, S. Z., Nasir, T., Saeed, S., & Almuhaideb, A. M. (2023). E-commerce and cybersecurity challenges: Recent advances and future trends. *Handbook of Research on Cybersecurity Issues and Challenges for Business and FinTech Applications*, 91-111.

Gull, H., Iqbal, S. Z., Saeed, S., Alqahtani, M. A., & Bamarouf, Y. A. (2021). U.S. Patent No. 11,055,137. Washington, DC: U.S. Patent and Trademark Office.

Gull, H., Saeed, S., Iqbal, S. Z., Bamarouf, Y. A., Alqahtani, M. A., Alabbad, D. A., & Alamer, A. (2022). An empirical study of mobile commerce and customers security perception in Saudi Arabia. *Electronics (Basel)*, 11(3), 293.

Hanlon, A., & Jones, K. (2023). Ethical concerns about social media privacy policies: Do users have the ability to comprehend their consent actions? *Journal of Strategic Marketing*, 1–18.

Hayes, R. M., Jiang, F., & Pan, Y. (2021). Voice of the customers: Local trust culture and consumer complaints to the CFPB. *Journal of Accounting Research*, 59(3), 1077–1121.

Henz, P. (2021). Ethical and legal responsibility for Artificial Intelligence. *Discover Artificial Intelligence*, 1, 1–5.

Hidayat, M., Salam, R., Hidayat, Y. S., Sutira, A., & Nugrahanti, T. P. (2022). Sustainable Digital Marketing Strategy in the Perspective of Sustainable Development Goals. Komitmen. *Jurnal Ilmiah Manajemen*, 3(2), 100–106.

Hutson, J., Coble, K., Kshetri, N., & Smith, A. (2023). Exploring the Intersection of Digital Marketing and Retail: Challenges and Opportunities in AI, Privacy, and Customer Experience. *Confronting Security and Privacy Challenges in Digital Marketing*, 50-72.

Infante, A., & Mardikaningsih, R. (2022). The Potential of social media as a Means of Online Business Promotion. *Journal of Social Science Studies (JOS3)*, 2(2), 45-49.

Jibril, A. B., Kwarteng, M. A., Chovancova, M., & Denanyoh, R. (2020, March). Customers' perception of cybersecurity threats toward e-banking adoption and retention: A conceptual study. In *ICCWS 2020 15th International Conference on Cyber Warfare and Security (Vol. 270)*. Academic Conferences and publishing limited.

Kushwaha, B. P., Singh, R. K., & Tyagi, V. (2021). Investigating privacy paradox: Consumer data privacy behavioural intention and disclosure behaviour. *Academy of Marketing Studies Journal*, 25(1), 1–10.

Limna, P., Kraiwanit, T., Siripipattanakul, S., Limna, P., Kraiwanit, T., & Siripipattanakul, S. (2023). The relationship between cyber security knowledge, awareness and behavioural choice protection among mobile banking users in Thailand. *International Journal of Computing Sciences Research*, 7, 1133–1151.

Mandal, P. C. (2023). Public Policy and Ethics in Marketing Research for Organizations: Concerns, Strategies, and Initiatives. [IJPSS]. *International Journal of Public Sociology and Sociotherapy*, 3(1), 1–12.

Mazur, N. (2023). CHALLENGES AND PROSPECTS OF DIGITAL MARKETING IN THE AGE OF ARTIFICIAL INTELLIGENCE. *Grail of Science*, (26), 75–77.

Nalbant, K. G., & Aydin, S. (2023). Development and transformation in digital marketing and branding with artificial intelligence and digital technologies dynamics in the Metaverse universe. *Journal of Metaverse*, 3(1), 9–18.

Naseer, A., Naseer, H., Ahmad, A., Maynard, S. B., & Siddiqui, A. M. (2023). Moving towards agile cybersecurity incident response: A case study exploring the enabling role of big data analytics-embedded dynamic capabilities. *Computers & Security*, 135, 103525.

Nunan, D., & Di Domenico, M. (2019). Older consumers, digital marketing, and public policy: A review and research agenda. *Journal of Public Policy & Marketing*, 38(4), 469–483.

Nuss, T., Chen, Y. J. M., Scully, M., Hickey, K., Martin, J., & Morley, B. (2023). Australian adults' attitudes towards government actions to protect children from digital marketing of unhealthy food and drink products. *Health Promotion Journal of Australia*.37286359

Ogbuke, N. J., Yusuf, Y. Y., Dharma, K., & Mercangoz, B. A. (2022). Big data supply chain analytics: Ethical, privacy and security challenges posed to business, industries and society. *Production Planning and Control*, 33(2-3), 123–137.

Oo, K. Z. (2019). Design and implementation of electronic payment gateway for secure online payment system. *Int. J. Trend Sci. Res. Dev*, 3, 1329–1334.

Page, M. J., McKenzie, J. E., Bossuyt, P. M., Boutron, I., Hoffmann, T. C., Mulrow, C. D., & Moher, D. (2021). The PRISMA 2020 statement: An updated guideline for reporting systematic reviews. *BMJ (Clinical Research Ed.)*, 372(71).33782057

Pandey, N., Nayal, P., & Rathore, A. S. (2020). Digital marketing for B2B organizations: Structured literature review and future research directions. *Journal of Business and Industrial Marketing*, 35(7), 1191–1204.

Pires, P. B., Santos, J. D., Pereira, I. V., & Torres, A. I. (Eds.). (2023). *Confronting Security and Privacy Challenges in Digital Marketing*. IGI Global.

Quach, S., Thaichon, P., Martin, K. D., Weaven, S., & Palmatier, R. W. (2022). Digital technologies: Tensions in privacy and data. *Journal of the Academy of Marketing Science*, 50(6), 1299–1323.35281634

Rauturier, S. (2023) What is Sustainable Digital Marketing? Solene Rauturier – Mindful Digital Marketing. https://www.solenerauturier.com/blog/sustainable-digital-marketing

Rodgers, W., & Nguyen, T. (2022). Advertising benefits from ethical artificial intelligence algorithmic purchase decision pathways. *Journal of Business Ethics*, 178(4), 1043–1061.

Rodrigues, D., & Martinez, L. F. (2020). The influence of digital marketing on recruitment effectiveness: A qualitative study. *European Journal of Management Studies*, 25(1), 23–44.

Saeed, S. (2019). Digital Business adoption and customer segmentation: An exploratory study of expatriate community in Saudi Arabia. *ICIC Express Letters*, 13(2), 133–139.

Saeed, S. (2023). A customer-centric view of E-commerce security and privacy. *Applied Sciences (Basel, Switzerland)*, 13(2), 1020.

Saeed, S. (2023). Digital Workplaces and Information Security Behavior of Business Employees: An Empirical Study of Saudi Arabia. *Sustainability*, 15(7), 6019.

Saeed, S., Altamimi, S. A., Alkayyal, N. A., Alshehri, E., & Alabbad, D. A. (2023). Digital transformation and cybersecurity challenges for businesses resilience: Issues and recommendations. *Sensors (Basel)*, 23(15), 6666.37571451

Saeed, S., Pipek, V., Rohde, M., Reuter, C., De Carvalho, A. F. P., & Wulf, V. (2019). Nomadic Knowledge Sharing Practices and Challenges: Findings From a Long-Term Case Study. *IEEE Access : Practical Innovations, Open Solutions*, 7, 63564–63577.

Saeed, S., Suayyid, S. A., Al-Ghamdi, M. S., Al-Muhaisen, H., & Almuhaideb, A. M. (2023). A Systematic Literature Review on Cyber Threat Intelligence for Organizational Cybersecurity Resilience. *Sensors (Basel)*, 23(16), 7273.37631808

Saeed, S., Wahab, F., Cheema, S. A., & Ashraf, S. (2013). Role of usability in e-government and e-commerce portals: An empirical study of Pakistan. *Life Science Journal*, 10(1), 8–13.

Saura, J. R. (2021). Using data sciences in digital marketing: Framework, methods, and performance metrics. *Journal of Innovation & Knowledge*, 6(2), 92–102.

Saura, J. R., Palacios-Marqués, D., & Ribeiro-Soriano, D. (2023). Digital marketing in SMEs via data-driven strategies: Reviewing the current state of research. *Journal of Small Business Management*, 61(3), 1278–1313.

Schlette, D., Caselli, M., & Pernul, G. (2021). A comparative study on cyber threat intelligence: The security incident response perspective. *IEEE Communications Surveys and Tutorials*, 23(4), 2525–2556.

Sundqvist, B., & Ohanisian, J. (2023). *Utilization of AI in Digital Marketing: An empirical study of Artificial Intelligence and the impact of effectiveness, ethics and regulations.*

Tariq, E., Alshurideh, M., Akour, I., & Al-Hawary, S. (2022). The effect of digital marketing capabilities on organizational ambidexterity of the information technology sector. *International Journal of Data and Network Science*, 6(2), 401–408.

Tatlow-Golden, M., & Garde, A. (2020). Digital food marketing to children: Exploitation, surveillance and rights violations. *Global Food Security*, 27, 100423.

Thomas, I. (2021). Planning for a cookie-less future: How browser and mobile privacy changes will impact marketing, targeting and analytics. *Applied marketing analytics*, 7(1), 6-16.

Winegar, A. G., & Sunstein, C. R. (2019). How much is data privacy worth? A preliminary investigation. *Journal of Consumer Policy*, 42, 425–440.

Wu, Y., Huang, H., Wu, N., Wang, Y., Bhuiyan, M. Z. A., & Wang, T. (2020). An incentive-based protection and recovery strategy for secure big data in social networks. *Information Sciences*, 508, 79–91.

Zhang, B., Ying, L., Khan, M. A., Ali, M., Barykin, S., & Jahanzeb, A. (2023). Sustainable digital marketing: Factors of adoption of m-technologies by older adults in the Chinese market. *Sustainability*, 15(3), 1972.

Zhang, J., Hassandoust, F., & Williams, J. E. (2020). Online customer trust in the context of the general data protection regulation (GDPR). *Pacific Asia Journal of the Association for Information Systems*, 12(1), 4.

Chapter 7
Global Ambitions, Local Realities:
Uber Eats' Marketing Strategy in India and Its Demise

Gurloveleen Kaur
https://orcid.org/0000-0002-0018-4423
Chitkara University, India

Megha Goyal
Chitkara University, India

ABSTRACT

This case examines Uber Eats' journey since its inception in 2014, focusing on its challenges in India. It showcases how Uber Eats adapted to serve customers globally, handling rapid growth, technological advancements, and partnerships. Despite facing hurdles like operational efficiency and the COVID-19 pandemic, Uber Eats emphasized innovation to stay ahead. The case also looks at Zomato's acquisition of Uber Eats in India, highlighting its impact on the food delivery industry and competition with Swiggy. It aims to offer insights into Uber Eats' performance, partnerships, and competition, providing valuable lessons for industry players. The case concludes with discussion questions to deepen understanding of strategic initiatives and industry trends.

INTRODUCTION

This case explores the revolutionary path taken by Uber Eats, a division of Uber Technologies, Inc., from its establishment in Los Angeles in 2014 to its current position as a prominent player in the worldwide meal delivery market but a failure in the Indian Market. It looks at how Uber Eats has adapted to serve a wide range of customers in thousands of cities throughout the globe by navigating through quick growth, technology breakthroughs, and clever alliances. To improve customer experience and keep its market leadership, Uber Eats has continuously invested in innovation, even in the face of obstacles like operational efficiency and adjusting to the COVID-19 pandemic's impact. In order to expand its products, Uber Eats has integrated services like groceries and alcohol delivery, and the piece also emphasizes the

DOI: 10.4018/979-8-3693-6660-8.ch007

Copyright ©2024, IGI Global. Copying or distributing in print or electronic forms without written permission of IGI Global is prohibited.

company's strategic approaches to partnerships and market expansion. Although Uber Eats enjoyed a strong start, it faced varying levels of customer satisfaction over time. Issues like tardy deliveries, inaccuracies in estimated arrival times (ETAs), and occasional drops in service quality emerged as the company grew. The inconsistent service, marked by occasional delays and communication mishaps, resulted in customer discontent, and consistently hindered the company's efforts to uphold high satisfaction levels. It also discusses the competitive environment in India, going over Zomato's acquisition of Uber Eats and its effects on the meal delivery industry.

The benefit from takeover by Zomato is discussed, which provides and enhances the knowledge related to the strategic alliances. Zomato got stronger in delivering meals in India by buying Uber Eats and bringing in its customers, restaurants, and delivery system. Even though there were some problems combining the two services, Zomato worked hard to make sure customers stayed happy. Buying Uber Eats made Zomato compete more with Swiggy, so they came up with new ways to attract customers, like cool ads and deals. Zomato wanted to keep growing and making more money, so they used the Uber Eats purchase to help them do that. They also got chances to try new things, like going into new markets and making money in different ways. This made Zomato's future look even brighter. Analysing Uber Eats' performance in the competitive landscape provides valuable insights for Zomato's strategy and contributes to industry discussions on meal delivery's evolution and its impact on all players involved. Moreover, the case offers insights into the elements influencing Uber Eats' performance and the difficulties it encounters in a competitive market through a thorough analysis. The questions are given at the end of the case, so that readers get a better understanding of the content. These questions will shed light on the concept of strategic initiatives undertaken by Uber Eats to expand its service offerings beyond traditional food delivery at global level. Thoroughly describes the impact of Uber Eats' acquisition by Zomato on the food delivery industry in India and the lessons learned by the uber eats case study that can be implemented for further improvement. This case study is written with the purpose to fully equip the readers about the starting of Uber Eats till the end of the brand in the Indian market.

Food Delivery Industry in India

Over the past few decades, the food delivery sector in India has experienced tremendous expansion and evolution due to a variety of factors including evolving consumer demands, technical advancements, and the introduction of new market participants. Before the advent of digital technology, the only places in India where people could get food delivered to their homes were neighbourhood eateries. Customers usually placed their orders by calling restaurants directly, using the outdated telephone-based ordering systems that were widely used. Delivery wait times were frequently lengthy, and the variety of cuisines offered was restricted to eateries in the vicinity. Online meal ordering services like Just Eat, Food panda, and Swiggy (established in 2014) began to appear in India in the early 2000s. These platforms increased the variety of restaurants and cuisines available to clients by providing them with the ease of ordering food online through websites or mobile apps.

Online food delivery services were not as widely used at this time due to poor smartphone usage and internet penetration. India's meal delivery business had a sharp rise in the mid-to late-2010s, driven by rising internet usage, smartphone adoption, and shifting customer habits. There were fierce competition as well-established firms like Uber Eats (which debuted in India in 2017), Swiggy, and Zomato (which was first established as Foodiebay in 2008) fought hard for market dominance. These platforms made significant investments in marketing, technology, and logistics to boost user experience, expedite deliv-

Global Ambitions, Local Realities

ery, and draw users. Discounts, promotions, and strategic alliances with eateries have become standard strategies to increase client acquisition and retention.

Market Share of Food Delivery Business

- The Online Food Delivery market in India is projected to reach a revenue of US$43.78bn in 2024.
- It is expected to show an annual growth rate (CAGR 2024-2028) of 16.95%.
- This growth will result in a projected market volume of US$81.91bn by 2028.
- In the Meal Delivery market in India, the number of users is expected to reach 346.6m users by 2028.

Figure 1. India online food ordering and delivery market

Source:https://www.techsciresearch.com/report/india-online-food-ordering-and-delivery-market/3952.html

Figure 1 explains Indian food ordering market share on regional basis in India, clarify that northern region has grabbed the largest share of food ordering market share in India as compared to west, east and south.

Uber Eats

Uber Eats is a division of Uber Technologies, Inc. that uses its network of logistics partners and technological platform to make meal delivery easier. With its global headquarters located in San Francisco, California, the organization serves thousands of towns in several nations. For order fulfilment and upkeep, it uses both internal employees and independent contractors (such delivery drivers). Uber Eats also keeps making investments in partnerships, innovation, and technology to improve its services and keep up its position as the market leader in food delivery.

Uber Eats first appeared in Los Angeles, California in 2014, before becoming available as a stand-alone app in other US regions. In 2015 and 2016, the service expanded internationally, touching major cities throughout the globe. Part of the reason for its rapid growth is partnerships with surrounding restaurants and franchises. In 2017, Uber Eats expanded its reach and added new services, such as real-time tracking, to its menu in 2018. Furthermore, it broadens the scope of services it provides in certain locations by introducing choices like food and alcohol delivery.

Uber Eats' priorities for 2019 and 2020 include operational optimization and profitability. It presents fresh efforts aimed at increasing productivity and streamlining delivery procedures. Uber Eats is forced to modify its offerings in response to shifting customer demands because of the COVID-19 pandemic's impact on the need for food delivery.

Market Entry Strategy

Since its launch in 2014, Uber Eats, a division of Uber Technologies, Inc., has undergone substantial expansion and change. Although there hasn't been a single incident or turning point, the platform has experienced a number of advancements and strategic changes that have contributed to its success.

They deal in Food Delivery: With Uber Eats, customers can order food to be delivered to their area, explore menus from a variety of restaurants, and place orders.

Grocery Delivery: Uber Eats provides grocery delivery services in some areas, enabling customers to order necessities from nearby shops and supermarkets.

Uber Eats offers alcohol delivery services, allowing customers to purchase beer, wine, and spirits in addition to their food, according to local rules.

Special Offers: To attract clients and increase revenue, Uber Eats regularly runs specials and discounts. These could include limited-time promotions, partnerships with eateries, and free delivery for new customers.

Figure 2. Marketing strategies used by Uber Eats

Source: Author's own contribution

- Partnerships and Acquisitions: To broaden its product offerings beyond traditional meal delivery, Uber Eats carefully forged alliances with several eateries, franchises, and supermarkets. It also bought smaller meal delivery services to improve its market position across several geographies.
- Market Expansion: By 2020, Uber Eats had quickly spread throughout 45 countries and over 6,000 cities. Due to its broad reach, the platform was able to provide a variety of cuisines and reach many users. After entering the Indian market, Uber Eats expanded to 41 cities, employing over 65,000 riders to transport food from 26,000 partner restaurants. Uber Eats has been dragging losses on the company's financials due to heavy discounts and low value orders in India's fiercely competitive delivery sector.
- Technology and innovation: Uber Eats consistently makes investments in technology and innovation to improve the user experience. This includes attributes like customized recommendations, expedited ordering procedures, and real-time tracking.
- Cost analysis: Uber Eats has redirected its attention on attaining profitability through cost reduction, operational optimization, and the application of dynamic pricing tactics. This involved modifying commissions, delivery costs, and driver incentives.

Figure 3. Revenue growth of grocery and meal delivery of Uber Eats from 2017 to 2028

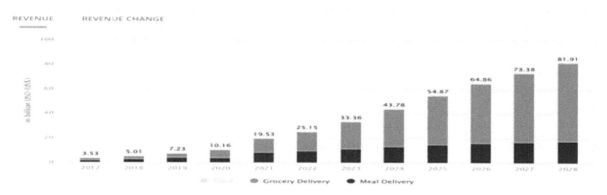

Source: https://www.statista.com

Figure 3 shows worldwide revenue earned by Uber Eats. It shows the revenue has increased significantly from 2017 to 2023 and is predicted to increase further till 2028. It has increased gradually in Grocery Delivery and Meal Delivery. Moreover, higher growth is observed in grocery delivery rather than meal delivery.

Target Audience of Uber Eats

Uber Eats knows the worth of people falling in varied ranges either its individual or chunk of people. A company attracted the individuals sitting at different places along with restaurants and businesses personnel.

Customers: Uber Eats mainly caters to people who are searching for quick and easy meal delivery services. This applies to everyone looking for a hassle-free method to enjoy meals from their favourite restaurants, including families, students, and busy professionals.

Restaurants and Businesses: Uber Eats offers delivery services to restaurants and food businesses looking to grow their customer base and boost revenue. It collaborates with regional restaurants as well as national chains to provide users with a wide variety of cuisines. As a full-service platform, Uber Eats concentrates on offering a wide range of features and services to clients as well as eateries.

USP of Uber Eats

It differentiated itself through cutting-edge technology integration, real-time tracking, and a diverse fleet of delivery vehicles. With an aggressive expansion strategy, it rapidly scaled its operations to 15 major urban centres within three years of inception, seamlessly catering to various culinary preferences. By the end of its fifth year, Uber Eats boasted operations in over 50 cities, serving a customer base exceeding 10 million active users monthly. The range of dining options catered to varied tastes and, enabling Uber Eats to position itself as a one-stop platform for numerous cuisines, from local favourites to international specialities.

Developing an AI-driven route optimisation algorithm showcased the company's dedication to improving operational efficiency. This proprietary technology reduced average delivery times by 25% and optimised routes dynamically based on real-time data, minimising delivery delays and enhancing overall service quality. Uber Eats 's unwavering dedication to service excellence is reflected in its consistently high customer satisfaction ratings, averaging over 4.5 out of 5. This achievement stemmed from a customer-centric approach, ensuring seamless ordering experiences, timely deliveries, and responsive customer support. The focus on maintaining and improving satisfaction levels contributed significantly to customer loyalty, repeat orders, and positive brand advocacy.

Business Model

Through the Uber Eats app or website, customers may access a wide range of restaurants and cuisines, providing convenience and choice. To guarantee that users have a flawless ordering and delivery experience, the platform makes investments in marketing, technology, and logistics.

In addition to charging delivery fees and restaurant commissions, Uber Eats may also make money through agreements with advertising networks and special promotions. To improve the user experience, it provides services including safe payment alternatives, customer assistance, personalized suggestions, and real-time purchase tracking. When opposed to less expensive options, the full-service model typically has slightly higher prices but places an emphasis on quality, dependability, and convenience.

Figure 4. Quarterly revenue from 2018 to 2022

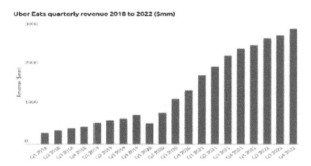

The graph shows how much money Uber Eats has made around the world over the years 2018 to 2022. Overall, revenue of Uber Eats jumped higher from 2018 to 2022. The highest portion of revenue was enjoyed by the company in fourth quarter of 2022.
Source: https://www.valueappz.com/blog/ubereats-business-model-uber-eats-make-money.

SWOT Analysis of Uber Eats

SWOT is done to know the actual strengths, weaknesses, opportunities, and threats of the company. Uber Eats is growing company which is clearly visible through generated revenue.

Figure 5. SWOT analysis

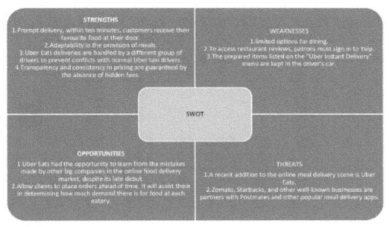

Source: Author's own contribution

Competitors

The India online food ordering and delivery market is characterized by intense competition and fragmentation, with key players such as Swiggy, Zomato, Uber Eats (now part of Zomato), and Foodpanda (merged with Ola). These platforms offer a diverse range of cuisines, catering to various consumer segments. The entry of Uber Eats (now integrated into Zomato) and Foodpanda has intensified competition, leveraging ride-hailing technology to enhance food delivery services

Swiggy: Founded in 2014, Swiggy is one of the leading players in the Indian food delivery market. Its strategies include:

- Extensive network: Swiggy has established a vast network of partner restaurants and delivery personnel across major cities in India, offering customers a wide selection of dining options.
- Technology and innovation: The company invests in technology and product development to enhance its app's user experience, introduce new features, and optimize delivery logistics.
- Diversification: Swiggy has diversified its services to include grocery delivery, alcohol delivery (in select markets), and cloud kitchens, catering to a broader range of customer needs.

Zomato: Originally founded as Foodiebay in 2008, Zomato is another major player in the Indian food delivery market. Its strategies include:

- Platform expansion: Zomato has expanded its platform beyond food delivery to include restaurant discovery, table reservations, and online ordering for groceries and essentials.
- Acquisitions and partnerships: The company has made strategic acquisitions and partnerships to strengthen its market position and diversify its offerings. For example, Zomato acquired Uber Eats' India business in 2020.

- International presence: Zomato has expanded its presence beyond India to international markets, further diversifying its revenue streams and customer base.

Figure 6. Orders taken by Swiggy, Zomato, and Uber Eats from 2016 to 2019

Source: https://ajuniorvc.com/foodtech-endgame-ubereats-acquisition-swiggy-zomato-amazon/

A Twisted Turn in the Tale

Uber Eats, the trailblazer in the food delivery sector, has experienced meteoric growth since its inception. However, as you dove into the company's operations, you quickly realised that behind the success stories lay many hurdles and complexities. From maintaining consistent delivery times in diverse locations to wrestling with customer dissatisfaction due to occasional delays and inaccurate estimates, the company was grappling with maintaining its once-impeccable reputation.

As Uber Eats expanded its services to multiple cities, maintaining consistent delivery times became a significant challenge. The complexities of operating in diverse locations with varying traffic patterns and logistical hurdles led to occasional delays in fulfilling orders. These inconsistencies resulted in customer dissatisfaction, as expectations for prompt deliveries were not consistently met. Occasional delays impacted Uber Eats's reputation for reliability and affected customer loyalty.

Moreover, challenges in effectively managing and allocating delivery personnel compounded these issues, leading to suboptimal route assignments and delays in order fulfilment. These inefficiencies impacted operational costs and service quality, requiring a more sophisticated and scalable operational infrastructure.

Despite its initial success, Uber Eats encountered fluctuating customer satisfaction levels. Factors such as late deliveries, inaccuracies in estimated arrival time (ETAs), and occasional lapses in service quality surfaced as the company expanded. Inconsistent service experiences caused by occasional delays and miscommunications led to customer dissatisfaction and consistently impacted the company's ability to maintain high satisfaction ratings.

Figure 7. Uber Eats growth and expenses in Indis during 2019-2020

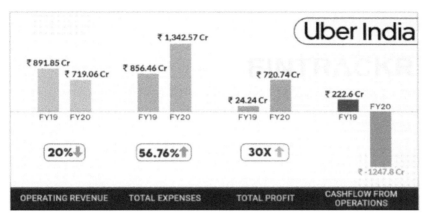

Source: https://entrackr.com/2021/04/the-curious-case-of-uber-indias-rs-721-cr-profit-jump-in-fy20/

Problems Faced by Uber Eats

- Uber Eats wants to reduce delivery time variations across different locations.
- Also, want to improve customer satisfaction ratings by addressing late deliveries and inaccurate ETAs.
- Need to manage the increasing fleet size, reducing operational costs related to vehicle acquisition and maintenance.

Solution to the Problems

- Uber Eats wants to reduce delivery time variations across different locations
    a. Allocating employees based on orders placed and improving vehicle condition would reduce the time variation. Using the predicting model time can be predicted considering the factors such as road density, delivery person age and distance between two locations.
- Also, we want to improve customer satisfaction ratings by addressing late deliveries and inaccurate ETAs.
    a. Ratings are highly influenced by ETAs and behavior of the employees. If delivery is done before ETAs, it would increase customer satisfaction. Equipping employees at cities with high orders and at time of high orders would ensure customer satisfaction. Offering additional discounts and offers would increase sales and hence customer satisfaction is achieved.
- Lastly, we need to manage the increasing fleet size, reducing operational costs related to vehicle acquisition and maintenance.

Global Ambitions, Local Realities

a. There is large no. of obsolete vehicles, removing them from the company would reduce fleet size and would lower the maintenance cost as well, as these vehicles would consume more fuel and take more time to deliver.

Zomato Acquired Uber Eats

Zomato purchased Uber Eats' Indian operation in January 2020. Zomato's position as one of the top players in the Indian meal delivery business was strengthened by this acquisition, which was a significant development in the market. As part of the agreement, Uber Eats stopped operating in India and switched its clients to Zomato's platform. Through the acquisition, Zomato was able to increase the size of its client base and the number of restaurant relationships it has, enhancing its market presence and competitiveness in relation to rivals like Swiggy. Additionally, it allowed Uber Eats to concentrate its resources on other worldwide critical markets and activities.

Impact of Acquisition

It made it possible for Zomato to solidify its place in India's fiercely competitive meal delivery industry. Second, it extended Zomato's geographic reach and gave it access to a bigger consumer base, particularly in major cities where Uber Eats was well-established. Furthermore, Zomato was able to perhaps realize economies of scale and raise its general level of market efficiency by purchasing the operations of Uber Eats.

Increasing Market Share: Zomato was able to maintain its position as one of the top companies in the Indian meal delivery market thanks to the purchase. Through the incorporation of Uber Eats' clientele, restaurant alliances, and delivery system, Zomato enhanced its market share and competitiveness vis-à-vis other significant companies such as Swiggy.

Operational Integration Challenges: Zomato had a lot of difficulties while combining the operations of two sizable meal delivery services. This involved coordinating restaurant alliances, coordinating logistics and delivery networks, coordinating technological platforms, and overseeing the shift for both clients and delivery partners. It was essential to overcome these integration obstacles in order to guarantee a smooth transition and preserve client satisfaction.

Impact on Competition: The acquisition changed how the Indian meal delivery business was competitive. Uber Eats' activities were consolidated into Zomato, which increased rivalry between Zomato and Swiggy, the other significant participant in the industry. Increased rivalry led to creative thinking, bold marketing plans, and customer-attracting and customer-retaining sales and promotions.

Long-Term Strategy and Growth Potential: Zomato's long-term strategy of growing its market leadership and presence in the meal delivery sector is in line with the acquisition of Uber Eats. Zomato sought to accomplish long-term sustainable development, higher profitability, and increased shareholder value by utilizing synergies from the purchase. Furthermore, the acquisition gave Zomato the chance to investigate new markets, diversify its sources of income, and penetrate related industry verticals.

Figure 8. Monthly users index of Swiggy, Zomato, and Uber Eats

Source: https://kr-asia.com/who-leads-the-food-delivery-race-between-zomato-and-swiggy-in-india

CONCLUSION

The experience of Uber Eats is a perfect example of how dynamic the food delivery sector is and how constant innovation and adaptability are essential. Uber Eats has made a significant impact on the world economy by skilfully navigating the obstacles of rapid expansion, intense competition, and shifting consumer preferences. An important turning point has been reached with Zomato's acquisition, which has changed the competitive environment and created opportunities for future expansion and innovation. Uber Eats is committed to enhancing service delivery and customer experience, even in the face of challenges like inconsistent delivery times and low customer satisfaction. This is demonstrated by the company's use of technology and strategic alliances. Uber Eats' capacity to innovate and adapt will be critical to maintaining its leading position and spurring future development as the food delivery industry continues to change. The lessons from Uber Eats journey highlight the importance of operational efficiency, customer focus, and strategic foresight in the fast-paced world of online food delivery.

REFERENCES

Ai, M. (2021, August 12). *Who leads the food delivery race between Zomato and Swiggy in India?*. KrASIA. https://kr-asia.com/who-leads-the-food-delivery-race-between-zomato-and-swiggy-in-india

Bhatt, T. (2024, April 5). *Uber Eats Business Model: Changing the Game in Food Delivery*. Intelivita. https://www.intelivita.com/blog/uber-eats-business-model/

India Online Food Ordering and Delivery Market Size and Trends 2029. (n.d.). TechsciResearch Pvt Ltd. https://www.techsciresearch.com/report/india-online-food-ordering-and-delivery-market/3952.html

A Junior VC. (2020, September 15). *Who Will Win FoodTech's Endgame?* A Junior VC. https://ajuniorvc.com/foodtech-endgame-ubereats-acquisition-swiggy-zomato-amazon/

Mitra, G., & Mitra, G. (2019, December 17). *What Led to Uber Eats' Failure in India? Here Are Insides from the Probable Uber Eats-Zomato Meger!* Express Computer. https://www.expresscomputer.in/news/uber-eats-failure-india/44393/

Statista - The Statistics Portal. (n.d.). Statista. https://www.statista.com

Streamlyn Academy. (2023, September 29). *A Comprehensive Uber Eats Case Study-2023*. Streamlyn Academy. https://streamlynacademy.com/blog/uber-eats-case-study/Tyagi, J. V. A. G. (2022, June 29). *The curious case of Uber India's Rs 721 Cr profit jump in FY20*. Entrackr. https://entrackr.com/2021/04/the-curious-case-of-uber-indias-rs-721-cr-profit-jump-in-fy20/

Yadav, M. (2023, December 3). *UberEats Business Model: How Does Uber Eats Make Money?* ValueAppz - Blog. https://www.valueappz.com/blog/ubereats-business-model-uber-eats-make-money

APPENDIX

Questions to be answered:

- What strategic initiatives did Uber Eats undertake to expand its service offerings beyond traditional food delivery?
- How did Uber Eats' acquisition by Zomato impact the food delivery industry in India?
- What are the lessons learned by the uber eats case study that can be implemented for further improvement?

Exhibit 1. Delivery Time Prediction

Figure 9. ETA for orders

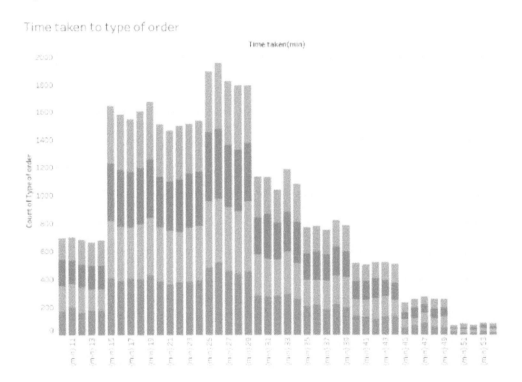

From the graph above we can infer that for every type of food it requires approx 20-30 min for preparation so including the delivery time 45 minutes should be the average predicted time.

Exhibit 2. No. of orders basis locality

Global Ambitions, Local Realities

Figure 10. No. of orders basis locality

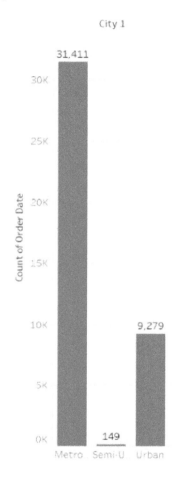

Bifurcating in the geographical aspect the cities can be classified into Metropolitan, Semi-urban and Urban. In Metropolitan cities there are more orders as compared to other regions, this can be due to high paying capacity and better infrastructure. In Semi- urban areas there is no proper infrastructure resulting in less orders.

Exhibit 3. Delivery Person Performance

Figure 11. Performance analysis of delivery persons basis age

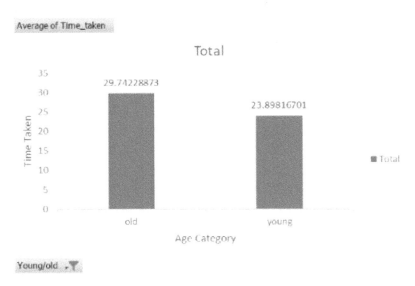

Analysed the delivery person's performance by considering their age, ratings, and vehicle condition. Identify factors that correlate with efficient and timely deliveries.

The age range covers the years 20 to 39. Thus, delivery staff members may be thirty years old on average. It has been observed that delivery employees over 30 typically have longer delivery times than their younger colleagues.

In particular, the average delivery time for employees under 30 is about 24 minutes, and for those over 30, it rises to about 30 minutes. This age-based difference in delivery times implies that older delivery staff members often take longer than their younger counterparts to finish deliveries.

Figure 12. Performance analysis of delivery persons basis volume

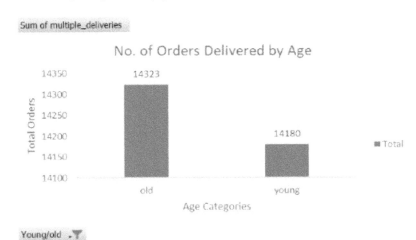

Global Ambitions, Local Realities

It has been observed that delivery employees who are older tend to manage a higher volume of deliveries than those who are younger.

This finding raises the possibility that older people's longer delivery durations are a result of their making more deliveries.

Exhibit 4. Customer Satisfaction

Figure 13. Relation between ETAs and customer satisfaction

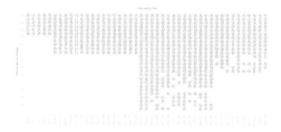

Delivery timings and driver ratings show a strong correlation. Delivery times are correlated with poorer ratings. Slower the delivery would result in lower ratings as timely delivery provides more customer satisfaction and meeting up with ETAs.

Exhibit 5. Delivery Person Allocation

Figure 14. Delivery person allocation

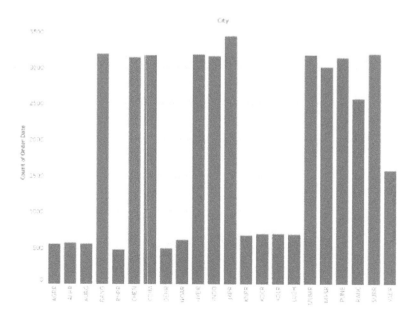

Based on the data, the following viz was prepared from this we can allocate our employees based on city with

105

high no. of orders.

Figure 15. Peak hours for delivery

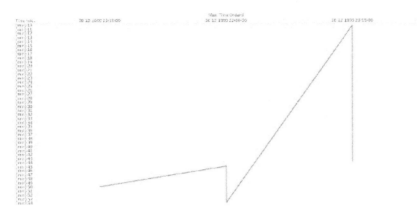

From the graph above we infer that most of the orders were placed at night. The results of the analysis show that a sizable portion of customers typically place their orders late at night. This implies that there was a significant need for delivery services at this time.

Orders placed late at night typically take longer to arrive. There could be several reasons for this, such as a spike in demand around specific times, possible staffing shortages, or an increase in the number of orders that need to be filled.

When managing delivery operations, it is crucial to consider the time of order placing, as seen by the observed pattern of early orders having shorter delivery times and late-night orders having longer delivery times. To satisfy the anticipated demand at various times of the day, it can assist firms in efficiently allocating resources, modifying employee levels, and optimizing delivery routes.

Exhibit 6. Cost Analysis

Global Ambitions, Local Realities

Figure 16. Relation between traffic density and cost

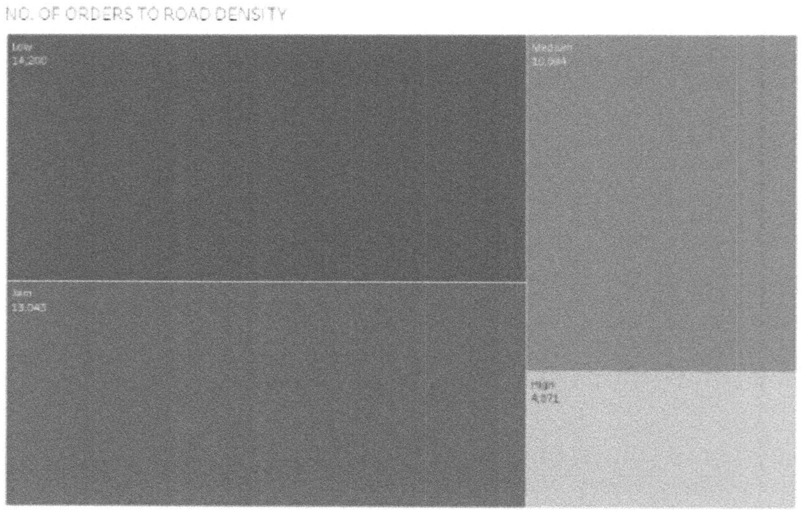

NO. OF ORDERS TO ROAD DENSITY
Low 14,200
Medium 10,984
Jam 13,043
High 4,971

Due to high traffic, there will be more fuel consumption resulting in increased cost. As we can see less no. of is placed when there is high traffic as delay in time would ultimately affect customer satisfaction.

Figure 17. Count of vehicles basis vehicle condition

VEHICLE DEGREE COUNT
VEHICLE_D..
BAD   13,815
GOOD   13,851
VERY GOOD   13,806

The vehicle conditions demonstrate that huge improvement is required in the area to achieve cost efficiency. The bad rated vehicles are similar to as of very good. If the company removes the bad vehicles their cost efficiency would increase as it will lower the maintenance cost, fuel consumption and would lower the delivery time as well approaching customer satisfaction.

Chapter 8
Impact of e-WOM on the Brand Image and Purchase Intention of the Consumer:
An Empirical Study

Namita Kochhar
GNA University, Phagwara, India

Nidhi Bhagat
Lovely Professional University, India

ABSTRACT

In this digital age, any information is just a click away, whether it is relating to business news or the fashion world. Consumers today do not rely on print media for any news; rather, they resort to online platforms for exploring the details with regard to the any product or services before making any buying decisions. In this chapter, the researcher has tried to explore how e-WOM has influenced the brand image and shaped consumers' perception towards product purchase decisions. The population of the study are the customers who use online platforms for purchasing or making purchase decisions. A structured questionnaire has been filled in by 341 respondents so as to analyse the impact of factors on the consumer's perception of purchase. The statistical technique used is SEM. The findings indicate that electronic word of mouth (e-WOM) significantly affects brand image and also has a substantial impact on purchase intentions. Further, brand image of a product also influences the consumer buying decisions.

INTRODUCTION

Most experts agree that word-of-mouth (WOM) communication has a significant impact on shaping consumer attitudes and intentions (Chatterjee, 2001; Chevalier and Mayzlin, 2006; Herr et al., 1991; Kiecker and Cowles, 2001; Sen and Lerman, 2007; Weinberger and Dillon, 1980; Xia and Bechwati, 2008).Research has shown that e-WOM has greater influence than communication from other sources, such as editorial recommendations or advertisements and moreover provides relatively reliable information (e.g. Bickart and Schindler, 2001; Smith et al., 2005; Trusov et al., 2009). (Gruen et al., 2006).

DOI: 10.4018/979-8-3693-6660-8.ch008

Copyright ©2024, IGI Global. Copying or distributing in print or electronic forms without written permission of IGI Global is prohibited.

As a result, due to its increased perceived reliability and dependability, this kind of communication is seen as being very convincing (e.g. Chatterjee, 2001; Godes and Mayzlin, 2004; Mayzlin, 2006). A less intimate but more common form of WOM communication emerged with the global spread of the internet, known as "online WOM communication," which replaced the earlier definition of WOM communication, which was person-to-person conversations between consumers about a product (Chatterjee, 2001; Sen and Lerman, 2007). (e.g. Brown et al., 2007; Chatterjee, 2001; Davis and Khazanchi, 2008; Godes and Mayzlin, 2004; Kiecker and Cowles, 2001; Xia and Bechwati, 2008). Because of its increased accessibility and wide audience, this new form of WOM communication has grown to be a significant platform for consumer opinions (Bickart and Schindler, 2001; Godes and Mayzlin, 2004; Hennig-Thurau et al., 2004; Mayzlin, 2006). It is believed to be even more effective than WOM communication in the offline world (Chatterjee, 2001). One of the most significant forms of online word-of-mouth (WOM) communication are product reviews that consumers post online (Schindler and Bickart, 2005; Sen and Lerman, 2007). It is becoming more and more common for consumers to search for online product reviews when obtaining pre-purchase product information (Adjei et al., 2009; Zhu and Zhang, 2010) and forming purchase intentions (Zhang and Tran, 2009). Additionally, a lot of industries have identified branding as their core capital. Robust brands have the potential to enhance consumers' confidence in the good or service they have chosen, as well as help them see and comprehend intangible elements more clearly. Yoo and Donthu (2001) posit that a company's brand image has the potential to impact various aspects of its operations, including future earnings and long-term cash flow, consumer willingness to pay premium pricing, stock prices, merger and acquisition decision-making, and marketing success. It is contended that online WOM communications posted in such an engaging and dynamic medium as the internet may have significant effects on brand image and, consequently, purchase intention, based on the theory that particularly vividly presented WOM communication has a strong impact on product judgments (Herr et al., 1991).

According to Keller (1993), brand image refers to how consumers perceive a brand based on the brand connections they have in their memory. Perceived service quality is a function of a consumer's consumption experiences, which in turn form the basis of their brand image. Therefore, brand image is strongly impacted by customers' perceptions of service quality (Aydin and Ozer, 2005). Customers are increasingly reliant on the interpersonal impact of e-WOM since intangibles, including after-sale services, cannot be assessed prior to the consuming experience. As a result, investing in intangible goods and services has a larger risk (Lewis and Chambers, 2000; Litvin et al., 2008).

Even though e-WOM has a big impact on the manufacturing sector, not much research has been done on the topic. e-WOM communications can influence brand image and purchase intention, based on the studies in the literature.

The experimental design methodology is used in this paper to investigate:

- how e-WOM messages affect a brand's image;
- how e-WOM communications affect consumers' intentions to buy; and
- the influence of brand perception on intention to buy.

REVIEW OF LITERATUIRE

Earlier Studies on the Impact of Electronic Word-of-Mouth

e-WOM has arisen as a result of people using the internet to research companies or products more frequently due to advancements in internet technologies. "Any positive or negative statement made by potential, actual, or former customers about a product or company which is made available to multitude of people and institutes via the Internet" is how Hennig-Thurau et al. (2004) defined e-WOM. Scholars are keen to explore the reasons behind the pursuit of electronic word-of-mouth (e-WOM) and the dissemination or expression of e-WOM (e.g., Hennig-Thurau et al., 2004; Lee et al., 2006), offering insights for marketers to enhance their comprehension of online consumer behavior. Stauss (1997, 2000) talked about how the increase in online consumer articulations presents both opportunities and risks for enterprises. According to a recent survey, the majority of consumers believe brand websites and internet opinions to be equally trustworthy (ACNielsen, 2007). Additionally, Rowley (2001) suggested that businesses attempt forming online communities as an alternative to just using the internet for online advertising. These findings demonstrate the significant potential influence e-WOM can have on the decision-making process of consumers. Senecal and Nantel (2004) used an experimental investigation of consumers' utilization of online suggestion sources to investigate how e-WOM effects product choice. Discussion boards and other online communication tools are examples of platforms that support electronic word-of-mouth (e-WOM) and are rapidly being acknowledged for their impact on the uptake and utilization of goods and services. (Rajagopalan and Subramani, 2003). According to Gilly et al., (1998), the risk of making a purchase is increased when there is insufficient information to differentiate products. Currently, a word-of-mouth message will serve as a crucial point of reference for customers as they formulate their purchasing decisions. According to certain relevant studies, e-WOM communications are a crucial way for customers to learn about the caliber of a product or service (Chevalier and Mayzlin, 2006). Furthermore, customers' perceptions of risk and uncertainty while making purchases of goods or services can be effectively reduced by this type of messaging, which can further impact the intention and decision-making of the consumer (Chatterjee, 2001).

Using publicly available data from two of the top online retailers, Chevalier and Mayzlin (2006) investigated the impact of online product reviews on the relative sales of two online bookshops. Their study's findings demonstrated how strongly these kinds of online interactions influence other customers' purchasing decisions. Despite the abundance of studies on the impact of electronic word-of-mouth (e-WOM) on purchase intention, no study has been done thus far to determine which specific e-WOM has a significant effect on brand image. There is, as far as we are aware, only one study that addresses our goal in this field. Negative online product reviews are one kind of word-of-mouth communication that Bambauer-Sachse and Mangold (2011) looked at in relation to consumer-based brand equity. Their empirical study's findings confirmed the hypothesis that unfavourable online product reviews had a negative impact on consumer-based brand equity. The aforementioned research demonstrates the fact that e-WOM has established itself as a crucial component of the online marketing mix by significantly influencing online consumers' perceptions of brands and their purchase decisions.

Past Studies on the Impact of Brand Image

Businesses have significantly raised the amount of money they invest in building and developing brands over the past ten years. In order to create a brand, one must communicate a specific brand image in a way that all of the target audiences of the company associate with the brand (and consequently, the services supplied under its name). "A set of brand assets and liabilities linked to a brand, its name and symbol that add to or subtract from the value provided by a product or service to a firm and/or to that firm's customers" is how Aaker (1991, p. 15) defines brand equity. Building on Aaker's research, Keller (1993) creates the behavioural concept of customer-based brand equity (CBBE), which is defined as the differential effect of brand knowledge on consumer response to the brand's marketing. CBBE consists of the two dimensions of brand awareness and brand image. According to Webster and Keller (2004), brand image refers to the characteristics and advantages that set a brand apart from competitors and help the company's product stand out. The descriptive characteristics that define a brand are called attributes. These include the consumer's perception of the brand, its characteristics, and the associated costs and benefits of purchasing or using it. Benefits are the perceived personal value that customers place on a brand's features, or what they believe the brand can do for them (Keller, 1993, 1998). Every encounter a business has with its clients becomes an input into its brand image in the context of firm-customer relationships. Service companies must ensure that all employees understand the significance of providing consistent, predictable, high-quality performance to the customer since a service brand expresses a commitment to give a particular kind of experience (Webster and Keller, 2004). B2C interactions can be severely disrupted for clients if product/service providers fall short of their expectations. As a result, clients usually depend on a limited group of reliable suppliers of goods or services who continuously provide superior products or render high-caliber services (Cousins and Menguc, 2006). Product and service companies rely heavily on a small number of important clients to generate the majority of their income. The fundamental intention of the brand is to arouse emotions of strength, durability, exclusivity, trust, confidence, security, and speed (Aaker, 1996; Keller, 1993). In the end, a strong product or service brand effectively communicates to consumers the organization's primary value proposition as well as that of the product or service. There are few researches that assess the impact of brand image on purchase intention, despite empirical data suggesting that brand equity can influence purchase intention in a variety of scenarios (Ashill and Sinha, 2004; Chang and Liu, 2009). Wang and Yang (2010) examined how customers' intentions to acquire a brand were affected by brand credibility, with a particular emphasis on the Chinese auto sector. They suggested that this link is moderated by brand awareness and brand image. Nonetheless, in the context of non-deceptive counterfeiting, Bian and Moutinho (2011) investigated the influence of customer purchase intention of counterfeits on perceived brand image, direct and indirect impacts (mediator and moderator effects) of product participation, and product knowledge. According to their findings, brand image does not act as a mediating factor between participation and knowledge's effects on purchase intention. Wu et al. (2011) also looked into how a private label brand's brand image and purchase intention were directly impacted by shop image and service quality. Their research showed that brand perception and purchase intention are directly and favourably impacted by shop image. They also demonstrated the direct and favourable relationship between service quality and brand image. According to Shukla (2010), branding signals and interpersonal effects influence consumers' willingness to acquire luxury goods. According to his study's findings, informational interpersonal impacts played a substantial role among consumers, but normative interpersonal influences were found to be important across national boundaries. Furthermore, a noteworthy moderator between normative interpersonal effects and aspirations to purchase luxury goods was brand image. Additionally, Davis et al. (2009) proposed that scales measuring brand equity, brand image, and brand awareness are valid and trustworthy when applied to logistics services.

The preceding reasons culminate in this study as hypotheses:

H1. Electronic word-of-mouth greatly affects the perception of a brand.

H2. The intention to buy is significantly influenced by electronic word of mouth.

H3. Purchase intention is significantly influenced by brand image.

Conclusion of the Literature Reviews

A review of research on the effects of online word-of-mouth (e-WOM) communication has revealed that e-WOM can influence factors including brand perception and purchase intent. The research model that serves as the foundation for the anticipated effect will be developed in this section, and the effect will be tested in a fresh empirical investigation. The hypothesised relationship between e-WOM and brand image has not yet been experimentally investigated; it will be done so in the empirical study that is going to be provided.

Figure 1. Research model

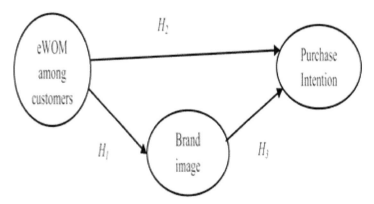

METHODOLOGY

Measurement

Based on the results of the literature research, a self-administered survey questionnaire was created in order to meet the study's objectives. Pretesting and revisions were made to the questionnaire. The following topics were covered in the four sections of the survey:

e-WOM, brand image, buying intention, and demographics are the first four factors.

Respondents were questioned about using online WOM conversations in the six-item e-WOM section (Bambauer-Sachse and Mangold, 2011). Respondents were asked to score their degree of agreement with three items in the brand image section addressing the significance of brand image in relation to automobile X (Davis et al., 2009). Respondents were questioned about their desire to buy this car in the three-item purchase intention section (Shukla, 2010). An electronic word-of-mouth, brand image, and purchase intention scale with seven points—from highly agree (1) to strongly disagree (7)—was used to measure the three variables. The benefit of using an interval scale is that, in addition to the arithmetic mean, standard deviation, product-moment correlations, and other statistics frequently used in marketing research, it enables the researchers to apply a variety of statistical techniques to data on nominal and ordinal scales (Malhotra, 1999). Table I lists the measurements. The final segment of the survey is the collected personal data about the participants, including their age, gender, level of education, and monthly earnings.

Data Analysis

Self-designed questionnaires were distributed using a cluster sampling technique in an automotive industry of cars car. After removing incomplete questionnaires, 341 acceptable samples were retrieved from the distribution of 400 questionnaires, resulting in an 85 percent response rate from those who consented to participate. The reliability of the internal consistency was confirmed using Cronbach's a. Descriptive statistics were performed using SPSS for data analysis, and the AMOS structural equation tool was used for structural equation modelling. The purpose of AMOS is to evaluate and estimate structural equation models (SEMs). Statistical models of linear relationships between manifest (observed) and latent (unobserved) variables are called SEMs. Its objective is to estimate a system of structural equations' coefficients. In order to examine the causal links for this study, AMOS is utilized, and the path coefficients are examined for goodness of fit and significance. The structural model's fit was assessed using the overall model fit metrics. The x^2 test was applied to estimate the goodness-of-fit indices (GFI) for measurement and structural models. Furthermore, as an absolute fit index, the root means square error of approximation (RMSEA) was employed. The indices for incremental fit that were employed were the comparative fit index (CFI), the incremental fit index (IFI), and the Tucker-Lewis index (TLI). The causal associations between the exogenous and endogenous constructs were reported using standardized estimates.

Table 1. Measures

Electronic Word of Mouth (Bambauer-Sachse and Mangold, 2011)	(e-WOM1) I often read other consumers' online product reviews to know what products/brands make good impressions on others
	(e-WOM2) To make sure I buy the right product/ brand, I often read other consumers' online product reviews
	(e-WOM3) I often consult other consumers' online product reviews to help choose the right product/ brand
	(e-WOM4) I frequently gather information from online consumers' product reviews before I buy a certain product/brand
	(e-WOM5) If I don't read consumers' online product reviews when I buy a product/ brand, I worry about my decision

continued on following page

Table 1. Continued

Electronic Word of Mouth (Bambauer-Sachse and Mangold, 2011)	(e-WOM1) I often read other consumers' online product reviews to know what products/brands make good impressions on others
	(e-WOM6) When I buy a product/brand, consumers' online product reviews make me confident in purchasing the product/brand
Brand image (Davis *et al.*, 2009)	(BI1) In comparison to another products/brand, this
	product/brand has high quality
	(BI2) This product/brand has a rich history
	(BI3) Customers (we) can reliably predict how this product/brand will perform
Purchase intention (Shukla, 2010)	(PI1) I would buy this product/brand rather than any
	other brands available
	(PI2) I am willing to recommend others to buy this product/brand
	(PI3) I intend to purchase this product/brand in the future

RESULT AND INTERPRETATION

Sample Profile

35.2 percent (120) and 64.8 percent (221) of the sample's total responders were female. The age ranges of the vast majority of responders were 26–35 (32.3 percent), 36–45 (36.7 percent), and 46–55 (24.9 percent). Fourteen percent of the respondents reported earning more than six hundred dollars a month. Furthermore, 53.1 percent of the respondents had an associate's degree or two years of college as their primary educational background. Table II presents descriptive statistics.

Model of Measurement

Structural Equation Modelling (SEM), which includes separate assessments of the significance of the relationships between the variables and a test of the overall model fit, was used to estimate the suggested structural model. These experiments revealed the connection between customers' purchase intentions, brand perception, and e-WOM communication. The measurement model's parameter estimations and overall fit index is presented below which is based on the approach of maximum likelihood (ML)

Table 2. Demographic characteristics of the respondents

Characteristic	Frequency	Percentage	CF (percent)
Age			
25 or under	12	3.5	3.5
26-35	110	32.3	35.8
36-45	125	36.7	72.4
46-55	85	24.9	97.4

continued on following page

Table 2. Continued

Characteristic	Frequency	Percentage	CF (percent)
Above 55	7	2.3	100
Gender			
Male	221	64.8	64.8
Female	120	35.2	100
Monthly income			
Under $200	21	6.2	6.2
$200-$299	56	16.4	22.6
$300-$600	124	36.4	58.9
Above $600	140	41.1	100
Education			
Below high school graduate	5	1.5	1.5
High school	25	7.3	8.8
Two-year college or associate's degree	181	53.1	61.9
Bachelor's degree	91	26.7	88.6
Postgraduate	39	11.4	100

The work meets or roughly approximates the fundamental requirements stated for the application of machine learning estimation (Byrne, 2001). In addition, the scale of observed variables is continuous, the sample size (n ¼ 341) cases is above the suggested 200 cases (Medsker et al., 1994), and there are no violations of multivariate normality in the survey replies. As shown in Table III, Cronbach's a was used to confirm the measurement items' reliability and evaluate the internal consistency of the applied model's components. Each construct had an acceptable level of internal consistency, with values ranging from 0.727 to 0.788, exceeding the minimum threshold of 0.60 (Hair et al., 1998). The measurement model's convergent validity was demonstrated by the fact that every measurement item had standardized loading estimates of 0.5 or above (varying from 0.518 to 0.702) at the 0.05 level. Each construct had adequate construct reliability, with values ranging from 0.801 to 0.836. Convergent validity was estimated using construct reliability, which was confirmed (Hair et al., 1998).

Furthermore, convergent validity was guaranteed because the average variance extracted (AVE) from all three components was greater than the minimum threshold of 0.5 (range from 0.593 to 0.670) (Hair et al., 1998). Correlations is estimated between the constructs to see if they were significantly different from 1, in order to test the discriminant validity of the measurement model. These results showed that the measurement model was discriminately valid because the confidence intervals of the correlations, which were calculated as correlations ~ 1.96 £ standard error of estimate, did not contain 1. Table IV displays the relationships for the constructs. These measurement results are generally favourable and indicate that moving further with the structural model evaluation is appropriate.

Table 3. Psychometric properties of measures

Construct	Item	Standardized loading	t- statistic	Mean	SD	Cronbach's a
Electronic word of mouth	EWOM1	0.702	9.483	4.72	1.202	0.788
(CR ¼ 0.836, AVE ¼ 0.631)	EWOM2	0.591	8.464	4.33	1.175	
	EWOM3	0.590	8.454	4.65	1.081	
	EWOM4	0.627	8.820	4.41	1.302	
	EWOM5	0.614	8.693	4.39	1.177	
	EWOM6	0.573	–	4.38	1.189	
Brand image	BI1	0.653	9.040	5.35	1.135	0.760
(CR ¼ 0.813, AVE ¼ 0.593)	BI2	0.567	8.184	5.32	1.194	
	BI3	0.604	–	4.86	1.298	
Purchase intention	PI1	0.518	–	6.16	0.801	0.727
(CR ¼ 0.801, AVE ¼ 0.670)	PI2	0.627	7.551	6.22	0.852	
	PI3	0.520	6.790	6.11	0.828	

Notes: CR, construct reliability; AVE, average variance extracted; EWOM, electronic word of mouth; BI, brand image; PI, purchase intention

Figure 2 displays the total explanatory power, the corresponding t-values of the research model's routes, and the standardized path regression coefficients that reveal the direct effects of the predictor upon the model's predicted latent components. Tables V and VI show the structural model's model fit indices as well as the cut-off value for each fit index. According to the goodness-of-fit statistics, the structural model did a fair job of fitting the data. A x^2 of 83.2 was obtained using the three-item model (df ¼ 51, p ¼ 0.003). It is generally known that this statistic is sensitive to large sample sizes, even though the overall x^2 for this measurement model was significant (p, 0.05) (e.g. Hair et al., 1998). The value of x^2 is sometimes divided by the degrees of freedom to lessen the sensitivity of the x^2 statistics. The re-calculated x^2 value was 1.631, and this new value falls within 1.0 to 3.0, which is an acceptable cut-off value range. The following met the suggested criterion of 0.90 or higher: Tucker-Lewis index (TLI ¼ 0.960, 1 ¼ maximum fit), incremental fit index (IFI ¼ 0.970), comparative fit index (CFI ¼ 0.969, 1 ¼ maximum fit), goodness of fit index (GFI ¼ 0.961, with 1 indicating maximum fit), and the comparative fit index (NFI ¼ 0.925, with 1 indicating maximum fit). Ultimately, the structural model was shown to be a fair fit by the root mean square error of approximation (RMSEA ¼ 0.043, with values,0.08 indicating good fit), one of the indices most suited to our model with a big sample. The outcomes of each test to determine the significance of the association between the variables are shown in Table V. Out of the three associations that were examined, two were significant at the 0.05 level and one was significant at the 0.01% level. With b ¼ 0.866, t ¼ 7.842, and p ¼ 0.000, e-WOM had a significantly favourable impact on brand image, suggesting that consumer e-WOM communication was a key antecedent of brand image.

continued on following page

Table 4. Continued
Table 4. Correlation matrix

	EWOM1	EWOM2	EWOM3	EWOM4	EWOM5	EWOM6	BI1	BI2	BI3	PI1	PI2
EWOM1	1.00										
EWOM2	0.356	1.00									
EWOM3	0.408	0.371	1.00								
EWOM4	0.396	0.395	0.381	1.00							
EWOM5	0.424	0.321	0.415	0.398	1.00						
EWOM6	0.387	0.352	0.347	0.408	0.402	1.00					
BI1	0.470	0.403	0.299	0.420	0.277	0.266	1.00				
BI2	0.316	0.342	0.306	0.275	0.269	0.244	0.335	1.00			
BI3	0.421	0.393	0.288	0.264	0.273	0.243	0.411	0.361	1.00		
PI1	0.478	0.269	0.255	0.323	0.332	0.342	0.329	0.299	0.327	1.00	
PI2	0.369	0.297	0.292	0.347	0.373	0.310	0.332	0.368	0.307	0.201	1.00
PI3	0.321	0.317	0.289	0.270	0.255	0.176	0.280	0.280	0.274	0.173	0.199

Figure 2. Standardized regression coefficients proposed model

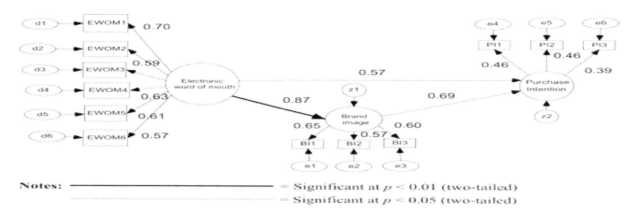

Table 5. Maximum likelihood estimates for research model (n ¼ 341)

Independent variable	Dependent Variable	Estimate	Standardized estimate	Standardized error	t- statistic	p
Electronic word of mouth	Brand image	0.997	0.866	0.127	7.842	**
Electronic word of mouth	Intention to purchase	0.312	0.574	0.140	2.224	0.026 *
Brand image	Intention to purchase	0.325	0.690	0.129	2.518	0.012 *
Electronic word of mouth	Intention to	0.312	0.574	0.140	2.224	0.026 *

Notes: *Significant at the p, 0.05 level (two-tailed); * *significant at the p, 0.001 level (two-tailed)

Table 6. Model fit statistics

Structural model	Fit statistics	Cut-off value
X^2	83.2	
df	51	
p-value	0.05	
Normed x^2	1.631	1.0-3.0
GFI	0.961	.0.90
NFI	0.925	.0.90
CFI	0.969	.0.90
TLI	0.960	.0.90
RMR	0.48	,0.50
RMSEA	0.043	,0.08[a]

Note: [a] Indicates good fit

Table 7. Decomposition of total effects for research model ($n^{1/4}$ 341)

Independent variable	Dependent variable	Total effect	Direct effect	Indirect effect
Electronic word of mouth	Brand image	0.866	0.866	0.000
Electronic word of mouth	Purchase intention	1.172	0.574	0.597
Brand image	Purchase intention	0.690	0.690	0.000

Additionally, purchase intention was strongly positively impacted by e-WOM (b ¼ 0.574, t ¼ 2.224, p ¼ 0.026). These findings imply that, in contrast to other forms of advertising, e-WOM communication is a significant predictor of consumers' behavioural intentions. At last, purchase intention was impacted by brand image, as evidenced by b ¼ 0.690, t ¼ 2.518, and p ¼ 0.012, which suggest that brand image was an antecedent of purchase intention. Three main conclusions were drawn from the statistical results, which are outlined in Table IV:
(1) Brand image is positively impacted by e-WOM communication;
(2) Buying intention is strongly positively impacted by e-WOM communication; and
(3) brand image affects buy intention.

Furthermore, forty percent of respondents stated they relied on company websites for their e-WOM, thirty percent utilized other media (such Facebook.com) and forty percent claimed they used email. A study of the standardized direct, indirect, and total effects was carried out in order to investigate the interaction between the two variables that influence intention to purchase (see Table VII). The direct relationship between e-WOM and purchasing intention (0.574) is very intriguing. Additionally, the data shows that e-WOM influences brand image, which in turn affects purchase intention (0.597) indirectly.

CONCLUSION AND IMPLICATIONS FOR FURTHER RESEARCH

This study examines the distinct impact of interpersonal factors on brand image and purchase intention in the automotive sector. This empirical research demonstrates that e-WOM, especially in the automotive sector, has a significant impact on brand image and indirectly influences purchase intention. Furthermore, the study demonstrated the significant direct impact of e-WOM on purchase intention. Several researches conducted before (e.g., Chevalier and Mayzlin, 2006) have established this fact, though not in the automotive sector. The current findings have a number of significant ramifications. For automakers in particular, the discovery that purchase intention can be influenced by online word-of-mouth communication is significant. Customers can read online product recommendations directly at the time of purchase while using the increasingly ubiquitous mobile internet, which could significantly influence their purchasing decisions. Thus, managers could start product trials as point-of-sale activities to encourage online word-of-mouth (WOM) communication by letting customers establish their own opinions. Numerous researches, including WOM communication, have looked into how customers perceive the quality of the services they receive and how that influences their behaviour intentions. According to Boulding et al. (1993), behavioural outcomes like loyalty and positive word-of-mouth (WOM) are positively impacted by service quality. In their model of the behavioural effects of service quality, Zeithaml et al. (1996) hypothesized a relationship between positive behavioural intents, such as word-of-mouth (WOM), buy intentions, complaint behaviour, and price sensitivity, and perceived service quality. Alexandris et al. (2002) found that 93% of the variance in word-of-mouth (WOM) could be explained by service quality, based on Zeithaml et al.'s study. Managers can further enhance the brand image by expanding the range of items, improving the quality of the products, pricing the products competitively, and giving after-sale services in a pleasant manner. These enhancements directly raise the products' intention to be purchased. Nonetheless, businesses possessing strong equity brands ought not to depend on the advantages of strong brand image, like devoted customers, as documented in previous studies (Aaker, 1991; Agarwal and Rao, 1996; Keller and Lehmann, 2006). Rather, these businesses need to be mindful of the dangers associated with negative online word-of-mouth (WOM) communication, as even strong brand equity can be severely undermined by it. Furthermore, these negative consequences will only worsen as network technology advances and becomes more widely used. Furthermore, due to the internet's accessibility, reach, and transparency, marketers and organizations are able to continuously monitor online word-of-mouth (WOM) communication about their businesses (Kozinets et al., 2010). Through online word-of-mouth (WOM), marketers can strive to change some of the negative connotations that customers have about the brand or the product by creating the right communication tools to educate people about certain brand or bank attributes. It's critical to note that positive word-of-mouth and electronic word-of-mouth (e-WOM) influence consumers' purchase intentions, build a positive perception of the business and its brand, and lower promotional costs. Additionally, since WOM communication may have a particularly significant impact on consumers' perceptions of goods and services with high credence qualities, it would be interesting to examine the effects of online WOM communication on brand image for more brands and in other product categories like financial services (Sweeney et al.,2008). Lastly, testing a broader model that incorporates functional, experiential, and attitudinal aspects of brand image might be helpful in order to better analyse brand image (Keller, 1993). Apart from examining this construct in internet networks, managers seeking to enhance the brand image of their products could benefit from investigating the antecedents of brand image.

REFERENCES

Aaker, D. (1996). *Building Strong Brands*. The Free Press.

Aaker, D. A. (1991). *Managing Brand Equity: Capitalizing on the Value of a Brand Name*. The Free Press.

ACNielsen. (2007), Trust in Advertising: A Global Nielsen Consumer Report. ACNielsen, New York, NY.

Adjei, M. T., Noble, S. M., & Noble, C. H. (2009). The influence of C2C communications in online brand communities on customer purchase behavior. *Journal of the Academy of Marketing Science*, 38(5), 634–653. 10.1007/s11747-009-0178-5

Agarwal, M. K., & Rao, V. R. (1996). An empirical comparison of consumer-based measures of brand equity. *Marketing Letters*, 7(3), 237–247. 10.1007/BF00435740

Alexandris, K., Dimitriadis, N., & Markata, D. (2002). Can perception of service quality predict behavioral intentions? An exploratory study in the hotel sector in Greece. *Managing Service Quality*, 12(4), 224–231. 10.1108/09604520210434839

Ashill, N. J., & Sinha, A. (2004). An exploratory study into the impact of components of brand equity and country of origin effects on purchase intention. *Journal of Asia-Pacific Business*, 5(3), 27–43. 10.1300/J098v05n03_03

Aydin, S., & Ozer, G. (2005). The analysis of antecedents of customer loyalty in the Turkish mobile telecommunication market. *European Journal of Marketing*, 39(7/8), 910–925. 10.1108/03090560510601833

Bambauer-Sachse, S., & Mangold, S. (2011). Brand equity dilution through negative online word-of-mouth communication. *Journal of Retailing and Consumer Services*, 18(1), 38–45. 10.1016/j.jretconser.2010.09.003

Bian, X., & Moutinho, L. (2011). The role of brand image, product involvement, and knowledge in explaining consumer purchase behaviour of counterfeits: Direct and indirect effects. *European Journal of Marketing*, 45(1/2), 191–216. 10.1108/03090561111095658

Bickart, B., & Schindler, R. M. (2001). Internet forums as influential sources of consumer information. *Journal of Interactive Marketing*, 15(3), 31–40. 10.1002/dir.1014

Boulding, W., Kalra, A., Staelin, R., & Zeithaml, V. A. (1993). A dynamic process model of service quality: From expectations to behavioral intention. *JMR, Journal of Marketing Research*, 30(1), 7–27. 10.1177/002224379303000102

Brown, J., Broderick, A. J., & Lee, N. (2007). Word of mouth communication within online communities: Conceptualizing the online social network. *Journal of Interactive Marketing*, 21(3), 2–20. 10.1002/dir.20082

Byrne, B. M. (2001). *Structural Equation Modelling with AMOS: Basic Concepts, Applications and Programming*. Lawrence Erlbaum Associates.

Chang, H. H., & Liu, Y. M. (2009). The impact of brand equity on brand preference and purchase intentions in the service industries. *Service Industries Journal*, 29(12), 1687–1706. 10.1080/02642060902793557

Chatterjee, P. (2001). Online reviews: Do consumers use them? *Advances in Consumer Research. Association for Consumer Research (U. S.)*, 28(1), 129–133.

Chevalier, J. A., & Mayzlin, D. (2006). The effect of word of mouth on sales: Online book reviews. *JMR, Journal of Marketing Research*, 43(3), 345–354. 10.1509/jmkr.43.3.345

Cousins, P. D., & Menguc, B. (2006). The implications of socialization and integration in supply chain management. *Journal of Operations Management*, 24(5), 604–620. 10.1016/j.jom.2005.09.001

Davis, A., & Khazanchi, D. (2008). An empirical study of online word of mouth as a predictor for multi-product category e-commerce sales. *Electronic Markets*, 18(2), 130–141. 10.1080/10196780802044776

Davis, D. F., Golicic, S. L., & Marquardt, A. (2009). Measuring brand equity for logistics services. *International Journal of Logistics Management*, 20(2), 201–212. 10.1108/09574090910981297

Gilly, M. C., Graham, J. L., Wolfinbarger, M. F., & Yale, L. J. (1998). A dyadic study of interpersonal information search. *Journal of the Academy of Marketing Science*, 26(2), 83–100. 10.1177/0092070398262001

Godes, D., & Mayzlin, D. (2004). Using online conversations to study word-of-mouth communication. *Marketing Science*, 23(4), 545–560. 10.1287/mksc.1040.0071

Goldsmith, R. E., & Horowitz, D. (2006). Measuring motivations for online opinion seeking. *Journal of Interactive Advertising*, 6(2), 1–16. 10.1080/15252019.2006.10722114

Gruen, T. W., Osmonbekov, T., & Czaplewski, A. J. (2006). EWOM: The impact of customer-to-customer online know-how exchange on customer value and loyalty. *Journal of Business Research*, 59(4), 449–456. 10.1016/j.jbusres.2005.10.004

Hair, J. F., Anderson, R. E., Tatham, R. L., & Black, W. C. (1998). *Multivariate Data Analysis* (5th ed.). Prentice Hall.

Harrison-Walker, L. J. (2001). The measurement of word-of-mouth communication and an investigation of service quality and customer commitment as potential antecedents. *Journal of Service Research*, 4(1), 60–75. 10.1177/109467050141006

Hennig-Thurau, T., Gwinner, K. P., Walsh, G., & Gremler, D. D. (2004). Electronic word-of-mouth via consumer-opinion platforms: What motivates consumers to articulate themselves on the internet? *Journal of Interactive Marketing*, 18(1), 38–52. 10.1002/dir.10073

Herr, P. M., Kardes, F. R., & Kim, J. (1991). Effects of word-of-mouth and product-attribute information on persuasion: An accessibility-diagnosticity perspective. *The Journal of Consumer Research*, 17(4), 454–462. 10.1086/208570

Keller, K. L. (1993). Conceptualizing, measuring, and managing customer-based brand equity. *Journal of Marketing*, 57(1), 1–22. 10.1177/002224299305700101

Keller, K. L. (1998). *Strategic Brand Management. Building, Measuring and Managing Brand Equity*. Prentice Hall.

Keller, K. L., & Lehmann, D. R. (2006). Brands and branding: Research findings and future priorities. *Marketing Science*, 25(6), 740–759. 10.1287/mksc.1050.0153

Kiecker, P., & Cowles, D. L. (2001). Interpersonal communication and personal influence on the internet: A framework for examining online word-of-mouth. *Internet Applications in Euromarketing*, 11(2), 71–88.

Kozinets, R. V., de Valck, K., Wojnicki, A. C., & Wilner, S. J. S. (2010). Networked narratives: Understanding word-of-mouth marketing in online communities. *Journal of Marketing*, 74(2), 71–89. 10.1509/jm.74.2.71

Lee, M. K. O., Cheung, C. M. K., Lim, K. H., & Sia, C. L. (2006). Understanding customer knowledge sharing in web-based discussion boards: An exploratory study. *Internet Research*, 16(3), 289–303. 10.1108/10662240610673709

Lewis, R. C., & Chambers, R. E. (2000). *Marketing Leadership in Hospitality. Foundations and Practices* (Vol. III). Wiley.

Litvin, S. W., Goldsmith, R. E., & Pan, B. (2008). Electronic word-of-mouth in hospitality and tourism management. *Tourism Management*, 29(3), 458–468. 10.1016/j.tourman.2007.05.011

Malhotra, N. K. (1999). *Marketing Research: An Applied Orientation* (3rd ed.). Prentice Hall.

Mayzlin, D. (2006). Promotional chat on the internet. *Marketing Science*, 25(2), 155–163. 10.1287/mksc.1050.0137

Medsker, G. J., Williams, L. J., & Holahan, P. J. (1994). A review of current practices for evaluating causal models in organizational behavior and human resources management research. *Journal of Management*, 20(2), 439–464. 10.1177/014920639402000207

Rowley, J. (2001). Remodelling marketing communications in an internet environment. *Internet Research*, 11(3), 203–212. 10.1108/10662240110397017

Sen, S., & Lerman, D. (2007). Why are you telling me this? An examination into negative consumer reviews on the web. *Journal of Interactive Marketing*, 21(4), 76–94. 10.1002/dir.20090

Senecal, S., & Nantel, J. (2004). The influence of online product recommendations on consumers' online choices. *Journal of Retailing*, 80(2), 159–169. 10.1016/j.jretai.2004.04.001

Shukla, P. (2010). Impact of interpersonal influences, brand origin and brand image on luxury purchase intentions: Measuring interfunctional interactions and a cross-national comparison. *Journal of World Business*, 46(2), 242–252. 10.1016/j.jwb.2010.11.002

Smith, D., Menon, S., & Sivakumar, K. (2005). Online peer and editorial recommendations, trust, and choice in virtual markets. *Journal of Interactive Marketing*, 19(3), 15–37. 10.1002/dir.20041

Smith, R. E., & Vogt, C. A. (1995). The effect of integrating advertising and negative word-of-mouth communications on message processing and response. *Journal of Consumer Psychology*, 4(2), 133–151. 10.1207/s15327663jcp0402_03

Stauss, B. (1997). Global word of mouth: Service bashing on the internet is a thorny issue. *Marketing Management*, 6(3), 28–30.

Stauss, B. (2000). Using new media for customer interaction: a challenge for relationship marketing. In Hennig-Thurau, T., & Hansen, U. (Eds.), *Relationship Marketing* (pp. 233–253). Springer. 10.1007/978-3-662-09745-8_13

Subramani, M. R., & Rajagopalan, B. (2003). Knowledge-sharing and influence in online social networks via viral marketing. *Communications of the ACM*, 46(12), 300–307. 10.1145/953460.953514

Sundaram, D. S., Mitra, K., & Webster, C. (1998). Word-of-mouth communications: A motivational analysis. *Advances in Consumer Research. Association for Consumer Research (U. S.)*, 25, 527–531.

Sweeney, J. C., Soutar, G. N., & Mazzarol, T. (2008). Factors influencing word of mouth effectiveness: Receiver perspectives. *European Journal of Marketing*, 42(3/4), 344–364. 10.1108/03090560810852977

Trusov, M., Bucklin, R. E., & Pauwels, K. (2009). Effects of word-of-mouth versus traditional marketing: Findings from an internet social networking site. *Journal of Marketing*, 73(5), 90–102. 10.1509/jmkg.73.5.90

Wang, X., & Yang, Z. (2010). The effect of brand credibility on consumers' brand purchase intention in emerging economies: The moderating role of brand awareness and brand image. *Journal of Global Marketing*, 23(3), 177–188. 10.1080/08911762.2010.487419

Webster, F. E.Jr, & Keller, K. L. (2004). A roadmap for branding in industrial markets. *Journal of Brand Management*, 11(5), 388–402. 10.1057/palgrave.bm.2540184

Weinberger, M. G., & Dillon, W. R. (1980). The effect of unfavourable product rating information. *Advances in Consumer Research. Association for Consumer Research (U. S.)*, 7(1), 528–532.

Westbrook, R. A. (1987). Product/consumption-based affective responses and post purchase process. *JMR, Journal of Marketing Research*, 24(3), 258–270. 10.1177/002224378702400302

Wu, P. C. S., Yeh, G. Y. Y., & Hsiao, C. R. (2011). The effect of store image and service quality on brand image and purchase intention for private label brands. *Australasian Marketing Journal*, 19(1), 30–39. 10.1016/j.ausmj.2010.11.001

Xia, L., & Bechwati, N. N. (2008). Word of mouth: The role of cognitive personalization in online consumer reviews. *Journal of Interactive Advertising*, 9(1), 108–128. 10.1080/15252019.2008.10722143

Yoo, B., & Donthu, N. (2001). Developing and validating a multidimensional consumer-based brand equity scale. *Journal of Business Research*, 52(1), 1–14. 10.1016/S0148-2963(99)00098-3

Zeithaml, V., Berry, L. L., & Parasuraman, A. (1996). The behavioral consequences of service quality. *Journal of Marketing*, 60(2), 31–46. 10.1177/002224299606000203

Zhang, R., & Tran, T. (2009). Helping e-commerce consumers make good purchase decisions: a user reviews-based approach. In Babin, G., Kropf, P., & Weiss, M. (Eds.), *E-technologies: Innovation in an Open World* (pp. 1–11). Springer. 10.1007/978-3-642-01187-0_1

Zhu, F., & Zhang, X. (2010). Impact of online consumer reviews on sales: The moderating role of product and consumer characteristics. *Journal of Marketing*, 74(2), 133–148. 10.1509/jm.74.2.133

Chapter 9
Revolutionizing Marketing by Utilizing the Power of Artificial Intelligence

Priya Jindal
Chitkara Business School, Chitkara University, Punjab India

Anju Rohilla
https://orcid.org/0009-0006-2111-376X
Panipat Institiute of Engineering and Technology, India

ABSTRACT

Industrial 4.0 redesigned the way the business manufactures and distributes their product among customers. Artificial intelligence occupies its place in almost every type of business and its operation. The chapter aims to explore the ways how the artificial intelligence is integrated into marketing domain and helps the marketers in making sound strategies. In order to understand the use of artificial intelligence in marketing and identifying its implication on marketing industry, the review of the available literature is conducted. The study shows that the employment of artificial intelligence in marketing operations aids the firm in identifying the target market, offering the highly personalized services, achieving the time and cost efficiency through automation, effectively engage the customers and enhances connectivity with customer across the multiple platforms. The study also reveals the various AI tools used by the firm to stimulate their marketing operations and to stay competitive in this digital era.

INTRODUCTION

In the era of Industrial 4.0, industries are moving toward automation which results in efficiency, and cost-effectiveness. The emergence of practical implications of AI has been hailed as one of the most significant advancements since the occurrence of the Industrial Revolution (Brynjolfsson & McAfee, 2014). It is often referred to as the next frontier for technological progress. The swift growth of artificial intelligence in recent years has been made possible by the expansion of cognitive mechanisms of AI and the ability of machines to learn based on the collected data (Davenport et al., 2020). Additionally, the possibility to create information that did not previously exist has also contributed to the quick develop-

DOI: 10.4018/979-8-3693-6660-8.ch009

ment of AI (Agrawal et al., 2023). Artificial intelligence is integrated into many fields and occupies an important place in our lives through automating daily life activities (Verma et. al. 2021). Siri and Alexa are the most common AI applications that assist users in finding hospitals near them filtering emails, playing songs, calling someone, answering user's queries etc. Artificial intelligence has transformed businesses through automation, providing the competency to learn from the data and analyse the customers and markets (Davenport et al., 2020). Artificial intelligence has garnered significant interest from engineers, IT specialists, and analysts. However, it is now expanding beyond its conventional domains and has brought about a dramatic transition in the contemporary corporate environment by making a more pronounced impact in the realms of management. Currently, artificial intelligence (AI) is becoming a crucial element in the expansion of businesses, leading to a significant increase in automation. It impacted the way operations are performed in any industry. Besides the IT sector, AI has wide applications in various sectors such as banking and finance, medicines, education, hospitality, health care etc. Marketing is one of the areas in which artificial intelligence has wide applications (Lim et al., 2021). AI is advantageous in several ways in the area of marketing. It assists marketers in conducting research, analyzing market trends, getting customer insights, developing competitive advantage, engaging the customers, connecting with the present and potential customers and measuring the effectiveness of the marketing strategy. AI is seen as a blessing in the field of marketing as AI enables the firm to develop tailor-made content and services by understanding and analyzing the needs of the customers and identifying the market trend, automating the operations of marketing. In addition to this, AI can predict market trends and help in enhancing customer satisfaction by identifying the patterns of the customer's behaviour (Nalini et. al., 2021). AI can process quantitative information through employing machine learning algorithms which enable the firms to handle voluminous data of the customers and assist them in the conversion of potential customers with a greater probability. With the growing developments in the field of AI, expands the use of AI to process qualitative information also. Now, AI can analyze not only the text but also images and audio-video information (Dhar, 2016). Through analyzing the quantitative and qualitative information, it enables the firms to develop complex and effective marketing strategies (Jankovic & Curovic, 2023). Marketing operations' efficiency can be enhanced by integrating artificial intelligence into marketing operations such as offering tailor-made services to the customers and designing personalized services based on the customers purchasing behaviour. The field of AI is ever-evolving and growing which demands organizations to look and evaluate how AI can impact their marketing operations. This study explores the implications of artificial intelligence in marketing.

LITERATURE REVIEW

Artificial Intelligence is one of those developments of computer science which are proven as a blessing to society, businesses and individuals too. With the help of the records or data, AI can provide intelligence to a machine which enables them to act similarly as humans do. Wirth (2018) has discussed the three types of artificial intelligence. These are narrow, hybrid and strong AI. Narrow AI utilizes a learning algorithm for performing a particular task only. It doesn't enable the machine to apply the acquired knowledge from performing that particular task to any other activity on its own. Whereas Hybrid AI is the combination of symbolic AI and non-symbolic AI (machine learning); which analyzes the data by employing a statistical model. Strong AI is the extended form of the narrow AI which enables the computer to learn from the available data or statistics. Furthermore, from time to time it has to ability to continuously learn, grow and develop its abilities. Analytical AI, Human-Inspired AI and Humanized AI are the various forms of artificial intelligence (Kaplan & Haenlein, 2019). Analytical AI depicts cognitive intelligence whereas human-inspired AI combines analytical AI with emotional intelligence. Whereas the Humanized AI, which is hypothesized AI; integrate the various forms of intelligence: cognitive, emotional and social.

Businesses are significantly affected by the development of artificial intelligence. Omdia-Tractica (2020) has projected exponential growth up to $126 billion in 2025 from $10.1 million in 2018. MIT Technology Review Insights (2020) surveyed the top officials of the companies and reported that in the United States, 24% of the companies are employing AI in their operations and the number of companies is expected to increase by 60% in 2022. Among the various domains of the business, the marketing domain is highly affected by the advancement of artificial intelligence. Artificial intelligence enables marketers to be more customer-centred and assists them in fulfilling their needs. Artificial intelligence utilises numerous technologies such as machine learning, natural language processing, deep learning etc. (Davenport et. al., 2020) which make it capable of handling and analyzing massive data and predicting market trends. It also helps the companies to conduct the analysis based on customer demand (Devang et. al, 2019). Artificial intelligence not only helps in developing a customer-centric strategy but also increases the efficiency of the firm by saving cost and time (Chintalapati & Pandey, 2022). Artificial intelligence has a wider application in marketing organizations. It assists the organization in automating marketing operations such as logistics and can enhance customer satisfaction through customer value delivery (Jarek & Mazurek, 2019). Artificial intelligence also significantly influences the marketing mix of the firm (Verma et al., 2021), boosts the profitability of the firm (Shahid & Li, 2019) and develops a competitive advantage over the competitor. Artificial intelligence also imposes some negative consequences on business as well as society such as job displacement and mischievous exploitation. The literature review concluded the potential benefits and the impact of AI in marketing and also focused the attention of the marketers to carefully implement AI.

INTEGRATION OF ARTIFICIAL INTELLIGENCE INTO MARKETING

Various scholars have examined and concluded in their study that the development of artificial intelligence has revolutionized the marketing landscape and transformed conventional marketing activities such as marketing channels, operations, research, and experimental projects. Artificial intelligence does just not automate operations but employs advanced algorithms and data analytics to develop personalized services and accurately target customers. Furthermore, artificial intelligence employs predictive analytics the enhance customer satisfaction and information distribution across the various marketing channels. Additionally, artificial intelligence regulates workflows and enhances customer engagement by delivering personalized services and streamlining resource allocation in marketing operations. Moreover, through employing artificial intelligence in marketing research marketing firms can handle the voluminous data and can interpret the complicated consumption pattern and behaviour which assist in the preparation of a customer-focused model for delivering the value to the customer. This section discusses the integration of artificial intelligence into the various operations of marketing.

Integration of AI in Marketing Strategies

Segmenting, targeting and positioning are the customer-centric strategic models of marketing which offer higher customer engagement and satisfaction (Pantano et. al., 2020). The incorporation of artificial intelligence applications in the developing marketing strategy provides the solutions the traditional programs of marketing such as how to fit luxury with mass-market benefits, versus customization. The emergence of e-commerce made it possible to serve niche and huge markets.

Integration of AI Into Segmentation, Targeting, and Positioning (Stp)

Identification of the target customer is one of the most important functions of marketing. It assists the marketers to provide more appropriate and desired information to the relevant group of customers. It not only saves the effort but also saves costs and enhances the sales of the firm. It assists in developing a good relationship with the customers. The integration of artificial intelligence in crafting marketing strategy (STP) transformed the conventional methods of segmenting the market from psychographics, demographics, and geographic to behavioural segmentation, and consumer preference analysis. It assists marketers in performing age cohorts, anticipating changes in consumer profiles and post-demographic consumption patterns (Vlačić et. al., 2021). Neural networks, Logistic Regression, and Multinomial Logit are employed for framing an effective segmentation strategy (Paschen et. al, 2019). Neural networks possess the ability to perform the tasks which are traditionally performed by human minds and can categorize potential customers into various categories for effective segmentation. Even the Neural networks can be applied for brand positioning and estimating its effectiveness. Li (2000) concluded in their study that the neural network is more efficient in drafting the segmentation, targeting and positioning in complicated business-to-business (B2B) settings. Moreover, in the telecommunications sector neural networks are employed for predicting customer turnover by analyzing the changes in the call pattern and subscriber contractual details. Predictive analysis is employed by marketers to target the customer. It lets marketers offer more customized services and create exceptional customer relationships. In addition to this, AI offers rationalization, customization, standardization, and synergy building (Huang &Rust, 2021).

Integration of AI into Customer Relationship Management

Artificial intelligence plays a significant role in building and managing relations with the customer. AI provides the answers to a few important questions to marketers such as who are their customers, what are their wants and needs, and how the firm can satisfy their needs. Human-inspired or the Feeling artificial intelligence is capable of conducting emotional analysis. It analyses the customer's feelings, inclinations, opinions and mindset which facilitates a better understanding of the needs and wants of the current and potential customers (Pathak & Sharma, 2022). Due to the ability of emotional intelligence, artificial intelligence helps marketers to develop long-term relationships with the customer. Marketers can employ artificial intelligence to identify the purchase intention and satisfaction level of the present as well as potential customers (Capatina et. al. 2020). Predicting the existing customer behaviour is much easier in comparison to the potential customer as the company possesses the information on the present customers' purchasing behaviour and present customer's preferences are highly stable in contrast to potential customers. In the case of potential customers, artificial intelligence can be put to use to conduct sentiment analysis to understand their wants. The automotive industry employs Automotive sentiment analysis to identify the emotions and behaviour of the drivers. Red Balloon utilizes the Albert AI which is an algorithm-based AI marketing platform that enables the firm to identify new customers (Sutton, 2018). Harley-Davidson is also employing the Albert AI to assist in performing marketing tasks such as developing the customized marketing drive and identifying the highly potential customers based on the analysis of information possessed by the company (Power, 2017). The sentimental analysis can be employed to understand the sentiments of the customers through the emotions and feelings shared by the customers in social media, online reviews or tweets. Moreover, it is enabled to detect the trends and patterns through analyzing the explicit and implicit responses (Humphreys & Wang, 2018).

Integration of AI into Marketing Mix

The integration of artificial intelligence in marketing assists marketers to decide their 4Ps (Product, Price, Place & Promotion) in harmony with the 4Cs (consumer, cost, convenience, and communication).

AI and Product Management

The product management comprises decisions from designing the product to its packaging, branding, and offering pre & post-sale customer services. Artificial intelligence assists marketers in multiple ways in product management from designing to the launching of products.

a) AI in Product Development Strategy

It helps in the development of novel and quality products for customers through the use of analytical analysis, machine learning, deep learning & generative designs (Dzyabura & Hauser, 2019). In the manufacturing sector, it enables automation of complex and onerous processes (Antons & Breidbach, 2018). In the development of skilled or artistic products, artificial intelligence tools such as Toogle3D. ai facilitate the development of 3D models and Nextech3D.ai transforms the CAD files into 3D models and 3D models into images similar to realistic products (photorealistic). AI facilitates the firms to research and understand the acceptability of the product by the target market. AI employs agile and design thinking to develop a solid strategy for product development. AI aids the developers in getting insights into the customer's feedback and trends of the market with the ability of big data to leverage the data for better strategic planning. Splunk AI is popularly used for designing product development strategies.

b) AI in Product Designing

A key component in designing the product is the development of the system infrastructure so that the firm can accurately meet the requirements of the customers which demands extensive experience and a high degree of precision. AI Design Assistants (AIDA) has revolutionized the product designing process by aligning customers' needs and requirements by getting insight into and analyzing the prior designs improving both precision and efficiency.

c) AI in Gathering Requirements Information

AI assists firms in streamlining the production process by automating the process of collection of requirements information which further leads towards the reduction of manual efforts and saves time too. An Artificial intelligence tool, IBM Watson enables the firm to cut the time by half spent on the collection of requirements.

d) AI in Quality Testing

Artificial intelligence eliminates human interventions and revolutionises quality assurance procedures by automating the analysis and identification of errors and assuring the delivery of high-quality products. The IT firm employs the Test. AI and DeepCode to automate the process of error detection which leads towards a more efficient, streamlined and faster product testing phase.

e) AI in Packaging Designing

With the help of artificial intelligence, marketers can develop aesthetic, alluring, edifying, and exclusive packaging designs. AI utilizes machine learning, deep learning and generative design algorithms to analyze the available information and to create tailor-made designs fit to the needs of the customer which boosts customer satisfaction too (Dekimpe, 2020). Pebblely, Designify, and Flair AI are the various AI tools that can be used to design unique packaging design.

AI and Pricing Management

Pricing decision involves in analyses of various factors such as production cost, selection of the distribution channel, mode of advertisements, competition and market forces (Kotler & Keller, 2006). The market forces (demand & supply) cause variations in the prices in real time. The predictive analysis in dynamic pricing utilizing AI assists the firms in automatically adjusting the prices based on the market forces in real time. Additionally, the AI-powered multiarmed bandit algorithm allows modifying the prices in real-time (Misra et al., 2019). It is possible through the AI algorithms-based real-time analysis of the information to predict demand and identify pricing trends. Bayesian inference-a machine learning algorithm is capable of modifying the prices of the product by analyzing the competitor's price (Bauer & Jannach, 2018). Additionally, the Optimal response pricing algorithm incorporates various factors to optimize the dynamic prices such as consumer choice and preferences, competitors' pricing strategy and supply chain dynamics (Dekimpe, 2020).

AI and Place Management

To ensure the availability of the product to the customer, marketers must create an efficient product distribution system. The product distribution system comprises of following areas such as logistics, inventory management, warehousing, networked relationships, and transportation (Kotler & Keller, 2006). The product distribution is highly mechanical and repetitive. Wholesalers often face problems in inventory management such as forecasting the demand precisely; harmonizing stock levels with the demand and managing the intricacies of massive orders. AI-empowered predictive analysis ensures the effective distribution of the product. To guarantee the timely and error-free delivery of the product the artificial intelligence analyses past data to assist in the preparation of realistic time frames.

Artificial intelligence allows the firm to build a competitive advantage, standardization and mechanization through the automated warehouse. These automated warehouses utilize big data analytics, and robotics in the distribution system such as cobots for packaging, employing predictive analysis for forecasting the demand, drones for delivery, and IoT for order tracking and replenishment (Huang & Rust, 2021). Additionally, Virtual assistant or chatbots allows customers to automatically place purchase orders. It helps to exercise control over the inventory in real time placing the purchase order and issuing the sales order immediately.

AI and Promotion Management

Promotion bridges the knowledge gap between the producer and the customer. It utilizes multiple approaches to disseminate information about the product to a broader audience (Kotler & Keller, 2006). The development of artificial intelligence allows the use of the physical as well as the digital strategies of promotion which are collectively known as "phygital" (Vlačić et al., 2021). AI employs machine learning and deep learning-based Predictive analysis to predict the pattern of consumer purchasing behaviour and forecast future possibilities and the content distribution approach to frame the distribution strategy to enhance the reach to the customer and increase customer engagement. Natural language processor allows analyzing customer preferences and choices for the development of customized content and advertisement (Huang and Rust, 2021). Additionally, the use of content analytics upgrades the value of the customer and delivers the highest satisfaction to them (Tripathi & Verma, 2018). Social media content (customer reviews) is also considered while designing a customized marketing strategy with the use of Netnography (Verma & Yadav, 2021). Real-time tracking of customer choices is possible through the utilization of the Emotive artificial intelligence algorithms (Tripathi & Verma, 2018; Verma, 2014)

Integration of Ai into Marketing Research

Philip Kotler defines marketing research as "Marketing research is systematic problem analysis, model building and fact-finding for improved decision-making and control in the marketing of goods and services." Integration of the various forms of artificial intelligence into marketing research enhances the speed of data collection as well as improves the analysis of the data and helps in better customer understanding.

Integration of AI into Data Collection

Marketing research comprises the analyses of the market, competitor, customers, industry and environment information. The mechanical form of artificial intelligence facilitates the automatic collection of data in real-time, sensing the data (Balducci & Marinova, 2018).In the era of digitalization, artificial intelligence eases the process of monitoring and real-time tracking of data. Data sensing assists in the efficient planning of marketing strategies by analyzing the needs, customer behaviour and market value. The customer information consists of data regarding their purchasing behaviour, reviews of the product, purchasing pattern and frequency, product usage and consumption experience (Ng & Wakenshaw, 2017) can be collected from the e-commerce website or through the connecting device (Cooke & Zubcsek, 2017). Insurance companies are calculating the insurance premium by analyzing driving behaviour (Soleymanian et. al., 2019).

Integration of AI into Market Analysis

The cognitive and mechanical form of artificial intelligence enables one to handle a large volume of market data (Kirkpatrick, 2020). It employs various AI-powered techniques for analyzing market information such as sentiment analysis, audio-video analysis, image recognition and analysis, predictive analysis, chatbots and virtual assistants, speech recognition and analysis, customer segmentation, customer journey analysis and demand forecasting. These AI-powered techniques facilitate the identification of upcoming market trends and are capable of forecasting market swings with precision. The predictive analysis permits the managers to preemptively update their strategy by the market analysis and integrate customer preferences to beat the competition and grab the opportunities for growth prospects (Markiewicz & Zheng, 2018). Automated text analysis facilitates customer research (identification of the consumption pattern, and customer satisfaction level (Humphreys & Wang, 2018); identifies the set of factors considered by the consumer while making a purchase decision (Dzyabura & Hauser, 2011) and forecasting and understanding the market shifts (Berger et. al., 2019). Machine learning algorithms and lexicon-based text classification enable the analysis of the customer reviews available online and high-volume social media data sets too (Humphreys & Wang, 2018). Market insights can be evaluated with the assistance of big data analysis (Berger et al. 2019). Artificial intelligence models such as Tensor Flow which are customized to address particular business problems specifically in the area of supply chain management and sales forecasting, improve decision-making by considering multiple factors. In addition to this, AI enables beta testing, which allows for collecting customer feedback in real time and redefines the AI- models accordingly. It guarantees the acceptance of the final product by the consumer and ensures commercial success.

Integration of AI in Customer Behavior Prediction

Consumer behaviour encompasses the study of the various tasks and the decisions taken by the consumer during making purchase decisions, using and disposing of the product or services (Kotler & Keller, 2006). Cultural, social and psychological factors play a major role in shaping cultural behaviour. Human-inspired AI aids marketers in understanding the needs of consumers and determining the behaviour of the consumer. AI assists in the determination of the pre-purchase customer behaviour through mapping the customer touch points from website, online customer reviews, online product searches and social media which facilitates getting insights into customer needs and the creation of personalized services for them. RedBallon is employing the AI-powered algorithm-based marketing platform "Albert AI" to identify new customers and enhance its reach to the customers (Sutton, 2018). Albert AI is employed by Harley-Davidson to analyze the customer relationship management database; determining the highly potential customers and drafting the customized marketing strategy to attract them (Power, 2017). Emotional intelligence enables the identification of the state of happiness through image recognition (Lieto et. al., 2019). In customer care centre emotional intelligence enables the identification of emotions such as anger through the analyses of the customer voice and also capable the satisfaction and dissatisfaction among the customer through text analyses in an online review.

IMPLICATIONS OF ARTIFICIAL INTELLIEGENCE IN MAREKTING

In the era of the industrial 4.0, the consumer choices are ever-evolving. The integration of artificial intelligence makes it possible to consider the ever-evolving needs of consumers while designing marketing strategies. This section of the study discusses the significant impact of AI on the marketing industry. Various scholars discussed the implications of artificial intelligence in the marketing industry, some of them are: that AI allows the marketer to analyze massive customer information (Sutton, 2018), and enables the creation of highly personalized content and recommendations (Goyal et al., 2019); identification of the new customers or target market (Power, 2017). AI made it possible to connect with the target audience in a better way and engage them (Tripathi & Verma, 2018). AI-powered application makes it feasible to handle a large amount of information and its processing (Huang & Rust, 2021). Analytical and mechanical AI enable to automate the repetitive tasks such as email campaigns, social media scheduling which result in cost and time saving (Humphreys & Wang, 2018). The automated collection of customer information raises privacy concerns (Verma, 2014). One of the biggest questions that arise with the integration of artificial intelligence into marketing functions is job displacement and filling the skills gap.

AI TOOLS EMPLOYED BY VARIOUS COMPANIES TO ASSIST MARKETING FUNCTION

In a corporate environment that is changing quickly, good marketing influences a company's overall competitiveness by forming consumer perceptions and responding to shifting market trends. Integrating cutting-edge technologies has become essential for staying ahead of the competition in the ever-changing world of modern marketing. Artificial Intelligence is one of these game-changing tools that is particularly effective in transforming the marketing industry. Table 1 provides a wide range of artificial intelligence tools that are transforming marketing processes, providing a thorough review of their uses and the significant influence they have on the always-changing marketing environment.

Table 1. Artificial tools used by various industries

S. NO.	Industry	Company	AI Tool	Application of AI Tool
1.	**Banking and Financial Services**	Capital Bank of Jordon	IBM Watson Studio	Interacting with consumers and creating customized offers as per their needs.
		Wells Fargo, Valley bank	Data Robot- Digital Wealth Management & Sales, Marketing and Relationship Management	Data Robot's capabilities to rapidly test and deploy predictive algorithms can be used to automatically rebalance portfolios with little human intervention, and help wealth managers match the right customer with the right product.
		Scotia Bank	Personetics	Increased Customer Engagement and Sales through Hyper- personalized, action insights and advice to customers
		Citi Bank	Wipro HOLMES	Enhances the Customer Experience by excelling the services to the customers in various areas such as business experience feedback, validations of the transactions and automated appointment booking & re-activation of a bank account.

continued on following page

Table 1. Continued

S. NO.	Industry	Company	AI Tool	Application of AI Tool
2.	E-Commerce	Myntra	MyfashionGPT	Generates a suitable product list for customers and uses natural speech-like text entry to find precise clothing requirements.
		Amazon Kindle	eBook recommender	personalized shopping recommendations
		Myntra	Vue.ai	Enables the visual search and personalized shopping
		Macy's	HubSpot AI	Outlining, drafting, rewriting, and repurposing content. Creating posts for social media. Generating images based on prompts.
3.	Aviation	Greater Toronto Airports Authority	Wipro HOLMES	Provides better Customer service and virtual assistance to the customers
		Delta Air Lines	Amazon Bedrock by Amazon web services	Conversational AI to enhance customer interaction.
		Boeing	Salesforce Einstein	Enhances the Passenger experience and passenger interactions with passengers through chatbots
		GE Aviation	Salesforce	Enhances the operational efficiency and serves as an analytical tool for customer data.
4.	Hotels	Marriott	Salesforce Marketing Cloud, WeChat, chatbots on Facebook, Google Assistant & simplify travel	Guest service and communication platform
		Hilton	IBM Watsons, Alliants	Personalized guest experiences
		La Casa del Camino	Intelity	In-room tablets for improving the guest experiences
		IHG Hotels & Resorts	Revinate	Guest feedback and reputation management
5.	Telecommunication	AT&T	Amdocs CES	Customer experience and billing management
		Reliance Jio	Guavus	Predictive analytics for network optimization
		NTT Communications	Amelia formerly known as Ipsoft	chatbots and conversational AI
		HCG Global Communication	Salesforce Einstein	To enhance the digital connections with the customers and communicate with them in simpler and more fulfilling ways
6.	Informational Technology	Adobe, Accenture, zendesk,	Marketo Engage	Marketing automation and lead management
		HubSpot/ KFC, Macy's, Airhelp, Axis Bank, ING	HubSpot AI	Inbound marketing and sales automation
		IBM	IBM Watson	AI-driven solutions for business processes
		Accenture, Infosys	Optimizely	Personalization and A/B testing

continued on following page

Table 1. Continued

S. NO.	Industry	Company	AI Tool	Application of AI Tool
7.	**Automobiles**	Tesla	Tesla AI, Marketo engage	Autonomous driving and predictive analytics
		Mercedes-Benz Group	Salesforce Einstein	Customer relationship management
		Ford, KeHe	Cognira	Predictive analytics for sales and marketing; Promotion, forecaster, promotion planning, promotion Analyzer, promotion advisor
		HARMAN	NVIDIA Drive IX	AI-powered infotainment and driver assistance
8.	**Health Care**	Olive Hospital & Clinic	Olive	Process automation and revenue cycle management
		Loyal Health	Loyal's HIPAA	Patient engagement and experience optimization
		GE Healthcare, alpha labs	Amelia formerly known as Ipsoft	Amelia is a conversational AI tool that enhances customer engagement, empowering the employees as well as operational efficiency.
		Cigna	Wipro HOLMES	Provides better Customer service and virtual assistance to the customers.
9.	**Transportation and Logistics**	Unilever, Arauco	Project44 + ClearMetal AI	Predictive logistics and supply chain visibility
		Maersk	IBM Watson Supply Chain	Supply chain optimization and risk management
		Ryder System	Turvo	Collaborative logistics platform for shippers and carriers
		Spark Logistic	TransVoyant ai.	Real-time supply chain visibility and predictive analytics
10.	**Social Media**	Instagram	Instagram: "Suggested for You"	Enhances the discovery of new information, and content and recommends the individuals of your interest based on your interest, activities and the people you follow.
		Youtube	YouTube: Intelligent advertising	Helpful in identifying the trends and improving ad efficiency.
		Twitter	Twitter Analytics	An effective tool that companies are utilizing with the Analytics dashboard to delve more into the performance of their Twitter campaigns.

Source: Author's Compilation[REMOVED HYPERLINK FIELD]

CONCLUSION

Artificial intelligence has become the transformative agent which transformed the traditional methods of working. Artificial intelligence provides the capability to think and perform tasks in machines in similar ways as humans do. Artificial intelligence employs machine learning, deep learning, big data analytics etc. to predict customer behaviour and aid in meeting customer expectations. This chapter provides information that how AI assists in the enhancement of customer satisfaction. Due to its ability, well-known companies are integrating AI into their routine tasks which results in improved customer engagement, accurate forecasting of consumer behaviour and market trends and efficient marketing operations. Marketers must ensure while incorporating AI into operations that it would inform which AI application is integrated into their strategy. To ensure a better future with AI, companies must consider and evaluate the ethical aspects, challenges and privacy concerns of the consumer while utilizing artificial intelligence.

REFERENCES

Agrawal, A., Gans, J. S., & Goldfarb, A. (2023). Artificial intelligence adoption and system-wide change. *Journal of Economics & Management Strategy*, 1–11.

Antons, D., & Breidbach, C. F. (2018). Big data, big insights? Advancing service innovation and design with machine learning. *Journal of Service Research*, 21(1), 17–39. 10.1177/1094670517738373

Balducci, B., & Marinova, D. (2018). Unstructured data in marketing. *Journal of the Academy of Marketing Science*, 46(4), 557–590. 10.1007/s11747-018-0581-x

Berger, J., Humphreys, A., Ludwig, S., Moe, W. W., Netzer, O., & Schweidel, D. A. (2020). Uniting the tribes: Using text for marketing insight. *Journal of Marketing*, 84(1), 1–25. 10.1177/0022242919873106

Brynjolfsson, E., & McAfee, A. (2014). *The second machine age: Work, progress, and prosperity in a time of brilliant technologies*. WW Norton & Company.

Capatina, A., Kachour, M., Lichy, J., Micu, A., Micu, A. E., & Codignola, F. (2020). Matching the future capabilities of an artificial intelligence-based software for social media marketing with potential users' expectations. *Technological Forecasting and Social Change*, 151, 119794. 10.1016/j.techfore.2019.119794

Chintalapati, S., & Pandey, S. K. (2022). Artificial intelligence in marketing: A systematic literature review. *International Journal of Market Research*, 64(1), 38–68. 10.1177/14707853211018428

Cooke, A. D., & Zubcsek, P. P. (2017). The connected consumer: Connected devices and the evolution of customer intelligence. *Journal of the Association for Consumer Research*, 2(2), 164–178. 10.1086/690941

Davenport, T., Guha, A., Grewal, D., & Bressgott, T. (2020). How artificial intelligence will change the future of marketing. *Journal of the Academy of Marketing Science*, 48(1), 24–42. 10.1007/s11747-019-00696-0

Dekimpe, M. (2020). Retailing and retailing research in the age of big data analytics. *International Journal of Research in Marketing*, 37(1), 3–14. 10.1016/j.ijresmar.2019.09.001

Devang, V., Chintan, S., Gunjan, T., & Krupa, R. (2019). Applications of artificial intelligence in marketing. *Annals of Dunarea de Jos University of Galati. Fascicle I.Economics and Applied Informatics*, 25(1), 28–36.

Dhar, V. (2016). The future of artificial intelligence. *Big Data*, 4(1), 5–9. 10.1089/big.2016.29004.vda27441580

Goyal, J., Singh, M., Singh, R., & Aggarwal, A. (2019). Efficiency and technology gaps in Indian banking sector: Application of meta-frontier directional distance function DEA approach. *The Journal of finance and data science*, 5(3), 156-172.

Huang, M. H., & Rust, R. T. (2021). A strategic framework for artificial intelligence in marketing. *Journal of the Academy of Marketing Science*, 49(1), 30–50. 10.1007/s11747-020-00749-9

Humphreys, A., & Wang, R. (2018). Automated text analysis for consumer research. *The Journal of Consumer Research*, 44(6), 1274–1306. 10.1093/jcr/ucx104

Jankovic, S. D., & Curovic, D. M. (2023). Strategic integration of artificial intelligence for sustainable businesses: Implications for data management and human user engagement in the digital era. *Sustainability (Basel)*, 15(21), 15208. 10.3390/su152115208

Jarek, K., & Mazurek, G. (2019). Marketing and Artificial Intelligence. *Central European Business Review, 8*(2).

Kaplan, A., & Haenlein, M. (2019). Siri, Siri, in my hand: Who's the fairest in the land? On the interpretations, illustrations, and implications of artificial intelligence. *Business Horizons*, 62(1), 15–25. 10.1016/j.bushor.2018.08.004

Kirkpatrick, K. (2020). Tracking shoppers. *Communications of the ACM*, 63(2), 19–21. 10.1145/3374876

Kotler, P., & Keller, K. L. (2006). *Marketing Management*. Pearson Prentice Hall.

Li, S. (2000). The development of a hybrid intelligent system for developing marketing strategy. *Decision Support Systems*, 27(4), 395–409. 10.1016/S0167-9236(99)00061-5

Lieto, A., Bhatt, M., Oltramari, A., & Vernon, D. (2017). Artificial Intelligence and Cognition. *Proceedings of the 4th International Workshop on Artificial Intelligence and Cognition co-located with the Joint Multi-Conference on Human-Level Artificial Intelligence (HLAI 2016)*. Technical University of Aachen.

Lim, W. M., Gupta, S., Aggarwal, A., Paul, J., & Sadhna, P. (2021). How do digital natives perceive and react toward online advertising? Implications for SMEs. *Journal of Strategic Marketing*, 1–35. 10.1080/0965254X.2021.1941204

Markiewicz, T., & Zheng, J. (2018). *Getting Started with Artificial Intelligence. A Practical Guide to Building Enterprise Applications*. O'Reilly.

Misra, K., Schwartz, E. M., & Abernethy, J. (2019). Dynamic online pricing with incomplete information using multiarmed bandit experiments. *Marketing Science*, 38(2), 226–252. 10.1287/mksc.2018.1129

Nalini, M., Radhakrishnan, D. P., Yogi, G., Santhiya, S., & Harivardhini, V. (2021). Impact of artificial intelligence (AI) on marketing. *International Journal of Aquatic Science*, 12(2), 3159–3167.

Ng, I. C. L., & Wakenshaw, S. Y. L. (2017). The internet-of-things: Review and research directions. *International Journal of Research in Marketing*, 34(1), 3–21. 10.1016/j.ijresmar.2016.11.003

Omdia-Tractica. (2020). *Artificial intelligence Software Market to Reach $126.0 Billion in Annual Worldwide Revenue by 2025*. Omdia. https://tractica.omdia.com/newsroom/press-releases/artificial-intelligence-software-market-toreach-126-0-billion-in-annual-worldwide-revenue-by-2025

Pantano, E., Pizzi, G., Scarpi, D., & Dennis, C. (2020). Competing during a pandemic? Retailers' ups and downs during the COVID-19 outbreak. *Journal of Business Research*, 116, 209–213. 10.1016/j.jbusres.2020.05.03632501307

Paschen, J., Kietzmann, J., & Kietzmann, T. C. (2019). Artificial intelligence (AI) and its implications for market knowledge in B2B marketing. *Journal of Business and Industrial Marketing*, 34(7), 1410–1479. 10.1108/JBIM-10-2018-0295

Pathak, A., & Sharma, S. D. (2022, December). Applications of Artificial Intelligence (AI) in Marketing Management. In *2022 5th International Conference on Contemporary Computing and Informatics (IC3I)* (pp. 1738-1745). IEEE.

Power, B. (2017). How Harley-Davidson used artificial intelligence to increase New York sales leads by 2,930%. *Harvard Business Review*.https://hbr.org/2017/05/howharley-davidson-used-predictive-analytics-to-increase-new-yorksales-leads-by-2930

Shahid, M. Z., & Li, G. (2019). Impact of artificial intelligence in marketing: A perspective of marketing professionals of Pakistan. *Global Journal of Management and Business Research*, 19(2), 27–33.

Soleymanian, M., Weinberg, C. B., & Zhu, T. (2019). Sensor data and behavioral tracking: Does usage-based auto insurance benefit drivers? *Marketing Science*, 38(1), 21–43. 10.1287/mksc.2018.1126

Sutton, D. (2018). How AI helped one retailer reach new customers. *Harvard Business Review*. https://hbr.org/2018/05/howai-helped-one-retailer-reach-new-customers

Technology Review Insights, M. I. T. (2020). *The global AI agenda: North America*. MIT Technology Review. mittrinsights.s3.amazonaws.com/AIagenda2020/NAAIagenda.pdf

Tripathi, S., & Verma, S. (2018). Social media, an emerging platform for relationship building: A study of engagement with nongovernment organizations in India. *International Journal of Nonprofit and Voluntary Sector Marketing*, 23(1), e1589. 10.1002/nvsm.1589

Verma, S. (2014). Online customer engagement through blogs in India. *Journal of Internet Commerce*, 13(3-4), 282–301. 10.1080/15332861.2014.961347

Verma, S., Sharma, R., Deb, S., & Maitra, D. (2021). Artificial intelligence in marketing: Systematic review and future research direction. *International Journal of Information Management Data Insights*, 1(1), 100002. 10.1016/j.jjimei.2020.100002

Verma, S., & Yadav, N. (2021). Past, present, and future of electronic word of mouth (EWOM). *Journal of Interactive Marketing*, 53, 111–128. 10.1016/j.intmar.2020.07.001

Vlačić, B., Corbo, L., Silva, S. C., & Dabić, M. (2021). The evolving role of artificial intelligence in marketing: A review and research agenda. *Journal of Business Research*, 128, 187–203. 10.1016/j.jbusres.2021.01.055

Chapter 10
Leveraging Artificial Intelligence in Education:
Enhancing Learning Experience

Sargunpreet Kaur
Lovely Professional University, India

Komal Budhraja
Fortune Institute of International Business, India

Anurag Pahuja
https://orcid.org/0000-0002-1170-5749
Lovely Professional University, India

Varun Nayyar
Chitkara University, India

Shefali Saluja
https://orcid.org/0000-0002-8560-5150
Chitkara University, India

ABSTRACT

The integration of artificial intelligence (AI) technologies into education has emerged as a promising avenue to revolutionize the learning experience. With the use of AI tools and methodologies, teachers can tailor educational pathways to suit their students' individual needs, respond to differences in teaching style and provide prompt feedback so that they are more engaged and comprehended. Various applications of artificial intelligence in the field of education such as intelligent tutoring systems, adaptive learning platforms, and natural language processing tools are examined to highlight their effectiveness for dealing with educational challenges and supporting student success. This chapter looks at the potential of artificial intelligence for improving education practices, with a focus on increasing learning processes and optimising student results. It highlights the importance of responsible use of AI to reduce biases and ensure equal opportunities for all in order to address concerns about ethics and possible problems related to integration of AI into education.

DOI: 10.4018/979-8-3693-6660-8.ch010

Leveraging Artificial Intelligence in Education

INTRODUCTION

Over the past few years, AI integration in education has emerged as a transformative force, promising to change traditional learning paradigms and improve learning experiences for learners around the world. Artificial intelligence technology has a wide range of opportunities for personalized learning, adapting to individual student needs and providing real time feedback in order to foster more efficient and interactive teaching environments. As stated by Siemens and Gašević (2012), the potential of artificial intelligence in education lies in its ability to analyse vast amounts of data to identify patterns and to adapt learning experiences, accordingly, ultimately leading to improved learning outcomes. Moreover, the connection of students around the world with AI education tools can facilitate collaboration learning experiences and overcome geographic obstacles (Buckingham et al., 2017). Moreover, as they can provide personalised guidance and assistance around the clock, AI powered virtual tutors and adaptive learning systems have shown promising results in increasing students' motivation and engagement (Nayyar, 2023; Woolf, 2010). Therefore, the integration of artificial intelligence into education has enormous potential to radically change the way we learn and teach, and to foster a more inclusive, adaptive, and efficient learning environment.

Overview of Artificial Intelligence in Education

The integration of AI in education has emerged as a promising approach to enhance the learning experience for students. A wide range of tools and techniques that can be used in a variety of educational settings, from traditional classrooms to online platforms, are covered by AI technologies. Using artificial intelligence, teachers can customize learning experiences, facilitate adaptive learning paths, and give students the most accurate feedback. The ability to analyse large datasets and identify patterns and insights on student learning behavior and performance is a key aspect of using artificial intelligence in education. This data driven approach allows teachers to gain invaluable insight into each student's strengths, weaknesses and educational preferences enabling them to adapt teaching according to his or her particular requirements in an effective manner.

Furthermore, based on the learning style and proficiency level of each student, AI powered educational platforms can provide personalised recommendations for resources such as textbooks, video clips or interactive exercises. This adaptive learning approach does not only help students to remain engaged, but also enables them to progress at a pace that leads to better education outcomes.

In addition, through technologies such as virtual reality (VR) and augmented reality (AR), Artificial Intelligence can facilitate the creation of immersive learning experiences. These tools allow students to study the complexities of concepts in a simulation environment and make learning more interactive and effective.

Automated administrative tasks, such as grading assignments and managing course materials, are another area where AI can have a significant impact. Leveraging these tasks to artificial intelligence systems will make it easier for teachers to offer personalised teaching and assistance to students.

Overall, the integration of AI into education has great potential to transform learning experience by making it more personalised, adaptive, and interactive. However, it is essential to address challenges such as data privacy concerns, ethical considerations, and the digital divide to ensure equitable access to AI-powered educational resources for all students.

Here is an overview of how AI can enhance the learning experience with relevant examples:

- **Personalized Learning**: In order to tailor the content and activities for individual needs, AI can analyse students' teaching habits, preferences, or strengths. This customization can enhance engagement and comprehension.

For iinstance, Adaptive learning platforms, such as Knew-ton and Dream-Box, adjust the difficulty level and content of the lesson based on the student's performance, providing targeted support and challenges.

- **Automated Grading & Assessment**: AI-powered grading systems can evaluate assignments, quizzes, and exams quickly and accurately, saving teachers time and providing students with immediate feedback.

For example: Grade scope uses artificial intelligence to analyse handwritten or typed student replies, providing detailed feedback and reducing the burden of grading for educators.

- **Virtual Teaching Assistants:** AI Chatbots or Virtual Assistants can provide students with instant and best study material with support and guidance, answering questions, explaining concepts, and offering resources.

For instance, by answering questions and providing practice exercises, IBM's Watson Assistant for Education and Duolingo's Chatbots are helping students learn languages.

- **Content Creation and Curation:** AI algorithms can create content educational content, curate resources, and recommend materials tailored to student's interest and learning objectives.

For Instance, Quillionz uses Natural Language Processing (NLP) to generate quiz questions from educational content, helping teachers create assessments efficiently.

- **Predictive Analysis**: AI Analytics can assess students at risk, forecast education outcomes and advise on interventions to support struggling learners.

An example: Bright-Bytes Clarity is using predictive analysis to detect students who may need additional support or intervention on the basis of different data points like attendance and school performance.

- **Language Learning & Translation:** AI- powered language learning platforms can provide personalised lessons, Pronunciation feedback, and translation services.

For example, Babbel and Rosetta stone are using artificial intelligence to modify language lessons for learners' level of proficiency, as well as providing practice exercises.

- **Augmented Reality & Virtual Reality:** Immersive learning experiences, allowing students to explore concepts in virtual environments, can be produced by AI driven technologies such as AR and VR.

For example, Space is offering educational solutions in the field of Augmented Reality and Virtual Reality, which allow students to interact with 3D models and simulations related to science and anatomy.

Scope and Introduction of AI in Education

AI is becoming more and more a part of education, with the aim of revolutionizing conventional teaching methods and methodologies so as to provide students with an overall experience. A wide range of applications, including personalised learning, intelligent coaching systems, educational data mining and virtual reality simulations are covered by artificial intelligence technologies. Such progress has enormous potential for transforming the way students learn, teachers provide instruction and institutions take on administrative tasks.

Personalized learning is one of the most important contributions of AI to education. To adapt teaching content and pacing to each student's specific needs, AI algorithms can analyse a large amount of data on individual students' performance, learning style or preferences. For instance, adaptive learning platforms such as DreamBox and Knewton leverage AI to provide personalized learning paths, adjusting the difficulty level of content based on students' mastery of concepts (Nayyar and Batra, 2020; Princeton, 2019). This personalised approach is not only beneficial for students' learning outcomes but also contributes to a more engaging and stimulating educational environment.

In addition to this, AI powered intelligent tutors offer real time feedback and guidance to students, which simulate interaction with a human tutor. These systems may identify areas of difficulty, provide specific remedial actions, and monitor student progress over time. For Instance, Carnegie Learning's Cognitive Tutor uses artificial intelligence algorithms to deliver interdisciplinary math classes, offering guidance and explanations that are tailored according to the students' understanding of their own misconceptions (Nayyar, 2018; Becker, 2017). By offering immediate feedback and scaffolding support, Intelligent Tutoring systems empower students to take ownership of their learning process and develop Problem-solving skills independently.

Moreover, AI facilitates mining educational data, enabling the educators to gain valuable information from large datasets that inform learning decisions. In order to optimise curriculum design and teaching strategies, teachers can identify patterns, trends, and areas of improvement through the analysis of student performance data.

For example, the use of predictive analytics can help identify students at risk of academic failure and enable early intervention initiatives to prevent dropout rates (Siemens & Gasevic, 2012). In addition, educators are provided with quantifiable data on student engagement, educational behaviour, performance metrics and decision making through the use of AI Learning Analytics platforms like Bright space Insights to allow them to make decisions based on data (D2L, n.d.).

In addition, through adaptive learning environments and assistive tools for students with diverse learning needs, AI technologies have the potential to improve accessibility and inclusion in education. For example, learning to speak for students with a speech impairment or ESL learners can be facilitated by technologies such as speech recognition and the use of Natural Language Processing Systems (Nayyar, 2022; Thrun & Pratt, 2012).

The integration of artificial intelligence into education offers transformative opportunities for improving learning experience, personalizing instruction, and improving educational outcomes for students. Enhancing the use of artificial intelligence technologies, such as personalised learning platforms, intelligent tutors, educational data mining and assistive tools, will enable teachers to meet the needs of individual students, optimise teaching practice and foster a more inclusive learning environment. However, it is very vital to ensure the ethical implementation of Artificial intelligence, addressing the concerns regarding data security and privacy, and provide adequate training and support for educators to harness the full potential of Artificial Intelligence(AI) in education.

THEORETICAL FOUNDATION OF AI IN EDUCATION

Definition and Evolution of Artificial Intelligence

The term "Artificial Intelligence" refers to the simulation of human intelligence processes by computer systems. Learning, reasoning, problem-solving, perception and language comprehension are some of the processes involved. The aim of AI technologies is to build systems capable of carrying out tasks that are traditionally based on human intelligence. It is possible to trace the evolution of AI through a number of stages:

- **Symbolic AI (1950s-1980s)**: To simulate human intelligence, early AI systems relied on symbolic logic and rule-based reasoning. By encoding humans' knowledge and expertise in computer programs, researchers have created expert systems to solve particular problems.
- **Connectionist AI (1980s-1990s)**: The evolution of neural networks and parallel distributed processing models inspired by the structure and function of the human brain took place in this era. Neural networks have enabled AI systems to learn from data and improve performance through experience, thus paving the way for advancement of machine learning and deep learning.
- **Statistical AI (2000s-2010s)**: Machine learning algorithms have become more and more prominent, which allow AI systems to analyse vast amounts of data and find accurate patterns. In areas such as natural language processing, computer vision, and robotics, techniques such as supervised learning, unsupervised learning, and reinforcement learning have revolutionized these areas.
- **Modern AI (2010s-Present)**: In recent years, advancements in deep learning, big data and computational power have led to substantial progress in artificial intelligence. Various thrust sectors, such as healthcare, finance, transport, and entertainment, are already covered by applications of artificial intelligence. The Current research is focused on improving the robustness, interpretability, and ethical considerations of AI.

Theoretical Framework for AI Integration in Education

he contemporary educational landscape, there is enormous potential for revolutionising traditional teaching and learning methods by integrating artificial intelligence. In order to improve the learning experience for students, this paper presents a conceptual framework on how artificial intelligence can be used effectively in education. This framework provides a structured approach to using AI technologies in order to optimise educational outcomes, based on various theories and models from education psychology, cognitive science, or artificial intelligence research.

The framework is based on key aspects, e.g., personalised learning, adaptive evaluation, smart tutoring systems and collaboration environments, all of which help to create dynamic and tailored educational experience. This framework provides insight on how AI can be used to address various learning needs and promote student engagement and achievement, by integrating it with existing educational theory.

Theoretical Foundation

- **Constructivism**
  1. AI can help constructivist learning by providing interactive and immersive experiences that allow students to develop their own understanding of concepts.
  2. Experiential engagement and experimentation, whereby students are able to study complex ideas in a dynamic environment, is encouraged through AI-powered simulations and Virtual environments.
- **Zone of Proximal Development**
  1. AI based tutors can adapt learning experiences to the students' individual ZPDs, providing appropriate level of support and challenge.
  2. Intelligent teaching systems use AI algorithms to determine the students' existing competences and provide focused interventions aimed at enabling them to attain greater levels of mastery.
- **Social Learning theory**
  1. AI can make it easier for students to engage, share ideas and work together on projects through the creation of Virtual Communities that allow them to do so.
  2. Socially intelligent artificial intelligence agents can help foster group cohesion and facilitate peer to peer learning experiences, fostering cooperation and knowledge sharing among students.
- **Cognitive Load Theory**
  1. AI Adaptive Learning Platforms can optimise teaching materials to take into account students' cognitive capabilities, minimize the overload of brain power and enhance educational efficiency.
  2. In order to align with students' cognitive abilities and prior knowledge, intelligent algorithms can dynamically adjust the presentation of information, scaffolding learning tasks.

Figure 1.

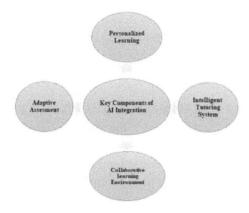

Source: Author's Own Creation

Cognitive Psychology and Learning Theories in AI-Based Education

Cognitive Psychology and learning theories play a crucial role in shaping AI-based education platforms and enhancing the learning experience. Here's how the principles are leveraged:

- **Personalized Learning:** The cognitive psychology stresses the fact that people have various learning styles and preferences. To provide learners with personalised experiences, AI pedagogical platforms use Machine Learning algorithms to analyse students' educational patterns, preferences and performance data. These platforms optimise learning efficiency through the adaptation of content, pace and difficulty levels to each student.
- **Adaptive Learning:** Learning theories like Constructivism emphasize the prominence of active engagement and building upon prior knowledge. AI in education can dynamically adapt content based on students' progress, providing scaffolding and support when needed. Adaptive learning systems can help in identifying misconceptions and provide targeted feedback to help students correct their understandings.
- **Feedback and Reinforcement:** Cognitive Psychology highlights the significance of feedback in the learning process.AI-based education platforms can offer immediate feedback on assessments, assignments, and interactive intellectual exercises. By providing the feedback on time and

Leveraging Artificial Intelligence in Education

specifically, these systems can be effectively reinforced for correct understanding and guidance towards mastery.
- **Natural-Language Processing:** NLP techniques are enabling AI systems to recognize and generate humans' languages. Natural-Language Processing facilitates a conversation interface between virtual tutors and Chatbots in the classroom. These AI assistants are capable of engaging students in natural language interactions, answering questions, providing explanations, and offering guidance in real time.
- **Data-Driven Decision Making:** Learning Analytics, rooted in cognitive psychology and educational theories, involves collection and analyses of data to inform the educational decisions. For the purpose of identifying trends, predicting performance and recommending interventions, AI algorithms can process large volumes of data produced by student interactions with learning content. Educators can use these insights to tailor instruction and provide support to the students more effectively.
- **Gamification & Motivation:** Cognitive theories of Motivation suggest that intrinsic motivation plays a decisive role in learning. In order to make students more engaged and motivated, AI gamification based educational platforms are increasingly incorporating elements such as badges, points or leader boards. By providing rewards and incentives, AI-based platforms encourage more participation and sustained efforts.
- **Deep-learning & Neural-Networks:** Various AI applications, including education, have been revolutionized by deep learning models inspired by neural networks. These models have the ability to probe large amounts of data, discover patterns and make predictions. Deep learning techniques are used in education to perform tasks such as recommendation of content, plagiarism detection and automated grading, streamlining the evaluation process and providing valuable information on students' educational development.

Overall, by integration of these principles from Cognitive Psychology to Learning theories, AI-based Education platforms can offer personalised, adaptive, and Experiential learning experiences that cater to the diverse needs of students and Educators.

APPLICATIONS OF AI IN EDUCATIONAL SETTINGS

AI has emerged as the most transformative force across various sectors, and its application in educational settings holds substantial promise for revolutionizing the learning experience.

Leveraging the power of Artificial Intelligence, teachers can customize their curricula, optimize teaching methods and offer tailored assistance to students. AI technologies are transforming traditional learning paradigms, from intelligent tutor systems to automated grading and feedback mechanisms that make learning more accessible, engaging or efficient. The inclusion of artificial intelligence in education not only improves educational results, but also develops crucial thinking, creativity and problem solving skills that are indispensable to success in the fast changing digital age.

The applications of artificial intelligence examine a range of ways in which AI is being used to enhance the learning environment, enabling more dynamic and flexible learning environments for students and teachers alike.

Intelligent Tutoring Systems (ITS)

Intelligent Tutoring system (ITS) symbolizes a subset of educational technology that aims to leverage AI to enhance the learning experience for students. These systems are using artificial intelligence techniques to provide personalised and adaptive learning, feedback and support for students. They've been set up to mimic the way humans' tutors behave, adapt to individual student needs, monitor their progress and provide real time assistance. In this explanation, we will be digging deep into the components, benefits, challenges, and examples of Intelligent Tutoring Systems.

Components of Intelligent Tutoring Systems (ITS)

- Knowledge Representation
- Student Model
- Pedagogical Model
- Domain Expertise
- Natural-Language

Benefits of Intelligent-Tutoring Systems (ITS)

- **Personalization:** ITS provides personalised training for each student according to his or her particular needs and abilities. These systems can optimise learning outcomes when content, pace and style of teaching are adapted (VanLehn, 2011).
- **Immediate Feedback:** The provision of timely and targeted feedback is one of the main advantages of ITS. In real time, students are receiving feedback on their responses that enable them to correct misunderstandings and learn from mistakes (Woolf, 2009).
- **Adaptive Learning Paths:** Based on the student's performance and progress, ITS may dynamically adjust the sequence and difficulty of learning activities. This adaptation approach guarantees that all learners receive the correct level of training at appropriate levels (Graesser et al., 2018).
- **Accessibility:** By providing a flexible educational option that is able to accommodate the various types of education, preferences and abilities, intelligent teaching systems can help increase accessibility. In addition, students with special needs or disabilities may be supported (Mittal et al., 2020; Nye et al., 2014).

Challenges and Limitations

- **Knowledge-Engineering:** It may be labour intensive to build a new knowledge base and a student model for and ITS, requiring expertise in both the subject matter and the use of artificial intelligence. It may also be difficult to maintain and update such models as new knowledge systems (VanLehn, 2011).

Leveraging Artificial Intelligence in Education

- **Scalability:** It is a major challenge to design an intelligent transport system which can effectively scale in order to accommodate the large numbers of students from different learning environments. Careful planning and allocation of resources is necessary to ensure that the system continues to respond as user numbers increase, while maintaining high quality instructions (Woolf, 2009).
- **Engagement and Motivation:** Maintaining student interest and motivation remains a challenge, even though ITS can provide personalised instruction. In order to maximise the effectiveness of such systems, it is necessary to create learning experiences that are stimulating, immersive and rewarding (Graesser et al., 2018).
- **Ethical Considerations:** Ethical implications related to the use of artificial intelligence in education, in particular with regard to data protection, algorithmic bias, and the potential for exacerbating existing inequalities, exist. These concerns need to be addressed and the deployment of ITS in an ethical and responsible manner needs to be ensured (Nye et al., 2014).

Examples of Intelligent Tutoring Systems (ITS)

- **Cognitive Tutor:** The Cognitive Tutor is an ITS providing personalised math instruction, developed and built by Carnegie Learning. It uses a combination of cognitive science principles and AI techniques to adaptively scaffold learning activities and provide feedback to students (Koedinger et al., 2012).
- **ASSISTments:** ASSISTments is an online learning platform that incorporates intelligent tutoring capabilities to support mathematics education. It offers personalized problem-solving assistance, immediate feedback, and data-driven insights to both students and teachers (Heffernan et al., 2014).
- **ALEKS (Assessment and Learning in Knowledge Spaces):** ALEKS is an adaptive learning system that assesses students' knowledge and skills, which provides personalised instruction in various areas such as mathematics, chemistry or accounting. Based on the student's knowledge of concepts, it uses artificial intelligence algorithms to continuously adjust its Curriculum (Piech et al., 2015)

Virtual Reality and Augmented Reality in Education

Virtual Reality (VR) and Augmented Reality (AR) have emerged as transformative technologies in education, offering immersive and interactive learning experiences. When combined with AI, these technologies can significantly enhance the learning process by providing personalized, adaptive, and engaging educational content. This will delve deep to explore more about the benefits of AR & VR in education, Their integration with AI, and the resulting benefits for the learners.

Virtual Reality in Education

The creation of a simulation environment that can be controlled by users is part of the VR process. Virtual Reality offers an opportunity to explore concepts in a hand on, immersive way, which transcends traditional classroom boundaries. For instance, students can take virtual field trips to historical landmarks, explore the human body in 3D, or even conduct science experiments in a virtual laboratory.

According to a study conducted by Ab Hamid, S. H., et al. (2020), VR technology provides an immersive and interactive learning environment that enhances students' motivation and engagement, leading to improved learning outcomes.

Augmented Reality in Education

Augmented Reality brings digital content to the real world and enhances learning experience by incorporating virtual objects into a physical environment. An interactive textbook, educational games and simulations that make abstract concepts tangible are among the applications of Augmented Reality in education.

The Dunavyle, Dede, and Mitchell (2009), research paper highlights the potential of Augmented Reality to facilitate real learning experiences by coupling conceptual concepts with actual world contexts in order to enhance students' understanding and retention.

Integration of AI in VR and AR

By personalizing content, providing real time feedback and adapting to different learning styles, AI can enhance VR and AR education experiences. In order to adapt educational materials, suggest personalised learning paths and offer targeted interventions where appropriate, AI algorithms can analyse student performance data.

According to a study conducted by Wu et al. (2013), research suggests that by adjusting the difficulty level of tasks according to their performance, thereby improving engagement and knowledge retention, AI-Powered Learning Adaptive Systems in Virtual Reality environments can substantially enhance students' education outcomes.

Benefits of AI-Enhanced VR and AR in Education

- **Personalized learning:** AI algorithms can analyse the data of students to design personalised learning experiences for each individual, according to their needs and preferences.
- **Increased engagement:** Immersive virtual and Augmented Reality environments combined with AI driven interactions can draw students' attention to the learning process, making them more engaged.
- **Enhanced Learning Outcomes:** AI-powered Virtual and Augmented Reality technologies can facilitate deeper understanding and long term retention of educational content by providing real time feedback, adaptive learning paths or interactive simulations.

Leveraging Artificial Intelligence in Education

BENEFITS AND CHALLENGES OF AI INTEGRATION IN EDUCATION

Integration of Artificial intelligence (AII) into education presents both benefits & challenges here are some key points:

Benefits

- **Personalized Learning**
AI algorithms can adapt the education content to a student's needs, pace and learning style, making them more engaged and aware. This facilitates the adaptation of learning systems to adapt content difficulty according to student's performance.

- **Enhanced Teaching Methods**
By analysing large amounts of learning data, finding patterns and indicating improvements, AI tools can assist teachers in developing more efficient teaching methods.

- **Automation of Administrative Tasks**
AI can automate administrative processes like scheduling, resource allocation, and grading; giving teachers more time to concentrate on deeper student connections.

Challenges

- **Ethical Concerns:** Ethical issues related to data protection, algorithm bias and the potential for AI to exacerbate existing inequalities in education are also addressed.
- **Technological Infrastructure:** In order to deliver effective AI solutions, a number of educational institutions may lack the required technical infrastructure and expertise resulting in problems with integration and maintenance.
- **Teacher Training& Resistance:** In order to make effective use of artificial intelligence tools in teaching, teachers may require training. The common barrier to adoption of artificial intelligence in education is resistance to changes and fear of job displacement.
- **Quality of AI-Solutions:** The effectiveness and accuracy of AI-Powered Education tools may be different; there is a need to carefully evaluate them for the purpose of ensuring pedagogical value.

Accessibility and Inclusivity in AI-Based Education

In the realm of education, leveraging AI has emerged as a powerful tool for enhancing the learning experience. Ensuring accessibility and inclusion of diverse learners in AI based learning systems, on the other hand, is essential to ensuring that they are properly addressed. Accessibility takes into account a number of considerations, such as accommodating students with disabilities, providing materials in multiple languages and providing alternative formats for the consumption of content.

By automating the process of creating accessible materials, such as converting text to speech for visually impaired students or providing real time language translation, AI can play a significant role in this respect. In addition, AI powered adaptive learning platforms can tailor the learning experience to meet the specific needs and preferences of each student, regardless of their background or ability, we can create a more equitable learning environment in which all students have the opportunity to thrive and succeed by making AI based education accessible and inclusive.

CASE STUDIES

Khan Academy: Personalized Learning With AI

- The potential of AI to deliver personalised learning experiences to students around the world has been embraced by Khan Academy, a pioneer in online learning. Through its adaptive learning platform, Khan Academy utilizes AI algorithms to analyse student performance data and dynamically adjust content delivery based on individual strengths, weaknesses, and learning pace (Khan Academy, n.d.).
- This personalised approach provides students with a tailor made education and support, enabling them to learn at their pace while understanding concepts more efficiently. The Khan Academy uses artificial intelligence to improve the learning experience by providing accessible educational resources for learners of all backgrounds and abilities, thereby promoting inclusiveness.
- In addition, the platform's commitment to free access ensures that quality education is available to anyone with an internet connection, democratizing learning on a global scale. The Khan Academy continues to be at the forefront of using technology to help learners and make education better, as artificial intelligence evolves.

Duolingo-Language Learning With AI

- One of the most prominent examples of using AI to enhance language learning experiences is Duolingo. Duolingo uses artificial intelligence algorithms to tailor the learning experience to each user's unique strengths, weaknesses, and learning preferences through its innovative platform.
- Duolingo's adaptive exercises, which adjust difficulty levels according to individual performance, ensuring that learners are constantly challenged without feeling overwhelmed, are one of the key features of Duolingo. In addition, the AI feedback mechanisms provide learners with instant corrections and explanations that allow them to learn from their mistakes in a timely manner while improving their language skills more efficiently.
- In addition, Duolingo's gamified approach to language learning reinforced by artificial intelligence is fostering engagement and motivation while encouraging users to stay focused on their language learning goals. Duolingo's use of artificial intelligence in language learning not only offers an ac-

cessible and inclusive platform for learners around the world, but also revolutionizes how languages are taught and learned, leading to more personalised, efficient or entertaining learning.

IMPLEMENTATION DIRECTIONS & EMERGING TRENDS

The implementation of AI in the education sector is set to revolutionize learning experience in a number of keyways, as it continues to grow. The integration of AI virtual tutors and assistants into educational settings, providing personalised support and guidance to students both inside and outside the classroom, is one of the emerging trends (Mittal et al., 2022; Banerjee & Beck, 2020).

In order to enhance the understanding and engagement of students, these virtual teachers will be able to adjust their training styles, preferences or pace so as to offer tailored assistance and feedback. In addition, educators can gain deeper insight into student performance and learning patterns through AI driven Analytics and Predictive Models, enabling them to make more informed decisions and targeted interventions.

Another direction is the development of AI-based content creation tools that automate the process of generating educational materials, such as interactive simulations, personalized quizzes, and adaptive learning pathways (Basu, 2019).

These tools allow teachers to create personalised learning experiences which meet the needs of a variety of students and help them understand concepts more deeply. In addition, the accessibility of educational content for learners with diverse linguistic backgrounds and breaking down language barriers and fostering inclusiveness are facilitated by AI Powered Language Translation and Transcription Technologies (Shah, 2020).

Overall, AI integration in education offers enormous potential for enhancing learning experience through personalised teaching, increasing educational outcomes and promoting accessibility and inclusion at global level.

CONCLUSION

The integration of AI in education holds immense potential for enhancing the learning experience of students. By leveraging AI technologies, educational institutions can personalize learning, provide timely feedback, and offer adaptive learning pathways tailored to individual student needs. AI-powered tools can also assist educators in automating administrative tasks, thus allowing them to focus more on delivering high-quality instruction and fostering meaningful student engagement.

In conclusion, the effective integration of AI in education has the power to revolutionize the learning experience, empowering students to reach their full potential and preparing them for success in an increasingly digital world.

REFERENCES

Ab Hamid, S. H., & Mat Zin, N. A. (2020). The Effects of Virtual Reality (VR) on Learning Motivation and Engagement: A Review. *Journal of Technical Education and Training*, 12(2), 1–12.

Aitken, J. M., & Van Hees, M. H. V. (2019). The importance of artificial intelligence in education: Perceptions of teachers and school administrators. *Journal of Technology and Teacher Education*, 27(2), 163–187.

Banerjee, P., & Beck, J. E. (2020). Emerging Trends in Artificial Intelligence for Education. In Beck, J. E., & Leighton, P. E. (Eds.), *Educational Data Mining: Applications and Trends* (pp. 3–18). Springer.

Basu, P. (2019). AI in Education: A Roadmap for Transformation. *Educational Technology*, 59(6), 49–53.

Becker, K. (2017). Carnegie Learning's Cognitive Tutor: A Case Study in Implementing Artificial Intelligence to Enhance Mathematics Instruction. *Journal of Educational Technology & Society*, 20(2), 75–86.

Buckingham Shum, S., Ferguson, R., & Martinez-Maldonado, R. (2019). Human-centred learning analytics. *Journal of Learning Analytics*, 6(2), 1–9. 10.18608/jla.2019.62.1

Dunleavy, M., Dede, C., & Mitchell, R. (2009). Affordances and limitations of immersive participatory augmented reality simulations for teaching and learning. *Journal of Science Education and Technology*, 18(1), 7–22. 10.1007/s10956-008-9119-1

Ferguson, R. (2018). Learning analytics: Drivers, developments and challenges. *International Journal of Educational Technology in Higher Education*, 15(1), 3.

Graesser, A. C., Li, H., Forsyth, C. M., & Elenzil, M. (2018). Conversational agents for learning, assessment, and coaching. In Fiore, S. M., & Salas, E. (Eds.), *Theories of Team Cognition: Cross-Disciplinary Perspectives* (pp. 283–299). Routledge.

Heffernan, N. T., Heffernan, C. L., Tuck, D., & Feldman, A. (2014). ASSISTments: Bringing classroom experiments into the digital age. *The Technology Innovations in Statistics Education, 8*(2).

Koedinger, K. R., & Corbett, A. T. (2012). Cognitive tutors: Technology bringing learning science to the classroom. In *Handbook of educational theories* (pp. 399–416). Routledge.

Mittal, A., Aggarwal, A., & Mittal, R. (2020). Predicting university students' adoption of mobile news applications: The role of perceived hedonic value and news motivation. [IJESMA]. *International Journal of E-Services and Mobile Applications*, 12(4), 42–59. 10.4018/IJESMA.2020100103

Mittal, A., Mantri, A., Tandon, U., & Dwivedi, Y. K. (2022). A unified perspective on the adoption of online teaching in higher education during the COVID-19 pandemic. [Top of Form]. *Information Discovery and Delivery*, 50(2), 117–132. 10.1108/IDD-09-2020-0114

Nayyar, V. (2018). 'My Mind Starts Craving'-Impact of Resealable Packages on the Consumption Behavior of Indian Consumers. *Indian Journal of Marketing*, 48(11), 56–63. 10.17010/ijom/2018/v48/i11/137986

Nayyar, V. (2022). Reviewing the impact of digital migration on the consumer buying journey with robust measurement of PLS-SEM and R Studio. *Systems Research and Behavioral Science*, 39(3), 542–556. 10.1002/sres.2857

Nayyar, V. (2023). The role of marketing analytics in the ethical consumption of online consumers. *Total Quality Management & Business Excellence*, 34(7-8), 1015–1031. 10.1080/14783363.2022.2139676

Nayyar, V., & Batra, R. (2020). Does online media self-regulate consumption behavior of INDIAN youth? *International Review on Public and Nonprofit Marketing*, 17(3), 277–288. 10.1007/s12208-020-00248-1

Nye, B. D., Graesser, A. C., & Hu, X. (2014). AutoTutor and family: A review of 17 years of natural language tutoring. *International Journal of Artificial Intelligence in Education*, 24(4), 427–469. 10.1007/s40593-014-0029-5

Piech, C., Huang, J., Chen, Z., Do, C., Ng, A., & Koller, D. (2015). Tuned models of peer assessment in MOOCs. In *Proceedings of the 28th International Conference on Neural Information Processing Systems* (pp. 1-9). IEEE.

Shah, V. (2020). Breaking Language Barriers in Education: The Role of AI-Powered Language Translation and Transcription Technologies. *International Journal of Educational Technology in Higher Education*, 17(1), 1–15.

Siemens, G., & Gasevic, D. (2012). Guest editorial-learning and knowledge analytics. *Journal of Educational Technology & Society*, 15(3), 1–2.

Thrun, S., & Pratt, L. (2012). Learning to Speak: AI tutors for language learning. *AI Magazine*, 33(3), 63–64.

Woolf, B. P. (2009). *Building intelligent interactive tutors*. Morgan Kaufmann Publishers Inc.

Woolf, B. P. (2010). *Building intelligent interactive tutors: Student-centered strategies for revolutionizing e-learning*. Morgan Kaufmann.

Yeung, S. C., Lee, W. L., Yue, Y., & Hui, S. C. (2014). Educational data mining: A survey and a data mining-based analysis of recent works. *Expert Systems with Applications*, 41(4), 1432–1462. 10.1016/j.eswa.2013.08.042

Chapter 11
Science Mapping of "Artificial Intelligence in Education" Literature Landscape:
A Bibliometric and Content Analysis Discourse

Ajay Chandel
https://orcid.org/0000-0002-4585-6406
Lovely Professional University, India

Anjali Sharma
https://orcid.org/0000-0002-4497-5489
Mittal School of Business, Lovely Professional University, India

Abbineni Praveen Chowdary
Lovely Professional University, India

Shefali Saluja
https://orcid.org/0000-0002-4497-5489
Chitkara University, India

ABSTRACT

Educational methods are being transformed by AI-powered systems that enable independent study, tailored instruction, and the gaining of varied disciplines. On the other hand, AI's use in education has also sparked a global debate on areas related to ethics in classroom education. The objective of this work is to present a thorough examination of academic literature about the application and challenges of artificial intelligence (AI) in educational settings. Through the use of sophisticated bibliometric methods such as co-citation analysis, bibliographic coupling, and keyword co-occurrence analysis, the of this work is to map out the ongoing debate on use of artificial intelligence in education and identify the underlying patterns, connections, and new developments in this area. The chapter proposes future routes for research and innovation in this quickly developing field in addition to providing insights on the historical evolution and current status of AI in education.

DOI: 10.4018/979-8-3693-6660-8.ch011

Copyright ©2024, IGI Global. Copying or distributing in print or electronic forms without written permission of IGI Global is prohibited.

Science Mapping of "Artificial Intelligence in Education" Literature Landscape

INTRODUCTION

The goal of artificial intelligence (AI) is to program technology to mimic human intellect in areas like learning, pattern recognition, and decision-making. Machine learning, computer vision, NLP, and robotics are all part of artificial intelligence (AI) (Wardat et al., 2024). The primary goal of artificial intelligence is to make machines act more intelligently than humans in areas such as data analysis, problem-solving, and situational adaptation. Artificial intelligence (AI) can revolutionize education by streamlining administrative processes, enhancing data-driven decision-making, and creating more tailored learning experiences for students (Xie et al., 2019). Teachers can improve their methods of instruction, cater lessons to the requirements of individual students, and create classrooms that are more welcoming and interesting for all students by utilizing AI.

In this age of Industry 4.0, it is critical to equip the future generation to face unknown challenges by incorporating Artificial Intelligence (AI) into education. More and more schools are embracing Industry 4.0 (Zhang et al., 2024) approaches to education, which use artificial intelligence to improve classroom instruction and student performance. Educational methods are being transformed by AI-powered systems that enable independent study, tailored instruction, and the gaining of varied disciplines. A further example of AI's revolutionary potential in the decision-making processes of higher education is the creation of chatbot platforms for educational advice. Educational institutions can gain significant insights from these platforms, which show excellent efficiency and customer satisfaction (Zhang et al., 2024).

Studies on the use of chatbots powered by artificial intelligence in the classroom have shown promising results, particularly in the area of social studies, where they have the ability to improve both student performance and the quality of instruction. In addition, according to Yi (2024), personalized education models that incorporate recommendation algorithms and semantic similarity analysis highlight the importance of AI in enhancing learning experiences and managing resources optimally. Yi (2024) argues that educational institutions may create a more flexible and personalized learning environment by using AI technology to detect user demands, improve teaching effectiveness, and adjust learning paths.

There are a lot of ways in which artificial intelligence (AI) can improve classroom instruction and student achievement. Chatbots and speech recognition platforms are examples of AI-powered solutions that can provide students with individualized learning experiences (Wang, 2023). Adaptive learning routes are made possible by these technologies, which let students go at their own speed while receiving specific help when they need it. Artificial intelligence also makes it easier to create dynamic classrooms where students actively participate, which in turn boosts their motivation. One example is how the use of AI chatbots in language classes has led to considerable gains in students' fluency and confidence when speaking the target language. Better learning outcomes and higher student satisfaction are the results of AI-driven educational platforms that maximize the use of resources and the efficiency of instruction (Huang, 2023). With the help of AI, teachers may improve classroom instruction, create more conducive settings for student collaboration, and meet the needs of students with a wide range of learning styles.

Nevertheless, there are other important factors to think about and obstacles to overcome before AI is widely used in classrooms. To make good use of AI tools in the classroom, there has to be extensive professional development and training for educators (Wang, 2023). The significance of continuous assistance and training programs should be underscored because many teacher educators have expressed uncertainty and incompetence when it comes to dealing with the consequences of AI in ILTE (Wang, 2023). Additionally, it is crucial to thoroughly handle ethical concerns related to AI use, including data protection, algorithmic prejudice, and the depersonalization of educational experiences. The necessity for open laws and procedures to regulate ethical AI use and reduce hazards is rising in tandem with the technology's widespread adoption in classrooms (Gouvea, 2024). Addressing socio-economic inequities and providing inclusive education for all students is crucial, especially in view of concerns about the digital divide and equitable access to AI-powered educational materials (Alam et al., 2024). Regardless of these obstacles, AI has enormous potential in the classroom, offering students all across the globe better learning outcomes, more efficiency, and individualized lessons.

A careful investigation of existing bibliometric studies on "Ai in Education" with minimum three citations, results into four publications (Table 1).

Table 1. Existing bibliometric investigation on 'AI in Education'

Authors	Title	TC	Methodology
Prahani et al. (2022)	Artificial Intelligence in Education Research During the Last Ten Years: A Review and Bibliometric Study	19	Database- SCOPUS Documents- 457 Period- 2011-2021
Maphosa and Maphosa (2023)	Artificial intelligence in higher education: a bibliometric analysis and topic modeling approach	4	Database- SCOPUS Documents- 304 Period- 2012-2021
Bozkurt (2023)	Unleashing the Potential of Generative AI, Conversational Agents and Chatbots in Educational Praxis: A Systematic Review and Bibliometric Analysis of GenAI in Education	3	Database- SCOPUS Documents- 513 Period- 2022-2024
Jaleniauskienė et al. (2023)	Artificial intelligence in language education: a bibliometric analysis	3	Database- SCOPUS Documents- 2609 Period- 2018-2022

Source: SCOPUS database and Authors' compilation

Current study differentiates itself from existing studies in many ways. First, this study uses the publications spanning 48 years (1976-2024), the longest period as compared to other studies on the topic. Two, this study uses a novel methodology of amalgamating bibliometric analysis with content analysis.

This study tries to decipher undermentioned research questions using science mapping technique of bibliometrics:

1.1 What are the key research themes or clusters emerging from co-citation networks in a specific discipline?
1.2 How does bibliographic coupling contribute to the identification of related research areas or subfields within a discipline?
1.3 How do patterns of keyword co-occurrence reflect the structure and evolution of research topics within a particular field?
1.4 What are the future research agendas to further AI research in education

RESEARCH METHODOLOGY

Bibliometrics

The development of bibliometric research methodologies was sparked by a widely acknowledged necessity to examine and classify the enormous volumes of bibliographic data in the library and information sciences (Broadus, 1987). More precisely, in the field of AI in Education, for example, bibliometric research creates representative summaries of the body of literature in order to assess and categorize vast amounts of bibliometric data. In order to address the research issues, two primary types of bibliographic analysis methodologies were utilized: scientific mapping, which highlighted the interdependencies among research aspects, and performance analysis, which concentrated on the performance of research components (Donthu et al., 2021). The tools utilized to do bibliometric analysis were VOSviewer and Biblioshiny, an R-based online interface for bibliometrics.

Keyword Identification

A two-way approach was utilized to choose the keywords that were used to locate pertinent literature on "AI in education." Five open-access articles were first reviewed by the writers. The list of keywords that were created in this manner were shown to five seasoned experts with appropriate experience in the next step. Experts were briefed about the purpose of the study and were requested to assess the preliminary keyword list (Chandel et al., 2022).

Data Procurement

Scopus was used to procure the bibliographic dataset (Bartol et al., 2014). A keyword search query "(TITLE("AI") OR TITLE("Artificial intelligence") AND TITLE("Education")) AND (LIMIT-TO (SRCTYPE,"j")) AND (LIMIT-TO (OA,"all")) AND (LIMIT-TO (DOCTYPE,"ar")) AND (LIMIT-TO (LANGUAGE,"English")))" led to the discovery of 1495 distinct documents released between 1976 and 2024 (April 8, 2024). In order to create a final dataset, these 1495 documents were subjected to PRISMA (Preferred reporting items for systematic reviews and meta-analysis), as suggested by Moher et al. (2009). "Artificial intelligence" and "Education" were essentially included in the article title search option of SCOPUS database. Figure 1 provides a thorough overview of the PRISMA framework & methodology (Chandel et al., 2023, 2024).

Figure 1. Preferred reporting items for systematic reviews and meta-analysis

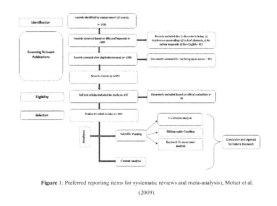

Figure 1: Preferred reporting items for systematic reviews and meta-analysis), Moher et al. (2009).

Moher et al. (2009)

Science Mapping

Studying the connections between research components is known as science mapping (Baker, Kumar, & Pandey, 2021). The analysis focuses on the research components' underlying relationships and intellectual exchanges. Co-citation analysis, bibliographic coupling, and keyword co-occurrence analysis are a few of the methods used in science mapping. These methods are essential for showing the intellectual and bibliometric structures of the research field when paired with network analysis (Baker et al., 2020). A review of the many science mapping approaches is shown in Table 3, emphasizing data concerns and usage.

ANALYSIS

Co-Citation Analysis

One way to find out how similar two research papers are to one other is to look at their co-citations. The term "co-cited" describes the practice of referencing two research papers in the same third document. The degree to which two papers are co-cited is determined by the number of referenced items that are identical. The strength of a CO-citation is defined as the perceived degree of association or relationship between texts according to the group of citing authors (Small, 1973). To illustrate the interconnectedness of important ideas, we might look at articles that have received a large number of citations from other researchers. Thus, core motifs in literature on AI in education were identified by co-citation analysis (Table 2 and Figure 2) in this inquiry.

Table 2. Co-citation analysis

Cluster No.	Cluster Name	Authors	Title	TC
1	AI-Enabled Learning Aggregates	Chen et al. (2020)	Artificial Intelligence in Education: A Review	482
		Huang et al. (2021)	A review on artificial intelligence in education	51
2	AI Innovations Shaping Education: ChatGPT and the Metaverse	Fütterer et al. (2023)	ChatGPT in education: global reactions to AI innovations	4
		Hwang and Chien (2022)	Definition, roles, and potential research issues of the metaverse in education: An artificial intelligence perspective	240
3	Ethical Challenges of AI	Holmes et al. (2022)	Ethics of AI in Education: Towards a Community-Wide Framework	126
		Roll I.; Wylie R. (2016)	Evolution and Revolution in Artificial Intelligence in Education	307
4	Sustainable Curriculum Design	Chiu and Chai (2020)	Sustainable curriculum planning for artificial intelligence education: A self-determination theory perspective	102
		Lee and Lee (2021)	Applying artificial intelligence in physical education and future perspectives	60
5	Bots to Books	Rudolph et al. (2023)	War of the chatbots: Bard, Bing Chat, ChatGPT, Ernie and beyond. The new AI gold rush and its impact on higher education	152
		Dogan et al. (2023)	The Use of Artificial Intelligence (AI) in Online Learning and Distance Education Processes: A Systematic Review of Empirical Studies	36

Source: SCOPUS database and Authors' compilation

Figure 2. Co-citation analysis

Figure 2: Co-citation analysis, Source- VOSviewer

Source- VOSviewer

Cluster-I: AI-Enabled Learning Aggregates

The cluster explores the far-reaching consequences of AI in the field of education, analyzing its various uses and revolutionary impacts. The research, which is based on a narrative and a framework for AI evaluation, focuses on the effects of AI on educational leadership, teaching, and learning. The research, which makes use of a qualitative methodology supported by extensive literature reviews, traces the development of artificial intelligence (AI) systems from simple computer-based systems to complex web-based platforms and humanoid robots, allowing them to perform either solo or collaborative roles in the classroom (Chen et al., 2020). Educators can optimize student engagement and learning results through the use of these innovations, which expedite administrative processes, boost teaching quality, and personalize curriculum delivery. The cluster also sheds light on how AI is being used in adaptive learning, evaluating teachers, and virtual classrooms, which could lead to better education overall. While these developments are encouraging, the cluster also highlights potential problems and consequences of using AI in the classroom, providing useful information for reform efforts in this area (Huang et al., 2021).

Cluster-II: AI Innovations Shaping Education: ChatGPT and the Metaverse

Two innovative technologies and their effects on teaching and learning are captured in the co-citation cluster. Educators throughout the world are talking about ChatGPT since its release, and they have different opinions on whether it will improve learning or make it easier to evade. A wide range of responses, from worries about cheating to talks about new learning opportunities, are shown by the study's analysis of a large dataset of Twitter conversations. Decisions made by those in positions of power have a major impact on how the public views new technologies, underscoring the nuanced nature of how people react to these developments in society (Fütterer et al., 2023). While the metaverse is being spoken about as a game-changing technology, it hasn't really been used much in classrooms yet. In an effort to fill this void, this position paper defines the metaverse and outlines its possible educational uses. The purpose of this study is to encourage future research in metaverse-based education by clarifying the functions of artificial intelligence (AI) in the metaverse and arguing for its incorporation into educational practice. Taken as a whole, these studies highlight how educational technology is constantly changing and how important it is to keep up with new technologies so that we can improve education (Hwang and Chien, 2022).

Cluster-III: Ethical Challenges of AI

Two innovative technologies and their effects on teaching and learning are captured in the co-citation cluster. Educators throughout the world are talking about ChatGPT since its release, and they have different opinions on whether it will improve learning or make it easier to evade. A wide range of responses, from worries about cheating to talks about new learning opportunities, are shown by the study's analysis of a large dataset of Twitter conversations. Decisions made by those in positions of power have a major impact on how the public views new technologies, underscoring the nuanced nature of how people react to these developments in society (Holmes et al., 2022). While the metaverse is being spoken about as a game-changing technology, it hasn't really been used much in classrooms yet. In an effort to fill this void, this position paper defines the metaverse and outlines its possible educational uses. The purpose of this study is to encourage future research in metaverse-based education by clarifying the functions of artificial intelligence (AI) in the metaverse and arguing for its incorporation into educational practice. Taken as a whole, these studies highlight how educational technology is constantly changing and how important it is to keep up with new technologies so that we can improve education (Roll & Wylie, 2016).

Cluster-IV: Sustainable Curriculum Design

The cluster explores the changing conversation around incorporating AI topics into K-12 education programs, drawing attention to the need for extensive research to help educators navigate this emerging area. In order to better understand what goes into creating, implementing, and updating AI curricula, one case study contrasts the viewpoints of K-12 teachers who have and have not taught AI before. The study presents a genuine curriculum creation cycle that places a priority on teachers' agency as orchestrators of learning experiences. It draws on four basic approaches to curriculum planning: content, process, praxis, and self-determination theory (SDT). At the same time, another research looks into the possibilities of AI in PE, highlighting the revolutionary effects it could have on pedagogy, information delivery, student assessment, and guidance techniques. The paper highlights the significance of future physical education teachers being fluent in artificial intelligence (AI), explores its practical ramifications, and proposes research directions to delve further into AI's uses in the classroom and on the field. Taken as a whole, these findings highlight how AI is changing the face of education and how important it is to help teachers become more fluent in the technology so that the next generation can thrive in an AI-powered society (Lee and Lee, 2021).

Cluster-V: Sustainable Curriculum Design

The cluster explores the rapid advancements in the chatbot domain, driven by an AI arms race with profound implications for higher education. It highlights promising chatbots in English and Chinese languages, examining their corporate backgrounds and performance in a multi-disciplinary test relevant to higher education. Surprisingly, despite sensationalist claims, the study finds no chatbots demonstrating A or B-grade performance, challenging prevailing notions of AI intelligence. GPT-4 and its predecessor emerge as top performers, while others lag behind (Rudolph et al.,2023). Recommendations for higher education stakeholders underscore the need for discernment and critical evaluation in integrating AI technologies into educational practices (Chiu and Chai, 2020). Concurrently, a systematic review of 276 publications delves into AI's impact on online distance education. Time trend analysis shows a steady increase in research, with China, India, and the United States leading contributions. Thematic analysis uncovers dominant clusters focusing on AI's role in teaching and learning processes, student behavior prediction, and adaptive learning. These studies collectively shed light on the evolving landscape of AI in education, emphasizing the importance of critical inquiry and ethical considerations in leveraging AI technologies effectively (Dogan et al., 2023).

Bibliographic Coupling

Bibliographic coupling is a science mapping technique based on the notion that works with a high number of shared references are probably on the same subject (Weinberg, 1974). According to Zupic and Cater (2014), the analysis works best when it is limited to a small time period and concentrates on grouping publications into theme clusters through shared references. By classifying publications according to their citing publications, bibliographic coupling (as opposed to co-citation analysis) aids in drawing attention to more recent and specialized publications. Given that this is a current snapshot, the analysis can be used to show how the field is currently doing (present).

The output of VOSviewer's bibliographic coupling (Chandel & Kaur, 2022) is shown in Figure 3 and table 3, which includes papers with at least 35 citation and those produced between 2022 and 2024. The six clusters that the threshold produced are described below:

Figure 3. Bibliographic coupling

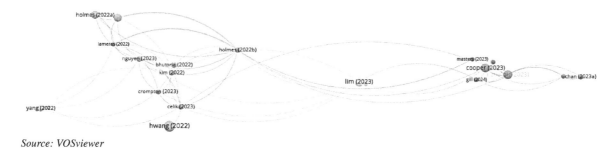

Source: VOSviewer

Table 3. Bibliographic coupling (2022-2024)

Cluster No	Cluster Name	Author(s)	Title	TC
1	AI in Education: Transformative Frameworks and Ethical Considerations	Cooper, (2023)	Examining Science Education in ChatGPT: An Exploratory Study of Generative Artificial Intelligence	161
		Rudolph et al., (2023)	War of the chatbots: Bard, Bing Chat, ChatGPT, Ernie and beyond. The new AI gold rush and its impact on higher education	152
2	Transparency and Ethics in Educational AI: Building a Foundation for Responsible Innovation	Holmes et al., (2022)	Ethics of AI in Education: Towards a Community-Wide Framework	126
		Khosravi et al., (2022)	Explainable Artificial Intelligence in education	121
3	Empowering Educators: Integrating AI and Metaverse Perspectives in Education	Hwang, (2022)	Definition, roles, and potential research issues of the metaverse in education: An artificial intelligence perspective	240
		Celik, (2023)	Towards Intelligent-TPACK: An empirical study on teachers' professional knowledge to ethically integrate artificial intelligence (AI)-based tools into education	60
4	Charting the Future: Perspectives on Generative AI and Chatbot Adoption in Education	Lim et al., (2023)	Generative AI and the future of education: Ragnarök or reformation? A paradoxical perspective from management educators	164
		Mohd Rahim et al., (2022)	AI-Based Chatbots Adoption Model for Higher-Education Institutions: A Hybrid PLS-SEM-Neural Network Modelling Approach	44
5	Fostering Collaboration: Learning Design and Personalization in AI-Enhanced Education	Bhutoria (2022)	Personalized education and Artificial Intelligence in the United States, China, and India: A systematic review using a Human-In-The-Loop model	73
		Kim et al., (2022)	Learning design to support student-AI collaboration: perspectives of leading teachers for AI in education	56
6	AI in Early Childhood Education: Curriculum Design and Implementation Strategies	Yang (2022)	Artificial Intelligence education for young children: Why, what, and how in curriculum design and implementation	93
		Su & Zhong (2022)	Artificial Intelligence (AI) in early childhood education: Curriculum design and future directions	40

Source: SCOPUS database and Authors' compilation

Cluster-I (Red Nodes)

Since late 2022, the dynamic field of AI-driven education has experienced exponential expansion in the chatbot environment, which is marked by intense competition and transformational possibilities. A comparative analysis shows that although chatbots like ChatGPT, Bing Chat, Bard, and Ernie are becoming indispensable tools for millions of academics, their cognitive ability nevertheless falls short of headline-grabbing claims (Cooper, 2023). While ChatGPT's potential congruence with research themes is highlighted by a separate inquiry into its usefulness in science education, it also raises ethical questions about its legitimacy and accountable use. To fully realize AI's revolutionary power in education, both studies emphasize the significance of critical analysis, adaptation, and ethical issues (Rudolph et al., 2023).

Cluster-II (Green Nodes)

Ethical issues are crucial in the field of "artificial intelligence in education" (AIED), but they are frequently disregarded. While promoting student learning is still a top priority, it is also critical to deal with concerns about bias, accountability, justice, and integrity. The ethical terrain around AIED is complicated, as recent investigations have shown (Holmes et al., 2022). To properly manage these problems, interdisciplinary frameworks and strong rules are necessary. Additionally, the use of explainable AI (XAI) in the classroom has the potential to improve the openness and dependability of AI systems. To address the unique requirements and potential hazards of XAI in educational contexts, a comprehensive framework called XAI-ED is suggested. Fostering ethical participation and open practices is crucial for the appropriate and effective application of AIED in education as it keeps on evolving (Khosravi et al., 2022).

Cluster-III (Blue Nodes)

Artificial intelligence's (AI) inclusion in education technology is still underdeveloped, which emphasizes the critical role that specialized expertise from teachers plays. To fill this vacuum, a new study offers a scale to assess instructors' competence with AI-based learning resources that takes ethical issues, pedagogical, and technological factors into account (Hwang, 2022). The results highlight the necessity of a combined technological pedagogical knowledge (TPK) for effective AI integration in education, while also highlighting the significance of teachers' technological knowledge (TK) in evaluating AI judgments. Furthermore, there is a lot of room for educational application with the recently developed idea of the metaverse, which is frequently disregarded in discussions on education. A position paper defines the metaverse and examines how AI and educational technologies intersect it. The study seeks to stimulate more research and discussion in this emerging topic by illuminating the features and educational opportunities of the metaverse (Celik, 2023).

Cluster-IV (Yellow Nodes)

Artificial intelligence (AI) integration presents opportunities as well as obstacles in the field of education. Though individualized instruction and meeting the requirements of each student are potential benefits of AI technology, integrating them into K–12 schools require considerable planning and thought. Instructors see capacity and subject-matter knowledge building as the best learning objectives, and they are at the center of the development of student-AI cooperation (SAC) in learning. As a learning partner,

AI's educational scaffolding and qualities facilitate transdisciplinary learning, authentic problem solving, and creative tasks necessary for facilitating SAC. Further considered important are a collaborative learning culture, adaptable school systems, and systematic AIED policy (Lim et al., 2023). In order to learn about AI, learn from AI, and learn together, teachers expect SAC to go through several phases. Concurrently, advances in Big Data, Machine Learning, and AI are facilitating a clear trend towards individualized education. Nonetheless, difficulties including resource limitations and data privacy concerns highlight the necessity of careful implementation and policy consideration. Regarding future instructional techniques, AI design, and educational policies that aim to improve individualized learning and SAC, these results hold significant implications (Mohd Rahim et al., 2023)

Cluster-V (Purple Nodes)

Although integrating generative artificial intelligence (AI) offers both benefits and challenges, it has the potential to completely transform education. This essay uses paradox theory and critical analysis to reconcile the arguments made for and against the use of generative AI in education, in an attempt to navigate this rapidly changing landscape. The paper provides guidance for management educators on how to embrace generative AI as a catalyst for educational reform by identifying four paradoxes inherent in the technology: its dual nature as both friend and foe, its capability coupled with dependency, its accessibility juxtaposed with restrictions, and its popularity amid controversy (Kim et al., 2023). Meanwhile, AI-driven chatbots are becoming powerful instruments for improving service quality and organizational efficiency in the field of customer support. Higher education institutions (HEIs) are just beginning to use AI chatbots, nevertheless, and obstacles like theoretical direction and preparation are making this happen slowly. In order to close this gap, a study looks into what influences chatbot adoption in higher education institutions (HEIs). The results show how important design, ethics, interactivity, perceived trust, and performance expectancy are in determining user behavior (Bhutoria, 2023). These results give important information for improving marketing tactics and productivity in addition to informing HEI student services. Collectively, these contributions illuminate the intricate relationship between AI technology and education, providing strategies for capitalizing on their revolutionary potential while averting unintended consequences.

Cluster VI (Orange Nodes)

Curricular frameworks that are specifically designed for early childhood education are necessary because artificial intelligence (AI) education presents special opportunities and problems. In light of this, this paper explores the fundamental issues of what, why, and how to include AI principles into early childhood education (ECE) (Yang, 2022). It promotes a cutting-edge pedagogical approach that emphasizes the organic character of AI literacy in a society growing more intelligent by integrating it with digital literacy. In addition to highlighting important AI principles like pattern recognition and prediction that are age-appropriate for young children, the model emphasizes the value of embodied, culturally relevant pedagogy in fostering meaningful interaction with AI devices. This pedagogical approach is exemplified by the excellent curriculum "AI for Kids," which offers educators opportunities for culturally sensitive inquiry that support young learners' knowledge of digital technology and STEM subjects. Furthermore, an investigation is conducted on the AI curriculum for kindergarten students, suggesting three fundamental competencies—AI Knowledge, AI Skill, and AI Attitude—and emphasizing the effectiveness of using social robots as teaching assistants. The paper promotes a thorough approach to AI education in early infancy, laying the groundwork for future generations to successfully navigate and utilize AI's potential using problem-based learning techniques (Su & Jhong, 2022).

Keyword Co-Occurrence Analysis

Bibliometricians examine the relationships between different keywords in a body of scholastic works using a method known as keyword co-occurrence analysis. A keyword co-occurrence inquiry can provide valuable insights into the thematic organization, linkages, and research trends within a topic. Through the display of correlated keywords, it facilitates the identification of recurrent themes, research clusters, and new topics of interest. The analysis can help clarify the relationships between various academic disciplines.

53 keywords met the criterion when using the Louvain cluster strategy, which required a minimum of 25 keyword co-occurrences out of a total of 1124 keywords. Twenty of these 53 keywords were manually removed while preserving the integrity of the analysis, depending on the authors' expertise and judgment (Blondel et al., 2008). Figure 5 presents the findings. Different colors designate each cluster on the network map. Five clusters are seen in the co-occurrence map, with each color on the map denoting a different cluster. Based on the emerging themes, this section attempts to elucidate these clusters (Figure 4):

Figure 4. Keyword co-occurrence analysis

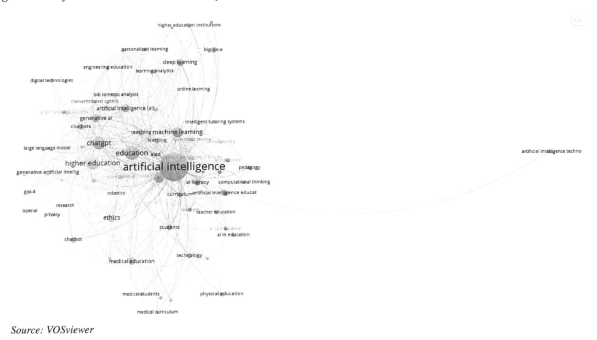

Source: VOSviewer

Cluster-I (Red): AI in education, AI literacy, Curriculum, Early childhood education, k-12 education, Pedagogy, Teacher education

The importance of artificial intelligence (AI) in transforming education at all levels—from K–12 to earlier childhood education—is highlighted by this cluster (Yang, 2022). It underscores the significance of AI literacy among educators in addition to highlighting the use of AI into conventional education approaches (Su & Yang, 2024). Educational institutions can adjust to the changing needs of students in a world that is becoming more and more digital by introducing AI into their courses. This cluster also discusses how important pedagogy and teacher preparation are to using AI to improve teaching methods and student participation (Su & Zhong, 2022).

Cluster-II (Green): AI, Chatbots, ChatGPT, Conversational technologies, Large language models, Learning, Teaching, Generative AI, Digital technologies

This cluster explores the various ways that AI technologies are being used in education, going beyond AI itself. This cluster explores how various tools, such as chatbots, conversational technologies, and massive language models like ChatGPT, are changing the face of education (Ismail et al., 2023). Teachers may give students more individualized and dynamic learning experiences by utilizing digital technology and generative AI. This cluster also emphasizes how AI may support adaptive learning strategies that adjust to the needs and preferences of each individual student (Bozkurt, 2023).

Cluster-III (Blue): AI, Adaptive learning, Big data, Deep learning, e-learning, Engineering education, Machine learning, Personalized learning, Learning analytics, Entrepreneurship education, Higher education institutes

In this case, the focus is on how AI-driven technologies—like machine learning, big data analytics, and adaptive learning—are transforming learning environments. Teachers can design individualized learning experiences that cater to the distinct skills and learning preferences of every student by utilizing these tools (Alqahtani, 2023). This cluster demonstrates how AI is changing the face of higher education institutions by examining how it intersects with disciplines like engineering and entrepreneurial courses. AI integration in curriculum design and delivery can help schools better educate students for professions in quickly changing fields (Nuseir et al., 2020).

Cluster-IV (Yellow): Academic integrity, Assessment, Education innovation, Generative AI, Ethics, Privacy, Research, Robotics, Higher education, OpenAI, GPT4

This cluster explores the moral questions raised by the application of AI in education, especially those about data security, privacy, and academic integrity. It is critical to address worries about the equality and openness of assessment procedures and the proper use of student data as AI technologies proliferate in educational settings (Su & Yang, 2023; Chan & Hu, 2023). This cluster also looks at how AI is influencing research and innovation in education, while also posing ethical concerns about the use of innovations like GPT4 (Lim et al., 2023).

Cluster-V (Purple): AI, AI Ethics, Automation, Medical curriculum, Medical students, Medical education, Technology

This cluster examines the consequences of AI in specialized disciplines like medical education, with a focus on the ethical aspects of the technology. There is an increasing need to include AI into medical curricula while ensuring ethical considerations are prioritized, as technology continues to transform the healthcare industry (Masters, 2023). Concerns regarding the automation of medical education and its possible effects on future healthcare professionals' training are also covered in this cluster. Through an analysis of the relationship between artificial intelligence and medical education, this cluster clarifies the intricate moral dilemmas that arise when technology is included in healthcare education (Holmes et al., 2022).

Cluster-VI (Teal): AIED, Intelligent tutoring system, Online learning, Virtual reality, AI in education

This cluster demonstrates how artificial intelligence (AI) is propelling the development of educational technology like virtual reality simulations, online learning environments, and intelligent tutoring systems (Nguyen et al., 2023). Teachers may design immersive, interactive learning environments that meet the needs of a wide range of students by utilizing AI-driven tools. Additionally, this cluster investigates how AI may improve diversity and accessibility in the classroom, especially for students who live far away or have disabilities. Education institutions can open up new avenues for learning and collaboration by embracing AI (Lameras & Arnab, 2023).

Cluster-VII (Orange): Anatomy education, ChatGPT, Large language models, Natural language processing

This cluster, which focuses on particular educational areas, looks at how artificial intelligence (AI) tools like ChatGPT and natural language processing are changing subjects like anatomy instruction. Teachers can give students dynamic, captivating learning experiences that improve their comprehension of difficult subjects by employing broad language models (Li et al., 2021). This cluster also highlights how AI may be used to tailor learning paths and meet the specific demands of each student, which will ultimately lead to better learning outcomes in specialized fields (Lazarus et al., 2024).

Cluster-VIII (Brown): AI technology, Civic education

Lastly, this cluster investigates how AI technology in education may have wider societal ramifications, especially in terms of promoting civic involvement and education. Education institutions can enable students to become knowledgeable and engaged citizens in a world that is becoming more complicated by incorporating AI-driven educational initiatives into curriculum design (Li et al., 2024). The significance of ethical issues and responsible AI governance in influencing the direction of education is also covered by this cluster. Through the use of AI technologies, educational institutions may foster the development of a new generation of engaged and socially responsible global citizens (Tang, 2023).

FUTURE RESEARCH AGENDAS

To identify the future research agendas unearthed, a content analysis of the 'Limitations and Scope for Future Research section' of the twelve recent publications (same as identified in bibliographic coupling; top two cited publications from each cluster) was conducted. The results were as follows in Table 4:

continued on following page

Table 4. Continued

Table 4. Future research agendas

Sr. No	Author(s)	Title	TC	Research agenda
1	Cooper (2023)	Examining Science Education in ChatGPT: An Exploratory Study of Generative Artificial Intelligence	161	Evaluating the effectiveness of using ChatGPT in scientific classes and how it affects students' learning results in various science areas.
2	Rudolph et al. (2023)	War of the chatbots: Bard, Bing Chat, ChatGPT, Ernie and beyond. The new AI gold rush and its impact on higher education	152	Carry out longitudinal research to monitor the changing face of chatbot use in higher education and assess the long-term impacts on methods of instruction and learning.
3	Holmes et al. (2022)	Ethics of AI in Education: Towards a Community-Wide Framework	126	Create a thorough framework that the entire community can use to solve ethical issues in AI-driven learning environments, and investigate how well it works in various educational contexts.
4	Khosravi et al. (2022)	Explainable Artificial Intelligence in education	121	Examine strategies for improving the explainability of artificial intelligence (AI) systems in the classroom and look at how they affect students' comprehension, involvement, and confidence in AI
5	Hwang (2022)	Definition, roles, and potential research issues of the metaverse in education: An artificial intelligence perspective	240	Examine how the metaverse might be used in educational settings and consider how AI-driven experiences could improve cooperation, teaching, and learning.
6	Celik (2023)	Towards Intelligent-TPACK: An empirical study on teachers' professional knowledge to ethically integrate artificial intelligence (AI)-based tools into education	60	Expand the research on the professional expertise of educators on the moral and efficient integration of AI-based tools into the classroom, with an emphasis on creating support systems and training curricula.
7	Lim et al. (2023)	Generative AI and the future of education: Ragnarök or reformation? A paradoxical perspective from management educators	164	Investigate the contradictory viewpoints of management educators regarding the use of generative AI in education. Analyze methods for utilizing AI technology to promote educational reformation while reducing possible hazards.
8	Mohd Rahim et al. (2022)	AI-Based Chatbots Adoption Model for Higher-Education Institutions: A Hybrid PLS-SEM-Neural Network Modelling Approach	44	Carry out comparative analyses to investigate the variables impacting the adoption of AI-driven chatbots in higher education establishments within various institutional and cultural contexts.
9	Bhutoria (2022)	Personalized education and Artificial Intelligence in the United States, China, and India: A systematic review using a Human-In-The-Loop model	73	Study the dynamics of student-AI collaboration in educational settings and investigate effective learning design strategies to maximize the benefits of such collaborations while addressing potential challenges
10	Kim et al. (2022)	Learning design to support student-AI collaboration: perspectives of leading teachers for AI in education	56	Study the factors contributing to success and challenges faced in each context when implementing personalized education using AI technologies.
11	Yang (2022)	Artificial Intelligence education for young children: Why, what, and how in curriculum design and implementation	93	Carry out longitudinal research to assess the long-term effects of AI-driven curriculum design on children's cognitive development and learning outcomes, as well as the efficacy of this approach in early childhood education.
12	Su & Jhong (2022)	Artificial Intelligence (AI) in early childhood education: Curriculum design and future directions	40	Examine cutting-edge methods to curriculum design, prospective future directions for research and practice, and emerging trends and best practices in AI integration in early childhood education.

Source: Authors' compilation

CONCLUSION

A complex tapestry of insights, difficulties, and opportunities originates from the dynamic nexus of artificial intelligence (AI) and education. The changing field of AI-driven education is examined via the prism of several research approaches, such as co-citation analysis, bibliographic coupling, keyword co-occurrence analysis, and future research goals. The interwoven web of ideas is illuminated by co-citation analysis, which reveals clusters of research ranging from sustainable curriculum design to AI-enabled learning aggregates. In addition to highlighting the complex effects of AI on curriculum delivery, teaching strategies, and educational leadership, it also sheds light on potential problems and ethical issues. Through the identification of emergent topics and research clusters, bibliographic coupling facilitates a greater understanding of the relationships between scholarly publications. Through the identification of emergent topics and research clusters, bibliographic coupling facilitates a greater understanding of the relationships between scholarly publications. It clarifies the evolving significance of ethics, transparency, and AI literacy in learning environments and highlights the revolutionary possibilities of AI-driven technologies such as generative AI and chatbots. A broad overview of the research trends and theme structure in the AI and education space is provided by keyword co-occurrence analysis. It offers a thorough overview of the various aspects of AI-driven education by outlining clusters ranging from curriculum design integration of AI to the ethical implications of AI technologies.

Last but not least, investigating potential study topics shows the way ahead and indicates important fields for investigation and creativity. There are countless chances for development in the future, ranging from assessing how well AI technologies work in educational contexts to resolving ethical issues and encouraging human-AI collaboration. Artificial Intelligence has the potential to significantly alter education, acting as a catalyst for both change and disruption. But, it is imperative to remember that people are at the core of education, even in the face of the swift growth of technology. Let's not waver in our dedication to creating meaningful learning opportunities, igniting curiosity, and equipping students with the skills they need to succeed in a world driven by artificial intelligence. The intersection of artificial intelligence and education presents both the opportunity for advancement and the necessity of exercising appropriate stewardship. Let's move forward on this path with knowledge, compassion, and a common goal in mind: to build a future in which education is a universal source of enlightenment and empowerment.

REFERENCES

Alam, S., Hameed, A., Madej, M., & Kobylarek, A. (2024). Perception and practice of using artificial intelligence in education: An opinion based study. *XLinguae*, 17(1), 216–233. 10.18355/XL.2024.17.01.15

Alqahtani, M. M. (2023). Artificial intelligence and entrepreneurship education: A paradigm in qatari higher education institutions after COVID-19 pandemic. *International Journal of Data and Network Science*, 7(2), 695–706. 10.5267/j.ijdns.2023.3.002

Bhutoria, A. (2022). Personalized education and artificial intelligence in the United States, China, and India: A systematic review using a human-in-The-Loop model. *Computers and Education: Artificial Intelligence*, 3, 100068. 10.1016/j.caeai.2022.100068

Bozkurt, A. (2023). Unleashing the potential of generative AI, conversational agents and chatbots in educational praxis: A systematic review and bibliometric analysis of GenAI in education. *Open Praxis*, 15(4), 261–270. 10.55982/openpraxis.15.4.609

Celik, I. (2023). Towards Intelligent-TPACK: An empirical study on teachers' professional knowledge to ethically integrate artificial intelligence (ai)-based tools into education. *Computers in Human Behavior*, 138, 107468. 10.1016/j.chb.2022.107468

Chan, C. K., & Hu, W. (2023). Students' voices on generative AI: Perceptions, benefits, and challenges in higher education. *International Journal of Educational Technology in Higher Education*, 20(1), 43. Advance online publication. 10.1186/s41239-023-00411-8

Chandel, A., Bhanot, N., Gupta, S., & Verma, R. (2024). Oil Spills-Where We Were, Where We Are, And Where We Will Be? A Bibliometric and Content Analysis Discourse. In *BIO Web of Conferences* (*Vol. 86,* p. 01050). EDP Sciences.

Chandel, A., Bhanot, N., & Sharma, R. (2023). A bibliometric and content analysis discourse on business application of blockchain technology. *International Journal of Quality & Reliability Management*. 10.1108/IJQRM-02-2023-0025

Chandel, A., Bhanot, N., & Verma, R. (2023). A Bibliometric Investigation of Ecocide Research: Tracing Trends and Shaping the Future. In *E3S Web of Conferences* (Vol. 453, p. 01044). EDP Sciences. 10.1051/e3sconf/202345301044

Chandel, A., & Kaur, T. (2022). Demystifying neuromarketing: a bibliometric analysis using vosviewer. In *Developing Relationships, Personalization, and Data Herald in Marketing 5.0* (pp. 256-283). IGI Global. 10.4018/978-1-6684-4496-2.ch016

Chen, L., Chen, P., & Lin, Z. (2020). Artificial intelligence in education: A review. *IEEE Access : Practical Innovations, Open Solutions*, 8, 75264–75278. 10.1109/ACCESS.2020.2988510

Chiu, T. K., & Chai, C. (2020). undefined. *Sustainability*, 12(14), 5568. 10.3390/su12145568

Cooper, G. (2023). Examining science education in ChatGPT: An exploratory study of generative artificial intelligence. *Journal of Science Education and Technology*, 32(3), 444–452. 10.1007/s10956-023-10039-y

Dogan, M. E., Goru Dogan, T., & Bozkurt, A. (2023). The use of artificial intelligence (AI) in online learning and distance education processes: A systematic review of empirical studies. *Applied Sciences (Basel, Switzerland)*, 13(5), 3056. 10.3390/app13053056

Donthu, N., Kumar, S., Mukherjee, D., Pandey, N., & Lim, W. M. (2021). How to conduct a bibliometric analysis: An overview and guidelines. *Journal of Business Research*, 133, 285–296. 10.1016/j.jbusres.2021.04.070

Fütterer, T., Fischer, C., Alekseeva, A., Chen, X., Tate, T., Warschauer, M., & Gerjets, P. (2023). ChatGPT in education: Global reactions to AI innovations. *Scientific Reports*, 13(1), 15310. Advance online publication. 10.1038/s41598-023-42227-637714915

Gouvea, J. S. (2024). Ethical dilemmas in current uses of AI in science education. *CBE Life Sciences Education*, 23(1), fe3. 10.1187/cbe.23-12-023938232237

Holmes, W., Porayska-Pomsta, K., Holstein, K., Sutherland, E., Baker, T., Shum, S. B., Santos, O. C., Rodrigo, M. T., Cukurova, M., Bittencourt, I. I., & Koedinger, K. R. (2021). Ethics of AI in education: Towards a community-wide framework. *International Journal of Artificial Intelligence in Education*, 32(3), 504–526. 10.1007/s40593-021-00239-1

Holmes, W., Porayska-Pomsta, K., Holstein, K., Sutherland, E., Baker, T., Shum, S. B., Santos, O. C., Rodrigo, M. T., Cukurova, M., Bittencourt, I. I., & Koedinger, K. R. (2021). Ethics of AI in education: Towards a community-wide framework. *International Journal of Artificial Intelligence in Education*, 32(3), 504–526. 10.1007/s40593-021-00239-1

Holmes, W., Porayska-Pomsta, K., Holstein, K., Sutherland, E., Baker, T., Shum, S. B., Santos, O. C., Rodrigo, M. T., Cukurova, M., Bittencourt, I. I., & Koedinger, K. R. (2021). Ethics of AI in education: Towards a community-wide framework. *International Journal of Artificial Intelligence in Education*, 32(3), 504–526. 10.1007/s40593-021-00239-1

Huang, D. (2024). undefined. *Applied Mathematics and Nonlinear Sciences*, 9(1). 10.2478/amns-2024-0835

Huang, J., Saleh, S., & Liu, Y. (2021). A review on artificial intelligence in education. *Academic Journal of Interdisciplinary Studies, 10*(3).

Hwang, G., & Chien, S. (2022). Definition, roles, and potential research issues of the metaverse in education: An artificial intelligence perspective. *Computers and Education: Artificial Intelligence*, 3, 100082. 10.1016/j.caeai.2022.100082

Hwang, G., & Chien, S. (2022). Definition, roles, and potential research issues of the metaverse in education: An artificial intelligence perspective. *Computers and Education: Artificial Intelligence*, 3, 100082. 10.1016/j.caeai.2022.100082

Ismail, F., Tan, E., Rudolph, J., Crawford, J., & Tan, S. (2023). Artificial intelligence in higher education. A protocol paper for a systematic literature review. *Journal of Applied Learning and Teaching*, 6(2).

Khosravi, H., Shum, S. B., Chen, G., Conati, C., Tsai, Y. S., Kay, J., & Gašević, D. (2022). Explainable artificial intelligence in education. *Computers and Education: Artificial Intelligence*, 3, 100074.

Kim, J., Lee, H., & Cho, Y. H. (2022). Learning design to support student-AI collaboration: Perspectives of leading teachers for AI in education. *Education and Information Technologies*, 27(5), 6069–6104. 10.1007/s10639-021-10831-6

Kingchang, T., Chatwattana, P., & Wannapiroon, P. (2024). Artificial intelligence chatbot platform: AI chatbot platform for educational recommendations in higher education. *International Journal of Information and Education Technology (IJIET)*, 14(1), 34–41. 10.18178/ijiet.2024.14.1.2021

Lazarus, M. D., Truong, M., Douglas, P., & Selwyn, N. (2022). Artificial intelligence and clinical anatomical education: Promises and perils. *Anatomical Sciences Education*, 17(2), 249–262. 10.1002/ase.222136030525

Lee, H. S., & Lee, J. (2021). Applying artificial intelligence in physical education and future perspectives. *Sustainability (Basel)*, 13(1), 351. 10.3390/su13010351

Li, Z., Qi, H., Zhang, S., & Ding, J. (2024). Enhancement of students' cognitive ability in civics informational education in colleges and universities in the era of artificial intelligence. *Applied Mathematics and Nonlinear Sciences*, 9(1), 20240671. 10.2478/amns-2024-0671

Mohd Rahim, N. I., & Iahad, A., N., Yusof, A. F., & A. Al-Sharafi, M. (2022). AI-based chatbots adoption model for higher-education institutions: A hybrid PLS-SEM-Neural network modelling approach. *Sustainability*, 14(19), 12726. 10.3390/su141912726

Moher, D., Liberati, A., Tetzlaff, J., & Altman, D. G. (2009). Preferred reporting items for systematic reviews and meta-analyses: The PRISMA statement. *Annals of Internal Medicine*, 151(4), 264–269. 10.7326/0003-4819-151-4-200908180-0013519622511

Nuseir, T., M., Basheer, M. F., & Aljumah, A. (2020). Antecedents of entrepreneurial intentions in smart city of Neom Saudi Arabia: Does the entrepreneurial education on artificial intelligence matter? *Cogent Business & Management*, 7(1), 1825041. 10.1080/23311975.2020.1825041

Roll, I., & Wylie, R. (2016). Evolution and revolution in artificial intelligence in education. *International Journal of Artificial Intelligence in Education*, 26(2), 582–599. 10.1007/s40593-016-0110-3

Rudolph, T. (2023). War of the chatbots: Bard, Bing chat, ChatGPT, Ernie and beyond. The new AI gold rush and its impact on higher education. *1*, 6(1). 10.37074/jalt.2023.6.1.23

Su, J., & Yang, W. (2023). AI literacy curriculum and its relation to children's perceptions of robots and attitudes towards engineering and science: An intervention study in early childhood education. *Journal of Computer Assisted Learning*, 40(1), 241–253. 10.1111/jcal.12867

Su, J., & Zhong, Y. (2022). Artificial intelligence (AI) in early childhood education: Curriculum design and future directions. *Computers and Education: Artificial Intelligence*, 3, 100072. 10.1016/j.caeai.2022.100072

Tang, C. (2023). *Innovation of ideological and political education based on artificial intelligence technology with wireless network*. ICST Transactions on Scalable Information Systems. 10.4108/eetsis.3829

Wardat, Y., Tashtoush, M., Alali, R., & Saleh, S. (2024). Artificial intelligence in education: Mathematics teachers' perspectives, practices and challenges. *Iraqi Journal For Computer Science and Mathematics*, 5(1), 60–77. 10.52866/ijcsm.2024.05.01.004

Yang, Q., Yuan, Y., Sun, J., & Cai, K. (2011). Semantic P2P-based learning resources personalized recommendation system design. *2011 Third Pacific-Asia Conference on Circuits, Communications and System (PACCS)*. IEEE. 10.1109/PACCS.2011.5990360

Yang, W. (2022). Artificial intelligence education for young children: Why, what, and how in curriculum design and implementation. *Computers and Education: Artificial Intelligence*, 3, 100061. 10.1016/j.caeai.2022.100061

Yi, J. (2023). Design and development of personalized education information management system based on artificial intelligence. *Applied Mathematics and Nonlinear Sciences*, 9(1), 20230633. 10.2478/amns.2023.2.00633

Zhang, C., & Liu, Z., B.R., A., & A, H. (. (2024). Synergizing language learning: Smalltalk AI in industry 4.0 and education 4.0. *PeerJ. Computer Science*, 10, e1843. 10.7717/peerj-cs.184338435575

Chapter 12
Role of Artificial Intelligence in Strategic Debt Sustainability Planning

Shveta Gupta
Chitkara University, India

Gurwinder Singh Badal
Chitkara University, India

Dhiresh Kulshrestha
Chitkara University, India

ABSTRACT

Artificial intelligence is being utilised to discover fiscal hazards, shady tendencies and patterns, and dangerous entities in revenue creation. Previously, public debt was regarded as a vital tool for temporarily increasing revenue or purchasing power in exchange for the government's commitment to repay the main sum borrowed and, in most cases, interest on that principal. However, it has now become a permanent feature. The purpose of the government borrowing is to fill up the gap between the government revenue and proposed spending for the fiscal year. The objective of the study is to examine the significance of artificial intelligence in estimating the public debt on fiscal deficit of the government's, and to examine the trends in the revenue and fiscal deficits, with the view to identify the factors responsible for the same. The secondary data has been collected from Union Government's budget documents of various years. Further economic surveys and various other publications of Government of India, RBI, and other regulatory bodies has also been used to collect data and other relevant information. To analyse the collected data, statistical techniques such as solow model, trend regression analysis, and ratio analysis etc., has been used. The analysis results found that liabilities and debt in relation to GSDP have been increasing, and this has been particularly noticeable throughout the UDAY scheme's execution era and efficiency can be achieved with the use of AI in the field. However, the debt-to-GDP ratio is significantly below the 25% target set by the fourteenth finance commission.

DOI: 10.4018/979-8-3693-6660-8.ch012

Copyright ©2024, IGI Global. Copying or distributing in print or electronic forms without written permission of IGI Global is prohibited.

INTRODUCTION AND LITERATURE REVIEW

The use of AI in debt sustainability of governments has consistently been a key field of study in public economics in recent scenario, for trans-borders as well as within a country at the sub-national level. However, the wider definition of sustainability does not provide a complete and accurate status of the fiscal health of federal systems. While the level of debt conveys the accumulated effect of governments borrowings due to the expenditure - revenue incompatibility, its size and composition are influenced by a number of other fiscal indicators. It is like a chain of events involving several policy variables, with the result being sustainability of debt. (Renjith and Shanmugam, 2020).

Hassan, H., & Akhter, A. (2014) examined the connection between budget deficit and growth of economy. They focused on connections between GDP relapsed with real interest rate, deficit in budget and gross investment from 1976 to 2012. The authors analysed data using Vector Error Correction, ADF (Augmented Dickey–Fuller) and Johansen Co-integration Model at second stage. Results state significant negative effects of deficit in budget on growth of economy of Bangladesh.

Bhoir, R. B., & Dayre, S. R. (2015) analysed the influence of fiscal deficit on of the Indian economic growth during 1991-2014. Among the concerned variables, no significant relationship was found under the method of OLS. The study suggests that the Indian Government must focus on indices of human development, like health, infrastructure development and education to boost the productivity of physical and human capital which in turn will fast-track growth in economy.

Nayab (2015) analysed the effects of Deficit in budget on development of economy for Pakistan using the technique of VAR granger causality test, co-integration technique and technique of vector error correction 1976 to 2007. The Discoveries demonstrate that there is significant +ve effect of budgetary deficit on Economic development. The author also asserted that the outcomes of his study are in sustenance with Keynesian views on budgetary deficit.

Navaratnam, R., & Mayandy, K. (2016) analysed the fiscal deficit effects and its impact on the economy for Bangladesh, Sri Lanka, Nepal and Pakistan and India for 1980 to 2014. Time series annual data was collected for the purpose. The analysis uses the techniques of econometric such as Granger causality test & co-integration to analyze the relation between variables selected under study. The outcomes confirm that the fiscal deficit has negatively affected the growth of these countries economically except Nepal, which has positive impact.

Ramu MR, A., & Gayithri, K. (2016) aimed to examine both the longrun and shortrun relationship between the growth and fiscal deficit of Indian economy for the period of 1971 to 2012. The study was done through the techniques of Johansen's co-integration test, VECM (Vector error Correction Model), and Granger causality Test. Study concluded that the fiscal deficits have a negative impact on GDP, lending support to the neoclassical theory. It contends that lowering the revenue deficit component of the fiscal deficit can boost capital formation and inspire private sector for more investment. The paper's control variables, had a positive relationship with GDP, whereas the rate of exchange and revenue from taxes had a negative relationship. The authors advocate "Golden Rule" for the public finance, arguing that for the formation of capital fiscal deficit should be used.

Objectives and Methods

1. To analyze the role of AI in estimating significance of public debt on fiscal deficit of the State Government of Haryana.

2. To examine the trends in the revenue and fiscal deficits through artificial intelligence, with the view to identify the factors responsible for the same.

The secondary data has been collected from Union Government's budget documents of various years. Further Economic Survey and various other publications of Government of India, RBI and other regulatory bodies has also been used to collect data and other relevant information. To analyse the collected data, statistical techniques such as Solow Model, Trend regression analysis and ratio analysis etc., has been used.

AI in Revenue Estimation for Long-Term Fiscal Deficit Reduction Plans

By utilising artificial intelligence and big data to discover fiscal hazards, shady tendencies and patterns, and dangerous entities in revenue creation, the fiscal sector has benefited from the advancement of technology. The future is projected to involve data analytics and artificial intelligence (AI). Thus, the Indian government is implementing technological advances in an intricate system like taxation in order to streamline tax filing more efficient and devoid of official prudence that is beneficial to both businesses and taxpayers. The government launched a project in 2021 called Advanced Analytics in Indirect Taxes, which makes use of both big data and artificial intelligence. The three goals of ADVAIT are to increase indirect tax income, broaden the base of taxpayers, and enhance data-driven tax policy.

In their daily work, fiscal responsibility law enforcers' use ADVAIT to help with everything from reporting taxation and adhering to finding tax evasion. With the 3 I's—Information, Insights, and Intelligence—in mind, ADVAIT was created, based on expertise data nature using some of the most cutting-edge analytics and solutions to problems in the world.

Role of AI in Revenue Estimation

Some uses of AI and data analytics in decision making for fiscal policymakers: Selecting situations for further examination that have a high chance of income increase and an elevated chance of tax evasion. Identifying taxpayers to whom push revenue tax notifications should be sent. Asking individual taxpayers about transactions that appear to be inconsistent with their Income Tax forms (ITR) so that those taxpayers can update their forms. Fiscal responsibility law enforcement personnel use big data tools to store information and conduct efficient searches. Using information analytics over frameworks of individuals and businesses to identify prospective transactions with potential risks and display the links between the general population. Using predictive analytics tools to segment individuals and businesses in order to concentrate the outreach effort on cases with a high likelihood of engaging in tax evasion.

Debt Sustainability

In every economy, total debt and liabilities are a significant macroeconomic metric for assessing sustainable government finances or the way in which the debt can be handled by these governments. The paper investigates many facets of debt and its long-term viability. Debt-sustainability can be defined as the capacity of a State to refund the government's credit and pay the debt maintenance expenses. Debt sustainability is mathematically represented in the Solow growth model as follows:

$\Delta b = b(r-y) - z$

Here the b = Ratio of Debt to GSDP
Δ = Change in b
r = Rate of Interest
y = GSDP Real Rate of Growth
z = Primary Surplus.

It means that the debt-to-GSDP ratio will drop whenever there is a primary surplus, which means debt can be governed and can be paid out of the own resources of the State. But it might increase, so that it could not be sustainable in the presence of a primary deficit. Secondly, irrespective of whether a country has a primarily deficit or surplus, it is possible to lower the debt-to-GDP ratio if the interest rates are below the actual growth rate for GSDP.

Table 1. Debt sustainability and fiscal variables

Year	Debt/GSDP	Interest Rates	Real GDP Growth Rate	Primary Deficit/ GSDP
2005 - 2006	15.161	10.97	9.2	-1.67
2006 - 2007	13.515	11.3	11.22	-2.68
2007 - 2008	11.225	11.69	8.45	-0.71
2008 - 2009	10.369	10.29	8.17	2.31
2009 - 2010	11.104	9.7	11.72	3.31
2010 - 2011	11.071	10.4	-	1.52
2011 - 2012	11.941	10.02	-	1.05
2012 - 2013	12.699	9.74	7.74	1.62
2013 - 2014	13.857	9.66	8.18	0.61
2014 - 2015	14.631	9.75	5.72	1.28
2015 - 2016	18.696	8.38	9	4.55
2016 - 2017	20.478	8.46	8.75	2.89
2017-2018	23.303	8.38	7.24	0.88
2018-2019	23.439	8.71	6.5	0.78
2019-2020	24.34	8.98	3.7	0.21
2020-2021 (Actuals)	23.93	8.77	-5.7	1.53
2021-2022(RE)	24.98	8.41	6.8	1.38
2022-2023(BE)	24.52	8.11	9.8	1.41

Author's Compilation from EPWRF data till 2019-20 and Budgetary documents of Haryana 2019 & 2020 for the years 2019-20, 2020-21 Actual, 2021-22 Revised and 2022-23 Budgeted Estimates.

Table 1 depicts that it was only in 2009-10 and 2015-16 during the study period that the rate of interest was less than real GDP growth rate and it is expected that 2022-23 also it would be less than real GSDP growth rate It also demonstrates the nominal fall in debt-to-GSDP ratio in 2010-11 due to the lower interest rates as compared to Real GDP growth rate in 2009-10 but unfortunately States were unable lower the debt-to-GSDP after 2015-16.

Figure 1. Public debt mechanism through fiscal variables

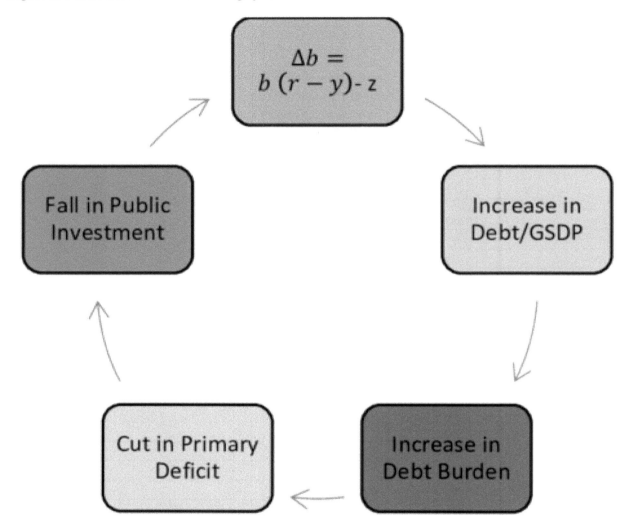

Sustainability of debt was examined using multiple criteria including interest and effective interest rates; rates of growth for GSDP; and debt to GDP ratios, total expenditure and total revenue, government's income, all the liabilities and debt.

For the measurement of total debt of Haryana Government, total liabilities outstanding are utilized by the State government amounts to Rs. 1,67,681 crores by end of March 2018. (RE). It is anticipated that Rs. 1,88,501 crores will be reached by 2018-2019 according to recent budget recommendations.

Results and Predictions for a Sustainable Debt Strategic Plan

Table highlights the findings for several fiscal variables as well as the debt-to-GDP ratio. At the revenue section, its own-tax-revenue (State) is expanding at a 14.2 percent of steady rate. During 2005-06 and 2016-17, the share of state in Central-taxes increased by 17.6 percent, and Central-grants increased by more than 15 percent. Non-tax revenue in the state, on the other hand, has been rising at a slightly slower rate of roughly 13.3 percent. According to the Centre's assurance, SGST will likely climb by at least 14 percent over the first five years. Overall, it is anticipated that there would be an increase by around 15.1 percent throughout the time under consideration of State's 'Non-debt-capital-receipts'. We believe it will continue to grow at this rate. Given prior patterns, the SGDP in nominal terms is expected to expand at a rate of 15.4 percent.

Table 2. Predictions based on trends regression from the period 2005 to 2019

Items	Trend ROG	2020	2021	2022	2023	2024	2025
OTR	0.1258	637.7	717.9	808.3	910	1024.5	1153.4
ONTR	0.0701	134.6	144	154.1	164.9	176.5	188.9
SGST	0.14	185.5	211.5	241.1	274.8	313.3	357.1
SCT	0.1558	129.2	149.4	172.7	199.6	230.6	266.6
CG	0.1508	92	105.9	121.9	140.3	161.4	185.8
TRE	0.1478	1184	1359	1559.8	1790.2	2054.7	2358.3
Interest Payment	0.1552	183.3	211.7	244.6	282.5	326.4	377
TE	0.1485	1419	1629.7	1871.7	2149.5	2468.6	2835
Non-Debt Receipts	0.1108	1047	1163.3	1292.2	1435.4	1594.5	1771.1
Public Debt	0.1792	2325	2742	3233	3812	4495	5301
(Public Debt) – Power Sector Debt	0.1715	1862	2182	2556	2994	3507	4108
GFD = Total Exp – Non-Debt Receipts		371.8	466.43	579.45	714.1	874.13	1063.9
GSDP	0.1444	9118	10435	11941	13665	15637	17895
(Public Debt)/GSDP (%)	Pessimistic	25.5	26.27	27.07	27.9	28.75	29.62
(Public Debt - Power Bonds)/GDP (%)	Optimistic	20.42	20.91	21.4	21.91	22.43	22.96
Interest Payment/T Exp.	Percent	12.9	13	13.1	13.1	13.2	13.3
Interest Payments /Non-Debt Receipts	Percent	17.5	18.2	18.9	19.7	20.5	21.3
Interest Payment /GSDP	Percent	2.01	2.03	2.05	2.07	2.09	2.11
GFD/GSDP	Percent	4.08	4.47	4.85	5.23	5.59	5.95
Interest Payment /Public Debt	Percent	7.9	7.7	7.6	7.4	7.3	7.1

Author's Calculations

Although on the side of spending, we see that expenditure of total-revenue, and total-expenditure' is growing at 16.4 percent and 16.9 percent, respectively.

So, based on the average growth of spending and revenue, table predicted that 'Gross-fiscal-deficit' will steadily grow and may exceed four percent by this year i.e., 2022-23, and 4.5 percent by 2024-25 and thereafter.

In terms of public debt, it is likely to grow as well. The Pessimistic scenario examines the Haryana Government debt-to-GSDP ratio considering Power sector Borrowings; while the Optimistic scenario examines the Haryana Government debt-to-GSDP ratio excluding Power sector Borrowings. This is based on the assumption that the both the Governments at Central and State levels will take exclusive care to encourage economic instruments to consider the fiscal consequences of the 'UDAY' plan, that has increased the State's-fiscal-deficit and even the Debt: GSDP ratio.

The Optimistic study predicts that the debt-to-GDP ratio (excluding Power sector Borrowings) would be in specified limit by 2025-26, reaching a peak of 25%.

If ignored, the state's debt problem is certain to worsen with time. As can be seen, the Pessimistic scenario indicates that the state's Public-Debt to SGDP ratio may exceed 31 percent by 2025-26. But it has been observed that Haryana has been one of the finer financially managed states, and there are no reasons to believe the state would not be able to maintain its status and remain fiscally careful.

Apart from the debt, the problem payments of interest must be resolved. Interest payments are expected to climb in tandem with the debt amount. It is expected that by 2025- 26 there will be an increase of 16% 'Non-Debt-Receipts'. This is not a vigorous trend, and the state exchequer needs to be carefully managed. As previously stated, it will have an immediate impact on the State's fiscal deficit. This will decrease the budgetary flexibility of the subsequent government, necessitating corrective action by the Finance Commission and the Centre to ensure that the state's finances are in profound figure for the years ahead.

Payments of interests as a percentage of total-expenditure are expected to climb at a gradual rate, rising from 11.6 percent in 2017-18 to around 12.7 percent in 2025-26. This would be unlikely to pose severe problem for administration, but debt repayment is definitely a major concern that requires sufficient attention.

The country, including the states, are confronting significant challenges as a result of the introduction of the demonetization and GST. The policy initiatives appear to have boosted the expansion of the economy's formal sector, but the informal economy has taken a hit, with negative consequences for jobs and income in this sector. The informal sector employs disproportionately poorer portions of the population, and when their earnings decrease, so does the economy's 'aggregate demand.' That is one of the reasons why private-sector investments are not taking up, and growth requires get-up-and-go motivation from investment by public-sector, which the central Government is doing its noblest to provide. It is the task for governments to ensure that incomes at the lowermost end of the distribution rise, as this will assure rising demand along with vicious cycle of growth. It could also assist to reduce the prevalence of poverty with in state, which has a higher 'Head-Count-ratio' despite having a per capita income at higher level.

The study suggests that inequalities with in state have increased for last decade, while all of the pitiable states have the contradictory response during the same time (Tendulkar Report, 2014).

As previously revealed, Haryana ranks quite low in social indicators, & by developing its social infrastructure, it might not only spur economic growth but also enhance the wellbeing of people. Policy-makers in the state must recognize that the economy and society must work together to enhance the state's overall status. The time has come for the public to build and upgrade infrastructure in order to improve not only economic but even social outcomes, as others, like Southern and Western successors have done.

The state of Haryana is relatively a tinier state as compared to India's geographical side, which contributes almost 3.6% to India's Gross Domestic product (GDP). Haryana has been constantly in deficit since 2008-2009. Fiscal deficit prevailing with a very high trend of growth rate expenditure namely interest payment and a huge debt burden in the power sector worsen the situation. These situations are the red flags of the Haryana state finance. The Finance Commission of the State mentioned that "Haryana's outstanding debt has seen an increasing trend in the growth rate of 20.2% between 2011-12 to 2018-19, and the debt-gross state domestic product (GSDP) ratio also increased from 18.33% in 2011-12 to 25.09% in 2018-19".

FINDINGS AND CONCLUSION

- Liabilities & Debt in relation to GSDP have been adding, and it has been particularly noticeable throughout the UDAY scheme's execution era. However, the debt-to-GDP ratio is significantly below the 25% target set by the Fourteenth Finance Commission.
- Growth rate & Debt Ratios in relation to gross domestic product (GSDP). Non-Debt-receipts and Total-expenditure were both more than one in the majority of study years.
- Debt servicing Burden has also been increasing, suggesting that sustainability in debt may come up as major issue in the coming years.
- Debt as a %age of non-debt-receipts was also excessively high and must be reduced.
- Furthermore, all through the study period, effective rates of interest are significantly smaller than those of Real GSDP growth rates, implying that debt may be sustainable.
- In 2014-15 and 2015-16, the debt-to-GDP ratio was less than 20%, and the fiscal deficit-to-GDP ratio was less than 3.25 percent, but both exceeded targets in later years due to the implementation of the UDAY plan.

The examination of Haryana state deficit shows that its accomplishments in the last decade 2006-2016 has enhanced compared to the post economic reforms period. However, as compared to other high-income states, Haryana's relative position has deteriorated. This state is not as futile as other states in refining its budgetary performance. As a result, one could argue that the potential exists and efforts must be made in right direction to achieve them.

Limitations

- Only selected direct and indirect taxes were taken for analysis on the basis of their significance in the research work, keeping objectives in mind and the size of amount contributed to the total revenue.
- The necessary data for this study have been collected from various secondary sources. The data for the last two years of the study are revised and budgeted estimates. The conclusions arrived at this study are subject to the limitations of the data.
- The data for few latest years is unavailable due to COVID-19 situation. Thus, when required, only available data has been used to arrive at various conclusions.
- The statistical tools of regression analysis have been employed in this study. The conclusions arrived at this study are subject to the limitations of the regression models.
- The study is restricted to the State of Haryana in India.

REFERENCES

Abhishek, A. (2019). Contribution of Agriculture, Industry, and Services on GDP in Recent Years. *Journal of Emerging Technologies and Innovative Research, 6*(5), 464-468.

Bernardi, L., & Fraschini, A. (2005). *Tax system and Tax Reforms in India*. Department of Public Policy and Public Choice.

Bhargava, D. P K (2007). Deteriorating Fiscal Measurement of States in India: Remedial Measures Needed. Thakur, Anil Kumar and M D Abdus Salam (ed.), *Indian Public Finance and Twelfth Finance Commission*. Deep and Deep Publishers, New Delhi.

Chakraborty, P. (2017). *Analysis of State Budgets 2017-18: Emerging Issues, NIPFP.*

Chaudhury, R. (2013). *Estimating True Fiscal Capacity of States and Devising a Suitable Rule for Granting Debt Relief based on Optimal Growth Requirement*. Fourteenth FC, Jadavpur University.

ADB. (n.d.). *Debt Dynamics, Fiscal Deficit, and Stability in Government Borrowing in India: A Dynamic Panel Analysis*. Asian Development Bank Institute https://www.adb.org/sites/default/files/publication/181400/adbi-wp557.pdf

Dhanasekaram, K. B. (2006). Sustaining the Finances of State Governments. In Srivastava, D. K., & Narasimhulu, M. (Eds.), *State Level Fiscal Reforms in the Indian Economy*. Deep and Deep Publication Pvt. Ltd.

Dhiresh, K. (2013). Relationship between economic growth and public expenditure through Wagner's law: an analytical study in Indian perspective. *International Journal of Entrepreneurship & Business Environment Perspectives, 2*(4).

Dhiresh, K. (2019). An Econometric Analysis of Agricultural Production and Economic Growth in India. *Indian Journal of Marketing*, 49(11), 56. 10.17010/ijom/2019/v49/i11/148276

Jana, P. (2009), *Review of the Compliance of the Provisions of the Haryana Fiscal Responsibility and Budget Management Act*. NIPFP.

Kapila, U. (2003). *"Fiscal Reforms in India: Policy Measures and Development", Indian Economy since Independence*. Academic Foundation Publication.

Nayyar, V. (2023). The role of marketing analytics in the ethical consumption of online consumers. *Total Quality Management & Business Excellence*, 34(7-8), 1015–1031. 10.1080/14783363.2022.2139676

Nayyar, V., Sugiat, M., Singla, B., Rojhe, K. C., & Sharma, S. (2023, August). Influence of Technology in Measuring the Purchase Intention of Indian Consumer. In *2023 International Conference on Digital Business and Technology Management (ICONDBTM)* (pp. 1-6). IEEE. 10.1109/ICONDBTM59210.2023.10327147

Sen, T., & Rao, R. K. (2000). *State Fiscal Studies*. NIPFP Study for World Bank.

Shveta, G. (2022). Review of Haryana State Spending Strategies and Growth Prospects. *International Journal of Research and Analytical Reviews, 9*(4), 663-672.

Chapter 13
Rise of Artificial Intelligence in Marketing:
Strategies for Ethical Implementation

Jaswinder Pal Singh
https://orcid.org/0000-0001-5515-6051
Chitkara University, Punjab, India

Neha Mishra
Chitkara University, Punjab, India

ABSTRACT

The chapter provides an overview of the wide-ranging impact of artificial intelligence (AI) on commercial opportunities, emphasizing its various applications and ethical considerations. It discusses AI's role in enhancing industry efficiency, banking transactions, marketing, and beyond, while also addressing concerns such as bias, discrimination, and data protection. The chapter underscores the importance of AI ethics and the need for responsible development and usage, as highlighted by the implementation of AI codes of ethics by tech companies. It further explores major ethical issues related to autonomous AI systems, including machine bias, privacy concerns, and job displacement, particularly in the marketing industry. Additionally, it mentions the European Commission's efforts to establish ethical principles for trustworthy AI and the legal implications of AI marketing, such as data privacy and consumer protection laws. Finally, it suggests the role of government and regulators in setting AI marketing technology laws to ensure fair competition and market practices.

INTRODUCTION

One of the technology developments that significantly impacted marketing is artificial intelligence (AI)(Winecoff & Watkins, 2022). It's rewriting the rule book on how businesses evaluate data and engage with customers, providing great competitive personalization and maximizing operational efficiency by harnessing data at scale and using state-of-the-art algorithms(Author & Maglaras, 2022). Given the numerous ethical dilemmas this reality triggers, a thorough review of the intersections between AI and

DOI: 10.4018/979-8-3693-6660-8.ch013

ethical marketing seems necessary. The list of concerns is long: privacy, algorithmic bias, data security (Huang & Yu, 2022).

The moral consideration revolving about AI in the field of marketing besides the transparency and the benefits of its usage is prevailing(Mogaji et al., 2021). The authors have provoked ethical interrogations of the AI-powered predictive marketing in this instance(Latham & Goltz, 2019). Esteemed moral instructions for multifarious AI challenges are also dealt with. On the contrary, it provides a sagacious vision on the ethical awareness and underlines the predicament of ethical ambition in the AI business(Wang, 2011). The mightier Technology for marketing AI must hence cling to the veracity of contemporary technology and should be fastened with the bow of moral conditions to ensure the soundness of the business well-being aspects alongside an evisceration to a moderate version of the public to reckon with(Guyo et al., 2023).

That is why it is crucial to scrutinize the ethics of the various AI systems used in marketing campaigns in this field. Concerns about the responsibility of increasingly independent AI systems have been growing, especially in instances where these systems' judgments could affect customers' privacy and consent(S. et al., 2023). As we rely more heavily on algorithmic processes, worries about AI decision-making's transparency and interpretability are mounting, potentially further isolating companies from their consumers(Campbell et al., 2020). This means we need to find ways to enhance the adoption of AI in marketing for targeted assistance while also addressing ethical concerns and data protection simultaneously. When employing AI for marketing purposes, one of the principals you should hold onto is ethical standards (Author & Maglaras, 2022). It is also crucial to form a moral code that thinks about the societal duties of each individual as well as their personal array of values.

The field of marketing and advertising frequently generates ethical and social dilemmas. Problems that arise relate to privacy, data security, bias, and transparency. Research findings suggest that AI models and data sets should not perpetuate unfairness or bias and must be transparent(Vlačić et al., 2021). It has become critical for enterprises to use varied information when calibration experiments though auditions are essential.

An example of this is the proposal of a new certification mechanism for AI-powered marketing systems at companies, in an attempted consider of the issues(Hermann et al., 2023). A program which strives to establish methods for evaluating marketing systems based on the criteria of acknowledged ethics, to boost customer trust and assure that companies of all scales are all playing by the identical rules(Saadi & Azdimousa, 2024). This program would thus be focused on the significance of AI marketing tricks and the ways in which the ethics of marketing could be altered by these mechanisms. The primary motive for this certification program is to assure that marketing technology further develops the industry while still maintaining its primary objective of holding all marketing systems, within the confines of ethical standards, sound and secure(Sharma & Sharma, 2023; Volkmar et al., 2022).

ARTIFICIAL INTELLIGENCE

The pursuit of artificial intelligence (AI) is fundamentally about creating computer systems with cognitive capabilities that are comparable to those of humans. "Artificial intelligence" is the expression that is used to describe the steps that are being taken to make computers perform tasks that require human intelligence a very practical way of doing it(Davenport et al., 2020; Sahai & Rath, 2021). Artificial intelligence is having a great impact on many different industries for example, steering in medicine from general diagnostics and treatment programs, to far more individualize and precise diagnostics and treatment plans(Drabiak, 2022; Kuzlu et al., 2023).In the banking industry, artificial intelligence is employed for both fraud detection and risk assessment(Hentzen et al., 2022). Although AI's benefits are widely understood, its implications for issues such as data protection and for discrimination and bias and the questions these may raise, for example about fairness and manipulation are less easily acknowledged(R. Kumar & Sharma, 2023).Like numerous other sectors, artificial intelligence (AI) is transforming marketing. Never have we seen such potential for AI to automate human interaction, offering highly customized marketing strategies and analyzing customer behavior(Hermann, 2022; Vlačić et al., 2021). AI-driven systems can sift efficiently through enormous data troves.

Automated data processing yields insights that are ripe for the gathering, which can be deployed to recalibrate your business's marketing flair. But that's not all. Those same algorithms will make themselves useful by handling tedious tasks, allowing you to free up your team's time to think more creatively. Additionally, because these algorithms can interact with your clients in real-time, we can now personalize our marketing tactics in ways that were nearly impossible just few years ago(Rodgers & Nguyen, 2022). The rapid integration of AI into advertising gives rise to significant legal and ethical considerations. Issues such as algorithmic discrimination, user approval, and data security are merely the most visible of many others(Rodgers & Nguyen, 2022). Addressing and managing the ethical and legal concerns correlated with AI are vital to guarantee productive use within marketing campaigns(Su et al., 2023).

AI ethics has become increasingly crucial, and as such, experts in the field argue that two considerations need to be made. First, the creation and Integration of AI systems must serve the populations who utilize them, as well as the broader societies in which they function. Second, the development or integration between AI and human beings-based and other human values and interests depend on prior analyses of those values and interests(Hajrasouliha, 2023; Volkmar et al., 2022). There is widespread interest, both inside and outside Large Technological Corporations, in how to ensure AI serves ethically defensible human Goals and values(Hermann, 2022). Your working definition of AI ethics is meant to guide the various stakeholders Governments, Global Industries, and Academia world figures around AI and shape the conversations, laws, and regulations that will drive us to a future that augments what people can doforging responsible AI agents that are beneficial for all of us(Davenport et al., 2020; Mahmoudian, 2021).

There is a vast spectrum of potential uses and interpretations for the phrase artificial intelligence (AI). The so-called Turing test, often dubbed an "imitation game," was presented by Alan Turing in his now-famous 1950 article on the question of whether machines can think. This was done long before the term "artificial intelligence" was used. Instead of focusing on whether computers can do abstract reasoning, Turing suggested we look at the prospect of developing AI systems that could make people believe they were interacting with a real person (Turing 1950). John McCarthy, Marvin L. Minsky, Nathaniel Rochester, and Claude E. Shannon were among the scholars that conceptualized the phrase "artificial intelligence" in 1955 during the illustrious two-month summer workshop at Dartmouth College on the "Study of Artificial Intelligence" in 1956. It was at this event that the field of artificial intelligence was born(*Ethics of Artificial Intelligence | Internet Encyclopedia of Philosophy*, n.d.).

Some potential elements of a strong AI code of ethics include minimizing environmental risks, avoiding bias, and safeguarding user and data privacy. Companies can implement AI ethics through internal codes of conduct, or the government can establish regulatory frameworks(*AI Ethics: What It Is and Why It Matters | Coursera*, n.d.). In tackling ethical AI concerns on a global scale and laying the groundwork for ethical AI in companies, both approaches help regulate AI. Discussions over the ethics of artificial intelligence (AI) have spread beyond the spheres of academia and nonprofits. Meta, IBM, and Google, alongside other companies, have united to address the ethical issues raised by the collection of vast data sets(*AI Ethics: What It Is and Why It Matters | Coursera*, n.d.). At the same time, governmental and international bodies are formulating ethical policies and regulations that are rooted in academic research.

UNESCO: AI WITH A HUMAN RIGHTS LENS

In order to address the Ethics of AI in a way that prioritizes human rights, UNESCO has put out ten fundamental principles(*Ethics of Artificial Intelligence | UNESCO*, n.d.).
1. Proportionality and Do No Harm: The use of AI systems must not go beyond what is necessary to achieve a legitimate aim. Risk assessment should be used to prevent harms which may result from such uses.
2. Safety and Security: Unwanted harms (safety risks) as well as vulnerabilities to attack (security risks) should be avoided and addressed by AI actors.
3. Right to Privacy and Data Protection: Privacy must be protected and promoted throughout the AI lifecycle. Adequate data protection frameworks should also be established.
4. Multi-stakeholder and Adaptive Governance & Collaboration: International law & nationalsovereignty must be respected in the use of data. Additionally, participation of diversestakeholders is necessary for inclusive approaches to AI governance.
5. Responsibility and Accountability: AI systems should be auditable and traceable. There shouldbe oversight, impact assessment, audit and due diligence mechanisms in place to avoid conflictswith human rights norms and threats to environmental wellbeing.
6. Transparency and Explain ability: The ethical deployment of AI systems depends on themtransparency & explains ability (T&E). The level of T&E should be appropriate to the context, asthere may be tensions between T&E and other principles such as privacy, safety and security.
7. Human Oversight and Determination: Member States should ensure that AI systems do notdisplace ultimate human responsibility and accountability.
8. Sustainability: AI technologies should be assessed against their impacts on 'sustainability', understood as a set of constantly evolving goals including those set out in the UN's SustainableDevelopment Goals.
9. Awareness & Literacy: Public understanding of AI and data should be promoted through open& accessible education, civic engagement, digital skills & AI ethics training, media &information literacy.
10. Fairness and Non-Decimation: AI actors should promote social justice, fairness, and non-discrimination while taking an inclusive approach to ensure AI's benefits are accessible to all.

PLAYERS INVOLVED IN THE ETHICAL CONSIDERATIONS OF ARTIFICIAL INTELLIGENCE

Responsible use and development of artificial intelligence requires industry participants to work together to create ethical standards. The impact of AI on politics, economics, and society must be considered by all parties involved if we are to discover a peaceful coexistence of people and machines. Everyone included here is vital to the cause of making AI less prejudiced and safer.

Governments, corporations, and organizations rely on the data, theories, and concepts provided by academics and lecturers at academic institutions(*AI Ethics: What It Is and Why It Matters | Coursera*, n.d.).

The government can help advance AI ethics through its national committees and agencies. For example, the 2016 NSTC paper Preparing for the Future of Artificial Intelligence explains AI in relation to public involvement, legislation, administration, economics, and security, among other sectors(Bundy, 2017).

The United Nations and the World Bank are examples of international organizations (IGOs) charged with educating the public about AI ethics and reaching agreements on this matter. In November 2021, the 193 member states of UNESCO adopted the first-ever worldwide accord on the Ethics of AI, with the aim of preserving human rights and dignity(*Ethics of Artificial Intelligence | UNESCO*, n.d.).Bodies that do not aim to generate a profit: A number of organizations are actively seeking to diversify the AI field, including Black in AI and Queer in AI. The Asilomar AI Principles, a set of 23 points outlined by the Future of Life Institute, described the possible risks, challenges, and outcomes of AI systems(Caner & Bhatti, 2020; Neuwirth, 2022).Companies that use AI should form ethical committees and adhere to standards of behavior that have been put in place by private sector executives. This encompasses a wide range of sectors, from banking and consulting to healthcare and internet businesses like Meta and Google. Other companies might feel compelled to do the same(Busis et al., 2024).

ARTIFICIAL INTELLIGENCE AND TECHNOLOGY ACCEPTANCE

Researchers have spent a lot of effort attempting to figure out why and how end consumers embrace AI. To get better services and more accurate choices, consumers nowadays are more reliant on AI and are prepared to give up some degree of autonomy and control over their environment. As a result, scientists have been trying to predict how these innovations would affect people. For his research, Muller zeroed in on the future of artificial intelligence and the ethical concerns it poses(Bundy, 2017). For instance, AI's potential for harm is contingent on its application; in other words, it won't do any damage unless its primary goal is to serve consumers or the company.

In order to shed light on why people embrace AI and other information systems, numerous foundational theories in technology acceptance have emerged in the past ten years. To begin, a prime example of a theory that attempts to explain human behavior is the Theory of Reasoned Action (TRA)(Beatty & Kahle, 1988; Heller et al., 2013). This theory sets out to explain and predict consumer behavior based on two premises: the individual's attitude toward the behavior their positive or negative feelings about the behavior and subjective norms their perception of how their peers believe they should or should not behave (Bock & Kim, 2002).

Second, the adaption of TRA designed to address users' adoption of information system technology is the Technology adoption Model (TAM), which was introduced by Fred Davis in 1986(Davis, 1989; Venkatesh et al., 2003). By analyzing several elements that impact consumers' decisions, the theory seeks to provide light on why technologies are adopted or not. On the other hand, the writers here didn't include attitude among the main considerations. Aiming to forecast when and how users will implement IT systems, TAM evaluates perceived ease of use (how easy the system is supposed to be to use), perceived usefulness (how much people think the system will help them do their jobs better), and how these factors impact behavioral intention(Venkatesh et al., 2003).

As a last step, we have the third iteration of the Technology Acceptance Model (TAM). The realm of IT systems' acceptability was one that Venkatesh persisted in exploring. Whatever the case may be, the system's complexity and the fact that it grew integral to organizational operations mean that adoption of the technology continues to be a challenge for a number of businesses. Companies suffer huge losses due to the low adoption of systems. The variables that impact the perceived utility and perceived simplicity of use, which in turn affect the behavioral intention, are the primary emphasis of this theory. In conclusion, while fundamental theories of acceptance were worked out, data and privacy concerns have been brought up in relation to new information systems, particularly in relation to the introduction of AI. But none of the earlier ideas accounted for ethical considerations in their models.

CONCERNS ABOUT ARTIFICIAL INTELLIGENCE ETHICS IN MARKETING

The great introductions by do a good job of presenting the big ethical problems that AI presents to human society (Schneider, 2023; Vlačić et al., 2021).Autonomous AI systems already pose serious ethical concerns, regardless of how AI is conceptualized. Consider the following examples: machine bias in the legal system, hiring decisions based on smart algorithms, chatbots that promote racism and sexism, and language translations that do not aim to eliminate gender bias. Concerns regarding deceit arise from the idea of AI which is sometimes defined as a computer "imitating" human intelligence and its incorporation into robots with human-like appearance and behavior(Hajrasouliha, 2023; Kim & Wang, 2023; Vlačić et al., 2021). "The greater the freedom of a machine, the more it will need moral standards" as Rosalind Picard correctly points out(Lin et al., 2012). In the context of autonomous mobility, for instance, this lends credence to the idea that any contact between humans and AI systems inherently involves an ethical component.

Among the primary aims of machine ethics research is the concept of embedding ethics into machines (Lin et al., 2012). Autonomous artificial intelligence systems are taking over increasingly formerly human-dominated tasks because they can do them more quickly, with fewer interruptions and less oversight, as shown by the stellar results achieved by many systems after they have overcome the debugging phase.Given the potential for AI systems to eventually match or surpass human capabilities, some have argued that the incorporation of strong moral principles into these systems could determine humanity's continued existence. A "technological singularity" occurred at this juncture. Notable figures such as Stephen Hawking, an astronomer, and Nick Bostrom, a philosopher, have both expressed concern about the potential risks of technological singularity in the event that artificially intelligent robots rebel against their human makers(Saadi & Azdimousa, 2024; Sharma & Sharma, 2023; Volkmar et al., 2022). Consequently, creating AI that is welcoming to humans is crucial, says Nick Bostrom (Bundy, 2017). Finally, there are many reasons why AI systems must adhere to ethical principles: to safeguard humanity from existential threats, to eliminate bias, to create AI that is amiable and willing to embrace our values, and to ensure that humanity thrives.

AI ethics matter because AI technology is meant to augment or replace human intelligence, but when it replicates human life, human judgment concerns might creep into the technology(Hermann et al., 2023; Pascual & de Uribe Gil, 2023). AI projects based on biased or erroneous data can affect underprivileged groups and individuals. If AI algorithms and machine learning models are constructed too quickly, engineers and product managers may struggle to correct taught biases. To reduce hazards, a code of ethics is easier to implement during development. AI's rapid rise has created various worldwide opportunities, from healthcare diagnosis to social media connections to labor efficiency through automated activities(Hermann et al., 2023; Pascual & de Uribe Gil, 2023). However, these rapid developments present serious ethical issues. AI systems can embed prejudices, degrade climate, harm human rights, and more. AI threats have already exacerbated inequities, harming underprivileged populations.Data captures, where consumers give AI personal data, classification, when AI makes personalized predictions, delegation, when AI performs some tasks, and social, when consumers communicate with AI, make up consumer AI experience(Engelmann et al., 2022). Thus, consumers may have many AI encounters daily.AI technology like machine learning, speech recognition, and natural language processing help businesses make smarter decisions.

Several technologies with better inputs have quickly supplanted human decision-making, according to study(Monteiro, 2023). This breakthrough allows customers to profit from digital assistants' decisions, which efficiently match personal preferences with available options without the cognitive and affective fatigue of decision-making. However, research shows that consumers can also enjoy their own decisions, and when they believe they cannot, it can lead to negative reactions and consequences, affecting choice and happiness(Benjelloun & Kabak, 2024).

Ethical decision-making entails recognizing moral awareness and issues and assessing their circumstances(Altinigne, 2024; Campbell et al., 2020). AI delivers huge benefits when used ethically, minimizing technology misuse and underuse(Benjelloun & Kabak, 2024). It lets organizations use social ideals to determine what society considers moral. However, it helps firms foresee and avoid costly blunders from unethical or inappropriate actions.

ETHICAL IMPLICATIONS OF AI IN MARKETING: CHALLENGES AND SOLUTIONS

AI could improve marketing efficiency and effectiveness. However, the growing use of AI in marketing has raised ethical issues that must be addressed to ensure ethical use (Vassileva & Palamarova, 2020). This section discusses AI marketing ethics and remedies.

Discrimination Prejudice: AI marketing poses severe ethical questions about bias and discrimination. AI algorithms in targeted advertising present high-paying job ads to men more than women, reinforcing gender bias (Shazly et al., 2020). Human data that is biased in favor of one group is used to train AI. Because AI systems frequently reflect and magnify prejudiced human judgments, this is a major cause for concern. Biases based on gender and race is particularly prevalent. A variety of technical and social solutions have been proposed by the Harvard academics to assist businesses. One of these is the idea that businesses should form "red teams" with outside specialists to review their work and make sure they've considered all potential ramifications before releasing new technology(Neuwirth, 2022).

Privacy Violations: Artificial intelligence in the context of marketing has created a predicament that is imbued with problems associated with privacy. The issue itself pivots on the extent to which AI, in its current iteration, is capable of collecting significant volumes of personal data, such as an individual's browser history or an individual's purchasing habits, without the individuals in question simply becoming aware that this process is taking place (Kopalle et al., 2022).Utilizing sensitive consumer data for targeted marketing purposes could lead to two pretty serious consequences: identity theft and psychological manipulation. The diversification of one's approach in the digital era, however, helps preserve the privacy of our AI personalities. It means cultivating a strong sense of how to guard against digital villainy, which can be as commonplace as cutting your teeth or as intellectually challenging as performing brain surgery (Tyagi & Rathore, 2023). Work to achieve this sense of diversification in the online realm; build strong passwords, read up on privacy rules to ensure that you understand how your data is being used, and pay two-factor authentication forward.

Controlling Customer Behavior: AI systems analyze client behavior and preferences to create effective marketing campaigns. However, marketing can become unethical(Mehmood et al., 2023). Using AI for marketing manipulating consumer behavior produces new ethical issues, and worries. Consumers can be targeted using AI-powered marketing which allows advertisers to message to the right individual based on psychological profile(Singh et al., 2023). Businesses may use AI-powered marketing ethically to prevent manipulating consumer behavior (Davenport et al., 2020). Companies can match AI marketing algorithms with consumers' beliefs using ethical design. Transparent data collection and consumer notification rules are also options. Participatory design helps AI-powered marketing techniques respect consumer values and interests. AI with human engagement can provide businesses the best of both worlds(Mohd Rahim et al., 2022).

Displaced Jobs: AI-driven marketing improves efficiency and reaction, but employment loss raises ethical problems. Robots can replace workers and create inequality(Glebova et al., 2024). AI-powered chatbots and virtual assistants increased customer service but cut jobs. Rescaling and up skilling can help businesses address job displacement. These programs teach job-relevant skills for a changing workforce. Employees can switch positions or careers through programmers. Companies can hybridize AI's efficiency with human workers' emotional intelligence.

Social Isolation: The difficulties of AI marketing include no human connection. AI-Powered chatbots and virtual assistant provide quick, efficient customer support. However, with quick service comes lack of empathy which could make the consumer upset and disregarded(Hermann, 2022; Lipschultz, 2023). Employees should be trained on AI-Powered software to have a more personalized and empathic services(Matei & Done, 2013).

Cyber security: AI marketing raises cyber security concerns. All digital systems can be hacked, but AI algorithms are especially vulnerable to data manipulation, which can lead to incorrect decisions (Sahai & Rath, 2021). Cybercriminals target AI in marketing because it collects and processes plenty of data. AI-specific cyber security laws are sparse, complicating problems. Companies can reduce risks using multi-layered cyber security. Multi-factor authentication, encryption, and vulnerability assessments are examples (D. Kumar & Suthar, 2024).

Cultural and Social Impact: Marketing using AI could affect society and culture, generating ethical concerns. AI-driven marketing may foster cultural norms, prejudices, and institutional distrust. AI in marketing may propagate cultural norms and prejudices, a serious ethical issue (Backholer et al., 2021). Data may teach AI systems social norms and reinforce them in marketing. To solve this issue, businesses may set ethical standards for AI-powered marketing that promote fairness, diversity, and cultural understanding "European Commission's High-Level Expert Group on AI, 2021"(Neuwirth, 2022). To address this issue companies, need to draw up ethical guidelines for AI-powered marketing techniques emphasizing responsible AI use and company values and societal obligations.Emerging businesses can also monitor and review AI-powered marketing activities to discover any reaching or even exceeding of goals or values of the company.Blockchain may alleviate data ownership and management difficulties. Blockchain technology may make data ownership and use transparent and safe. By securely storing and exchanging data, Blockchain technologies may prevent data breaches and attacks(Kumar & Suthar, 2024).

Unexpected Outcomes: AI-powered marketing has "unintended consequences" when unintended. The future of AI is promising, but marketing algorithms may be surprising(Adarsh et al., 2023; Arango et al., 2023). AI marketing is unethical since these unexpected findings could harm customers. To reduce risk, companies can avoid AI-driven marketing strategy-related unintended consequences. Ethical guidelines for AI-driven marketing created by companies could underscore things like transparency and accountability(Kuzlu et al., 2023).

Duty and Dedication: AI marketing can also raise moral considerations about duty and accountability. The paper suggested ethical marketing AI case studies that need engineers to demonstrate: Openness—sharing marketing goals, algorithms, data, targeting, and appeal Responsible for marketing actions that may create emotional distress, influence decision-making, or exploit youngsters(Sullins, 2014). Ethical marketing AI promotes solely the best interests of individuals, communities, and society. The European Commission's High-Level Expert Group on AI released ethical principles for trustworthy AI in 2021 (Herath Pathirannehelage et al., 2024; Neuwirth, 2022). Companies must promote ethics and regulate staff AI use.Notifying employees of their job's ethical implications and creating AI-driven marketing accountability channels are examples (Neuwirth, 2022).

Assessment of Environmental Impacts: Most people don't consider the environmental affects, but in fact AI has a huge impact on the environment. AI algorithms go through a certain system where they're processed and it takes a lot of energy to process all of the information (Hermann, 2022). Companies can reduce their environmental impact with sustainable computing. Use renewable energy, utilize computational resources, and use energy-efficient gear. Cloud computing requires less energy than data centers. Pooling computing resources saves energy and carbon. Green AI creates efficient, eco-friendly algorithms(Saadi & Azdimousa, 2024). Energy-efficient algorithms or hardware improvements may be needed. Circular economies reduce environmental impact. Making things that can be repaired, recycled, or biodegraded lowers waste and maximizes resources (Backholer et al., 2021; Shen et al., 2011).

Exploiting AI for Dubious Purposes: Marketing AI can deceive customers and exploit weak people. Action is needed to address these ethical challenges. The ethical implications, challenges, and solutions of deploying AI for destruction are discussed here. AI algorithms can modify media, produce deep fakes, and spread misinformation(Bose et al., 2024). These actions can affect people and corporate trust. Openness, liability, and conscientious use could be ethical guidelines for AI-driven marketing (European Commission, 2021). Companies may protect AI algorithms and data with cyber security. Data collection and usage rules and customer data ownership rights can be enforced by businesses (EU Commission, 2019; Neuwirth, 2022). Malicious AI Is unethical, irresponsible and causes accountability issues.

Emotional Impact: Artificial intelligence and Marketing can have impacts of client mental health. AI marketing's impacts of revenues by exposing client preferences, implementing advertising techniques and enacts consumer emotions(R. Kumar & Sharma, 2023). Customer, intrusion, anxiety and dependence are some of the psychological impacts(McStay, 2020). Organizations need to deploy AI based marketing's responsibly and inform the public(Furey & Blue, 2018). There can be a hybrid strategy where AI-based technologies can be coupled with human efforts to provide a more personalized and empathetic experience to customers(Lin et al., 2012).

Figure 1. Ethical implications of AI

IMPLICATIONS OF ARTIFICIAL INTELLIGENCE IN MARKETING

In order to be complaint with laws and regulations, it is necessary that companies handle the legal issues brought on by the artificial intelligent marketing. Some of the issues that come with using artificial intelligence in marketing will be covered in this section.

Intellectual Property Rights Protection: When the AI creates work that is too similar to copyrighted material, it will violate copyright. Any corporation without the IP for AI's products might be sued and penalized. AI marketing challenges content ownership(Doroshuk, 2021). AI-created IP can be licensed and protected by companies. Avoiding copyright infringement in AI marketing is difficult. Companies that violate IP rights may be fined(Huang & Yu, 2022). AI can mimic copyright content. Creative commons licenses allow copyrighted material use under specified conditions. Companies can market AI-generated content without violating IP(Sahin & Soylemez, 2024).

Privacy and Data Security: AI-powered marketing will make consumer data collecting and use more vital. Companies must obtain consumer authorization before using their data under data privacy rules(Deslée & Cloarec, 2024). Violating these rules might result in legal and financial penalties. Personal data must be legally collected and used, making AI marketing challenging (Schneider, 2023).

Consumer Protection: There are many issues for consumer protection with AI marketing. AI systems are collecting massive amounts of data on customers to then mine and analyze. With the accumulation of data, security is the first issue at hand(Bundy, 2017). Consumers must be provided with a certain level of safety. No one wants a leak of personal information from the companyThe company cannot advertise something beyond the limits(Liu et al., 2023). However, consumer protection laws requiring companies to inform the public of how the AI algorithms are being used in their marketing campaign.

Obligation: AI in Marketing is going to touch legal obligation and accountability. As AI systems become more complicated and self-ruler, assigning duty for mistakes or destruction may become more difficult. This may create a legal issue for AI driven agency(Bundy, 2017). AI systems pose some inherent challenges or complications for current regulations, which examples of a lack of clarity for example duty and explainability. While initiatives with AI for marketing are legal, there is a clear line that should not be crossed. Keeping a close eye on the proceedings and initiatives of the European Commission's High-Level Expert Group on AI, particularly focusing on their endeavors concerning the ethical considerations and optimal strategies in the realm of AI-driven marketing practices (Neuwirth, 2022). These principles emphasize openness, fairness, and accountability in AI marketing respectively. Businesses can further mitigate their AI marketing liabilities by utilizing risk management tools such as insurance. Companies should also have clear and transparent data collection and use policies that inform customers and obtain consent before using their data (Schneider, 2023).

Trademark and Brand Protection: Another legal issue of AI marketing is trademark and brand protection. Counterfeit products may be made and sold more as more AI marketing is used (Sahin & Soylemez, 2024). Proof of false items and endorsements will be safeguarded and blocked of trademarks and brand protection. Social media and online marketplaces might be checked by businesses with AI to uncover fake items and endorsements. Secure, unalterable records of product legitimacy with blockchain could be utilized by businesses for trademarks and brand protection (Tamayo Salazar et al., 2023). This can be managed with cohesive and effective trademark and brand protection plans by worldwide businesses in concert with international organizations and governments.

Competition Legislation and Conflicts of Interest: The utilization of AI in marketing gives rise to concerns regarding antitrust and competition law. AI algorithms in marketing may give certain dominant companies market power that can be used to anticompetitive purpose and antitrust law offences. In marketing dominant companies may use AI algorithms to approve unfair advantage over weaker competitors (Latham & Goltz, 2019; Neuwirth, 2022). Leaders may use AI to acquire and analyze huge volumes of customer data quantities giving them marketing edge. This may impede market competitiveness and entry of smaller firms. To address these concerns, antitrust and competition authorities may require openness and accountability in AI- based marketing algorithm development and deployment. These guidelines also address the concern that AI algorithms could encourage price-fixing, collusions and other anti-competitive arrangements (Neuwirth, 2022). Companies also need to establish ethical standards for use of AI algorithms in marketing highlighting fair competition, market processes. For instance, companies may commit not to aim competitors with AI algorithms (Kashyap et al., 2024; Perry et al., 2023).

Licenses and Agreements: As AI marketing technology advances, the significance of licenses and contracts rises. In the interactions between AI provider and client, licenses and contracts are employed to handle the data's ownership and usage(McAlister et al., 2024). For AI marketing technologies, however, conventional licenses frameworks are burdened by two main problems: identifying who is responsible for the decisions the algorithms make and data privacy concerns (D. Kumar & Suthar, 2024). The new AI marketing tool licensing and contractual arrangements can solve these problems(*Ethics of Artificial Intelligence | UNESCO*, n.d.).Blockchain technology allows "smart contracts" to automate contract execution and give data usage and ownership transparency. Contract risk-sharing can address AI system liability and accountability(*Ethics of Artificial Intelligence | UNESCO*, n.d.). AI marketing technology is increasing rapidly, needing regulatory reform. Governments and regulators may help establish AI marketing technology laws. It may be necessary to establish AI marketing tool legislation and monitoring and enforcement systems.

Lack of Laws: The growing use of AI in marketing has produced a regulatory vacuum that has overtaken legislation, worrying corporations and consumers. Technology, including AI, has long had legal loopholes. The internet brought copyright, data privacy, and e-commerce difficulties in the 1990s that took years to settle. Social media users are concerned about free speech, data ownership, and misinformation (Lipschultz, 2023; Monteiro, 2023; Mühlhoff & Willem, 2023). Companies struggle to determine legality due to unclear legal frameworks. Lack of transparency promotes data abuse and unfair commercial practices. The industry can establish morality and best practices. These transparent, responsible, and just rules can be developed by customers, workers, and regulators (Heinze et al., 2020; Milan et al., 2023).

IMPLICATIONS OF THE STUDY

Due of ethical and regulatory implications, AI-driven marketing tactics require a thorough theoretical framework. AI in marketing raises significant ethical and legal challenges that have yet to be answered. This may fit Von Schomberg's 2011 responsible innovation framework(Commission et al., 2011). A multifaceted approach must consider technological, economic, social, ethical, and legal elements for responsible innovation. This technique involves engaging stakeholders, predicting and decreasing risks and uncertainties, and fairly allocating innovation advantages and risks. Rodgers and Nguyen (2006) identified ethical leadership as a key theoretical paradigm(Rodgers & Nguyen, 2022). Ethical leaders encourage ethical behavior, decision-making, and accountability. This method can be utilized to build and implement AI-driven marketing campaigns that prioritize ethical leadership from CEOs to professionals. Additionally, ethical decision-making frameworks (EDMF) can help create and implement AI-driven marketing strategies. EDMFs assist companies rate ethical issues, estimate risks and rewards, and create ethical mitigation plans (Altinigne, 2024). Although ethical and regulatory issues exist, AI in marketing may be beneficial.

PRACTICAL IMPLICATIONS

Marketing professionals need to address AI's ethical guidelines and regulatory implications. AI experts must educate clients in data collection, targeted advertising and marketing AI algorithms. Promoting transparency and understandability will help marketers build customer trust and reduce cloudiness (Lin et al., 2012; Mühlhoff & Willem, 2023). Marketing professionals should moreover create ethical criteria for AI driven initiatives. Adhering to these ethical standards will help marketing practitioners employ AI legally, ethically and humanly. Marketers must invest in bias-detection and privacy-enhancing technology to mitigate AI risks(Kunz & Wirtz, 2024). These methods and technologies will be able to detect and eliminate biases in AI algorithms and at the same time maintain user privacy.

LIMITATIONS

This research on the ethical and legal challenges of AI in marketing is a promising work however it has its limitations. In this chapter firstly we have provided ethical and legal challenges on AI technology in marketing, on our future studies, it may be checked on the intellectual property rights, condition of the contract and also should be combined full condition of likeness. This study has covered a lot of ethical and legal issues, however their effectiveness and pragmatism in real-world scenarios is unknown and may vary. Rapid growth in the technology raises ethical and legal issues in the AI in marketing, further research and discussion should be carried out harvesting this technology.

FUTURE EXPLORATION POSSIBILITIES

Future research will be needed to understand AI's complicated effects on marketing. This requires examining AI algorithms' marketing biases and discovering ways to eliminate them. New laws, ethics, and norms can ensure AI marketing is done right. Explore blockchain technology for client privacy and data protection. Testing AI-driven marketing success requires unique methodologies like experiments and randomized controlled trials. To maximize AI's benefits and limit its negatives, hybrid systems with human control are essential. Use natural language processing and visualization to simplify AI systems for non-experts. To minimize socioeconomic inequities and cultural norms, AI in marketing must consider its sociological and cultural effects. Ethical AI use requires marketing professional training and certification. The study promotes openness, transparency, and ethics in AI-driven marketing across disciplines. To alleviate AI-based troubling, researchers and practitioners have proposed bias-detection, privacy-enhancing, and contractual agreements. The study propose further scope for researchers and practitioners to understand the current landscape and additional research in the domain of AI in marketing.

CONCLUSION

Artificial intelligence (AI) is the biggest commercial opportunity in today's world. Artificial intelligence is defined robots. AI has chosen lots of different ways through which it can perform its tasks effectively such as voice recognition, chess moves, smart cars, deep Blue, Watson, etc. The aim to research on AI is helping to produce computers or other machines of cognitive abilities that human have. Work can be easily done by AI that humans are not able to do. AI utilizes theories and techniques from many fields such as neuroscience and computer science. AI is a wide-ranging discipline that includes everything from the very basic to the very complex. The new applications for AI are constantly being developed. This inevitably means that there will be new fields, techniques, and AI applications with the passage of time. AI systems can produce human-like responses. For example, the Turing Test, proposed by the mathematically British logician and crypt metadata can convince people in believing that they are interacting with another human. In order to ensure that AI is developed and used responsibly, many of the tech companies have launched their AI codes. One of the biggest criticisms of AI is its role in issues such as bias, discrimination, and data protection. Companies should prioritize protection against cyber-attacks, and work to make AI available to everyone despite abilities, etc to nourish AI's long-term impact. Companies must follow the policies and regulations created by government and international agencies. Governmental and international agencies have their codes and standards that they set to make machines safe to use.

AI marketing also presents some ethical issues that may influence the future of job in the marketing industry. Marketers must address three important ethical challenges in the AI evolution area: job displacement, isolation, and transparency. Companies must retain their employees for new job placements when AI machines come in for jobs in which humans were previously used. The job displacement is one of the most ethical issues that the marketers must address. The AI program replaces people in their job at a company. Companies should use their technology platform to persuade or teach people for the skills that are necessary for the job during the time that they are still under the company payroll. It is the company's responsibility to ensure its employees are gainfully employed. The perfect solution is the right combination of artificial intelligence and human's hybrid strategy. The combination of both is the ultimate dynamic duo. AI has the speed or efficiency and humans has the emotional intelligence. Companies must allow customers to receive personal and empathic service/products from intelligent humans. The hybrid strategy allows customers to be served with a human sense of personalization. Most millennial prefer going online, because the shopping center after Trump shut down its last store. Another underrated ethical issue with AI marketing program is cyber security. Companies must be able to monitor and supervise their AI programs either with a physical presence or decision trees.

AI marketing also has some unintended outcomes which raise questions about ethical duties and responsibilities. The European Commission's High-Level Expert Group on AI created ethical principles for trustworthy AI in 2021, to promote accountability and transparency through their trustworthy AI framework. AI marketing has significant legal implications for consumer protection. This includes data privacy, consumer protection and obligation. By these businesses must get consumer consent prior to utilizing the consumers' information under the data privacy rules, data will have to be encrypted and anonyms and businesses will have to follow GDPR Government and regulators can help set AI marketing technology laws.

REFERENCES

Adarsh, R., Pillai, R. H., Krishnamurthy, A., & Bi, A. (2023). Innovative Business Research in Finance and Marketing System Based on Ethically Governed Artificial Intelligence. *Proceedings of 8th IEEE International Conference on Science, Technology, Engineering and Mathematics, ICONSTEM 2023*. IEEE. 10.1109/ICONSTEM56934.2023.10142836

AI Ethics: What It Is and Why It Matters. (n.d.). Coursera. https://www.coursera.org/articles/ai-ethics

Altinigne, N. (2024). The importance and limitations of artificial intelligence ethics and digital corporate responsibility in consumer markets: Challenges and opportunities. In *Globalized Consumer Insights in the Digital Era* (pp. 150–168). IGI Global. 10.4018/979-8-3693-3811-7.ch007

Arango, L., Singaraju, S. P., & Niininen, O. (2023). Consumer Responses to AI-Generated Charitable Giving Ads. *Journal of Advertising*, 52(4), 486–503. 10.1080/00913367.2023.2183285

Beatty, S. E., & Kahle, L. R. (1988). Alternative hierarchies of the attitude-behavior relationship: The impact of brand commitment and habit. *Journal of the Academy of Marketing Science*, 16(2), 1–10. 10.1007/BF02723310

Benjelloun, A., & Kabak, S. (2024). Ethical Challenges and Managerial Implications of Artificial Intelligence in Digital Marketing. In K. S., B. K., K. J.H., & B. J.C. (Eds.), *Lecture Notes in Networks and Systems* (pp. 439–445). Springer Science and Business Media Deutschland GmbH. 10.1007/978-981-99-9040-5_32

Bock, G. W., & Kim, Y. G. (2002). Breaking the Myths of Rewards: An Exploratory Study of Attitudes about Knowledge Sharing. [IRMJ]. *Information Resources Management Journal*, 15(2), 14–21. 10.4018/irmj.2002040102

Bundy, A. (2017). Preparing for the future of Artificial Intelligence. *AI & Society*, 32(2), 285–287. 10.1007/s00146-016-0685-0

Busis, N. A., Marolia, D., Montgomery, R., Balcer, L. J., Galetta, S. L., & Grossman, S. N. (2024). Navigating the U.S. regulatory landscape for neurologic digital health technologies. *NPJ Digital Medicine*, 7(1), 94. 10.1038/s41746-024-01098-538609447

Campbell, C., Sands, S., Ferraro, C., Tsao, H.-Y. J., & Mavrommatis, A. (2020). From data to action: How marketers can leverage AI. *Business Horizons*, 63(2), 227–243. 10.1016/j.bushor.2019.12.002

Caner, S., & Bhatti, F. (2020). A conceptual framework on defining businesses strategy for artificial intelligence. *Contemporary Management Research*, 16(3), 175–206. 10.7903/cmr.19970

Commission, E., & Innovation, D.-G. for R. and, & Schomberg, R. (2011). *Towards responsible research and innovation in the information and communication technologies and security technologies fields* (R. Schomberg (Ed.)). Publications Office. https://doi.org/doi/10.2777/58723

Davenport, T., Guha, A., Grewal, D., & Bressgott, T. (2020). How artificial intelligence will change the future of marketing. *Journal of the Academy of Marketing Science*, 48(1), 24–42. 10.1007/s11747-019-00696-0

Davis, F. D. (1989). Perceived usefulness, perceived ease of use, and user acceptance of information technology. *Management Information Systems Quarterly*, 13(3), 319–339. 10.2307/249008

Deslée, A., & Cloarec, J. (2024). Safeguarding privacy: Ethical considerations in Data-Driven Marketing. In *The Impact of Digitalization on Current Marketing Strategies* (pp. 147–161). Emerald Group Publishing Ltd., 10.1108/978-1-83753-686-320241009

Doroshuk, H. (2021). Prospects and efficiency measurement of artificial intelligence in the management of enterprises in the energy sector in the era of Industry 4.0. *Polityka Energetyczna*, 24(4), 61–76. 10.33223/epj/144083

Drabiak, K. (2022). Leveraging law and ethics to promote safe and reliable AI/ML in healthcare. *Frontiers in Nuclear Medicine*, 2, 983340. 10.3389/fnume.2022.983340

Engelmann, S., Ullstein, C., Papakyriakopoulos, O., & Grossklags, J. (2022). What People Think AI Should Infer From Faces. *ACM International Conference Proceeding Series*, 128–141. 10.1145/3531146.3533080

Furey, E., & Blue, J. (2018). She just doesn't understand me! Curing Alexa of her Alexithymia. In B. J., D. J., B. R., J. A.C., & B. R. (Eds.), *CEUR Workshop Proceedings* (Vol. 2259, pp. 244–255). CEUR-WS. https://www.scopus.com/inward/record.uri?eid=2-s2.0-85058234360&partnerID=40&md5=04babd4b045a7162ddf26ff3922b8363

Hajrasouliha, A. H. (2023). Applications, Approaches, and Ethics of the Extended Reality in Urban Design and Planning. *Journal of the American Planning Association*, 1–17. Advance online publication. 10.1080/01944363.2023.2275123

Heller, L. J., Skinner, C. S., Tomiyama, A. J., Epel, E. S., Hall, P. A., Allan, J., LaCaille, L., Randall, A. K., Bodenmann, G., Li-Tsang, C. W. P., Sinclair, K., Creek, J., Baumann, L. C., Karel, A., Andersson, G., Hanewinkel, R., Morgenstern, M., Puska, P., Bucks, R. S., & Denollet, J. (2013). Theory of Reasoned Action. In *Encyclopedia of Behavioral Medicine* (pp. 1964–1967). Springer New York. 10.1007/978-1-4419-1005-9_1619

Hentzen, J. K., Hoffmann, A., Dolan, R., & Pala, E. (2022). Artificial intelligence in customer-facing financial services: A systematic literature review and agenda for future research. *International Journal of Bank Marketing*, 40(6), 1299–1336. 10.1108/IJBM-09-2021-0417

Herath Pathirannehelage, S., Shrestha, Y. R., & von Krogh, G. (2024). Design principles for artificial intelligence-augmented decision making: An action design research study. *European Journal of Information Systems*, 1–23. 10.1080/0960085X.2024.2330402

Hermann, E. (2022). Leveraging Artificial Intelligence in Marketing for Social Good—An Ethical Perspective. *Journal of Business Ethics*, 179(1), 43–61. 10.1007/s10551-021-04843-y34054170

Hermann, E., Williams, G. Y., & Puntoni, S. (2023). Deploying artificial intelligence in services to AID vulnerable consumers. *Journal of the Academy of Marketing Science*. 10.1007/s11747-023-00986-8

Huang, G., & Yu, Y. (2022). The Application of Artificial Intelligence in Organizational Innovation Management: Take the Autonomous Driving Technology of Tesla as an Example. *Lecture Notes on Data Engineering and Communications Technologies*, 135, 690–697. 10.1007/978-3-031-04809-8_63

Kashyap, B., Sachdeva, V., Shirahatti, A., Singh, G., Arya, A., Jagatheesan, S., & Kumar, C. (2024). A Novel Approach for Human Behaviour Prediction Using Deep Learning Algorithms. *International Journal of Intelligent Systems and Applications in Engineering*, 12(1), 793–801. https://www.scopus.com/inward/record.uri?eid=2-s2.0-85182487249&partnerID=40&md5=be67f71a2ee0cecdb48ded1d5f681e50

Kopalle, P. K., Gangwar, M., Kaplan, A., Ramachandran, D., Reinartz, W., & Rindfleisch, A. (2022). Examining artificial intelligence (AI) technologies in marketing via a global lens: Current trends and future research opportunities. *International Journal of Research in Marketing*, 39(2), 522–540. 10.1016/j.ijresmar.2021.11.002

Kumar, D., & Suthar, N. (2024). Ethical and legal challenges of AI in marketing: An exploration of solutions. *Journal of Information. Communication and Ethics in Society*, 22(1), 124–144. 10.1108/JICES-05-2023-0068

Kumar, R., & Sharma, V. (2023). The AI revolution: Financial services in the age of intelligent machines. In *Leveraging AI and Emotional Intelligence in Contemporary Business Organizations* (pp. 287–305). IGI Global. 10.4018/979-8-3693-1902-4.ch017

Kumar, V., Ashraf, A. R., & Nadeem, W. (2024). AI-powered marketing: What, where, and how? *International Journal of Information Management*, 102783. Advance online publication. 10.1016/j.ijinfomgt.2024.102783

Kuzlu, M., Xiao, Z., Sarp, S., Catak, F. O., Gurler, N., & Guler, O. (2023). The Rise of Generative Artificial Intelligence in Healthcare. *12th Mediterranean Conference on Embedded Computing, MECO 2023*. IEEE. 10.1109/MECO58584.2023.10155107

Latham, A., & Goltz, S. (2019). A survey of the general public's views on the ethics of using AI in education. In I. S., M. E., O. A., M. B., H. P., & L. R. (Eds.), *Lecture Notes in Computer Science (including subseries Lecture Notes in Artificial Intelligence and Lecture Notes in Bioinformatics),* (pp. 194–206). Springer Verlag. 10.1007/978-3-030-23204-7_17

Lin, P., Abney, K., & Bekey, G. A. (2012). *Robot ethics : the ethical and social implications of robotics*. 386.

Liu, R., Gupta, S., & Patel, P. (2023). The Application of the Principles of Responsible AI on Social Media Marketing for Digital Health. *Information Systems Frontiers*, 25(6), 2275–2299. 10.1007/s10796-021-10191-z34539226

Maglaras, L. (2022). Artificial Intelligence: Practical and Ethical Challenges. In *Studies in Computational Intelligence, 1025*. Springer Science and Business Media Deutschland GmbH. 10.1007/978-3-030-96630-0_3

Matei, M., & Done, I. (2013). The social responsibility: Conceptual interferences and motivational factors specific to corporations. In *Sustainable Technologies, Policies, and Constraints in the Green Economy* (pp. 204–218). IGI Global. 10.4018/978-1-4666-4098-6.ch011

McAlister, A. R., Alhabash, S., & Yang, J. (2024). Artificial intelligence and ChatGPT: Exploring Current and potential future roles in marketing education. *Journal of Marketing Communications*, 30(2), 166–187. 10.1080/13527266.2023.2289034

McStay, A. (2020). Emotional AI, soft biometrics and the surveillance of emotional life: An unusual consensus on privacy. *Big Data & Society*, 7(1). Advance online publication. 10.1177/2053951720904386

Milan, A., Sahu, R., & Sandhu, J. K. (2023). Impact of AI on Social Marketing and its Usage in Social Media: A Review Analysis. *Proceedings of the International Conference on Circuit Power and Computing Technologies, ICCPCT 2023*, (pp. 1749–1754). IEEE. 10.1109/ICCPCT58313.2023.10245676

Mogaji, E., Soetan, T. O., & Kieu, T. A. (2021). The implications of artificial intelligence on the digital marketing of financial services to vulnerable customers. *Australasian Marketing Journal*, 29(3), 235–242. 10.1016/j.ausmj.2020.05.003

Mohd Rahim, N. I., & Iahad, A., N., Yusof, A. F., & A. Al-Sharafi, M. (. (2022). AI-Based Chatbots Adoption Model for Higher-Education Institutions: A Hybrid PLS-SEM-Neural Network Modelling Approach. *Sustainability (Switzerland)*, 14(19). 10.3390/su141912726

Monteiro, S. (2023). Gaming faces: Diagnostic scanning in social media and the legacy of racist face analysis. *Information Communication and Society*, 26(8), 1601–1617. 10.1080/1369118X.2021.2020867

Pascual, J. M., & de Uribe Gil, C. E. (2023). Renewing Ethics in Public Relations: A Case Study. *Revista Espanola de la Transparencia*, 18, 406–425. 10.51915/ret.263

Perry, V. G., Martin, K., & Schnare, A. (2023). Algorithms for All: Can AI in the Mortgage Market Expand Access to Homeownership? *AI*, 4(4), 888–903. 10.3390/ai4040045

S., Y., A., H., P.K., A., & H., K. (Eds.). (2023). 2nd International Conference on Mechanical and Energy Technologies, ICMET 2021. *Smart Innovation, Systems and Technologies, 290*. https://www.scopus.com/inward/record.uri?eid=2-s2.0-85134330558&partnerID=40&md5=2bc4dbd7343017a23de838fad58f769a

Sharma, A. K., & Sharma, R. (2023). Considerations in artificial intelligence-based marketing: An ethical perspective. *Applied Marketing Analytics, 9*(2), 162–172. https://www.scopus.com/inward/record.uri?eid=2-s2.0-85184230627&partnerID=40&md5=1de1ed003a445b409d307f81cd3915f2

Shen, H., Han, Y., Zhang, Z., & Zeng, Z. (2011). Notice of Retraction: Marketing strategies for Chinese public legal services companies. *2011 2nd International Conference on Artificial Intelligence, Management Science and Electronic Commerce, AIMSEC 2011 - Proceedings*, 3105–3108. 10.1109/AIMSEC.2011.6011125

Singh, C., Dash, M. K., Sahu, R., & Kumar, A. (2023). Artificial intelligence in customer retention: A bibliometric analysis and future research framework. *Kybernetes*. 10.1108/K-02-2023-0245

Tyagi, S., & Rathore, R. (2023). Unveiling the Dynamic Journey from Data Insights to Action in Data Science. *2023 IEEE International Conference on Research Methodologies in Knowledge Management, Artificial Intelligence and Telecommunication Engineering, RMKMATE 2023*. IEEE. 10.1109/RMKMATE59243.2023.10369698

Venkatesh, V., Morris, M. G., Davis, G. B., & Davis, F. D. (2003). User Acceptance of Information Technology: Toward a Unified View. *Management Information Systems Quarterly*, 27(3), 425–478. 10.2307/30036540

Vlačić, B., Corbo, L., Costa e Silva, S., & Dabić, M. (2021). The evolving role of artificial intelligence in marketing: A review and research agenda. *Journal of Business Research*, 128, 187–203. 10.1016/j.jbusres.2021.01.055

Volkmar, G., Fischer, P. M., & Reinecke, S. (2022). Artificial Intelligence and Machine Learning: Exploring drivers, barriers, and future developments in marketing management. *Journal of Business Research*, 149, 599–614. 10.1016/j.jbusres.2022.04.007

Wang, C. (2011). Analyses of underlying causes on the abnormal marketing ethics of Chinese enterprises. *2011 2nd International Conference on Artificial Intelligence, Management Science and Electronic Commerce, AIMSEC 2011 - Proceedings*. IEEE. 10.1109/AIMSEC.2011.6010191

Winecoff, A. A., & Watkins, E. A. (2022). Artificial concepts of artificial intelligence: Institutional compliance and resistance in ai startups. *AIES 2022 - Proceedings of the 2022 AAAI/ACM Conference on AI, Ethics, and Society*. ACM. 10.1145/3514094.3534138

Chapter 14
Unveiling the Transformative Landscape:
A Bibliometric Exploration of AI Integration in Healthcare

Ajay Chandel
https://orcid.org/0000-0002-4585-6406
Lovely Professional University, India

Krishan Gopal
Lovely Professional University, India

Anurag Pahuja
https://orcid.org/0000-0002-1170-5749
Lovely Professional University, India

Varun Nayyar
Chitkara University, India

ABSTRACT

This study uses bibliometric analysis to investigate the methods, thematic insights, and revolutionary possibilities of AI integration in healthcare. It provides insights into the evolution of AI in healthcare through topic mapping, keyword co-occurrence, co-citation, and bibliographic coupling. Keyword co-occurrence highlights important themes like federated learning, digital healthcare, and the internet of things, while co-citation analysis identifies emerging subjects like federated machine learning. The relationships between different research streams and the effects of explainable AI and machine learning on healthcare IT are made clear by the bibliographic coupling. Thematic mapping offers a graphic synopsis of several subjects, from systemic modifications to technical innovations. By educating stakeholders, this study helps them make decisions and sets the stage for future research. It directs efforts to maximize AI's potential for bettering patient outcomes and providing healthcare to practitioners, policymakers, and researchers.

DOI: 10.4018/979-8-3693-6660-8.ch014

INTRODUCTION

The use of AI in medical settings has recently attracted the interest of scholars and professionals all over the globe. Roboticquet and Ramsundar (2019) state that artificial intelligence's ability to mimic human intellect and do out activities that often necessitate human cognition might drastically alter numerous facets of patient care, diagnosis, and therapy. In the face of increasing demand and decreasing resources, the healthcare business is confronted with a multitude of difficulties, including the need to improve patient outcomes, increase operational effectiveness, and manage costs (Obermeyer & Emanuel, 2016). Artificial intelligence (AI) stands out as a game-changing technical advancement in this regard.

One of the most well-known uses of artificial intelligence in healthcare is medical diagnosis. The use of complicated algorithms and machine-learning techniques allows AI-driven systems to sift through mountains of patient data, such as genetic information, medical records, and imaging studies, assisting doctors in arriving at correct diagnoses and treatment choices (Davenport & Kalakota, 2019). Some areas where AI-driven diagnostic technologies have proven to be more accurate than human specialists include cancer, neurological illnesses, and cardiovascular ailments.

In addition, AI makes it possible to personalize treatment approaches based on each patient's unique traits, preferences, and genetic makeup. Healthcare practitioners can give individualized treatments that improve efficacy while avoiding bad effects by evaluating huge databases and predicting patient reactions to various medications (Gulshan et al., 2016). The goal of healthcare organizations using AI-powered predictive analytics is to avoid and respond to public health disasters by allowing them to foresee disease outbreaks, identify vulnerable populations, and allocate resources efficiently. Artificial intelligence algorithms can improve healthcare delivery systems and disease surveillance by analyzing data from various sources, including environmental factors, socioeconomic determinants of health, and electronic health records (EHRs). This, in turn, allows for proactive interventions and informed policy decisions (Lipton et al., 2015).

There are a number of issues that need fixing before AI may be used extensively in healthcare. It is important to give serious thought to the ethical and practical concerns raised by data openness, privacy, security, and prejudice (Rajkomar et al., 2018). To make sure AI helps out, not hurts, the human side of healthcare delivery, experts in the field need specific training on how to use AI tools and understand what they mean (Char et al., 2018).

Notwithstanding these obstacles, artificial intelligence (AI) has the potential to revolutionize healthcare administration and clinical practice by fostering creativity, entrepreneurship, and teamwork. Synergies between artificial intelligence (AI), robots, big data analytics, and the IoT have the potential to inspire innovative medical research and reshape healthcare delivery paradigms (Topol, 2019).

Collaboration among stakeholders is being fostered through public-private partnerships, research consortia, and AI innovation centers to speed up the development and use of AI in healthcare (Krittanawong et al., 2018). Using science mapping in bibliometric analysis, this research seeks to delve into the complex ways in which AI is changing healthcare, with a focus on how it affects healthcare administration, clinical procedures, and the final results for patients. The research tries to accomplish undermentioned research questions:

RQ1. How do different methods of science mapping, including co-citation analysis, bibliographic coupling, and keyword co-occurrence analysis, contribute to our understanding of applications of AI in Healthcare?

Unveiling the Transformative Landscape

RQ2. What insights can be gained from exploring the interconnections and relationships between scholarly documents and concepts using science mapping techniques?

RQ3. Thematic mapping of various themes on applications of AI in Healthcare

RQ4. Identifying future research agendas

RESEARCH METHODOLOGY

To accomplish the objectives of the study, bibliometric and content analyses were carried out. The field of bibliometrics assesses the impact and significance of scholarly articles by employing statistical methods (Guest et al., 2006). Through content analysis, researchers can measure the importance, frequency, and relationships among specific terms, concepts, or ideas. Researchers seeking to look at more data than systematic literature reviews allow triangulation to succeed by maintaining scientific rigor, objectivity, and generalizability.

Database Curation

Academic articles published between 1997 and 2024 were subjected to a bibliometric study. To gather bibliometric data, the most extensive database of its kind, SCOPUS, was chosen. In addition, SCOPUS is a popular choice because of its advisory council, content selection procedure (which guarantees that only the top papers are catalogued), and extensive coverage of worldwide academic literature (Chandel & Kaur, 2022)

Keyword Identification

The authors first reviewed 10 relevant open-access publications (SCOPUS, Q1), comprising systematic reviews, to identify potential keywords for a subsequent search of the SCOPUS database. The second step involved providing an inventory of discovered keywords to ten healthcare academics with the necessary experience (Chandel et al., 2023). Researchers gave academics a rundown of the study's goals and asked for their feedback on the initially selected keyword. Some keywords were added, and others were eliminated based on recommendations from experts.

Procurement of Articles for Bibliometric Analysis

Summary, heading, and pertinent search terms Using the search tool of SCOPUS and a variety of keywords, 3664 papers were extracted. The Preferred Reporting Items for the Systematic Review methodology was used to further select the relevant publications. There are four steps to the PRISMA framework: finding and documenting studies through database searches, screening studies, determining study eligibility, and finally, selecting studies. Here is a quick rundown of the approach and a diagram of the PRISMA process that was used to select the publications:

To achieve the stated goals of this study, the procedure led to the ultimate selection of 1,201 papers that were analysed. 1,201 articles were included in the final sample for the bibliometric study of inclusive education. proposed two primary study methods: scientific mapping and performance analysis.

Table 1. Preferred reporting items for systematic review, Moher et al., (2009)

Identification	Search query: ((TITLE("AI") OR TITLE-ABS-KEY ("Artificial Intelligence") AND TITLE("Healthcare")); n= 2962	Records removed before Screening (Chapters, Erratum, Letters, Short surveys, Note), n=1022
Screening	Records screened; n=1940	Records removed before eligibility (Non-English, Not open access, Abstract and Author keywords missing), n=713
Eligibility	Records accessed for eligibility, n=1227	Records removed based on critical review, n=43
Selection	Records included in final dataset, n=1201	

Scientific Mapping

Researchers in the field of bibliometrics can benefit from science mapping in several ways: it helps them better understand the structure and evolution of scientific knowledge, identifies emerging fields of study and trends, measures the quality of collaborations across disciplines, and ultimately informs decisions about funding, partnerships, and policy. It is a powerful resource for navigating the vast landscape of scholarly literature and better understanding the interdependent study topics, disciplines, and communities (Chandel et al., 2023). This study deploys co-citation analysis, Keyword co-occurrence analysis, Bibliographic coupling and thematic maps using VOSviewer and Biblioshiny (R based web interface).

ANALYSIS AND DISCUSSION OF RESULTS

Scientific Mapping

This section presents the results of scientific mapping, which summarize the analysis of blockchain technology's business applications by highlighting the conceptual, intellectual, and social frameworks around the subject.

Keyword Co-Occurrence Analysis

This analysis aimed to determine the frequency with which the dataset and the SCOPUS-assigned keywords appeared in each article. The Louvain cluster method was used to group the 56 most frequently used keywords.

A word's proximity to the network map's center is proportional to the number of times it appears there. The more keywords' authors utilize simultaneously, the stronger and closer the links. Additionally, the bigger the bubble indicating the frequency of usage, the more often academics employ a particular keyword. No two clusters have the same color scheme (Chandel et al., 2024).

An era of revolutionary potential has dawned on the expansive landscape of healthcare innovation, with the combination of artificial intelligence (AI) with cutting-edge technologies such as deep learning, blockchain, and the Internet of Things (IoT). Numerous trend and theme clusters were identified, which together make up the digital health landscape.

Unveiling the Transformative Landscape

Figure 1. Keyword co-occurrence analysis

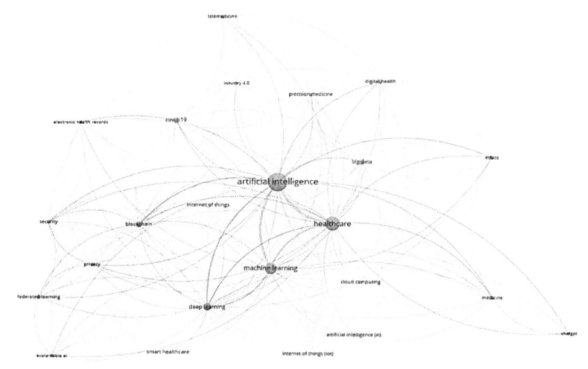

Source: VOSviewer

Figure 2. Cluster wise keyword co-occurrence analysis

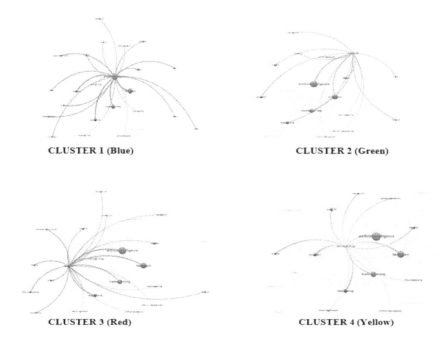

Cluster-I

Artificial intelligence (AI) is revolutionizing healthcare by improving medical diagnostics, streamlining operations, and providing more personalized care to patients. Technologies driven by artificial intelligence enhance the efficacy and efficiency of robotic surgery and predictive analytics, among others. This group examines how AI could change healthcare delivery by highlighting new ideas and putting the patient first (Kumar et al., 2022; Nayyar and Batra, 2020). The foundation of Cluster-I is the idea that AI will govern the future hospital. When fed massive amounts of medical data, machine learning can uncover previously unseen patterns that aid in patient diagnosis and treatment. By connecting various devices to the internet, medical professionals can keep tabs on their patients from afar and add new data points all the time (Sharma & Bikshandi, 2020). While blockchain ensures the security of sensitive data, explainable AI ensures that doctors can understand the machine's reasoning. The future of healthcare is bright because of this technological convergence, which will allow for personalized preventative care.

Cluster-II

An analysis of Cluster-II demonstrates how AI drives the futuristic healthcare system. Big data, which comprises an abundance of medical records, machine learning can diagnose and treat patients with an unprecedented level of accuracy. Through the use of watchful internet of things (IoT) devices, doctors are able to remotely monitor their patients. The use of explainable AI ensures that clinicians can understand the machine's thinking, and the use of blockchain technology safeguards this data. This technical marvel prevents disease in its early stages, heralding a future of individualized treatment.

Cluster III

Cluster III keywords were centered around themes that investigated the use of AI in the healthcare sector. The medical landscape is being drastically changed by AI and its friends. At its foundation lies artificial intelligence, with machine learning and deep learning serving as its apprentices (Nayyar, 2022). Large volumes of medical data, or "big data," are processed by machine learning, which then applies deep learning to enhance the patterns discovered in order to deliver more precise diagnosis and tailored care. This change is being driven by a network of devices called the internet of things (IoT), which continuously monitors patients' health. This data stream generates an ever-growing knowledge base when integrated with electronic health records (EHRs). To safeguard this private information, blockchain technology steps in. Explainable AI (XAI), however, is essential with this powerful technology. XAI ensures moral decision-making and builds confidence by making the AI's logic understandable to physicians.

Together, big data, blockchain, IoT, AI, and XAI are transforming healthcare and paving the way for earlier diagnosis and more effective treatment of disease.

Cluster IV

Cluster IV's keywords centered on how artificial intelligence affects the healthcare sector. AI is at the core of this transformation, using cutting-edge technologies like machine learning and deep learning. Machine learning from medical imaging and electronic health records (EHRs) consumes large volumes of medical data, or "big data," which uncovers hidden patterns to improve diagnosis. Deep learning is then used to hone these discoveries further to deliver precise, personalized care. There is more information available.

The Internet of Things (IoT), which employs devices to monitor patients' health remotely, adds another layer. Because of this continuous information flow, the data pool keeps growing. But with such a powerful resource, security is essential. Blockchain technology enables a secure, tamper-proof system to protect sensitive patient data. But enormous authority also entails accountability. This is where explainable AI, or XAI, comes in handy. Thanks to XAI, doctors can now understand the AI's decision justification. This openness guarantees moral decision-making that enhances patient outcomes by building trust between medical personnel and AI. Healthcare is revolutionizing through powerful alliances, including IoT, AI, big data, and XAI. This future may consist of preemptive measures, individualized care, and a setting where illness may be contained before it spreads.

Co-Citation Analysis

In bibliometrics, co-citation analysis investigates the connections between papers by examining how frequently other publications cite them together. Co-citation analysis is based on the fundamental premise that texts that are frequently cited together are either thematically linked or have similar themes.

Figure 3. Cluster wise co-citation analysis

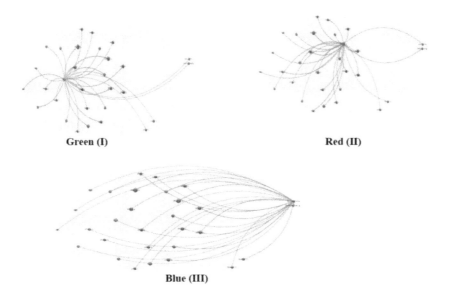

Cluster I: Advancements in Healthcare Technology

A promising new approach to data privacy, federated machine learning (FL) is driving expansion in the area where machine learning meets healthcare. The development of personalized models was prompted by the fact that traditional FL techniques encounter difficulties in Non-IID circumstances (Wang et al., 2022; Lu et al., 2022; Yang et al., 2020; Tucker at el., 2020 and Laranjo et al., 2018). Using batch normalization statistics, FedAP is suggested to handle domain shifts and provide local customers with customized models. Healthcare 4.0, which is driven by manufacturing-based technologies, ushers in a new age of homecare robotic systems (HRS), which integrate cyber-physical systems (CPS) to improve intelligence and speed. Research into synthetic data production to bypass privacy constraints is also being driven by the desire for advanced artificial intelligence technology in healthcare. A more realistic synthetic dataset can be created with the help of graphical modeling, outlier analysis, latent variable identification, and resampling, which reduces the chances of patient re-identification(Nayyar, 2018). There is growing hope for conversational agents that can understand and respond to natural language as a tool in the healthcare industry. Full potential of these medicines in healthcare settings can only be realized with more rigorous trial designs and consistent reporting, since there has been limited evaluation of them so far.

Cluster II: Emerging Technologies in Healthcare

The release of ChatGPT, an artificial intelligence chatbot created by OpenAI, exemplifies the considerable interest in the intersection of cutting-edge technology and healthcare. Like other recent AI innovations, such as AlphaGo and self-driving cars, ChatGPT has attracted a lot of attention and shows

Unveiling the Transformative Landscape

promise for new ways that people in the medical field and the general public can interact with AI (Ali et al., 2023; Chen et al., 2023; Kim et al., 2022; Li et al., 2024). Nevertheless, it is important to exercise caution, particularly in the healthcare industry, despite the enthusiasm. The present limits of ChatGPT in achieving strong clinical performance are highlighted by a systematic assessment of its healthcare utilization, which emphasizes the need for specialized natural language processing models that are suited to biomedical datasets for crucial applications (Nayyar, 2023; Mittal et al., 2020). Despite its limitations due to biases and errors, ChatGPT shows promise as an AI tool for clinicians to use in report interpretation and information access. As a whole, smart healthcare is changing due to developments in artificial intelligence and data fusion. The proliferation of healthcare data from multiple sources makes automatic information fusion crucial for making the best decisions. Addressing issues like privacy concerns in cloud storage systems through creative deduplication techniques, research in this area seeks to offer insights into future paths for smart health. Taken together, these advancements demonstrate how new healthcare technology have the ability to revolutionize the industry, paving the path for solutions that are accessible, efficient, and mindful of patients' privacy.

Cluster III: Multimodal Decision-Making in Smart Healthcare Systems

Intelligent healthcare systems are undergoing a sea change as a result of the advent of a data-driven multimodal approach, which is transforming the way diseases are analyzed, triaged, diagnosed, and treated (Cai et al., 2019; Haleem et al., 2023; Kumar et al., 2023; and Saraswat et al., 2022). This change is fuelling the fast adoption of AI in healthcare by highlighting the need for new approaches to data management and decision-making. The decision-making procedures in smart healthcare systems are the primary subject of this all-encompassing review, which aims to cover cutting-edge methods and current trends. The review begins with an examination of multimodal association mining techniques, with a focus on alignment, entity association mining, semantic perception, and other forms of fine-grained data semantics. Second, it explores methods for cross-border association and multimodal data fusion. The article concludes by discussing intelligent decision support systems, interactive decision-making, and panoramic decision frameworks, and by demonstrating how these tools might be used for data privacy and knowledge discovery. Summing up the ever-changing world of smart healthcare systems, this synthesis heralds a new age of revolutionary healthcare solutions.

Bibliography Coupling

Figure 4. Bibliography coupling analysis

Source: VOSviewer

Cluster I (Red nodes): Advancements in Healthcare Technology and AI

Artificial intelligence (AI) and machine learning (ML) are transforming healthcare, yet their black-box nature impedes widespread adoption (Loh et al., 2022; Mittal et al., 2022). Explainable AI (XAI) addresses this, guiding areas like bio signal anomaly detection and clinical note analysis (de Hond et al., 2022). Guidance for AI-based prediction models (AIPMs) is robust in early phases but lacking in later stages, highlighting the need for comprehensive support (Saraswat et al., 2022). Healthcare 5.0 emphasizes real-time monitoring and privacy compliance, with XAI enhancing transparency. Wearable devices hold promise for tracking health, but market translation lags. Continued research and innovation are vital in bridging these gaps (Sabry et al., 2022).

Cluster II (Green Nodes): Artificial Intelligence in Healthcare

By improving diagnostic precision and decision-making procedures, artificial intelligence (AI) has tremendous promise to radically alter the healthcare system. Machine learning (ML), a branch of artificial intelligence, simplifies medical practitioners' work, which is especially helpful in healthcare systems that are already struggling due to a lack of trained personnel (Manickam et al., 2022). ML may be used to improve efficiency and decrease costs in healthcare by identifying ideal trial samples, detecting early indicators of epidemics, and personalizing therapies. There are a number of ethical and legal questions that arise when AI is used in healthcare, such as privacy, prejudice, and the value of human judgment (Javaid et al., 2022). The current absence of regulations that tackle these matters highlights the critical importance of implementing cybersecurity safeguards, protecting privacy, and promoting algorithmic openness. To guarantee the ethical and responsible application of AI technologies, it is vital to carefully consider these concerns as AI continues to impact the future of healthcare (Naik et al., 2022).

Cluster III (Blue Nodes): Metaverse and AI in Healthcare

Medical practices are changing as a result of new paradigms brought about by the integration of digitalization, automation, and cutting-edge tech like the Metaverse and artificial intelligence (AI). These innovations provide new ways to provide patients with high-quality, immersive care at a reasonable cost (Chengoden et al., 2023). The combination of physical and virtual worlds in the Metaverse has the potential to transform medical technology and clinical practice, especially in the areas of artificial intelligence (AI)-based medical imaging and therapy. Further, there have been notable advancements in medical imaging analysis made possible by the use of AI in the diagnosis of brain tumors, particularly using deep learning techniques such as convolutional neural networks (CNNs) (Wang et al., 2022). Full use of these technologies in healthcare will need resolving concerns like privacy, security, and inequity, notwithstanding their revolutionary promise (Arabahmadi et al., 2022).

Cluster IV (Yellow Nodes): Advancements in Healthcare Technology

Recent advancements in healthcare technology, particularly in the Internet of Medical Things (IoMT) and artificial intelligence (AI), have led to the emergence of Smart Healthcare, addressing concerns such as privacy and security through technologies like machine learning (ML), blockchain (BC), and federated learning (FL) (Nguyen et al., 2022; Rehman et al, 2022). FL, a distributed AI paradigm, has gained prominence for its ability to train models without compromising data privacy, particularly suited for the high scalability and privacy concerns of modern healthcare networks. Concurrently, deep learning techniques are revolutionizing healthcare, notably in arrhythmia classification using electrocardiography (ECG) data. To address privacy and explainability concerns, a novel framework combining federated learning and explainable AI (XAI) is proposed, achieving high accuracy in arrhythmia detection while ensuring privacy and interpretability of results. These advancements underscore the transformative potential of emerging technologies in revolutionizing healthcare delivery and patient outcomes (Raza et al., 2022).

Cluster V (Purple Nodes): Healthcare Transformation Through IoT and AI

Proactive healthcare tactics and smart city efforts are being made possible by the revolutionary impact of the confluence of the Internet of Things (IoT) and artificial intelligence (AI). By facilitating precise illness prediction and preventative care measures, predictive analytics—driven by sophisticated AI and ML—is revolutionizing the healthcare sector. When it comes to managing sequential time-series data from electronic health records, deep learning—a subset of ML—offers unrivaled capabilities for evaluating enormous datasets. The precision of illness prediction models is improved by combining Internet of Things (IoT) devices with cloud-based analytics tools (Nancy et al., 2022). An innovative smart healthcare system that utilizes bidirectional long short-term memory (Bi-LSTM) outperforms current methods in forecasting the risk of heart disease. It produces exceptional results in terms of accuracy, precision, sensitivity, specificity, and F-measure. Furthermore, in smart city settings, remote healthcare monitoring (RHM) systems based on the Internet of Things (IoT) and powered by artificial intelligence and machine learning are crucial for improving healthcare efficiency and patient care. This extensive study highlights critical Internet of Things (IoT) applications in healthcare, assesses applicable systems and technologies, provides insights into monitoring applications, and suggests areas for further research. In altering healthcare delivery and increasing patient outcomes, these achievements highlight the transformational potential of AI and the Internet of Things (Alshamrani et al., 2022).

Thematic Map

Figure 6 is a thematic map of the area that helps readers understand the breadth and depth of the authors' topics covered throughout the years. This study uses the co-occurrence keywords + parameter to generate thematic maps. Because they allow researchers to see how themes emerge in the four corners based on their centrality (X-axis) and density (Y-axis), thematic maps are straightforward and easy to grasp (Cobo et al., 2012). Specifically, centrality assesses the degree to which an important subject is interrelated with other themes in a given field or the degree to which there is interaction between clusters. The degree of cohesion within individual clusters is measured by density, however. The degree to which a cluster's interconnected topics provide the basis for a topic.

Motor Themes

Inquiries for "federated learning," "medical services," "digital healthcare," and "internet of things" are densely concentrated and highly centralized on this map. This indicates that these are important and related topics in healthcare AI. Using federated learning, many sources of patient data can be used to train AI models without compromising patient privacy. This is essential for building accurate AI models for healthcare. AI-powered automated diagnoses and personalized treatment regimens are reshaping the healthcare industry. Virtual healthcare is another sector growing rapidly, with innovations like telemedicine, remote patient monitoring, and AI-powered chatbots proliferating. One potential benefit of the Internet of Things (IoT) is the ability for medical devices to collect and exchange data with AI systems; this could lead to better early illness detection and preventative healthcare.

Niche Themes

Despite their frequent mention, the specialty areas of healthcare systems, health politics, and information technology don't appear to pertain much to the primary issue of artificial intelligence in healthcare. This suggests that the technological developments (federated learning, medical services, etc.) propelling this field should receive greater attention than larger systemic or policy issues in healthcare. These small difficulties may nonetheless be relevant to the exploration of artificial intelligence in healthcare, despite their lesser centrality. For instance, the role of AI in the present healthcare system or health policy could be an interesting area to investigate.

Emerging or Declining Themes

The map's priority of terms like "digital healthcare," "medical services," "internet of things," and "federated learning" demonstrates an emphasis on the technological aspects of integrating AI into healthcare procedures. It would be a mistake to disregard these minor themes entirely. They might provide a helping hand: For artificial intelligence (AI) healthcare apps to be successful, qualitative research is essential for understanding user demands and experiences.

Basic Themes

The integration of AI, smart healthcare, clinical decision support, explainability, and machine learning heralds a new era of revolutionary change in contemporary healthcare. The combination of these factors improves the precision of diagnoses, the efficiency of treatments, and the final results for patients. Healthcare practitioners optimize resource usage while delivering individualized, proactive treatment through the use of data-driven insights, transparent algorithms, and integrated systems. More than merely technical progress, this convergence heralds a sea change in the healthcare system towards one that is smarter, more efficient, and focused on the individual patient.

Unveiling the Transformative Landscape

Figure 5. Thematic map

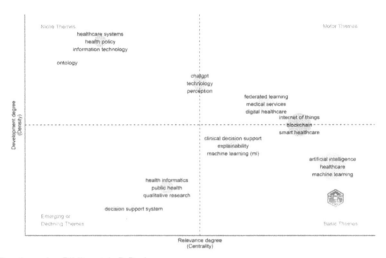

Sources(s): *Author's Creation using Bibliometrix R-Package*

CONCLUSION

This research delves at the application of artificial intelligence (AI) in the healthcare industry, unveiling a scene full of inventiveness, cooperation, and game-changing possibilities. Through the use of a multi-dimensional analysis that takes into account co-citation, bibliographic coupling, thematic mapping, and keyword co-occurrence, the dynamic evolution of this field is revealed.

Federated learning, digital healthcare, and the Internet of Things were found to be important subjects by keyword co-occurrence analysis, underscoring their interdependence and centrality in healthcare AI. Co-citation analysis demonstrated the growing importance of subjects such as federated machine learning and smart healthcare systems in academic discourse. Furthermore, by highlighting connections between several fields of study, bibliographic coupling analysis demonstrated how developments in explainable AI and machine learning are set to transform healthcare IT.

These results were summarized through thematic mapping, which clarified the range and complexity of topics covered, from systemic changes in healthcare delivery to technological breakthroughs. The development of the discipline was fueled by motor themes like digital healthcare and federated learning, while healthcare systems and health politics became side issues.

The dataset tells a captivating story of artificial intelligence's revolutionary effects on healthcare, from improving treatment results to improving diagnostic accuracy. As the healthcare sector adjusts to AI-driven breakthroughs, ethical and privacy considerations must be taken into consideration to enable the equitable and responsible integration of AI technologies.

The study also tries to capture future research agenda by review ten most cited publications (2 each year, 2020-2024). The table 2 below shows the future research agendas in "AI in healthcare" research:

Table 2. Future research agendas

Sr. No	Authors	Title	TC	Research agenda
1	Zhou et al. (2024)	"Natural Language Processing for Smart Healthcare"	23	Developments in Natural Language Processing (NLP) for Healthcare: More research is being done to determine how NLP can be used in smart healthcare environments to improve patient care, clinical judgment, and the provision of healthcare.
2	Ueda et al. (2024)	"Fairness of artificial intelligence in healthcare: review and recommendations"	5	Ethical Considerations in AI Implementation: Research on guaranteeing justice and equity in the application of AI technology in healthcare should continue, with an emphasis on creating standards and suggestions for moral AI application.
3	Sallam (2023)	"ChatGPT Utility in Healthcare Education, Research, and Practice: Systematic Review on the Promising Perspectives and Valid Concerns"	396	ChatGPT's Place in Healthcare teaching and Practice: A more thorough analysis of ChatGPT's applicability in healthcare environments is needed, with a focus on both encouraging viewpoints and legitimate concerns, in order to maximize its incorporation into clinical practice, research, and teaching.
4	Cascella (2023)	"Evaluating the Feasibility of ChatGPT in Healthcare: An Analysis of Multiple Clinical and Research Scenarios"	174	Examining ChatGPT's Viability in Medical Situations: More research is needed to determine whether ChatGPT is feasible in different clinical and research settings in order to evaluate its efficacy, drawbacks, and potential to improve healthcare workflows.
5	Nguyen et al. (2022)	"Federated Learning for Smart Healthcare: A Survey"	151	Further investigation into federated learning techniques in smart healthcare systems is necessary to solve data privacy issues and enhance data sharing, model training, and predictive analytics for better patient outcomes. Federated learning is one way to improve healthcare systems.
6	Loh et al., (2022)	"Application of explainable artificial intelligence for healthcare: A systematic review of the last decade (2011–2022)"	149	Applications of Explainable AI (XAI) in Healthcare: Research into XAI methods to improve the interpretability, openness, and reliability of AI-powered healthcare systems is ongoing. This will help patients and healthcare providers accept and comprehend these systems better.
7	Ghazal et al. (2021)	"IoT for smart cities: Machine learning approaches in smart healthcare—A review"	259	Integration of IoT and Machine Learning in Smart Healthcare: To optimize data collecting, analysis, and decision-making processes for better healthcare management and patient care, more research should be done on machine learning techniques inside IoT-enabled smart healthcare systems.
8	Secinaro et al. (2021)	"The role of artificial intelligence in healthcare: a structured literature review"	205	Organized Literature Reviews of AI's Various Applications in Healthcare: Ongoing analysis of AI's various applications in healthcare, with an emphasis on recognizing new trends, obstacles, and areas for further study and application.
9	Amann et al. (2020)	"Explainability for artificial intelligence in healthcare: a multidisciplinary perspective"	410	Multidisciplinary Views on AI Explainability in Healthcare: To create thorough frameworks and recommendations, more research should be done on multidisciplinary perspectives on AI explainability, taking into account the opinions of data scientists, healthcare practitioners, ethicists, and legislators.
10	Bohr et al. (2020)	"The rise of artificial intelligence in healthcare applications"	326	Examining Novel and Emerging AI Applications in Healthcare: This study examines novel and emerging AI applications in healthcare, taking into account technological innovations, creative use cases, and possible effects on patient outcomes and healthcare delivery.

Researchers, policymakers, and healthcare professionals can use this bibliometric study as a guide for future initiatives aimed at optimizing the use of AI in healthcare delivery and enhancing patient outcomes.

REFERENCES

Ali, H., Qadir, J., Alam, T., Househ, M., & Shah, Z. (2023). Revolutionizing healthcare with Foundation AI models. *Studies in Health Technology and Informatics*. 10.3233/SHTI23053337387067

Alshamrani, M. (2022). IoT and artificial intelligence implementations for remote healthcare monitoring systems: A survey. *Journal of King Saud University. Computer and Information Sciences*, 34(8), 4687–4701. 10.1016/j.jksuci.2021.06.005

Arabahmadi, M., Farahbakhsh, R., & Rezazadeh, J. (2022). Deep learning for smart healthcare—A survey on brain tumor detection from medical imaging. *Sensors (Basel)*, 22(5), 1960. 10.3390/s22051960 35271115

Cai, Q., Wang, H., Li, Z., & Liu, X. (2019). A survey on multimodal data-driven smart healthcare systems: Approaches and applications. *IEEE Access : Practical Innovations, Open Solutions*, 7, 133583–133599. 10.1109/ACCESS.2019.2941419

Chandel, A., Bhanot, N., Gupta, S., & Verma, R. (2024). Oil Spills-Where We Were, Where We Are, And Where We Will Be? A Bibliometric and Content Analysis Discourse. In *BIO Web of Conferences* (Vol. 86, p. 01050). EDP Sciences.

Chandel, A., Bhanot, N., & Sharma, R. (2023). A bibliometric and content analysis discourse on business application of blockchain technology. *International Journal of Quality & Reliability Management*. 10.1108/IJQRM-02-2023-0025

Chandel, A., Bhanot, N., & Verma, R. (2023). A Bibliometric Investigation of Ecocide Research: Tracing Trends and Shaping the Future. In *E3S Web of Conferences* (Vol. 453, p. 01044). EDP Sciences. 10.1051/e3sconf/202345301044

Chandel, A., & Kaur, T. (2022). Demystifying neuromarketing: a bibliometric analysis using vosviewer. In *Developing Relationships, Personalization, and Data Herald in Marketing5.0* (pp. 256-283). IGI Global. 10.4018/978-1-6684-4496-2.ch016

Char, D. S., Shah, N. H., & Magnus, D. (2018). Implementing machine learning in health care—Addressing ethical challenges. *The New England Journal of Medicine*, 378(11), 981–983. 10.1056/NEJMp1714229 29539284

Chen, X., Xie, H., Li, Z., Cheng, G., Leng, M., & Wang, F. L. (2023). Information fusion and artificial intelligence for smart healthcare: A bibliometric study. *Information Processing & Management*, 60(1), 103113. 10.1016/j.ipm.2022.103113

Chengoden, R., Victor, N., Huynh-The, T., Yenduri, G., Jhaveri, R. H., Alazab, M., Bhattacharya, S., Hegde, P., Maddikunta, P. K., & Gadekallu, T. R. (2023). Metaverse for healthcare: A survey on potential applications, challenges and future directions. *IEEE Access : Practical Innovations, Open Solutions*, 11, 12765–12795. 10.1109/ACCESS.2023.3241628

Cobo, M. J., López-Herrera, A. G., Herrera-Viedma, E., & Herrera, F. (2012). SciMAT: A new science mapping analysis software tool. *Journal of the American Society for Information Science and Technology*, 63(8), 1609–1630. 10.1002/asi.22688

Davenport, T. H., & Kalakota, R. (2019). The potential for artificial intelligence in healthcare. *Future Healthcare Journal*, 6(2), 94–98. 10.7861/futurehosp.6-2-9431363513

De Hond, A. A., Leeuwenberg, A. M., Hooft, L., Kant, I. M., Nijman, S. W., Van Os, H. J., Aardoom, J. J., Debray, T. P., Schuit, E., Van Smeden, M., Reitsma, J. B., Steyerberg, E. W., Chavannes, N. H., & Moons, K. G. (2022). Guidelines and quality criteria for artificial intelligence-based prediction models in healthcare: A scoping review. npj. *Digital Medicine*, 5(1), 2. Advance online publication. 10.1038/s41746-021-00549-735013569

Esteva, A., Robicquet, A., Ramsundar, B., Kuleshov, V., DePristo, M., Chou, K., Cui, C., Corrado, G., Thrun, S., & Dean, J. (2019). A guide to deep learning in healthcare. *Nature Medicine*, 25(1), 24–29. 10.1038/s41591-018-0316-z30617335

Guest, G., Bunce, A., & Johnson, L. (2006). How many interviews are enough? An experiment with data saturation and variability. *Field Methods*, 18(1), 59–82. 10.1177/1525822X05279903

Gulshan, V., Peng, L., Coram, M., Stumpe, M. C., Wu, D., Narayanaswamy, A., & Webster, D. R. (2016). Development and validation of a deep learning algorithm for detection of diabetic retinopathy in retinal fundus photographs. *jama*, 316(22), 2402-2410.

Haleem, A., Javaid, M., Pratap Singh, R., & Suman, R. (2023). Exploring the revolution in healthcare systems through the applications of digital twin technology. *Biomedical Technology*, 4, 28–38. 10.1016/j.bmt.2023.02.001

Kim, J., Ryu, S., & Park, N. (2022). Privacy-enhanced data Deduplication computational intelligence technique for secure healthcare applications. *Computers, Materials & Continua*, 70(2), 4169–4184. 10.32604/cmc.2022.019277

Krittanawong, C., Zhang, H., Wang, Z., Aydar, M., & Kitai, T. (2017). Artificial intelligence in precision cardiovascular medicine. *Journal of the American College of Cardiology*, 69(21), 2657–2664. 10.1016/j.jacc.2017.03.57128545640

Kumar, A., Mani, V., Jain, V., Gupta, H., & Venkatesh, V. (2023). Managing healthcare supply chain through artificial intelligence (AI): A study of critical success factors. *Computers & Industrial Engineering*, 175, 108815. 10.1016/j.cie.2022.10881536405396

Kumar, K. P., Baskaran, P., & Thulasisingh, A. (2022). *Artificial intelligence in healthcare analytics. Applications of Artificial Intelligence and Machine Learning in Healthcare.* 10.36647/AAIM-LH/2022.01.B1.Ch011

Laranjo, L., Dunn, A. G., Tong, H. L., Kocaballi, A. B., Chen, J., Bashir, R., Surian, D., Gallego, B., Magrabi, F., Lau, A. Y. S., & Coiera, E. (2018). Conversational agents in healthcare: A systematic review. *Journal of the American Medical Informatics Association : JAMIA*, 25(9), 1248–1258. 10.1093/jamia/ocy07230010941

Li, J., Dada, A., Puladi, B., Kleesiek, J., & Egger, J. (2024). ChatGPT in healthcare: A taxonomy and systematic review. *Computer Methods and Programs in Biomedicine*, 245, 108013. 10.1016/j.cmpb.2024.10801338262126

Lipton, Z. C., Kale, D. C., Elkan, C., & Wetzel, R. (2015). *Learning to diagnose with LSTM recurrent neural networks.* arXiv preprint arXiv:1511.03677.

Loh, H. W., Ooi, C. P., Seoni, S., Barua, P. D., Molinari, F., & Acharya, U. R. (2022). Application of explainable artificial intelligence for healthcare: A systematic review of the last decade (2011–2022). *Computer Methods and Programs in Biomedicine*, 226, 107161. 10.1016/j.cmpb.2022.10716136228495

Lu, W., Wang, J., Chen, Y., Qin, X., Xu, R., Dimitriadis, D., & Qin, T. (2024). Personalized federated learning with adaptive Batchnorm for healthcare. *IEEE Transactions on Big Data*, 1–1. 10.1109/TBDATA.2022.3177197

Mittal, A., Aggarwal, A., & Mittal, R. (2020). Predicting university students' adoption of mobile news applications: The role of perceived hedonic value and news motivation. [IJESMA]. *International Journal of E-Services and Mobile Applications*, 12(4), 42–59. 10.4018/IJESMA.2020100103

Mittal, A., Mantri, A., Tandon, U., & Dwivedi, Y. K. (2022). A unified perspective on the adoption of online teaching in higher education during the COVID-19 pandemic. *Information Discovery and Delivery*, 50(2), 117–132. 10.1108/IDD-09-2020-0114

Moher, D., Shamseer, L., Clarke, M., Ghersi, D., Liberati, A., Petticrew, M., Shekelle, P., & Stewart, L. A. (2015). Preferred reporting items for systematic review and meta-analysis protocols (PRISMA-P) 2015 statement. *Systematic Reviews*, 4(1), 1. 10.1186/2046-4053-4-125554246

Nancy, A. A., Ravindran, D., Raj Vincent, P. M., Srinivasan, K., & Gutierrez Reina, D. (2022). IoT-cloud-Based smart healthcare monitoring system for heart disease prediction via deep learning. *Electronics (Basel)*, 11(15), 2292. 10.3390/electronics11152292

Nayyar, V. (2018). 'My Mind Starts Craving'-Impact of Resealable Packages on the Consumption Behavior of Indian Consumers. *Indian Journal of Marketing*, 48(11), 56–63. 10.17010/ijom/2018/v48/i11/137986

Nayyar, V. (2022). Reviewing the impact of digital migration on the consumer buying journey with robust measurement of PLS-SEM and R Studio. *Systems Research and Behavioral Science*, 39(3), 542–556. 10.1002/sres.2857

Nayyar, V. (2023). The role of marketing analytics in the ethical consumption of online consumers. *Total Quality Management & Business Excellence*, 34(7-8), 1015–1031. 10.1080/14783363.2022.2139676

Nayyar, V., & Batra, R. (2020). Does online media self-regulate consumption behavior of INDIAN youth? *International Review on Public and Nonprofit Marketing*, 17(3), 277–288. 10.1007/s12208-020-00248-1

Nguyen, D. C., Pham, Q. V., Pathirana, P. N., Ding, M., Seneviratne, A., Lin, Z., Dobre, O., & Hwang, W. J. (2022). Federated learning for smart healthcare: A survey. *ACM Computing Surveys*, 55(3), 1–37. 10.1145/3501296

Obermeyer, Z., & Emanuel, E. J. (2016). Predicting the future—Big data, machine learning, and clinical medicine. *The New England Journal of Medicine*, 375(13), 1216–1219. 10.1056/NEJMp160618127682033

Rajkomar, A., Oren, E., Chen, K., Dai, A. M., Hajaj, N., Hardt, M., Liu, P. J., Liu, X., Marcus, J., Sun, M., Sundberg, P., Yee, H., Zhang, K., Zhang, Y., Flores, G., Duggan, G. E., Irvine, J., Le, Q., Litsch, K., & Dean, J. (2018). Scalable and accurate deep learning with electronic health records. *NPJ Digital Medicine*, 1(1), 1–10. 10.1038/s41746-018-0029-131304302

Raza, A., Tran, K. P., Koehl, L., & Li, S. (2022). Designing ECG monitoring healthcare system with federated transfer learning and explainable AI. *Knowledge-Based Systems*, 236, 107763. 10.1016/j.knosys.2021.107763

Rehman, A., Abbas, S., Khan, M. A., Ghazal, T. M., Adnan, K. M., & Mosavi, A. (2022). A secure healthcare 5.0 system based on blockchain technology entangled with federated learning technique. https://doi.org/10.31219/osf.io/gvkqc

Sabry, F., Eltaras, T., Labda, W., Alzoubi, K., & Malluhi, Q. (2022). Machine learning for healthcare wearable devices: The big picture. *Journal of Healthcare Engineering*, 2022, 1–25. 10.1155/2022/465392335480146

Saraswat, D., Bhattacharya, P., Verma, A., Prasad, V. K., Tanwar, S., Sharma, G., Bokoro, P. N., & Sharma, R. (2022). Explainable AI for healthcare 5.0: Opportunities and challenges. *IEEE Access : Practical Innovations, Open Solutions*, 10, 84486–84517. 10.1109/ACCESS.2022.3197671

Saraswat, D., Bhattacharya, P., Verma, A., Prasad, V. K., Tanwar, S., Sharma, G., Bokoro, P. N., & Sharma, R. (2022). Explainable AI for healthcare 5.0: Opportunities and challenges. *IEEE Access : Practical Innovations, Open Solutions*, 10, 84486–84517. 10.1109/ACCESS.2022.3197671

Sharma, D., & Bikshandi, B. (2020). Artificial empathy – An artificial intelligence challenge. *Artificial Intelligence*, 321–326. 10.4324/9780429317415-19

Topol, E. J. (2019). High-performance medicine: The convergence of human and artificial intelligence. *Nature Medicine*, 25(1), 44–56. 10.1038/s41591-018-0300-730617339

Tucker, A., Wang, Z., Rotalinti, Y., & Myles, P. (2020). Generating high-fidelity synthetic patient data for assessing machine learning healthcare software. *npj. Digital Medicine*, 3(1), 147. 10.1038/s41746-020-00353-933299100

Wang, C., Zhang, J., Lassi, N., & Zhang, X. (2022). Privacy protection in using artificial intelligence for healthcare: Chinese regulation in comparative perspective. *Health Care*, 10(10), 1878. 10.3390/healthcare1010187836292325

Wang, G., Badal, A., Jia, X., Maltz, J. S., Mueller, K., Myers, K. J., Niu, C., Vannier, M., Yan, P., Yu, Z., & Zeng, R. (2022). Development of metaverse for intelligent healthcare. *Nature Machine Intelligence*, 4(11), 922–929. 10.1038/s42256-022-00549-636935774

Yang, G., Pang, Z., Jamal Deen, M., Dong, M., Zhang, Y., Lovell, N., & Rahmani, A. M. (2020). Homecare robotic systems for healthcare 4.0: Visions and enabling technologies. *IEEE Journal of Biomedical and Health Informatics*, 24(9), 2535–2549. 10.1109/JBHI.2020.299052932340971

Chapter 15
Examining the Impact of AI on Education:
Ethical, Psychological, and Pedagogical Perspectives

Anurag Pahuja
https://orcid.org/0000-0002-1170-5749
Lovely Professional University, India

Sargunpreet Kaur
Lovely Professional University, India

Komal Budhraja
Fortune Institute of International Business, India

Sakshi Kathuria
Fortune Institute of International Business, India

ABSTRACT

Education is a fundamental aspect of human development, crucial for both individuals and societies. This chapter provides a comprehensive exploration of education, its significance, and its multifaceted nature. Education encompasses the acquisition of knowledge, skills, values, and attitudes through formal and informal means. It empowers individuals to understand their environment, make informed decisions, and contribute to society's betterment. However, the integration of artificial intelligence (AI) in education raises ethical, psychological, and pedagogical concerns. AI's capability to generate coherent responses may compromise academic integrity and undermine critical thinking. Furthermore, excessive dependence on AI may diminish students' motivation and self-efficacy, leading to passive learning and eroding trust in the educational system. Pedagogically, AI cannot replace the nuanced guidance and personalized feedback offered by teachers, potentially disrupting the traditional teacher-student dynamic.

DOI: 10.4018/979-8-3693-6660-8.ch015

Copyright ©2024, IGI Global. Copying or distributing in print or electronic forms without written permission of IGI Global is prohibited.

INTRODUCTION

"Education is the most Powerful Weapon Which Can use to change the World."

This profound statement by Nelson Mandela encapsulates the belief that education equips individuals with the tools to challenge existing norms, address social injustices, and contribute to the betterment of their communities. It underscores the idea that education is an essential educational birth right that has the implicit to break cycles of poverty, inequality, and ignorance. Education drives economic growth, social mobility, and personal development, fostering critical thinking, problem-solving, and creativity. Moreover, it promotes social cohesion, equality, and democratic values by providing equal opportunities and fostering understanding and tolerance.

AI, developed by OpenAI, 2023 is an advanced language model that has the potential to greatly impact education. This AI-powered tool can be used in various educational settings to enhance literacy skills, provide substantiated instruction, and offer valuable support to both students and educators. One of the main benefits of AI in education is its capability to epitomize literacy. Through its natural language processing capabilities, AI can engage with students in a conversational manner, understanding their queries and providing customized explanations or resources. This personalized approach caters to individual learning styles and paces, resulting in a more adaptive and effective learning experience. Additionally, AI serves as a valuable resource for students seeking instant explanations or fresh information on academic topics. Whether it is answering questions about complex concepts, offering real-time feedback on assignments, or providing supplementary learning materials, AI acts as a virtual assistant, supporting students in their academic pursuits. Furthermore, AI can assist educators in various ways. It can help create interactive lesson plans, generate educational content, and even automate administrative tasks such as grading assignments or providing personalized feedback on student work. By streamlining these processes, educators have more time to engage with students on a deeper level and address their individual needs. Similarly, AI has the potential to support language learning endeavours by engaging learners in meaningful interactions and providing opportunities for language practice. Its ability to comprehend and generate human-like responses makes it a valuable tool for language acquisition. However, it is important to consider privacy, data security, and ethical use when implementing AI in educational settings. Safeguarding sensitive student information and ensuring responsible AI usage are crucial factors that need to be addressed.

Despite its usefulness to students in the field of education, the rise of AI has raised concerns among teachers and academics (Smith, 2020). This is because AI lacks human interaction, which can lead to issues such as plagiarism, cheating, and other misleading practices (Jones & Brown, 2019). These negative impacts on education include a lack of creativity, inaccurate feedback, and a deficiency in emotional intelligence (Garcia et al., 2021). One of the main drawbacks of AI is its tendency to stifle creativity, resulting in a lack of original and engaging ideas (Lee & Wang, 2018). The frequent use of AI services further diminishes the use of human creativity (Chen & Liu, 2020). While AI provides quick feedback, much of it is flawed and lacks specificity (Johnson, 2017). Although there are on-going efforts to improve this area, most of the work done by AI is generalized and lacks individual attention (Thompson et al., 2022). While AI is generally effective and known for its human-like gestures, it lacks empathy and human instincts (Robinson, 2019). This occasionally leads to mechanical or robotic responses that lack genuine human understanding (Adams & White, 2021).

Examining the Impact of AI on Education

Artificial Intelligence (AI) has emerged as a transformative force in various domains, and its integration into education is reshaping traditional teaching and learning paradigms. As AI technologies continue to advance, they offer promising opportunities to enhance educational practices, personalize learning experiences, and improve educational outcomes. However, along with these advancements come ethical, psychological, and pedagogical considerations that must be carefully examined to ensure that AI in education serves the best interests of students, educators, and society as a whole.

While Artificial Intelligence offers multitudinous benefits similar as substantiated literacy and instant access to information, there are Concerns about its implicit negative impact on education. This impact can be anatomized from Ethical, Psychological, and pedagogical perspectives.

Figure 1.

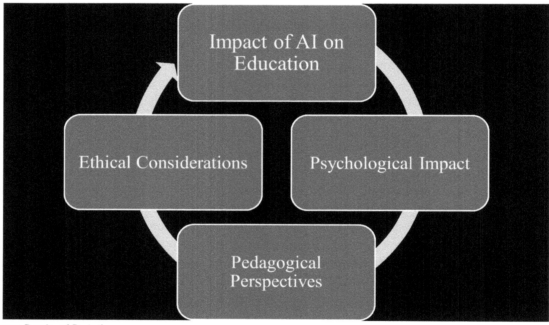

Source: *Developed By Author*

This paper is structured into several distinct sections for clarity and coherence. Firstly, Section 1 serves as an introduction, setting the stage for the subsequent discussion. Moving on to Section 2, a comprehensive literature review is provided, offering insights into existing research and knowledge. Ethical considerations are thoroughly explored in Section 3, delving into the moral implications inherent in the utilization of AI. Section 4 is dedicated to elucidating the psychological dimensions of AI in education, examining its impact from a psychological standpoint. Pedagogical aspects of AI in education are extensively discussed in Section 5, providing a detailed examination of its instructional implications. Section 6 presents significant case studies, offering real-world examples to illustrate key concepts and applications. Future directions and considerations are outlined in Section 7, offering insights into potential advancements and challenges. Finally, Section 8 offers a succinct conclusion, summarizing key findings and implications drawn from the preceding sections.

Overview of Ethical, Psychological, and Pedagogical Aspects

- *Ethical Perspectives*

Ethical considerations surrounding AI in education encompass a range of issues, including privacy, bias, fairness, and equity. AI-powered learning systems often collect vast amounts of student data, raising concerns about data privacy and security (Floridi, 2019). Additionally, AI algorithms can perpetuate biases present in the data they are trained on, potentially exacerbating inequalities in educational opportunities (Crawford & Paglen, 2019). Ensuring fairness and equity in AI-driven educational environments is crucial to promoting equal access to quality education for all learners (Sarwar et al., 2020).

- *Psychological Perspectives*

From a psychological standpoint, AI in education influences factors such as cognitive load, motivation, engagement, and emotional well-being. AI tools can alleviate cognitive load by providing personalized support and adaptive learning experiences tailored to individual student needs (Koedinger & Corbett, 2012). Moreover, AI-driven learning environments have the potential to enhance student motivation and engagement through interactive feedback mechanisms and gamification elements (Baker et al., 2010). However, concerns also arise regarding the emotional impact of AI tutoring systems and the need to prioritize students' psychological well-being in technology-mediated learning environments (Baylor & Kim, 2009).

- *Pedagogical Perspectives*

Pedagogical considerations related to AI in education focus on the integration of AI technologies into teaching practices, curriculum design, and assessment strategies. AI enables personalized learning experiences by adapting instructional content and pacing to suit individual student preferences and learning styles (VanLehn, 2011). Furthermore, AI-driven content creation tools facilitate the development of interactive educational materials tailored to specific learning objectives and student needs (Woolf, 2010). However, questions arise regarding the role of teachers in AI-integrated classrooms and the implications for pedagogical autonomy and professional expertise (Luckin et al., 2016).

This paper aims to comprehensively examine the impact of AI on education from ethical, psychological, and pedagogical perspectives. By exploring the ethical implications of AI technologies, assessing their psychological effects on students, and analysing their pedagogical implications for teaching and learning, this paper seeks to provide insights into the opportunities and challenges of integrating AI into educational practices. Ultimately, the goal is to inform educators, policymakers, and stakeholders about the ethical, psychological, and pedagogical considerations associated with AI in education and to propose recommendations for promoting responsible and effective use of AI technologies in educational settings.

THE GIST OF LITERATURE

Despite the popularity and attention, less work has been done in the literature to investigate the study of ChatGPT in educational environments.

Review of important studies on Education and Artificial Intelligence has been presented in Table 1. The Existing Studies Highlight both Limitations and Capabilities that ChatGPT might offer in Different Disciplines of Education.

Authors /Reference	Focus	Limitations
Currie (2023)	Challenges and potentials of ChatGPT in nuclear medicine	Healthcare Centered
Eggmann et al. (2023)	Implications of ChatGPT in dental Education.	Healthcare Focused
Emenike and Emenike (2023)	Implicit use of ChatGPT for Tutoring, Exploration and Professional Activities.	A method of development has not been Provided.
Eysenbach (2023)	Impact of ChatGPT on medical education	Healthcare Focused
Gardner and Giordano (2023)	Oral examinations	Costly Deployment
Gentile et al. (2023)	Critical dimensions related to the teacher figure	Dimensions may need to be contextualized
Miao and Ahn (2023)	Impact of ChatGPT on nursing education	Healthcare Focused
Lo (2023)	Impact of ChatGPT on education	Majority of papers are Preprints
Ray (2023)	Impact of ChatGPT on nursing education	Healthcare Focused
Sallam (2023)	ChatGPT utility in health education	Broad and often distant topics in healthcare, the majority of papers on preprints
Thurzo et al. (2023)	Use of AI in dental education	AI feeling anatomy versus AI memorizing anatomy
Wu and Yu (2023)	Analysis of the impact of AI Chatbots on students' learning outcomes.	Codification of research questions and reliance on statistical outcomes for 24 studies

Further exploration is demanded to completely understand the impact of Artificial Intelligence in the field of education, particularly in non-medical subjects where issues may not be as well-defined. While there have been studies conducted on the use of Chatbots in education, there's still important work to be done to epitomize the current state of the art. One area that requires farther disquisition is how ChatGPT can be employed in subjects that do not have easily defined issues, similar as understanding the physiology of the mortal body and maintaining ideal fleshly conditions. In these fields, the use of virtual intelligence may not be as straightforward as it is in other subjects with further constrained issues.

In addition to medical settings, consider how Artificial Intelligence could revolutionize fields such as history or literature. While AI might assist in diagnosing and treating patients by suggesting treatment options based on symptoms, its application in subjects like history or literature may demand more nuanced approaches due to the absence of singular correct answers or outcomes. This highlights the potential for Digital Intelligence to adapt and enhance decision-making processes in diverse domains.

One potential application of ChatGPT in non-medical education could be as a tool for facilitating discussions and debates. Students could interact with AI powered Co-pilots to explore different perspectives on a topic, ask questions, and engage in critical thinking. This could help foster a deeper understanding of complex subjects and encourage students to think critically and independently.

Another area where Virtual Intelligence could be beneficial is in providing personalized feedback and guidance to students. By analysing their responses and providing tailored suggestions, ChatGPT could help students improve their writing skills, problem-solving abilities, and overall understanding of the subject matter.

However, there are challenges that need to be addressed when using Chatbots in education. One major concern is the potential for bias in the model's responses. ChatGPT learns from vast amounts of data, which can include biased or incorrect information. It is crucial to ensure that the model's responses are accurate, unbiased, and aligned with educational standards. Additionally, there is a need for further research on how to effectively integrate Artificial Intelligence into existing educational frameworks. Teachers and educators play a vital role in guiding students' learning experiences, and it is important to explore how ChatGPT can complement their expertise rather than replace it.

In the field of healthcare, Machine Learning has been explored for a variety of applications, such as triage, diagnosis, and patient communication. However, as Emenike and Emenike (2023) note, the findings of these studies may not be generalizable or transferable to other contexts. Similarly, Eggmann(2023) and Eysenbach (2023) highlight the limitations of using AI in healthcare, such as the need for high-quality training data and the potential for bias in AI decision-making.

In the field of nursing education, Ray (2023) and Miao and Ahn(2023) have explored the use of AI in tutoring and literacy. Still, as Thurzo etal.(2023) note, AI may fall suddenly in understanding mortal deconstruction and the mortal experience of healthcare professionals.

While Conducting Literature Review, the major end was to cover the studies on Artificial Intelligence and explore colorful approaches. In doing so, we came following exploration questions.
1. What ways are used when studying AI in education literature?
2. What are the capabilities for Chatbots in education literature?
3. What are the limitations and challenges for ChatGPT in education literature?

This disquisition contributes to our understanding of AI and builds its capacity for disquisition in educational surrounds. In the styles section that follows, we describe our quest process and codification scheme which mainly comprises open and axial coding as seen in rested proposition disquisition. We purposefully used rested proposition as our regular approach to enable analysis and discussion of imperative disquisition on Chatbots. The results section provides a summary of findings girding our three disquisition questions noted above. In the discussion, we further give implicit challenges and future capabilities of AI in education predicated on our emulsion of the reviewed studies. The pivotal donation of this disquisition is in offering an in-depth emulsion of literature and furnishing a discussion on future considerations for AI tools in education.

ETHICAL PERSPECTIVES

Definition of Ethical AI in Education

Ethical AI in education refers to the application of artificial intelligence technologies in ways that uphold principles of fairness, transparency, accountability, and respect for human rights and dignity. It involves designing, developing, and deploying AI systems in educational settings while considering the potential ethical implications and ensuring that these technologies align with societal values and norms (Floridi, 2019).

In the context of education, ethical AI encompasses various aspects, including data privacy, algorithmic transparency, bias mitigation, and the promotion of inclusive and equitable learning opportunities. It involves adhering to ethical guidelines and standards to safeguard the interests and well-being of students, educators, and other stakeholders involved in the educational process (UNESCO, 2020).

Privacy Concerns in AI-Powered Learning Environments

Privacy concerns arise in AI-powered learning environments due to the collection, storage, and analysis of vast amounts of student data. These environments often rely on data-driven algorithms to personalize learning experiences and provide targeted recommendations, which require access to sensitive information such as student demographics, academic performance, and behavioral patterns (Morrison, 2018).

However, the indiscriminate use of student data raises significant privacy risks, including unauthorized access, data breaches, and potential misuse of personal information. Moreover, the lack of transparency regarding data collection practices and the algorithms used in AI systems exacerbates privacy concerns and undermines trust in educational institutions and technology providers (OECD, 2019).

Bias and Fairness Issues in AI Algorithms

Bias and fairness issues are prevalent in AI algorithms used in educational contexts, leading to inequalities and discrimination against certain groups of students. AI systems can inherit biases from the data they are trained on, reflecting existing social, cultural, and historical biases present in society (Crawford & Paglen, 2019).

For example, AI algorithms may exhibit racial or gender biases in decision-making processes, such as grading assignments or recommending courses, leading to disparities in educational outcomes. Addressing bias in AI algorithms requires careful consideration of the data used for training, as well as the development of algorithmic fairness techniques to mitigate biases and ensure equitable treatment for all students (Barocas & Selbst, 2016).

Equity and Access in AI-Enhanced Education

Equity and access are fundamental ethical considerations in AI-enhanced education, as these technologies have the potential to either exacerbate or alleviate existing inequalities in educational opportunities. While AI can personalize learning experiences and provide targeted support to students with diverse needs and backgrounds, there is a risk of widening the digital divide and perpetuating socioeconomic disparities (Luckin et al., 2019).

Ensuring equity and access in AI-enhanced education requires proactive measures to address barriers to participation and promote inclusivity for marginalized and underserved communities. This includes designing AI systems that are accessible to individuals with disabilities, providing equitable access to technology resources, and fostering digital literacy skills to empower all learners to benefit from AI-enabled educational experiences (UNESCO, 2020).

Figure 2.

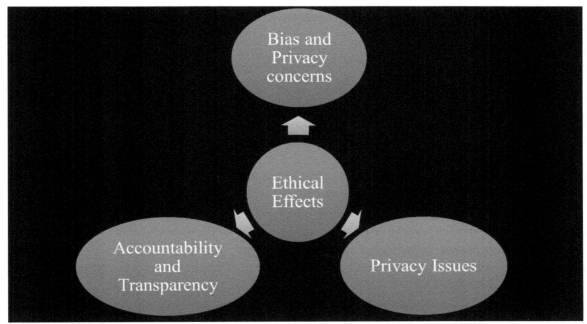

Source: *Developed By Author*

PSYCHOLOGICAL PERSPECTIVES

Cognitive Load and Learning Efficiency With AI Tools

AI tools in education have the potential to optimize cognitive load and enhance learning efficiency by providing personalized learning experiences tailored to individual student needs. For example, intelligent tutoring systems can dynamically adjust the difficulty level of learning tasks based on the student's performance, thereby optimizing cognitive resources and promoting deeper learning (Koedinger & Corbett, 2012).

Additionally, AI-powered educational platforms can offer adaptive feedback and scaffolding to support learners in overcoming cognitive challenges and mastering complex concepts. By tailoring instructional content and pacing to match the learner's cognitive abilities and learning preferences, AI tools can help optimize learning outcomes and improve retention rates (VanLehn, 2011).

Student Motivation and Engagement in AI-Supported Learning

One of the key benefits of AI-supported learning is its potential to enhance student motivation and engagement. AI-powered educational applications often incorporate interactive features, gamification elements, and personalized recommendations to captivate students' interest and sustain their engagement over time (Baker et al., 2010).

For example, language learning applications may use AI algorithms to generate interactive exercises and quizzes tailored to the learner's proficiency level and interests, thereby fostering a sense of autonomy and accomplishment. Similarly, AI-driven virtual tutors can provide real-time feedback and encouragement, boosting students' motivation and confidence in their learning abilities (Baylor & Kim, 2009).

Emotional Intelligence and AI Tutoring Systems

Emotional intelligence plays a crucial role in effective teaching and learning, and AI tutoring systems are increasingly incorporating features designed to recognize and respond to students' emotional states. For instance, affective computing technologies can investigate facial expressions, vocal intonations, and other physiological signals to infer students' emotions and adapt instructional strategies accordingly (D'Mello & Graesser, 2012).

By integrating emotional intelligence into AI tutoring systems, educators can create more empathetic and supportive learning environments that cater to students' social and emotional needs. For example, an AI tutor might detect signs of frustration or confusion in a student's facial expressions and respond with encouraging messages or alternative explanations to help alleviate emotional distress and promote positive learning experiences (Pardos & Heffernan, 2010).

Psychological Well-Being and Mental Health Implications

The integration of AI in education raises important questions about its impact on students' psychological well-being and mental health. While AI tools have the potential to enhance learning experiences and support students' academic progress, there are concerns about the potential negative effects of excessive screen time, social isolation, and dependency on technology (Twenge, 2019).

Furthermore, the use of AI-driven assessment tools and performance metrics may inadvertently contribute to students' anxiety, stress, and self-esteem issues, particularly if they feel pressured to meet predetermined benchmarks or compete against algorithmically generated standards (Conley et al., 2019).

To mitigate these risks, educators and developers must prioritize the holistic well-being of students and incorporate strategies for promoting mental health awareness, self-care practices, and healthy technology use habits into AI-supported learning environments (Kramer et al., 2020).

Figure 3.

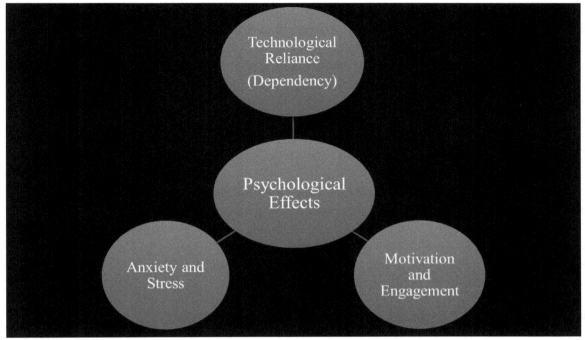

Source: *Developed By Author*

PEDAGOGICAL ASPECTS

Personalization and Adaptive Learning With AI

AI enables personalized learning experiences tailored to individual student needs and preferences. Adaptive learning platforms use AI algorithms to examine student performance data and adjust instructional content and pacing accordingly (VanLehn, 2011).

For example, Khan Academy's adaptive learning platform offers personalized practice exercises and instructional videos based on students' skill levels and learning progress. By dynamically adapting to each student's strengths and weaknesses, these AI-powered systems optimize learning outcomes and promote mastery of subject matter (Khan Academy, n.d.).

Teacher Roles and Collaboration in AI-Integrated Classrooms

AI-integrated classrooms redefine the role of teachers as facilitators and mentors rather than traditional lecturers. Teachers collaborate with AI systems to create engaging learning experiences, provide targeted support, and assess student progress (Luckin et al., 2016).

For instance, the Teach to One personalized learning program uses AI algorithms to create individualized schedules and learning pathways for each student, allowing teachers to focus on small-group instruction and differentiated learning activities. This collaborative approach leverages the strengths of both teachers and AI technologies to maximize student learning outcomes (Teach to One, n.d.).

Curriculum Design and AI-Driven Content Creation

AI-driven content creation tools revolutionize curriculum design by generating interactive educational materials tailored to specific learning objectives and student needs (Woolf, 2010).

For example, Carnegie Learning's AI-driven textbooks use natural language processing algorithms to analyse student responses and provide personalized feedback in real time. These adaptive textbooks adapt to students' learning styles and progress, offering targeted support and scaffolding to facilitate comprehension and mastery (Carnegie Learning).

Assessment and Feedback in AI-Empowered Education

AI empowers educators to conduct more effective assessments and provide timely feedback to students. AI-powered assessment tools use machine learning algorithms to examine student responses, identify patterns of understanding, and generate personalized feedback (Baker et al., 2010).

For instance, Turnitin's Feedback Studio uses AI algorithms to provide students with detailed feedback on their writing assignments, highlighting areas for improvement in grammar, style, and plagiarism detection. By leveraging AI for assessment and feedback, educators can streamline grading processes, provide targeted support, and promote continuous improvement in student learning (Turnitin).

Figure 4.

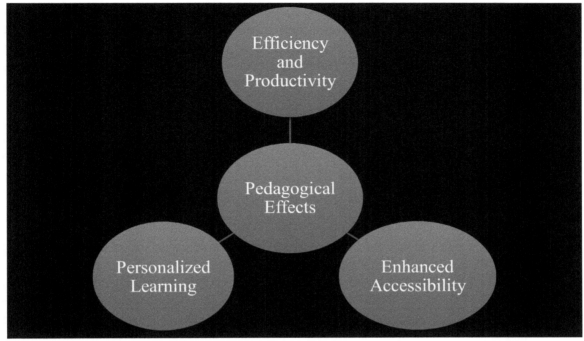

Source: *Developed By Author*

CASE STUDIES

1. IBM Watson Education:

    - Overview: IBM Watson Education is an AI-powered platform that offers personalized learning experiences, data-driven insights, and teacher support tools.
    - Success Story: The Georgia State University used IBM Watson Education to improve graduation rates and reduce achievement gaps among its diverse student population. By analysing student data and providing targeted interventions, the university increased graduation rates by 22% and narrowed the achievement gap between Black and white students by 70% (IBM).
    - Challenges: Implementing AI technologies like IBM Watson Education requires significant investment in infrastructure, training, and support services. Moreover, ensuring data privacy and security remains a major challenge, as educational institutions must navigate complex regulatory requirements and safeguard sensitive student information (Coughlin et al., 2020).

2. Duolingo:

- Overview: Duolingo is a popular language learning platform that uses AI algorithms to personalize learning experiences and optimize learning outcomes.
- Success Story: Duolingo's AI-powered adaptive learning system has enabled millions of users worldwide to learn new languages at their own pace and convenience. The platform offers interactive exercises, quizzes, and gamified challenges tailored to each user's proficiency level and learning goals. As a result, Duolingo has achieved high user engagement and retention rates, making language learning accessible to learners of all ages and backgrounds (Vesselinov & Grego, 2012).
- Challenges: Despite its success, Duolingo faces challenges in ensuring the quality and accuracy of its AI-driven language courses. Balancing personalized learning experiences with standardized curriculum requirements and language proficiency standards remains an on-going challenge for the platform (Chaudron et al., 2019).

3. SMART Learning Suite:

- Overview: SMART Learning Suite is an AI-enhanced platform that offers interactive whiteboard technology, collaborative learning tools, and personalized content creation features.
- Success Story: The Toronto District School Board (TDSB) implemented SMART Learning Suite to enhance teaching and learning experiences in its classrooms. By leveraging AI-driven analytics and assessment tools, TDSB teachers gained valuable insights into student progress and learning needs. Additionally, SMART Learning Suite's interactive features and multimedia resources improved student engagement and participation, leading to better learning outcomes (SMART Technologies, n.d.).
- Challenges: Integrating AI technologies like SMART Learning Suite into existing educational infrastructures requires extensive professional development and training for teachers. Moreover, ensuring equitable access to technology resources and support services remains a challenge for school districts with limited funding and resources (Harris et al., 2019).

These case studies and examples highlight the diverse applications of AI in education and the potential benefits of AI-driven technologies for enhancing teaching and learning experiences. However, they also underscore the importance of addressing challenges such as data privacy, infrastructure, and professional development to maximize the impact of AI in education.

FUTURE DIRECTIONS AND CONSIDERATIONS

Emerging Trends in AI and Education

- **Adaptive Learning:** AI-driven adaptive learning systems will continue to evolve, offering increasingly personalized and responsive learning experiences tailored to individual student needs and preferences (VanLehn, 2011).

- **Natural Language Processing (NLP):** NLP technologies will enable more sophisticated interactions between students and AI tutors, facilitating natural language communication, conversational agents, and intelligent feedback mechanisms (D'Mello & Graesser, 2012).
- **Augmented Reality (AR) and Virtual Reality (VR):** AR and VR technologies will transform educational experiences by providing immersive learning environments, virtual simulations, and interactive content creation tools (Dalgarno & Lee, 2010).
- **Data Analytics and Learning Analytics:** Advanced data analytics techniques will enable educators to gain deeper insights into student learning behaviors, performance trends, and instructional effectiveness, informing evidence-based decision-making and personalized interventions (Baker & Siemens, 2014).

Ethical Guidelines and Regulatory Frameworks:

- **Data Privacy and Security:** Ethical guidelines and regulatory frameworks must prioritize the protection of student data privacy and security, ensuring compliance with laws such as the General Data Protection Regulation (GDPR) and the Family Educational Rights and Privacy Act (FERPA) (Floridi, 2019).
- **Algorithmic Transparency and Accountability:** Educational institutions and technology providers should promote transparency and accountability in AI algorithms used in educational settings, disclosing how data is collected, processed, and utilized to inform decision-making processes (OECD, 2019).
- **Equity and Inclusivity:** Ethical guidelines should prioritize equity and inclusivity in AI-enhanced education, addressing concerns about algorithmic bias, digital divide, and accessibility barriers that may disproportionately affect marginalized and underserved communities (UNESCO, 2020).

Opportunities and Challenges for Further Research and Development

- **Teacher Training and Professional Development:** Further research is needed to explore effective strategies for integrating AI technologies into teacher training programs and professional development initiatives, empowering educators to harness the full potential of AI in education (Luckin et al., 2016).
- **Longitudinal Studies and Impact Assessment:** Longitudinal studies are necessary to assess the long-term impact of AI on teaching and learning outcomes, examining factors such as student achievement, retention rates, and career readiness (Koedinger & Corbett, 2012).
- **Ethical Design and Responsible Innovation:** Future research should focus on developing ethical design principles and responsible innovation practices for AI technologies in education, promoting values such as transparency, fairness, and human-centricity (Floridi, 2019).

- **Cross-Disciplinary Collaboration:** Collaboration between educators, researchers, policymakers, and industry stakeholders is essential for advancing AI in education research and development, fostering interdisciplinary approaches to address complex challenges and seize opportunities for innovation (Luckin et al., 2019).

By addressing these future directions and considerations, stakeholders can ensure that AI technologies in education are ethically designed, effectively implemented, and responsibly governed to maximize their potential benefits for learners, educators, and society as a whole.

CONCLUSION

This paper has explored the multifaceted impact of artificial intelligence (AI) on education, examining ethical, psychological, and pedagogical perspectives. Through an analysis of current research and real-world examples, several key findings and insights have emerged.

Firstly, AI technologies hold tremendous potential to revolutionize education by offering personalized learning experiences, optimizing cognitive load, and enhancing student motivation and engagement. Adaptive learning systems, AI-driven tutoring platforms, and intelligent content creation tools have demonstrated promising results in improving learning outcomes and promoting equity and inclusivity in educational settings (Baker et al., 2010; Luckin et al., 2016).

However, the integration of AI in education also raises important ethical considerations, including data privacy, algorithmic bias, and equity concerns. Safeguarding student data privacy, ensuring algorithmic transparency and fairness, and addressing digital divide challenges are critical for promoting responsible AI adoption in education (Floridi, 2019; OECD, 2019).

Moreover, the psychological impact of AI on learners' well-being and mental health cannot be overlooked. While AI technologies have the potential to support students' cognitive and emotional development, there are concerns about the potential negative effects of excessive screen time, social isolation, and dependency on technology (Twenge, 2019).

From a pedagogical standpoint, AI offers new opportunities for personalized instruction, collaborative learning, and data-driven decision-making. Teachers play a crucial role as facilitators and mentors in AI-integrated classrooms, collaborating with AI systems to create engaging learning experiences and provide targeted support to students (VanLehn, 2011).

In light of these findings, educators, policymakers, and stakeholders must work together to harness the potential of AI in education while addressing its ethical, psychological, and pedagogical implications. This requires investing in teacher training and professional development, implementing robust data privacy regulations, and promoting equity and inclusivity in AI-enhanced learning environments (UNESCO, 2020).

Looking ahead, the future of AI in education holds immense promise for transforming teaching and learning practices, fostering innovation, and advancing global education agendas. By embracing responsible AI adoption and prioritizing the well-being and development of learners, we can unlock the full potential of AI to create a more equitable, inclusive, and empowering educational landscape for all (Luckin et al., 2019).

In summation, while challenges and complexities lie ahead, the opportunities presented by AI in education are vast and transformative. By navigating these challenges thoughtfully and collaboratively, we can shape a future where AI enhances, rather than detracts from, the quality and accessibility of education for learners worldwide.

REFERENCES

Adams, T., & White, E. (2021). Understanding the Impact of Artificial Intelligence on Education: A Comprehensive Analysis. *Educational Technology Research Journal*, 25(3), 67–82.

Baker, R. S., D'Mello, S. K., Rodrigo, M. M. T., & Graesser, A. C. (2010). Better to be frustrated than bored: The incidence, persistence, and impact of learners' cognitive–affective states during interactions with three different computer-based learning environments. *International Journal of Human-Computer Studies*, 68(4), 223–241. 10.1016/j.ijhcs.2009.12.003

Barocas, S., & Selbst, A. D. (2016). Big data's disparate impact. *California Law Review*, 104, 671–732.

Baylor, A. L., & Kim, Y. (2009). Pedagogical agent design: The impact of agent realism, gender, ethnicity, and instructional role. In *Workshop on Educational Software Agents: Crossing the Chasm* (pp. 1-8). Research Gate.

Chen, S., & Liu, W. (2020). Artificial Intelligence in Education: Current and Future Trends. *Journal of Educational Technology*, 14(2), 45–59.

Conley, C. S., Durlak, J. A., & Dickson, D. A. (2013). An evaluative review of outcome research on universal mental health promotion and prevention programs for higher education students. *Journal of American College Health*, 61(5), 286–301. 10.1080/07448481.2013.80223723768226

Crawford, K., & Paglen, T. (2019). *Excavating AI: The politics of images in machine learning training sets*.

D'Mello, S. K., & Graesser, A. C. (2012). Dynamics of affective states during complex learning. *Learning and Instruction*, 22(2), 145–157. 10.1016/j.learninstruc.2011.10.001

Dalgarno, B., & Lee, M. J. W. (2010). What are the learning affordances of 3-D virtual environments? *British Journal of Educational Technology*, 41(1), 10–32. 10.1111/j.1467-8535.2009.01038.x

Egbemhenghe, A., Ojeyemi, T., Iwuozor, K. O., Emenike, E. C., Ogunsanya, T. I., Anidiobi, S. U., & Adeniyi, A. G. (2023). Revolutionizing water treatment, conservation, and management: Harnessing the power of AI-driven ChatGPT solutions. *Environmental Challenges*, 13, 100782. 10.1016/j.envc.2023.100782

Eggmann, F., Weiger, R., Zitzmann, N. U., & Blatz, M. B. (2023). Implications of large language models such as ChatGPT for dental medicine. *Journal of Esthetic and Restorative Dentistry*, 35(7), 1098–1102. 10.1111/jerd.1304637017291

Eysenbach, G. (2023). The role of ChatGPT, generative language models, and artificial intelligence in medical education: A conversation with ChatGPT and a call for papers. *JMIR Medical Education*, 9(1), e46885. 10.2196/4688536863937

Floridi, L. (2019). *The logic of information: A theory of philosophy as conceptual design*. Oxford University Press. 10.1093/oso/9780198833635.001.0001

Koedinger, K. R., & Corbett, A. T. (2012). Cognitive tutors: Technology bringing learning science to the classroom. [). Academic Press.]. *Psychology of Learning and Motivation*, 57, 1–55.

Lee, J., & Wang, L. (2018). The Influence of Artificial Intelligence on Creativity in Education: A Review. *Educational Psychology Review*, 24(3), 387–401.

Liu, J., & Liu, S. (2023). *The application of ChatGPT in nursing education.*

Miao, H., & Ahn, H. (2023). Impact of ChatGPT on interdisciplinary nursing education and research. *Asian/Pacific Island Nursing Journal*, 7(1), e48136. 10.2196/4813637093625

Mogavi, R. H., Deng, C., Kim, J. J., Zhou, P., Kwon, Y. D., Metwally, A. H. S., & Hui, P. (2023). *Exploring user perspectives on ChatGPT: Applications, perceptions, and implications for ai-integrated education.* arXiv preprint arXiv:2305.13114.

Morrison, D. (2018). Ethical implications of datafication in education. *Learning, Media and Technology*, 43(4), 369–382.

OECD. (2019). *Education in the digital age: Making the case for an ethical, responsible, and inclusive digital future.* OECD Publishing.

Panagopoulou, F., Parpoula, C., & Karpouzis, K. (2023). *Legal and ethical considerations regarding the use of ChatGPT in education.* arXiv preprint arXiv:2306.10037. 10.31235/osf.io/c5hf3

Pardos, Z. A., & Heffernan, N. T. (2010). Modeling individualization in a Bayesian Networks implementation of knowledge tracing. In *Proceedings of the 3rd International Conference on Educational Data Mining* (pp. 61-70). Springer. 10.1007/978-3-642-13470-8_24

Ray, A., Ray, S., Daniel, M. S., & Kumar, B. (2021). Change in attitudes and perceptions of undergraduate health profession students towards inter-professional education following an educational experience in post-natal care. *medical journal armed forces india*, 77, S173-S179.

Sarwar, S., Imran, M., & Hussain, S. (2020). The role of artificial intelligence in achieving sustainable development goals: A review. *Sustainable Development*, 28(1), 146–158.

Smith, K. (2020). The Impact of AI on Education: Perspectives from Teachers and Academics. *The Journal of Educational Research*, 45(1), 55–67.

Surovková, J., Haluzová, S., Strunga, M., Urban, R., Lifková, M., & Thurzo, A. (2023). The New Role of the Dental Assistant and Nurse in the Age of Advanced Artificial Intelligence in Telehealth Orthodontic Care with Dental Monitoring: Preliminary Report. *Applied Sciences (Basel, Switzerland)*, 13(8), 5212. 10.3390/app13085212

UNESCO. (2020). *Steering AI and advanced ICTs for knowledge societies: A rights, openness, access, and multistakeholder perspective.* UNESCO.

VanLehn, K. (2011). The relative effectiveness of human tutoring, intelligent tutoring systems, and other tutoring systems. *Educational Psychologist*, 46(4), 197–221. 10.1080/00461520.2011.611369

Vesselinov, R., & Grego, J. (2012). *Duolingo effectiveness study.* Duolingo Inc.

Woolf, B. P. (2010). *Building intelligent interactive tutors: Student-centered strategies for revolutionizing e-learning.* Morgan Kaufmann.

Chapter 16
Addressing Ethical Concerns in Digital Marketing:
Challenges, Strategies, and Industry Participation

Gurloveleen Kaur Maan
https://orcid.org/0000-0002-0018-4423
Chitkara University, India

Navleen Kaur
https://orcid.org/0009-0002-6858-9993
Sri Guru Granth Sahib World University, India

ABSTRACT

The study comprises social and cultural issues pertaining to buying and selling on the digital platform. Ethics in marketing plays a vital role in building sustainable goals. The aim of writing the chapter is to throw light on the psychological influences of the customers while ethically imparting the product information through the marketers. The varied marketing strategies like remarketing, pay per click, demographic targeting, emotional and social bond connectivity, etc., are discussed with real cases of Abbot shoes, Surf excel, Red Label, Patagonia, and others. Market research, data collection, truthful branding, ethical digital advertising, regulatory compliances, and others are a few challenges observed in the proper execution of digital marketing. It is not just a mere saying by companies that we are following the right practices; they need to follow the same in their day-to-day operations. Tata Steel, Wipro, Just Water, Ocado, Hello Fresh, People Tree's and others are few renowned organizations using the sources of digital marketing in the right direction.

INTRODUCTION

Before the emergence of the word e-marketing, the 'digital marketing' term was utilized during period of 1990's. The swift advancement in digital world paved the way for fresh avenues and opportunities in advertising and marketing. The concept of Internet marketing, 'online marketing' or 'web marketing', digital marketing gained a prominent place gradually in some specific regions and were often used

DOI: 10.4018/979-8-3693-6660-8.ch016

Copyright ©2024, IGI Global. Copying or distributing in print or electronic forms without written permission of IGI Global is prohibited.

interchangeably. While 'online marketing' remains prevalent in United States of America and 'Web Marketing' is the norm in Italy, 'digital marketing' has become the widely accepted terminology in the UK and globally. When transactions involving products or services occur through computer networks via Internet, lead and is termed as E-commerce.

E-marketing encompasses a range of digital tools and strategies, such as, 'email marketing, website and micro site development, search engine advertising, SEO (Search Engine Optimization) & various methods which are technology operated. It involves facilitating website functionality, establishing virtual storefronts, managing customer databases, exchanging business-to-business data, communicating with customers via email or fax, engaging in business-to-business transactions, and other related practices within the digital realm.

When this practice of selling the products and services online has become so common, companies' distrust and unprofessional activities recognized by others, especially by customers, a term 'ethical digital marketing' coined. Ethics and values in the globe of digital marketing entails endorsing of tangible and intangible items on the internet in a manner that upholds principle of assurance & responsibility, while considering beliefs & ethics the target customer carry, especially 'Z' and 'Y' generation. In today's time the effect of environment is of utmost importance like the change in weather wherein the strategies of digital marketing resonate with the demographic's values. Hence building the trust and sustainable liaisons with their clientele.

REVIEW OF LITERATURE

Chaffey (2002) expands on this concept, defining e-marketing as the application of digital technology to enhance marketing endeavors, with the primary objectives of profit generation and customer retention through augmenting customer understanding and fostering integrated communication via online channels tailored to individual customer preferences. Chaffey and Smith (2008) further assert that marketing via digital, electronic and internet media are interchangeable words referred to as marketing through web resources encompassing activities such as website utilization, online advertising, and engagement through various digital devices and interactive platforms.

Loyalty, the extent to which customers consistently patronize a business and maintain a disposition aligned with their preferences during making purchase decisions. And makes a deep impression on the customer's minds whereby leading to the commitment for a specific brand (Sudhahar et al., 2006). Kotler (2016) defined ethical marketing practices, which uphold ethical standards, encompass actions, regulations, and policies governing privacy, the collection of personal information, and the safeguarding of user data when employing digital marketing as a sales channel. According to Chen (2018), companies are expected to conduct their marketing endeavors with honesty, accurately representing their products and assuming responsibility for their claims.

According to Fauzan and Ida (2014), business ethics are founded on the principles of fairness, honesty, and trust. In digital marketing, interactions with buyers can indirectly lead to conflicts, which marketers aim to mitigate by offering high-quality products at reasonable prices. Limbu et al. (2011) conducted research highlighting four dimensions of perceived ethics in online marketing: security, privacy, absence of fraud, and fulfillment. Violations of any of these dimensions may be interpreted as a breach of ethics by the seller.

Romain (2007) coined the term "online fraud" to describe situations where goods were deliberately not delivered to customers. Trust emerges as a crucial factor in determining overall ethical behavior. Misleading claims were identified as the primary contributor to variance, indicating that the retailers doing online business must refrain from any mis leading and fabricated communication and other tactics that builds false picture. It is imperative for online retailers to avoid making unsubstantiated claims and using ambiguous statements that require customers to make assumptions about the intended message (Gundlach & Murphy, 1993; Ruiz, 2005).

Sagala (2017) outlines a procedure for making purchase decisions, which includes analyzing needs, gathering data on products and services, assessing choices, making the purchase, and post-purchase behavior. According to Sharma and Wang (2015), buyers are inclined to make purchases when they perceive a product as meeting their needs and providing benefits. However, if the product proves unsuitable or if unethical promotional tactics are detected, buyers may opt to cancel the purchase. Attanayake (2005) conducted research on gaining competitive advantage through ethical interaction in digital marketing, assessing various aspects such as website advertisements, email promotions, and customer profiles.

Sutrisno (2016) emphasizes that service quality is determined by the extent to which professionals adhere to standards when delivering products and services that align with consumer expectations. Khan and Mahapatra (2009) highlight the role of technology in enhancing service quality. Sathya (2017) noted that web-based service standards, a technological development, enable businesses to integrate various functions through web design and applications for consumer purchases. In Siti and Setyo's research (2020), ease of access and transparency in product and service information significantly impact purchasing decisions. Attanayake (2005) notes a positive response to electronic purchases in Europe and North America, creating a competitive advantage through ethical interactivity. Sharma and Li (2012) stress the need to address ethical issues such as privacy laws, policies, and regulations in digital transactions. Ensuring quality service in online marketing, according to Berry and Parasuraman (2004), involves offering competitive prices, leading to customer satisfaction and positive word-of-mouth.

Research Methodology

The study comprises secondary data which is gathered from the websites of the companies doing & claiming the adoption of the ethical digital marketing practices. The other information related to social & ethical issues, strategies chosen, challenges involved, internet engagement, targeting the children by companies, etc was collected from the relevant sources. Those companies who are dealing with the businesses related to grocery, beverages, cosmetics, perfumes, daily uses products, skin care and such as others, either Indian or foreign were chosen for the broader coverage of the study. The marketing strategies of selling the products by Trivago, Nike, Amazon, etc are also mentioned in the research work that explains their way of unique selling and targeting the customers.

Data Discussion

This era is totally a part of technology and digital media and companies are well aware about the role of digital technology in the promotion of their products and services. Hardly, we find any company who is not using the technology for the company's growth and advancement. Moreover, the use unethical and emotional practices are too common amongst the corporations. Despite knowing the negative consequences of unethical digital marketing standards, many companies just used the sentiments of the people. There is not any doubt that a lot of social and ethical issues are involved in digital marketing. The following section explains the same in detail.

Social and Ethical Issues Involved in Digital Marketing

The current adherence to ethical standards by online marketers raises significant concerns, particularly regarding consumer privacy. Maintaining integrity and sustainability in the market becomes a critical issue. It is imperative to weigh the pros and cons of digital marketing, especially considering the moral principles involved in interactions with social media users. Digital marketing differs from news and entertainment content, requiring transparency in product promotion. Maintaining consumer privacy is paramount, with stringent measures necessary to prevent the dissemination and potential misuse of data by unauthorized parties (Chen, 2018).

There exists a concerning trend that individuals must be aware of before engaging with any online marketing initiatives. Several aspects pertaining to online marketing should be highlighted for consumer awareness:

Individual privacy: Online marketing success depends on the ability to target consumers based on their demographics and present them in an ethical manner using cookies and online tracking. Before interacting with customers, any ethical internet marketing strategies should make their privacy regulations clear.

Violation of copyright: Ethical challenges in online marketing often intersect with copyright law. For instance, 'Google bombing' exploits the ranking system by linking a specific website's content to another highly-ranked site. Copyright infringement can severely undermine any campaign.

Security of personal data: Ethical handling of customer data mandates safeguarding personal information and obtaining consent before disclosure. However, the increasing sophistication of hackers poses a threat, compromising the security measures of ethical marketers and potentially leading to illegal use of private data.

Figure 1. Social and ethical issues

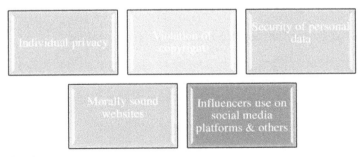

Source: Author's own collaboration

Morally sound websites: While online marketers often utilize third-party websites for advertising, it is crucial to ensure alignment with the company's ethics and values to maintain integrity. Alshurideh et al. (2016) concluded that marketing ethics hold significant value and exert influence within marketing literature.

Addressing Ethical Concerns in Digital Marketing

Influencers use on social media platforms: Social media influencers wield considerable sway over consumer behavior. However, transparency regarding paid promotions is essential for preserving campaign effectiveness and authenticity. Employing ethical influencers who disclose any agreements ensures transparency and ethical marketing practices.

Promoting environmental sustainability by decreasing the environmental impact of digital marketing efforts, which includes lowering energy usage, minimizing waste, and reducing carbon emissions. Taking responsibility for the influence of advertising campaigns on humanity, the atmosphere, and entities, and addressing any negative consequences or unintended harm and others are the factors, companies need to consider before doing any digital marketing activity. Basically, awareness of ethical considerations is supreme in steering the complexities of online marketing, safeguarding consumer trust, and upholding ethical standards in digital advertising. Ethics presents a nuanced and subjective discussion, as individuals possess differing perspectives on what constitutes right and wrong. Consequently, marketing ethics serve as a broad framework to aid companies or organizations in evaluating new marketing strategies (Kotler, 2016).

Strategies Opted by Companies to Sell Online Products

Companies bring into play the speckled mode to magnetize the new customers for buying their products and services. Innovative strategies and techniques are continued to allure and hit the consumers mind for their goods. For instance, Patagonia claims 'Gear is built for generations of fun' (https://www.patagonia.com/home/). Strategies such as product suggestions, remarketing, email marketing, pay-per-click advertising, demographic targeting, and others are frequently used by multiple businesses to widen the operations and demand for the products/services. Product Suggestions: Most online shoppers have encountered this scenario, when the customers opt to check out, a pop up in the window showing the items bought together with those lying in customer's cart. This technique, is termed as suggested selling which is strategized to allure the customers with cross-selling or up-selling chances. Its effectiveness is impressive, with methods like cross-selling and category-penetration, such as product suggestions, leading to escalation of sales by 20% and generation of profits by 30%, as cited by McKinsey & Company.

Figure 2. Strategies used by corporations to sell their products online

Source: Author's own collaboration

Remarketing: For companies using the social media apps such as Facebook, YouTube and others for marketing, employing strategies of retargeting and remarketing that can provide an exclusive way for increasing their sales. Remarketing involves reintroducing pages or products previously viewed by a customer, displaying them again after they have left the website. This renewed exposure to products offers an opportunity to drive traffic to the website and potentially generate sales.

Email Marketing: While several businesses integrate this approach into their business strategies, only a few can take proper benefit of this behavioral segmentation. An example of this approach is evident in abandoned cart emails. Marketing and selling teams of the corporations start sending personal emails to the people who keep the products in their carts for a specific time, it goes to remind them that they forget to buy these products and can place the order. Ultimately, this strategy enhances a more personalized experience for the customer.

Pay-Per-Click (PPC) Advertising: In PPC advertising, platforms such as Google Ads, Bing Ads and others are used to target the would-be customers of the products. These ads provide the information regarding the products and directly take the expected customers to the home page, from where customers can buy the articles.

Demographic targeting: Companies are frequently using demographic targeting practices, where they assess the certain factors like location, gender, age, area, etc and start sending them messages via different social media platforms as per their interests and preferences. Their browsing history is also scrutinized to sense their understanding of the products.

Through the integration of marketing automation and machine learning technologies, companies can harness their extensive data repositories to predict consumer behavior well ahead of time, allowing for more proactive and targeted marketing strategies. Singla et al. (2017) investigated ethical issues in digital marketing and identified several problematic areas, including excessive spamming of promotional emails, concerns regarding privacy and misuse of personal data by companies, and mismatches between advertising and products. Some websites displayed pop-ups that were unrelated to customers' search data.

How Companies Play With the Mind of Consumers

Companies know better how to do behavioral advertisement and marketing of their products or services that fascinate the customers to buy. Such as, Nike has established itself as a frontrunner in the marketing arena, renowned for its innovative advertising campaigns featuring athletes that motivate both youngsters and adults to embrace an active lifestyle. Beyond these traditional marketing efforts, Nike has also cultivated a remarkable digital marketing strategy. The remarketing ad highlighted above may appear straightforward, but it holds significant potential in redirecting prospective shoe buyers back to the Nike website.

In contemporary society, it is not unusual to see customers checking over a business's website multiple times before making a purchase. This kind of conduct is especially common in travel and transportation-related companies. Re marketing advertisements are so very important. Trivago, for instance, witnesses numerous visitors exploring vacation destinations on its website. However, most individuals do not make a purchase during their initial visit. To remain forefront in consumers' minds, Trivago employs remarketing ads on platforms like Facebook and Google. These ads display updated offers for hotels in previously searched locations, enticing potential customers to revisit the site and potentially make a booking.

Amazon has mastered the art of suggestive advertising, dominating the market with its highly effective approach. Within its website, users encounter advertisements and curated sections suggesting products based on their past purchases, browsing history, or items currently in their shopping cart. Additionally, Amazon provides insights into what previous buyers have purchased alongside the item currently in the user's cart.

This level of personalized recommendation has significantly influenced consumer behavior, shifting many individuals from purchasing single items to multiple items and leading most of their shopping from Amazon's platform.

Here, the Research Question Arises: Do Companies Need to Follow Ethical Digital Practices?

Maintaining ethical standards in digital marketing is not just a moral obligation but a necessity for establishing sustainable relationships with consumers. In the internet sphere, unethical behavior can seriously harm a brand's reputation and have serious consequences. Marketing platforms and search engines are getting more and more aggressive in penalizing unethical activities. Techniques like content scraping, link manipulation, and keyword stuffing can cause a website's search engine ranks to collapse, which will reduce its online visibility and reputation. Sharma and Li (2012) emphasize that digital marketing allows sellers to provide information, collaborate, interact, and address potential ethical concerns. Penalties for such actions can range from reduced visibility to complete removal from search engine indexes, effectively making a business invisible to potential customers. Rita et al. (2019) proposes a four-dimensional model of electronic service quality affecting customer satisfaction and behavior. Javalgi and Russel (2015) argue that ethics are crucial for marketing managers to influence consumer purchasing decisions successfully.

In addition, a lot of digital marketing solutions have built-in systems for upholding moral principles. For example, social media and email marketing platforms use algorithms to identify false material, spam, and phony interaction. Few companies like 'Abbot Shoes' highlighted the concept where grandmother learned bicycle from her grand child and exclaimed in joy with saying 'I am flying' at the end. Also, give the message to 'Live the life to the fullest'.

Challenges to Take Consistent Ethical Digital Marketing in Practices

It is not easy for the corporations to ethically impart the digital marketing practices in their business strategies. They need to be vigilant and must properly consider the rules and regulations set by the authorities. Few prominent areas where the companies face the issues are market research and data collection, truthful branding and marketing, and ethical digital advertising.

The basic challenge involves in the process of getting the data from customers is their consent of share their personal information. Further, companies must ensure the safety and privacy of the collected data. Another challenge is to do the truthful marketing of the brands and bring transparency in their activities or strategies chosen to promote the brand in front of others. Founding trust with clients through translucent communication is crucial for decent business performs.

Figure 3. Challenges for ethical digital marketing

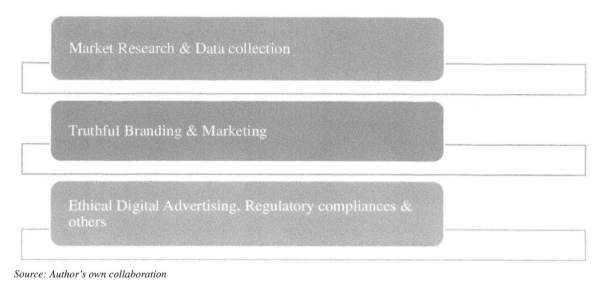

Source: Author's own collaboration

Imparting ethics in organization practices, conveying clear information about the products and services to misguide the customers. Corporations need to know that they are not going to become part of such race where showing false and unclear information is common. Companies should deliver true content to their clients and not misguiding them, not even at the sake of just making profits and fetch more customers.

Corporations Imparting Genuine Digital Marketing Practices

The following part of the study discusses the cases of few corporations using ethical and genuine digital marketing practices in the advertisement and marketing of their products.

Patagonia showcases its commitment to the environment through its "1% for the Planet" initiative, demonstrating a dedication to sustainability by donating a portion of its revenue to environmental nonprofits. This strategic marketing approach emphasizes a voluntary "Earth tax" that the environmentally-conscious company contributes toward environmental causes. Patagonia's "Wornwear" ad hits shots at the quick fashion industry, much like its "Don't Buy" campaign. Through its online store, it encourages customers to recycle and buy used clothing, upending the rapid fashion cycle and drastically lowering the carbon, waste, and water footprint of each item. Roughly 85 percent of clothing is burned or ends up in landfills. Increasing the lifespan of items and lowering our overall consumption are two of the best things we can do for the environment. This entails exchanging equipment when it is no longer needed, fixing more, and making fewer purchases (https://wornwear.patagonia.com/).

Through its "Activism" efforts, Patagonia not only promotes social change but also facilitates consumer engagement in activism at the local level through its Action Works page. Patagonia effectively integrates ethical marketing throughout its brand identity, evident from the moment one visits its website and consistently upheld on every subsequent page.

Addressing Ethical Concerns in Digital Marketing

Figure 4. Companies using ethical digital marketing practices

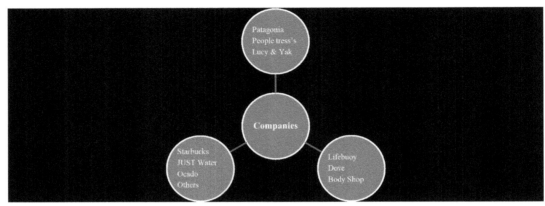

Source: Author's own collaboration

Starbucks, by procuring all its coffee sustainably and optimizing its sustainable sourcing methods using the C.A.F.E. (Coffee and Farmer Equity Practices) system, Starbucks shows its dedication to sustainability. Four fundamental ideas form the basis of the C.A.F.E. system: environmental leadership, social responsibility, economic transparency, and quality. Fair pricing for coffee is a top priority for the organization, which also makes sure that ethical procedures are followed throughout the entire coffee production process, from planting and harvesting to processing and buying. Starbucks' ethical sourcing requirements are now considered industry norms, and the company's programs have engaged over 170,000 farmers, generating billions of dollars in income annually.

People Tree's "Our Blue Planet" collection is a perfect example of how businesses may work together to develop a moral marketing initiative. The apparel brand and BBC Earth collaborated in 2019 to spread awareness about marine life and ocean conservation. This collaboration, their second, encourages consumers to embrace trendy yet sustainable choices by wearing garments that are GOTS Certified. With increasing numbers of marine and animal species facing endangerment, creating a clothing line that promotes awareness represents a responsible and accessible form of activism at the consumer level.

JUST Water sets itself apart from the competition by presenting evidence against the notion that all water products are naturally sustainable. Although water itself is renewable, there are other factors to consider in addition to the product's ingredients. Jaden Smith's JUST Water brand takes a holistic approach to social and environmental justice, much like Dr. Bronner's. They make investments in infrastructure and ethically source recycled materials to actively minimize carbon emissions. The money made goes toward projects like renovating the water business model and fixing old water mains. JUST Water's commitment to forestry contributes even more to its marketing success. The paperboard bottles show off their dedication to sustainable forestry techniques by prominently displaying their FSC accreditation. Additionally, their website provides a plethora of material to enlighten visitors about their sustainability initiatives, including informative infographics and photos.

Few companies set the leading examples for others, where they advise the appealing customers to use that product either of any other brands too just for their wellbeing's. Example, **Lifebuoy**, its advertisement comes with this way that suggest to 'Use Any Soap', because personal hygiene is essential. Additionally, safety transcends brand loyalty or personal preference, and in this regard, Lifebuoy deserves commendation for its ethical stance. The recent Lifebuoy advertisement, which demonstrates proper handwashing techniques, has likely been viewed by a significant portion of the population. At the end of the demonstration, the ad emphasizes that any soap can be used, placing importance on the word 'any.' This message underscores the importance of hand hygiene above promoting a specific brand, aligning with ethical principles prioritizing public health and safety.

Dove soap launched a highly visible advertising campaign featuring 'real' models, aimed at promoting realistic body images and encouraging girls to embrace their appearance, regardless of whether they conformed to traditional supermodel standards. This campaign marked a significant departure from previous Dove advertisements, which often featured stereotypically beautiful models whose images were digitally altered to conceal imperfections.

The Ethisphere Institute, a well-known worldwide authority on ethical business practices, has named **Tata Steel** and **Wipro** as two of the most ethical firms in the world. Their dedication to maintaining the highest ethical standards in their business practices is demonstrated by this acknowledgment (Source: https://economictimes.indiatimes.com). As the first-ever global provider of carbon-neutral meal kits, Hello Fresh stands out. Apart from its primary goal of transforming people's eating habits, Hello Fresh is committed to environmental sustainability and actively looks for ways to help people offset their carbon emissions.

Ocado is an online grocery retailer known for its commitment to sustainability, exemplified by its utilization of Carbon Balanced packaging. Recognizing the urgency of addressing climate change, Ocado has made sustainability one of its primary focuses.

The **Body Shop,** well-known for its pure skincare products, is intensely devoted to environmental preservation, principally in protecting the rainforests with pioneering initiatives. One distinguished effort comprises the unveiling of the 'Rainforest Haircare' range, that allows clients to donate for safeguarding the specific extent of the Atlantic Rainforest at REGUA, Brazil.

The Body Shop launched its Wood Positive program in 2012 to reduce the amount of paper and cardboard used in both product and transportation packaging throughout its global supply chain. The company looked for extra steps to address the wood used in their packaging, even though they were trying to reduce packing. This resulted in the formation of a relationship with the World Land Trust, whose mission is to provide money for the restoration and preservation of habitats in the Andean foothills of Southern Ecuador and the Brazilian Atlantic Rainforest. As a result, the program guarantees that 10% more wood is planted and maintained than is consumed, making it a genuinely Wood Positive effort.

Lucy & Yak is a custom clothing brand that offers stylish dresses, skirts, shorts, and pants in addition to their distinctive, vividly colored dungarees. Lucy & Yak is wholly committed to combating the problems brought about by quick fashion.

No doubt, organizations are following the good ethical practices during the promotion of their products or services, but not all. In fact, they use smart ways to disclose the true information in front of public; normally people fail to understand the same. Numerous, ethical issues and challenges involved here. ***The ethical challenges in digital marketing are increasingly prevalent as the internet continues to evolve.*** With this evolution, moral principles regarding what is considered good or bad, right or wrong, are intertwined with the ethical issues arising in digital marketing. Legal difficulties in marketing include laws, rules, obligations, and terms and conditions that control marketing strategies. Ethical quandaries in marketing might be exacerbated by controversies and conflicts pertaining to cases or rulings.

Addressing Ethical Concerns in Digital Marketing

Where the ethical boundary in digital marketing should be drawn is a matter of concern, given the increasing sophistication and capability of technical tools that can be used to target individuals in an invasive way. For marketers in the digital age, finding a balance between the need to efficiently contact consumers and their right to privacy and autonomy is a constant issue (Singh & Singh, 2023).

A well-executed marketing campaign has the potential to transform prospective clients into loyal customers for life. In an ideal scenario, marketing initiatives increase awareness of a product or service, leading to mutually beneficial outcomes for both the business and the consumer. This win-win situation occurs when marketing efforts effectively communicate the value proposition of the offering, resonating with the target audience and fostering long-term relationships built on trust and satisfaction.

These ethical and legal difficulties in digital marketing are also linked to marketing methods, details are given in the below section. Moreover, **'Clarity and Trust'** is considered as the most challenging factor in ethical digital marketing. Balancing the ethical concerns surrounding the utilization of big data in marketing entails carefully managing the extraction of valuable audience insights while upholding transparency and trust with consumers. To tackle this issue effectively, businesses need to emphasize the importance of honesty and transparency in their marketing strategies (Saluja, et al., 2022). One approach to deal is to provide clear and proper information in appropriate way, not use jargons that confuse or misguide the consumers. Corporations must convey the correct information about the use of collected data and protection of the data to their consumers. Additionally, companies need to obey the good governance practices in their operations. By ensuring transparency, honesty, responsibility towards the users personal data, they all win the hearts of their customers. This practice also conveys the users that these organizations using the true ethical digital marketing practices for uplifting their businesses.

Few social media apps or websites such as facebook, google, youtube, snapchat, etc fetched the personal details, interests, beliefs, and sentiments of the users, further pass the collected details to the interested corporations and charge money for the same. This practice of making money is not so ethically. As, companies start using this information for their own personal motives and disturb the people during their leisure time. Smart phones, smart watches, smart speakers etc also come in this line. Companies must prioritize the security and privacy of their customers, ensuring that data collection and usage are done responsibly, with clear consent and transparency. Additionally, lawmakers and regulatory bodies play a crucial role in implementing safeguards and enforcing legislation to prevent the misuse of personal information.

Targeting Children for Marketing of Products or Services

Children are easily exposed to marketing messages through various digital channels, influencing their interests and identities. Businesses must approach to children with caution, prioritizing educational content over promotional material. Moreover, companies should be mindful of the potential negative impacts of marketing products like e-cigarettes to children.

Spamming, or inundating individuals with unsolicited advertising, is unethical and undermines consumer trust. Businesses should avoid spamming tactics and instead focus on providing relevant and valuable content to their audience. Ethical email marketing involves transparency about the frequency of communications and a commitment to delivering meaningful content.

This issue can be tackled with the help of truthful advertising that is paramount in maintaining consumer trust. Businesses should refrain from making false statements or promises in their advertising campaigns. Transparency and honesty are essential elements of ethical marketing, as demonstrated by the success of brands like KFC, which openly acknowledged and addressed issues with their supply chain. Overall, digital media presents a range of ethical issues, including transparency, trust, integrity, and ownership of information. By prioritizing ethical considerations in their marketing practices, businesses can build stronger relationships with consumers and contribute to a more trustworthy and responsible digital landscape.

Future of Ethical Digital Marketing

It is of much demand to run ethics in marketing through the digital resource, with the rise in consumer awareness for standardized and pure products. As the consumers are growing smarter as far as the knowhow of consequences are concerned after making purchases, they look forward for more of ethical brands that gives them a sense of trust and confidence. This paradigm shift in the behavior of the consumers gives a kick to the marketers to adapt more of the ethical practices for the online marketing of the goods. The principle of transparency, reliability, assurance, empathy, and societal responsibility enhances the value of the brand in the world of competition online and inculcates a sense of confidence amongst customers towards those brands. It fosters in building long-term relationship with the target audience.

With the advent of more innovations in tech- driven marketing, the marketers must become proactive of developments and make use of advanced tools and techniques. Thereby facilitating the personalized orientation and lovely experiences while safeguarding the privacy of consumers. This involves ethically managing pool of information, with explicit consent and opt-out options are also made available. Thus, the future of digital marketing while making it ethical, relies on the consumer's perception and satisfaction, playing massive role in shaping the brand narratives. not just by being the passive recipients of advertising messages. By attentively listening to consumer preferences and needs, the strategists can establish coherent and deep connections with them.

The ethical digital marketing not only meets the expectations of today's consumers but also lays the foundation for a sustainable future where brands thrive while contributing positively to society.

CONCLUSION

The digitization is poised to enter in every remarkable sphere of global village. The heart of marketing the products and services lie in building trust with its customers which is sensed blurred in majority of the cases. The morality by virtue of transparency and honesty in marketing of products and services lays the foundation of customer satisfaction. With every passing age, the online marketing is taking its place in the form of social media concept, buzz-marketing, viral marketing, and the like. The fake representation, false information and deceptive promotions are posing threat to the scenario of online marketing. The varied strategies and practices are adopted by companies to sell and differentiate their products from others.

The advertisement strategies of few organizations such as Surf Excel, Nestle, Kit Kat, Red Label, Domino's Pizza, Maggie, etc put the emotions and try to connect the people with their brand products. For example, Surf excel advertisement often claims "Stains are Good" after interlinking the emotional bond of grandkid with granny or with some other social help. Red Lable tried to unite two religious community together at one platform, where Hindu and muslin family sit together to share a cup of tea together in one advertisement.

The study highlighted the significance of ethical digital approaches in product promotion, addressing social and ethical concerns and examining the diverse strategies employed by corporations of all sizes. It also delved into how companies influence the perceptions of their target audience and shed light on the hurdles encountered in implementing ethical digital practices. Moreover, it underscores the crucial role of ethical digital marketing practices in today's landscape.

REFERENCES

Alshurideh. (2016). Marketing Ethics and Relationship Marketing. *International Business Research*, 9(9), 78-90. .10.5539/ibr.v9n9p78

Arjoon and Rambocas. (2011). Ethics and Customer Loyalty: Some Insights into Online Retailing Services. *International Journal of Business and Social Science*, 2(14).

Assegaf, S. (2016). The Effect of Services Quality to Customer Satisfaction by Using Internet Banking Service in Jambi. *The Asian Journal of Technology Management*, 9(1), 21–36. 10.12695/ajtm.2015. 9.1.3

Attanayake. (2005). *Ethical emarketing for competitive advantage*. [Dissertation, Sri Lanka: University of Moratuwa].

Chen. (2018). Multinational Corporate Power, Influence and Responsibility in Global Supply Chains. *Journal Business Ethics, 148*, 365- 375. https://doi.org/.10.1007/s10551- 016-3033

Dwivedi. (2020). Set the future of digital and social media marketing research: Perspectives and research propositions. *International Journal of Information Management, 2*(1), 31-42. .10.1016/j.ijinfomgt.2020.102168

Fauzan and Ida. (2014). The Effect of Quality of Service, Image, and Business Ethics on Satisfaction and Loyalty of Patients in Hospitals in Makassar City. *International Journal of Management Progress*, 1(2), 1–22. 10.21067/jem.v10i1.774

Gundlach, G. T., & Murphy, P. E. (1993). Ethical and Legal Foundations of Relational Marketing Exchanges. *Journal of Marketing*, 57(4), 35–46. 10.1177/002224299305700403

Hoge and Cecil. (1993). Dissimilarity of e-marketing vs. traditional marketing. *The Electronic Marketing Manual ABA Journal*, 22, 175–185.

Khan, M. S., Mahapatra, S. S., & Sreekumar, N. A. (2009). Service quality evaluation in internet banking: An empirical study in India. *International Journal Indian Culture and Business Management*, 2(1), 30–46. 10.1504/IJICBM.2009.021596

Kotler (2016). Marketing Management, 15th Edition New Jersey: Pearson Prentice Hall, Inc.

Limbu, Y. B., Wolf, M., & Lunsford, D. L. (2011). Consumers' perception of online ethics and its effect on satisfaction and loyalty. *Journal of Research in Interactive Marketing*, 5(1), 71–89. 10.1108/17505931111121534

Nurfadila, S. (2020). The Impact of Influencers in Consumer Decision-Making: The Fashion Industry. *IDJ*, 1(1), 1–14. 10.19184/ijl.v1i1.19146

https://wornwear.patagonia.com/

https://economictimes.indiatimes.com

Parasuraman, A., Zeithaml, V. A., & Berry, L. L. (1985). A conceptual model of service quality and its implications for future research. *Journal of Marketing*, 49(64), 41–50. 10.2307/1251430

Paulo, R. (2019). The impact of e-service quality and customer satisfaction on customer behavior in online shopping. *Heliyon*, 5(10), 1–14. 10.1016/j.heliyon.2019.e0269031720459

Romain. (2007). The Ethics of Online Retailing: A Scale Development and Validation from the Consumers. *Perspective. Journal of Business Ethics,* 72(2), 131-148.

Ruiz (2005). Relationship Outcomes of Perceived Ethical Sales Behavior: The Customer's Perspective. *Journal of Business Research,* 8(4), 439–445.

Saluja, S., Aggarwal, A., & Mittal, A. (2022). Understanding the fraud theories and advancing with integrity model. *Journal of Financial Crime*, 29(4), 1318–1328. 10.1108/JFC-07-2021-0163

Sathya (2017). A Study on Digital Marketing and its Impact. *International Journal of Science and Research,* 6(2), 866-868. ISSN: 2319-7064.

Sharma, G., & Baoku, L. (2012). E-Marketing on Online Social Networks and Ethical Issues. *International Journal of Online Marketing*, 2(4), 1–14. 10.4018/ijom.2012100101

Sharma, G., & Lijuan, W. (2015). The effects of online service quality of e-commerce Websites on user satisfaction. *The Electronic Library*, 33(3), 468–485. 10.1108/EL-10-2013-0193

Singh, A., & Singh, A. (2023). *The Impact of Social Marketing on SMEs in India: A Theoretical Perspective*. Strengthening SME Performance Through Social Media Adoption and Usage. 10.4018/978-1-6684-5770-2.ch013

Singla. (2017). Role of Ethics in Digital Marketing. *Imperial Journal of Interdisciplinary Research,* 3(7), 371-375.

Compilation of References

A Junior VC. (2020, September 15). *Who Will Win FoodTech's Endgame?* A Junior VC. https://ajuniorvc.com/foodtech-endgame-ubereats-acquisition-swiggy-zomato-amazon/

Aaker, D. (1996). *Building Strong Brands*. The Free Press.

Aaker, D. A. (1991). *Managing Brand Equity: Capitalizing on the Value of a Brand Name*. The Free Press.

Ab Hamid, S. H., & Mat Zin, N. A. (2020). The Effects of Virtual Reality (VR) on Learning Motivation and Engagement: A Review. *Journal of Technical Education and Training*, 12(2), 1–12.

Abhishek, A. (2019). Contribution of Agriculture, Industry, and Services on GDP in Recent Years. *Journal of Emerging Technologies and Innovative Research*, 6(5), 464-468.

ACNielsen. (2007), Trust in Advertising: A Global Nielsen Consumer Report. ACNielsen, New York, NY.

Adams, T., & White, E. (2021). Understanding the Impact of Artificial Intelligence on Education: A Comprehensive Analysis. *Educational Technology Research Journal*, 25(3), 67–82.

Adarsh, R., Pillai, R. H., Krishnamurthy, A., & Bi, A. (2023). Innovative Business Research in Finance and Marketing System Based on Ethically Governed Artificial Intelligence. *Proceedings of 8th IEEE International Conference on Science, Technology, Engineering and Mathematics, ICONSTEM 2023*. IEEE. 10.1109/ICONSTEM56934.2023.10142836

ADB. (n.d.). *Debt Dynamics, Fiscal Deficit, and Stability in Government Borrowing in India: A Dynamic Panel Analysis*. Asian Development Bank Institute https://www.adb.org/sites/default/files/publication/181400/adbi-wp557.pdf

Adjei, M. T., Noble, S. M., & Noble, C. H. (2009). The influence of C2C communications in online brand communities on customer purchase behavior. *Journal of the Academy of Marketing Science*, 38(5), 634–653. 10.1007/s11747-009-0178-5

Agarwal, M. K., & Rao, V. R. (1996). An empirical comparison of consumer-based measures of brand equity. *Marketing Letters*, 7(3), 237–247. 10.1007/BF00435740

Agrawal, A., Gans, J. S., & Goldfarb, A. (2023). Artificial intelligence adoption and system-wide change. *Journal of Economics & Management Strategy*, 1–11.

Ahmad, A., Khan, M. N., & Haque, M. A. (2020). Employer branding aids in enhancing employee attraction and retention. *Journal of Asia-Pacific Business*, 21(1), 27–38. 10.1080/10599231.2020.1708231

Ahmed, A. M. A. A. (n.d.). *The impact of artificial intelligence in digital marketing*. Diva-portal.org. https://www.diva-portal.org/smash/get/diva2:1663148/FULLTEXT01.pdf

Ahmed, S. A. (2015). Correlates of Citizen Reaction to Demarketing Strategies. In *Proceedings of the 1985 Academy of Marketing Science (AMS) Annual Conference* (pp. 355-358). Cham: Springer International Publishing. 10.1007/978-3-319-16943-9_75

AI Ethics: What It Is and Why It Matters. (n.d.). Coursera. https://www.coursera.org/articles/ai-ethics

Compilation of References

Ai, M. (2021, August 12). *Who leads the food delivery race between Zomato and Swiggy in India?*. KrASIA. https://kr-asia.com/who-leads-the-food-delivery-race-between-zomato-and-swiggy-in-india

Aitken, J. M., & Van Hees, M. H. V. (2019). The importance of artificial intelligence in education: Perceptions of teachers and school administrators. *Journal of Technology and Teacher Education*, 27(2), 163–187.

Akerkar, R. (2019). *Artificial Intelligence for Business*. Springer Cham. 10.1007/978-3-319-97436-1

Alam, S., Hameed, A., Madej, M., & Kobylarek, A. (2024). Perception and practice of using artificial intelligence in education: An opinion based study. *XLinguae*, 17(1), 216–233. 10.18355/XL.2024.17.01.15

Alexandris, K., Dimitriadis, N., & Markata, D. (2002). Can perception of service quality predict behavioral intentions? An exploratory study in the hotel sector in Greece. *Managing Service Quality*, 12(4), 224–231. 10.1108/09604520210434839

Ali, H., Qadir, J., Alam, T., Househ, M., & Shah, Z. (2023). Revolutionizing healthcare with Foundation AI models. *Studies in Health Technology and Informatics*. 10.3233/SHTI23053337387067

Alkhatib, S., Kecskés, P., & Keller, V. (2023). Green Marketing in the Digital Age: A Systematic Literature Review. *Sustainability*, 15(16), 12369.

Allen, F., McAndrews, J., & Strahan, P. (2002). E-finance: An introduction. *Journal of Financial Services Research*, 22(Aug), 5–27. 10.1023/A:1016007126394

Alqahtani, M. M. (2023). Artificial intelligence and entrepreneurship education: A paradigm in qatari higher education institutions after COVID-19 pandemic. *International Journal of Data and Network Science*, 7(2), 695–706. 10.5267/j.ijdns.2023.3.002

Alshamrani, M. (2022). IoT and artificial intelligence implementations for remote healthcare monitoring systems: A survey. *Journal of King Saud University. Computer and Information Sciences*, 34(8), 4687–4701. 10.1016/j.jksuci.2021.06.005

Alshurideh. (2016). Marketing Ethics and Relationship Marketing. *International Business Research, 9*(9), 78-90. .10.5539/ibr.v9n9p78

Altinigne, N. (2024). The importance and limitations of artificial intelligence ethics and digital corporate responsibility in consumer markets: Challenges and opportunities. In *Globalized Consumer Insights in the Digital Era* (pp. 150–168). IGI Global. 10.4018/979-8-3693-3811-7.ch007

Ameen, N., Tarba, S., Cheah, J. H., Xia, S., & Sharma, G. D. (2024). Coupling artificial intelligence capability and strategic agility for enhanced product and service creativity. *British Journal of Management*.

Ameen, N., Tarhini, A., Reppel, A., & Anand, A. (2021). Customer experiences in the age of artificial intelligence. *Computers in Human Behavior*, 114, 106548.32905175

Ando, Y., Thawonmas, R., & Rinaldo, F. 2013. Inference of viewed exhibits in a metaverse museum. In: *2013 International Conference on Culture and Computing*. IEEE. 10.1109/CultureComputing.2013.73

Andreev, R., Andreeva, P., Krotov, L., & Krotova, E. L. (2018). Review of blockchain technology: Types of blockchain and their application. *Intellekt. Sist. Proizv*, 16(1), 11–14. 10.22213/2410-9304-2018-1-11-14

André, Q., Carmon, Z., Wertenbroch, K., Crum, A., Frank, D., Goldstein, W., Huber, J., Boven, L., Weber, B., & Yang, H. (2018). Consumer choice and autonomy in the age of artificial intelligence and big data. *Customer Needs and Solutions*, 5(1), 28–37. 10.1007/s40547-017-0085-8

Andrew, J., & Baker, M. (2021). The general data protection regulation in the age of surveillance capitalism. *Journal of Business Ethics*, 168, 565–578.

Anshari, M., Hamdan, M., Ahmad, N., Ali, E., & Haidi, H. (2023). COVID-19, artificial intelligence, ethical challenges and policy implications. *AI & Society*, 38(2), 707–720.35607368

Antons, D., & Breidbach, C. F. (2018). Big data, big insights? Advancing service innovation and design with machine learning. *Journal of Service Research*, 21(1), 17–39. 10.1177/1094670517738373

Arabahmadi, M., Farahbakhsh, R., & Rezazadeh, J. (2022). Deep learning for smart healthcare—A survey on brain tumor detection from medical imaging. *Sensors (Basel)*, 22(5), 1960. 10.3390/s2205196035271115

Arango, L., Singaraju, S. P., & Niininen, O. (2023). Consumer Responses to AI-Generated Charitable Giving Ads. *Journal of Advertising*, 52(4), 486–503. 10.1080/00913367.2023.2183285

Arjoon and Rambocas. (2011). Ethics and Customer Loyalty: Some Insights into Online Retailing Services. *International Journal of Business and Social Science*, 2(14).

Armstrong Soule, C. A., & Reich, B. J. (2015). Less is more: Is a green demarketing strategy sustainable? *Journal of Marketing Management*, 31(13-14), 1403–1427. 10.1080/0267257X.2015.1059874

Arsenijevic, U., & Jovic, M. (2019). Artificial Intelligence Marketing: Chatbots. *2019 International Conference on Artificial Intelligence: Applications and Innovations (IC-AIAI)*, (pp. 19–193). Research Gate.

Artificial intelligence (AI) and data privacy for companies. (n.d.). Consent Management Platform (CMP) Usercentrics. https://usercentrics.com/knowledge-hub/data-privacy-artificial-intelligence/

Artificial Intelligence and Privacy - Issues and Challenges. (2021, April 13). Office of the Victorian Information Commissioner; Office of Victorian Information Commissioner. https://ovic.vic.gov.au/privacy/resources-for-organisations/artificial-intelligence-and-privacy-issues-and-challenges/

Ashill, N. J., & Sinha, A. (2004). An exploratory study into the impact of components of brand equity and country of origin effects on purchase intention. *Journal of Asia-Pacific Business*, 5(3), 27–43. 10.1300/J098v05n03_03

Assegaf, S. (2016). The Effect of Services Quality to Customer Satisfaction by Using Internet Banking Service in Jambi. *The Asian Journal of Technology Management*, 9(1), 21–36. 10.12695/ajtm.2015. 9.1.3

Attanayake. (2005). *Ethical emarketing for competitive advantage*. [Dissertation, Sri Lanka: University of Moratuwa].

Aydin, S., & Ozer, G. (2005). The analysis of antecedents of customer loyalty in the Turkish mobile telecommunication market. *European Journal of Marketing*, 39(7/8), 910–925. 10.1108/03090560510601833

Azad, A. (n.d.). *Marketing chatbots: The ultimate solution for 2023 and beyond*. Engati. https://www.engati.com/blog/chatbots-for-marketing

Azhar, A., Rehman, N., Majeed, N., & Bano, S. (2024). Employer branding: A strategy to enhance organizational performance. *International Journal of Hospitality Management*, 116, 103618. 10.1016/j.ijhm.2023.103618

Baker, R. S., D'Mello, S. K., Rodrigo, M. M. T., & Graesser, A. C. (2010). Better to be frustrated than bored: The incidence, persistence, and impact of learners' cognitive–affective states during interactions with three different computer-based learning environments. *International Journal of Human-Computer Studies*, 68(4), 223–241. 10.1016/j.ijhcs.2009.12.003

Balducci, B., & Marinova, D. (2018). Unstructured data in marketing. *Journal of the Academy of Marketing Science*, 46(4), 557–590. 10.1007/s11747-018-0581-x

Bambauer-Sachse, S., & Mangold, S. (2011). Brand equity dilution through negative online word-of-mouth communication. *Journal of Retailing and Consumer Services*, 18(1), 38–45. 10.1016/j.jretconser.2010.09.003

Compilation of References

Banaeian Far, S., & Imani Rad, A. (2022). What are the benefits and opportunities of launching a metaverse for neom city? *Security and Privacy*, 6(3), e282. 10.1002/spy2.282

Bandara, R., Fernando, M., & Akter, S. (2021). Managing consumer privacy concerns and defensive behaviours in the digital marketplace. *European Journal of Marketing*, 55(1), 219–246.

Banerjee, P., & Beck, J. E. (2020). Emerging Trends in Artificial Intelligence for Education. In Beck, J. E., & Leighton, P. E. (Eds.), *Educational Data Mining: Applications and Trends* (pp. 3–18). Springer.

Barocas, S., & Selbst, A. D. (2016). Big data's disparate impact. *California Law Review*, 104, 671–732.

Barrow, S., & Mosley, R. (2005). *The employer brand: Bringing the best of brand management to people at work*. John Wiley and Sons, Ltd.

Basu, P. (2019). AI in Education: A Roadmap for Transformation. *Educational Technology*, 59(6), 49–53.

Baum, T., & Hai, N. T. T. (2019). Applying sustainable employment principles in the tourism industry: Righting human rights wrongs? *Tourism Recreation Research*, 44(3), 371–381. 10.1080/02508281.2019.1624407

Baylor, A. L., & Kim, Y. (2009). Pedagogical agent design: The impact of agent realism, gender, ethnicity, and instructional role. In *Workshop on Educational Software Agents: Crossing the Chasm* (pp. 1-8). Research Gate.

Beatty, S. E., & Kahle, L. R. (1988). Alternative hierarchies of the attitude-behavior relationship: The impact of brand commitment and habit. *Journal of the Academy of Marketing Science*, 16(2), 1–10. 10.1007/BF02723310

Becker, K. (2017). Carnegie Learning's Cognitive Tutor: A Case Study in Implementing Artificial Intelligence to Enhance Mathematics Instruction. *Journal of Educational Technology & Society*, 20(2), 75–86.

Benjelloun, A., & Kabak, S. (2024). Ethical Challenges and Managerial Implications of Artificial Intelligence in Digital Marketing. In K. S., B. K., K. J.H., & B. J.C. (Eds.), *Lecture Notes in Networks and Systems* (pp. 439–445). Springer Science and Business Media Deutschland GmbH. 10.1007/978-981-99-9040-5_32

Berger, J., Humphreys, A., Ludwig, S., Moe, W. W., Netzer, O., & Schweidel, D. A. (2020). Uniting the tribes: Using text for marketing insight. *Journal of Marketing*, 84(1), 1–25. 10.1177/0022242919873106

Bernardi, L., & Fraschini, A. (2005). *Tax system and Tax Reforms in India*. Department of Public Policy and Public Choice.

Bernhard, M., Bracciali, A., & Gudgeon, L. (2021). Financial Cryptography and Data Security. In: *Proceedings of FC: 25th International Conference on Financial Cryptography and Data Security*. Springer, Berlin, Heidelberg.

Bharadwaj, S., Khan, N. A., & Yameen, M. (2022). Unbundling employer branding, job satisfaction, organizational identification and employee retention: A sequential mediation analysis. *Asia-Pacific Journal of Business Administration*, 14(3), 309–334. 10.1108/APJBA-08-2020-0279

Bhargava, D. P K (2007). Deteriorating Fiscal Measurement of States in India: Remedial Measures Needed. Thakur, Anil Kumar and M D Abdus Salam (ed.), *Indian Public Finance and Twelfth Finance Commission*. Deep and Deep Publishers, New Delhi.

Bhatt, T. (2024, April 5). *Uber Eats Business Model: Changing the Game in Food Delivery*. Intelivita. https://www.intelivita.com/blog/uber-eats-business-model/

Bhutoria, A. (2022). Personalized education and artificial intelligence in the United States, China, and India: A systematic review using a human-in-The-Loop model. *Computers and Education: Artificial Intelligence*, 3, 100068. 10.1016/j.caeai.2022.100068

Bian, X., & Moutinho, L. (2011). The role of brand image, product involvement, and knowledge in explaining consumer purchase behaviour of counterfeits: Direct and indirect effects. *European Journal of Marketing*, 45(1/2), 191–216. 10.1108/03090561111095658

Bickart, B., & Schindler, R. M. (2001). Internet forums as influential sources of consumer information. *Journal of Interactive Marketing*, 15(3), 31–40. 10.1002/dir.1014

Biswas, B., Sanyal, M. K., & Mukherjee, T. (2023). AI-Based Sales Forecasting Model for Digital Marketing. [IJEBR]. *International Journal of E-Business Research*, 19(1), 1–14.

Bleier, A., Goldfarb, A., & Tucker, C. (2020). Consumer privacy and the future of data-based innovation and marketing. *International Journal of Research in Marketing*, 37(3), 466–480.

Bock, G. W., & Kim, Y. G. (2002). Breaking the Myths of Rewards: An Exploratory Study of Attitudes about Knowledge Sharing. [IRMJ]. *Information Resources Management Journal*, 15(2), 14–21. 10.4018/irmj.2002040102

Bogani, R., Theodorou, A., Arnaboldi, L., & Wortham, R. H. (2022). Garbage in, toxic data out: A proposal for ethical artificial intelligence sustainability impact statements. *AI and Ethics*, •••, 1–8.36281314

Boulding, W., Kalra, A., Staelin, R., & Zeithaml, V. A. (1993). A dynamic process model of service quality: From expectations to behavioral intention. *JMR, Journal of Marketing Research*, 30(1), 7–27. 10.1177/002224379303000102

Bozkurt, A. (2023). Unleashing the potential of generative AI, conversational agents and chatbots in educational praxis: A systematic review and bibliometric analysis of GenAI in education. *Open Praxis*, 15(4), 261–270. 10.55982/openpraxis.15.4.609

Brien, A. (2014). Do I want a job in hospitality? Only Till I get a Real Job. In *Proceedings of the New Zealand Tourism and Hospitality Research Conference* (pp. 35–42). Victoria University of Wellington.

Brough, A. R., & Martin, K. D. (2021). Consumer privacy during (and after) the COVID-19 pandemic. *Journal of Public Policy & Marketing*, 40(1), 108–110.

Brown, J., Broderick, A. J., & Lee, N. (2007). Word of mouth communication within online communities: Conceptualizing the online social network. *Journal of Interactive Marketing*, 21(3), 2–20. 10.1002/dir.20082

Brynjolfsson, E., & McAfee, A. (2014). *The second machine age: Work, progress, and prosperity in a time of brilliant technologies*. WW Norton & Company.

Buckingham Shum, S., Ferguson, R., & Martinez-Maldonado, R. (2019). Human-centred learning analytics. *Journal of Learning Analytics*, 6(2), 1–9. 10.18608/jla.2019.62.1

Budden, M. C., & Hossain, N. (1987). Tobacco demarketing campaigns and role model selection in developing countries: The case of Bangladesh. *Health Marketing Quarterly*, 4(2), 63–67. 10.1300/J026v04n02_0810282181

Bundy, A. (2017). Preparing for the future of Artificial Intelligence. *AI & Society*, 32(2), 285–287. 10.1007/s00146-016-0685-0

Busis, N. A., Marolia, D., Montgomery, R., Balcer, L. J., Galetta, S. L., & Grossman, S. N. (2024). Navigating the U.S. regulatory landscape for neurologic digital health technologies. *NPJ Digital Medicine*, 7(1), 94. 10.1038/s41746-024-01098-538609447

Byrne, B. M. (2001). *Structural Equation Modelling with AMOS: Basic Concepts, Applications and Programming*. Lawrence Erlbaum Associates.

Cai, Q., Wang, H., Li, Z., & Liu, X. (2019). A survey on multimodal data-driven smart healthcare systems: Approaches and applications. *IEEE Access : Practical Innovations, Open Solutions*, 7, 133583–133599. 10.1109/ACCESS.2019.2941419

Çakar, K., & Uzut, İ. (2020). Exploring the stakeholder's role in sustainable degrowth within the context of tourist destination governance: The case of Istanbul, Turkey. *Journal of Travel & Tourism Marketing*, 37(8-9), 917–932. 10.1080/10548408.2020.1782307

Campbell, C., Sands, S., Ferraro, C., Tsao, H.-Y. J., & Mavrommatis, A. (2020). From data to action: How marketers can leverage AI. *Business Horizons*, 63(2), 227–243. 10.1016/j.bushor.2019.12.002

Caner, S., & Bhatti, F. (2020). A conceptual framework on defining businesses strategy for artificial intelligence. *Contemporary Management Research*, 16(3), 175–206. 10.7903/cmr.19970

Canhoto, A. I., & Clear, F. (2020). Artificial intelligence and machine learning as business tools: A framework for diagnosing value destruction potential. *Business Horizons*, 63(2), 183–193. 10.1016/j.bushor.2019.11.003

Capatina, A., Kachour, M., Lichy, J., Micu, A., Micu, A. E., & Codignola, F. (2020). Matching the future capabilities of an artificial intelligence-based software for social media marketing with potential users' expectations. *Technological Forecasting and Social Change*, 151, 119794. 10.1016/j.techfore.2019.119794

Capuano, N., Greco, L., Ritrovato, P., & Vento, M. (2021). Sentiment analysis for customer relationship management: An incremental learning approach. *Applied Intelligence*, 51, 3339–3352.

Celik, I. (2023). Towards Intelligent-TPACK: An empirical study on teachers' professional knowledge to ethically integrate artificial intelligence (ai)-based tools into education. *Computers in Human Behavior*, 138, 107468. 10.1016/j.chb.2022.107468

Chaffey, D., & Ellis-Chadwick, F. (2019). *Digital marketing*. Pearson uk.

Chakraborty, P. (2017). *Analysis of State Budgets 2017-18: Emerging Issues, NIPFP*.

Chan, C. K., & Hu, W. (2023). Students' voices on generative AI: Perceptions, benefits, and challenges in higher education. *International Journal of Educational Technology in Higher Education*, 20(1), 43. Advance online publication. 10.1186/s41239-023-00411-8

Chandel, A., & Kaur, T. (2022). Demystifying neuromarketing: a bibliometric analysis using vosviewer. In *Developing Relationships, Personalization, and Data Herald in Marketing 5.0* (pp. 256-283). IGI Global. 10.4018/978-1-6684-4496-2.ch016

Chandel, A., Bhanot, N., Gupta, S., & Verma, R. (2024). Oil Spills-Where We Were, Where We Are, And Where We Will Be? A Bibliometric and Content Analysis Discourse. In *BIO Web of Conferences* (Vol. 86, p. 01050). EDP Sciences.

Chandel, A., Bhanot, N., & Sharma, R. (2023). A bibliometric and content analysis discourse on business application of blockchain technology. *International Journal of Quality & Reliability Management*. 10.1108/IJQRM-02-2023-0025

Chandel, A., Bhanot, N., & Verma, R. (2023). A Bibliometric Investigation of Ecocide Research: Tracing Trends and Shaping the Future. In *E3S Web of Conferences* (Vol. 453, p. 01044). EDP Sciences. 10.1051/e3sconf/202345301044

Chang, H. H., & Liu, Y. M. (2009). The impact of brand equity on brand preference and purchase intentions in the service industries. *Service Industries Journal*, 29(12), 1687–1706. 10.1080/02642060902793557

Char, D. S., Shah, N. H., & Magnus, D. (2018). Implementing machine learning in health care—Addressing ethical challenges. *The New England Journal of Medicine*, 378(11), 981–983. 10.1056/NEJMp171422929539284

Chatterjee, P. (2001). Online reviews: Do consumers use them? *Advances in Consumer Research. Association for Consumer Research (U. S.)*, 28(1), 129–133.

Chaudhury, R. (2013). *Estimating True Fiscal Capacity of States and Devising a Suitable Rule for Granting Debt Relief based on Optimal Growth Requirement*. Fourteenth FC, Jadavpur University.

Chawla, N., & Kumar, B. (2022). E-commerce and consumer protection in India: The emerging trend. *Journal of Business Ethics*, 180(2), 581–604. 10.1007/s10551-021-04884-334257470

Chen, R. (2019). *Policy and regulatory issues with digital businesses*. World Bank Policy Research Working Paper. https://documents.worldbank.org/en/publication/documents-reports/documentdetail/675241563969185669/policy-and-regulatory-issues-with-digital-businesses.

Chen, Y., & Bellavitis, C. (2019). Decentralized finance: blockchain technology and the quest for an open financial system. In: *Stevens Institute of Technology School of Business Research Paper*. SIT. 10.2139/ssrn.3418557

Chen. (2018). Multinational Corporate Power, Influence and Responsibility in Global Supply Chains. *Journal Business Ethics, 148*, 365- 375. https://doi.org/.10.1007/s10551- 016-3033

Chengoden, R., Victor, N., Huynh-The, T., Yenduri, G., Jhaveri, R. H., Alazab, M., Bhattacharya, S., Hegde, P., Maddikunta, P. K., & Gadekallu, T. R. (2023). Metaverse for healthcare: A survey on potential applications, challenges and future directions. *IEEE Access : Practical Innovations, Open Solutions*, 11, 12765–12795. 10.1109/ACCESS.2023.3241628

Chen, L., Chen, P., & Lin, Z. (2020). Artificial intelligence in education: A review. *IEEE Access : Practical Innovations, Open Solutions*, 8, 75264–75278. 10.1109/ACCESS.2020.2988510

Chen, S., & Liu, W. (2020). Artificial Intelligence in Education: Current and Future Trends. *Journal of Educational Technology*, 14(2), 45–59.

Chen, X., Xie, H., Li, Z., Cheng, G., Leng, M., & Wang, F. L. (2023). Information fusion and artificial intelligence for smart healthcare: A bibliometric study. *Information Processing & Management*, 60(1), 103113. 10.1016/j.ipm.2022.103113

Chevalier, J. A., & Mayzlin, D. (2006). The effect of word of mouth on sales: Online book reviews. *JMR, Journal of Marketing Research*, 43(3), 345–354. 10.1509/jmkr.43.3.345

Chintalapati, S., & Pandey, S. K. (2022). Artificial intelligence in marketing: A systematic literature review. *International Journal of Market Research*, 64(1), 38–68. 10.1177/14707853211018428

Chiu, T. K., & Chai, C. (2020). undefined. *Sustainability*, 12(14), 5568. 10.3390/su12145568

Choudhary, N., Gautam, C., & Arya, V. (2020). Digital marketing challenge and opportunity with reference to tiktok-a new rising social media platform. *Editorial Board*, 9(10), 189–197.

Cobo, M. J., López-Herrera, A. G., Herrera-Viedma, E., & Herrera, F. (2012). SciMAT: A new science mapping analysis software tool. *Journal of the American Society for Information Science and Technology*, 63(8), 1609–1630. 10.1002/asi.22688

Comm, C. L. (1998). Demarketing products which may pose health risks. *Health Marketing Quarterly*, 15(1), 95–102. 10.1300/J026v15n01_0610179066

Commission, E., & Innovation, D.-G. for R. and, & Schomberg, R. (2011). *Towards responsible research and innovation in the information and communication technologies and security technologies fields* (R. Schomberg (Ed.)). Publications Office. https://doi.org/doi/10.2777/58723

Compilation of References

Conley, C. S., Durlak, J. A., & Dickson, D. A. (2013). An evaluative review of outcome research on universal mental health promotion and prevention programs for higher education students. *Journal of American College Health*, 61(5), 286–301. 10.1080/07448481.2013.80223723768226

Cooke, A. D., & Zubcsek, P. P. (2017). The connected consumer: Connected devices and the evolution of customer intelligence. *Journal of the Association for Consumer Research*, 2(2), 164–178. 10.1086/690941

Cooper, G. (2023). Examining science education in ChatGPT: An exploratory study of generative artificial intelligence. *Journal of Science Education and Technology*, 32(3), 444–452. 10.1007/s10956-023-10039-y

Cousins, P. D., & Menguc, B. (2006). The implications of socialization and integration in supply chain management. *Journal of Operations Management*, 24(5), 604–620. 10.1016/j.jom.2005.09.001

Crawford, K., & Paglen, T. (2019). *Excavating AI: The politics of images in machine learning training sets*.

Cvelbar, L. K., & Dwyer, L. (2013). An importance–performance analysis of sustainability factors for long-term strategy planning in Slovenian hotels. *Journal of Sustainable Tourism*, 21(3), 487–504. 10.1080/09669582.2012.713965

D'Mello, S. K., & Graesser, A. C. (2012). Dynamics of affective states during complex learning. *Learning and Instruction*, 22(2), 145–157. 10.1016/j.learninstruc.2011.10.001

Dalgarno, B., & Lee, M. J. W. (2010). What are the learning affordances of 3-D virtual environments? *British Journal of Educational Technology*, 41(1), 10–32. 10.1111/j.1467-8535.2009.01038.x

Dastane, D. O. (2020). Impact of digital marketing on online purchase intention: Mediation effect of customer relationship management. *Journal of Asian Business Strategy*.

Davenport, T. H., & Kalakota, R. (2019). The potential for artificial intelligence in healthcare. *Future Healthcare Journal*, 6(2), 94–98. 10.7861/futurehosp.6-2-9431363513

Davenport, T., Guha, A., Grewal, D., & Bressgott, T. (2020). How artificial intelligence will change the future of marketing. *Journal of the Academy of Marketing Science*, 48(1), 24–42. 10.1007/s11747-019-00696-0

Davis, A., & Khazanchi, D. (2008). An empirical study of online word of mouth as a predictor for multi-product category e-commerce sales. *Electronic Markets*, 18(2), 130–141. 10.1080/10196780802044776

Davis, D. F., Golicic, S. L., & Marquardt, A. (2009). Measuring brand equity for logistics services. *International Journal of Logistics Management*, 20(2), 201–212. 10.1108/09574090910981297

Davis, F. D. (1989). Perceived usefulness, perceived ease of use, and user acceptance of information technology. *Management Information Systems Quarterly*, 13(3), 319–339. 10.2307/249008

De Hond, A. A., Leeuwenberg, A. M., Hooft, L., Kant, I. M., Nijman, S. W., Van Os, H. J., Aardoom, J. J., Debray, T. P., Schuit, E., Van Smeden, M., Reitsma, J. B., Steyerberg, E. W., Chavannes, N. H., & Moons, K. G. (2022). Guidelines and quality criteria for artificial intelligence-based prediction models in healthcare: A scoping review. npj. *Digital Medicine*, 5(1), 2. Advance online publication. 10.1038/s41746-021-00549-735013569

De Mauro, A., Sestino, A., & Bacconi, A. (2022). Machine learning and artificial intelligence use in marketing: A general taxonomy. *Italian Journal of Marketing*, 2022(4), 439–457. 10.1007/s43039-022-00057-w

Dekimpe, M. (2020). Retailing and retailing research in the age of big data analytics. *International Journal of Research in Marketing*, 37(1), 3–14. 10.1016/j.ijresmar.2019.09.001

Deslée, A., & Cloarec, J. (2024). Safeguarding privacy: Ethical considerations in Data-Driven Marketing. In *The Impact of Digitalization on Current Marketing Strategies* (pp. 147–161). Emerald Group Publishing Ltd., 10.1108/978-1-83753-686-320241009

Devang, V., Chintan, S., Gunjan, T., & Krupa, R. (2019). Applications of artificial intelligence in marketing. *Annals of Dunarea de Jos University of Galati. Fascicle I.Economics and Applied Informatics*, 25(1), 28–36.

Dhanasekaram, K. B. (2006). Sustaining the Finances of State Governments. In Srivastava, D. K., & Narasimhulu, M. (Eds.), *State Level Fiscal Reforms in the Indian Economy*. Deep and Deep Publication Pvt. Ltd.

Dhar, V. (2016). The future of artificial intelligence. *Big Data*, 4(1), 5–9. 10.1089/big.2016.29004.vda27441580

Dhiresh, K. (2013). Relationship between economic growth and public expenditure through Wagner's law: an analytical study in Indian perspective. *International Journal of Entrepreneurship & Business Environment Perspectives, 2*(4).

Dhiresh, K. (2019). An Econometric Analysis of Agricultural Production and Economic Growth in India. *Indian Journal of Marketing*, 49(11), 56. 10.17010/ijom/2019/v49/i11/148276

Di Vaio, A., Palladino, R., Hassan, R., & Escobar, O. (2020). Artificial intelligence and business models in the sustainable development goals perspective: A systematic literature review. *Journal of Business Research*, 121(Dec), 283–314. 10.1016/j.jbusres.2020.08.019

Dias, A., Silva, G. M., Patuleia, M., & González-Rodríguez, M. R. (2020). Developing sustainable business models: Local knowledge acquisition and tourism lifestyle entrepreneurship. *Journal of Sustainable Tourism*, 1–20.

Dogan, M. E., Goru Dogan, T., & Bozkurt, A. (2023). The use of artificial intelligence (AI) in online learning and distance education processes: A systematic review of empirical studies. *Applied Sciences (Basel, Switzerland)*, 13(5), 3056. 10.3390/app13053056

Donthu, N., Kumar, S., Mukherjee, D., Pandey, N., & Lim, W. M. (2021). How to conduct a bibliometric analysis: An overview and guidelines. *Journal of Business Research*, 133, 285–296. 10.1016/j.jbusres.2021.04.070

Doroshuk, H. (2021). Prospects and efficiency measurement of artificial intelligence in the management of enterprises in the energy sector in the era of Industry 4.0. *Polityka Energetyczna*, 24(4), 61–76. 10.33223/epj/144083

Drabiak, K. (2022). Leveraging law and ethics to promote safe and reliable AI/ML in healthcare. *Frontiers in Nuclear Medicine*, 2, 983340. 10.3389/fnume.2022.983340

Drenten, J., & McManus, K. (2016). Religion-related research in the Journal of Macromarketing, 1981-2014. *Journal of Macromarketing*, 36(4), 377–387. 10.1177/0276146715623051

Dube, M., Musungwini, S., Mudzimba, E., & Watyoka, N. (2023). Mixed Reality in Confronting Consumer Security and Privacy Issues in Digital Marketing: Integrating the Best of Both Worlds for Better Interaction With Users. In *Confronting Security and Privacy Challenges in Digital Marketing* (pp. 252-266). IGI Global.

Dunleavy, M., Dede, C., & Mitchell, R. (2009). Affordances and limitations of immersive participatory augmented reality simulations for teaching and learning. *Journal of Science Education and Technology*, 18(1), 7–22. 10.1007/s10956-008-9119-1

Dwivedi. (2020). Set the future of digital and social media marketing research: Perspectives and research propositions. *International Journal of Information Management*, 2(1), 31-42. .10.1016/j.ijinfomgt.2020.102168

Compilation of References

Egbemhenghe, A., Ojeyemi, T., Iwuozor, K. O., Emenike, E. C., Ogunsanya, T. I., Anidiobi, S. U., & Adeniyi, A. G. (2023). Revolutionizing water treatment, conservation, and management: Harnessing the power of AI-driven ChatGPT solutions. *Environmental Challenges*, 13, 100782. 10.1016/j.envc.2023.100782

Eggmann, F., Weiger, R., Zitzmann, N. U., & Blatz, M. B. (2023). Implications of large language models such as ChatGPT for dental medicine. *Journal of Esthetic and Restorative Dentistry*, 35(7), 1098–1102. 10.1111/jerd.1304637017291

Ekici, A., Genc, T. O., & Celik, H. (2021). The future of macromarketing: Recommendations based on a content analysis of the past twelve years of the Journal of Macromarketing. *Journal of Macromarketing*, 41(1), 25–47. 10.1177/0276146720966654

El Zoghbi, E., & Aoun, K. (2016). Employer branding and social media strategies. In *Information and Communication Technologies in Organizations and Society: Past, Present and Future Issues* (pp. 277-283). Springer International Publishing. 10.1007/978-3-319-28907-6_18

Emami-Naeini, P., Dixon, H., Agarwal, Y., & Cranor, L. F. (2019, May). Exploring how privacy and security factor into IoT device purchase behavior. In *Proceedings of the 2019 CHI Conference on Human Factors in Computing Systems* (pp. 1-12).

Engelmann, S., Ullstein, C., Papakyriakopoulos, O., & Grosslags, J. (2022). What People Think AI Should Infer From Faces. *ACM International Conference Proceeding Series*, 128–141. 10.1145/3531146.3533080

Eser, H. (2022, May). Big Data, Social Media and Employer Branding: An exploratory study from the hospitality industry. In *International Conference on Tourism Research* (Vol. 15, No. 1, pp. 110-116). 10.34190/ictr.15.1.273

Esteva, A., Robicquet, A., Ramsundar, B., Kuleshov, V., DePristo, M., Chou, K., Cui, C., Corrado, G., Thrun, S., & Dean, J. (2019). A guide to deep learning in healthcare. *Nature Medicine*, 25(1), 24–29. 10.1038/s41591-018-0316-z30617335

Eysenbach, G. (2023). The role of ChatGPT, generative language models, and artificial intelligence in medical education: A conversation with ChatGPT and a call for papers. *JMIR Medical Education*, 9(1), e46885. 10.2196/4688536863937

Ezechukwu, N. V. (2023). Consumer Protection and Trade Governance: A Critical Partnership? *Journal of Consumer Policy*, 46(2), 191–221. 10.1007/s10603-023-09538-7

Far, S. B., & Rad, A. I. (2022). Applying digital twins in metaverse: User interface, security and privacy challenges. *J. Metaverse*, 2(1), 8–15.

Fauzan and Ida. (2014). The Effect of Quality of Service, Image, and Business Ethics on Satisfaction and Loyalty of Patients in Hospitals in Makassar City. *International Journal of Management Progress*, 1(2), 1–22. 10.21067/jem.v10i1.774

Feng, H. (2023, August 2). *How AI-powered chatbots are transforming marketing and sales operations*. IBM Blog. https://www.ibm.com/blog/how-ai-powered-chatbots-are-transforming-marketing-and-sales-operations/

Fennell, D. A., & Bowyer, E. (2019). Tourism and Sustainable transformation: A discussion and application to tourism food consumption. *Tourism Recreation Research*, 45(1), 119–131. 10.1080/02508281.2019.1694757

Ferguson, R. (2018). Learning analytics: Drivers, developments and challenges. *International Journal of Educational Technology in Higher Education*, 15(1), 3.

Fernandes, P. M., Sousa, B. B., Veloso, C. M., & Valeri, M. (2023). The role of endomarketing in human capital management: A study applied to the Minho Urban Quadrilateral. *EuroMed Journal of Business*. 10.1108/EMJB-12-2022-0212

Fernandes, R., Sousa, B. B., Fonseca, M., & Oliveira, J. (2023). Assessing the Impacts of Internal Communication: Employer Branding and Human Resources. *Administrative Sciences*, 13(6), 155. 10.3390/admsci13060155

Ferretti, S., & D'Angelo, G. (2020). On the ethereum blockchain structure: A complex networks theory perspective. *Concurrency and Computation*, 32(12), e5493. 10.1002/cpe.5493

Floridi, L. (2019). *The logic of information: A theory of philosophy as conceptual design*. Oxford University Press. 10.1093/oso/9780198833635.001.0001

From chatbots to predictive analytics: Using AI marketing tools to enhance customer experience. (2023, June 30). AI-Contentfy. https://aicontentfy.com/en/blog/from-chatbots-to-predictive-analytics-using-ai-marketing-tools-to-enhance-customer-experience

Furey, E., & Blue, J. (2018). She just doesn't understand me! Curing Alexa of her Alexithymia. In B. J., D. J., B. R., J. A.C., & B. R. (Eds.), *CEUR Workshop Proceedings* (Vol. 2259, pp. 244–255). CEUR-WS. https://www.scopus.com/inward/record.uri?eid=2-s2.0-85058234360&partnerID=40&md5=04babd4b045a7162ddf26ff3922b8363

Furukawa, G. (n.d.). *Revolutionizing marketing strategy: The power of AI chatbots*. Marketerhire.com. https://marketerhire.com/blog/marketing-chatbots

Fütterer, T., Fischer, C., Alekseeva, A., Chen, X., Tate, T., Warschauer, M., & Gerjets, P. (2023). ChatGPT in education: Global reactions to AI innovations. *Scientific Reports*, 13(1), 15310. Advance online publication. 10.1038/s41598-023-42227-637714915

Gai, K., Qiu, M., & Sun, X. (2018). A survey on fintech. *Journal of Network and Computer Applications*, 103(Feb), 262–273. 10.1016/j.jnca.2017.10.011

Gilly, M. C., Graham, J. L., Wolfinbarger, M. F., & Yale, L. J. (1998). A dyadic study of interpersonal information search. *Journal of the Academy of Marketing Science*, 26(2), 83–100. 10.1177/0092070398262001

Godes, D., & Mayzlin, D. (2004). Using online conversations to study word-of-mouth communication. *Marketing Science*, 23(4), 545–560. 10.1287/mksc.1040.0071

Golden, L. L., & Suder, A. J. (1994). Disease demarketing: The college AIDS challenge. *Health Marketing Quarterly*, 11(3-4), 105–124. 10.1300/J026v11n03_1010137011

Goldsmith, R. E., & Horowitz, D. (2006). Measuring motivations for online opinion seeking. *Journal of Interactive Advertising*, 6(2), 1–16. 10.1080/15252019.2006.10722114

Gössling, S., Scott, D., & Hall, C. M. (2015). Inter-market variability in CO2 emission-intensities in tourism: Implications for destination marketing and carbon management. *Tourism Management*, 46, 203–212. 10.1016/j.tourman.2014.06.021

Gouvea, J. S. (2024). Ethical dilemmas in current uses of AI in science education. *CBE Life Sciences Education*, 23(1), fe3. 10.1187/cbe.23-12-023938232237

Goyal, J., Singh, M., Singh, R., & Aggarwal, A. (2019). Efficiency and technology gaps in Indian banking sector: Application of meta-frontier directional distance function DEA approach. *The Journal of finance and data science*, 5(3), 156-172.

Graesser, A. C., Li, H., Forsyth, C. M., & Elenzil, M. (2018). Conversational agents for learning, assessment, and coaching. In Fiore, S. M., & Salas, E. (Eds.), *Theories of Team Cognition: Cross-Disciplinary Perspectives* (pp. 283–299). Routledge.

Gruen, T. W., Osmonbekov, T., & Czaplewski, A. J. (2006). EWOM: The impact of customer-to-customer online know-how exchange on customer value and loyalty. *Journal of Business Research*, 59(4), 449–456. 10.1016/j.jbusres.2005.10.004

Guest, G., Bunce, A., & Johnson, L. (2006). How many interviews are enough? An experiment with data saturation and variability. *Field Methods*, 18(1), 59–82. 10.1177/1525822X05279903

Compilation of References

Guillou-Landreat, M., Dany, A., Le Reste, J. Y., Le Goff, D., Benyamina, A., Grall-Bronnec, M., & Gallopel-Morvan, K. (2020). Impact of alcohol marketing on drinkers with Alcohol use disorders seeking treatment: A mixed-method study protocol. *BMC Public Health*, 20(1), 1–8. 10.1186/s12889-020-08543-632264848

Gu, J., Wang, J., Guo, X., Liu, G., Qin, S., & Bi, Z. (2023). A metaverse-based teaching building evacuation training system with deep reinforcement learning. *IEEE Transactions on Systems, Man, and Cybernetics. Systems*, 53(4), 2209–2219. 10.1109/TSMC.2022.3231299

Gull, H., Alabbad, D. A., Saqib, M., Iqbal, S. Z., Nasir, T., Saeed, S., & Almuhaideb, A. M. (2023). E-commerce and cybersecurity challenges: Recent advances and future trends. *Handbook of Research on Cybersecurity Issues and Challenges for Business and FinTech Applications*, 91-111.

Gull, H., Iqbal, S. Z., Saeed, S., Alqahtani, M. A., & Bamarouf, Y. A. (2021). U.S. Patent No. 11,055,137. Washington, DC: U.S. Patent and Trademark Office.

Gull, H., Saeed, S., Iqbal, S. Z., Bamarouf, Y. A., Alqahtani, M. A., Alabbad, D. A., & Alamer, A. (2022). An empirical study of mobile commerce and customers security perception in Saudi Arabia. *Electronics (Basel)*, 11(3), 293.

Gülşen, U., Yolcu, H., Ataker, P., Erçakar, İ., & Acar, S. (2021). Counteracting Overtourism Using Demarketing Tools: A Logit Analysis Based on Existing Literature. *Sustainability (Basel)*, 13(19), 10592. 10.3390/su131910592

Gulshan, V., Peng, L., Coram, M., Stumpe, M. C., Wu, D., Narayanaswamy, A., & Webster, D. R. (2016). Development and validation of a deep learning algorithm for detection of diabetic retinopathy in retinal fundus photographs. *jama*, 316(22), 2402-2410.

Gundlach, G. T., & Murphy, P. E. (1993). Ethical and Legal Foundations of Relational Marketing Exchanges. *Journal of Marketing*, 57(4), 35–46. 10.1177/002224299305700403

Hadi Kiapour, M., Han, X., & Lazebnik, S. (2015). Where to buy it: matching street clothing photos in online shops. In: *Proceedings of the IEEE International Conference on Computer Vision*. IEEE.

Hair, J. F., Anderson, R. E., Tatham, R. L., & Black, W. C. (1998). *Multivariate Data Analysis* (5th ed.). Prentice Hall.

Hajrasouliha, A. H. (2023). Applications, Approaches, and Ethics of the Extended Reality in Urban Design and Planning. *Journal of the American Planning Association*, 1–17. Advance online publication. 10.1080/01944363.2023.2275123

Haleem, A., Javaid, M., Asim Qadri, M., Pratap Singh, R., & Suman, R. (2022). Artificial intelligence (AI) applications for marketing: A literature-based study. *International Journal of Intelligent Networks*, 3, 119–132. 10.1016/j.ijin.2022.08.005

Haleem, A., Javaid, M., Pratap Singh, R., & Suman, R. (2023). Exploring the revolution in healthcare systems through the applications of digital twin technology. *Biomedical Technology*, 4, 28–38. 10.1016/j.bmt.2023.02.001

Hanlon, A., & Jones, K. (2023). Ethical concerns about social media privacy policies: Do users have the ability to comprehend their consent actions? *Journal of Strategic Marketing*, 1–18.

Happonen, M., Rasmusson, L., Elofsson, A., & Kamb, A. (2023). Aviation's climate impact allocated to inbound tourism: Decision-making insights for "climate-ambitious" destinations. *Journal of Sustainable Tourism*, 31(8), 1885–1901. 10.1080/09669582.2022.2080835

Harrison-Walker, L. J. (2001). The measurement of word-of-mouth communication and an investigation of service quality and customer commitment as potential antecedents. *Journal of Service Research*, 4(1), 60–75. 10.1177/109467050141006

Hawkins, M. (2022). Metaverse live shopping analytics: Retail data measurement tools, computer vision and deep learning algorithms, and decision intelligence and modeling. *J. Self Govern. Manag. Econ.*, 10(2), 22–36. 10.22381/jsme10220222

Hayes, R. M., Jiang, F., & Pan, Y. (2021). Voice of the customers: Local trust culture and consumer complaints to the CFPB. *Journal of Accounting Research*, 59(3), 1077–1121.

Heffernan, N. T., Heffernan, C. L., Tuck, D., & Feldman, A. (2014). ASSISTments: Bringing classroom experiments into the digital age. *The Technology Innovations in Statistics Education, 8*(2).

Hein, A. Z., Elving, W. J., Koster, S., & Edzes, A. (2024). Is your employer branding strategy effective? The role of employee predisposition in achieving employer attractiveness. *Corporate Communications*, 29(7), 1–20. 10.1108/CCIJ-07-2022-0070

Heller, L. J., Skinner, C. S., Tomiyama, A. J., Epel, E. S., Hall, P. A., Allan, J., LaCaille, L., Randall, A. K., Bodenmann, G., Li-Tsang, C. W. P., Sinclair, K., Creek, J., Baumann, L. C., Karel, A., Andersson, G., Hanewinkel, R., Morgenstern, M., Puska, P., Bucks, R. S., & Denollet, J. (2013). Theory of Reasoned Action. In *Encyclopedia of Behavioral Medicine* (pp. 1964–1967). Springer New York. 10.1007/978-1-4419-1005-9_1619

Hennig-Thurau, T., Gwinner, K. P., Walsh, G., & Gremler, D. D. (2004). Electronic word-of-mouth via consumer-opinion platforms: What motivates consumers to articulate themselves on the internet? *Journal of Interactive Marketing*, 18(1), 38–52. 10.1002/dir.10073

Hentzen, J. K., Hoffmann, A., Dolan, R., & Pala, E. (2022). Artificial intelligence in customer-facing financial services: A systematic literature review and agenda for future research. *International Journal of Bank Marketing*, 40(6), 1299–1336. 10.1108/IJBM-09-2021-0417

Henz, P. (2021). Ethical and legal responsibility for Artificial Intelligence. *Discover Artificial Intelligence*, 1, 1–5.

Herath Pathirannehelage, S., Shrestha, Y. R., & von Krogh, G. (2024). Design principles for artificial intelligence-augmented decision making: An action design research study. *European Journal of Information Systems*, 1–23. 10.1080/0960085X.2024.2330402

Hermann, E. (2022). Leveraging artificial intelligence in marketing for social good—An ethical perspective. *Journal of Business Ethics*, 179(1), 43–61. 10.1007/s10551-021-04843-y34054170

Hermann, E., Williams, G. Y., & Puntoni, S. (2023). Deploying artificial intelligence in services to AID vulnerable consumers. *Journal of the Academy of Marketing Science*. 10.1007/s11747-023-00986-8

Herr, P. M., Kardes, F. R., & Kim, J. (1991). Effects of word-of-mouth and product-attribute information on persuasion: An accessibility-diagnosticity perspective. *The Journal of Consumer Research*, 17(4), 454–462. 10.1086/208570

Hesse, A., & Rünz, S. (2022). 'Fly Responsibly': A case study on consumer perceptions of a green demarketing campaign. *Journal of Marketing Communications*, 28(3), 232–252. 10.1080/13527266.2020.1842483

Hewitt, J., Parker, L., McQuilten, G., & Khan, R. (2023). Sustainability Chic and the Future of Fashion Marketing. In *BEYOND THE DARK ARTS* (pp. 125–147). Advancing Marketing and Communication Theory and Practice. 10.1142/9789811276064_0007

Hidayat, M., Salam, R., Hidayat, Y. S., Sutira, A., & Nugrahanti, T. P. (2022). Sustainable Digital Marketing Strategy in the Perspective of Sustainable Development Goals. Komitmen. *Jurnal Ilmiah Manajemen*, 3(2), 100–106.

Hoge and Cecil. (1993). Dissimilarity of e-marketing vs. traditional marketing. *The Electronic Marketing Manual ABA Journal*, 22, 175–185.

Hollensen, S., Kotler, P., & Opresnik, M. O. (2022). Metaverse–the new marketing universe. *The Journal of Business Strategy*, 44(3), 119–125. 10.1108/JBS-01-2022-0014

Compilation of References

Holmes, W., Porayska-Pomsta, K., Holstein, K., Sutherland, E., Baker, T., Shum, S. B., Santos, O. C., Rodrigo, M. T., Cukurova, M., Bittencourt, I. I., & Koedinger, K. R. (2021). Ethics of AI in education: Towards a community-wide framework. *International Journal of Artificial Intelligence in Education*, 32(3), 504–526. 10.1007/s40593-021-00239-1

How Chatbots are Changing the Landscape of AI Marketing. (2023, May 30). *AIContentfy*. https://aicontentfy.com/en/blog/how-chatbots-are-changing-landscape-of-ai-marketing

Hoxby, C. M. (1996). Are efficiency and equity in school finance substitutes or complements? *The Journal of Economic Perspectives*, 10(4), 51–72. 10.1257/jep.10.4.51

https://economictimes.indiatimes.com

https://wornwear.patagonia.com/

Huang, J., Saleh, S., & Liu, Y. (2021). A review on artificial intelligence in education. *Academic Journal of Interdisciplinary Studies, 10*(3).

Huang, D. (2024). undefined. *Applied Mathematics and Nonlinear Sciences*, 9(1). 10.2478/amns-2024-0835

Huang, G., & Yu, Y. (2022). The Application of Artificial Intelligence in Organizational Innovation Management: Take the Autonomous Driving Technology of Tesla as an Example. *Lecture Notes on Data Engineering and Communications Technologies*, 135, 690–697. 10.1007/978-3-031-04809-8_63

Huang, M. H., & Rust, R. T. (2021). A strategic framework for artificial intelligence in marketing. *Journal of the Academy of Marketing Science*, 49(1), 30–50. 10.1007/s11747-020-00749-9

Humphreys, A., & Wang, R. (2018). Automated text analysis for consumer research. *The Journal of Consumer Research*, 44(6), 1274–1306. 10.1093/jcr/ucx104

Hutson, J., Coble, K., Kshetri, N., & Smith, A. (2023). Exploring the Intersection of Digital Marketing and Retail: Challenges and Opportunities in AI, Privacy, and Customer Experience. *Confronting Security and Privacy Challenges in Digital Marketing*, 50-72.

Hwang, G., & Chien, S. (2022). Definition, roles, and potential research issues of the metaverse in education: An artificial intelligence perspective. *Computers and Education: Artificial Intelligence*, 3, 100082. 10.1016/j.caeai.2022.100082

Hyde, R., & Cartwright, P. (2023). Exploring Consumer Detriment in Immersive Gaming Technologies. *Journal of Consumer Policy*, 46(3), 335–361. 10.1007/s10603-023-09544-9

India Online Food Ordering and Delivery Market Size and Trends 2029. (n.d.). TechsciResearch Pvt Ltd. https://www.techsciresearch.com/report/india-online-food-ordering-and-delivery-market/3952.html

Infante, A., & Mardikaningsih, R. (2022). The Potential of social media as a Means of Online Business Promotion. *Journal of Social Science Studies (JOS3), 2*(2), 45-49.

Islam, G. (2020). Psychology and business ethics: A multi-level research agenda. *Journal of Business Ethics*, 165(1), 1–13. 10.1007/s10551-019-04107-w

Ismail, F., Tan, E., Rudolph, J., Crawford, J., & Tan, S. (2023). Artificial intelligence in higher education. A protocol paper for a systematic literature review. *Journal of Applied Learning and Teaching*, 6(2).

Ismail, M. H., Khater, M., & Zaki, M. (2017). Digital business transformation and strategy: What do we know so far. *Cambridge Service Alliance*, 10, 1–35.

Jana, P. (2009), *Review of the Compliance of the Provisions of the Haryana Fiscal Responsibility and Budget Management Act*. NIPFP.

Jankovic, S. D., & Curovic, D. M. (2023). Strategic integration of artificial intelligence for sustainable businesses: Implications for data management and human user engagement in the digital era. *Sustainability (Basel)*, 15(21), 15208. 10.3390/su152115208

Jarek, K., & Mazurek, G. (2019). Marketing and Artificial Intelligence. *Central European Business Review, 8*(2).

Jibril, A. B., Kwarteng, M. A., Chovancova, M., & Denanyoh, R. (2020, March). Customers' perception of cybersecurity threats toward e-banking adoption and retention: A conceptual study. In *ICCWS 2020 15th International Conference on Cyber Warfare and Security (Vol. 270)*. Academic Conferences and publishing limited.

Jiménez-Barreto, J., Loureiro, S., Braun, E., Sthapit, E., & Zenker, S. (2021). Use numbers not words! Communicating hotels' cleaning programs for COVID-19 from the brand perspective. *International Journal of Hospitality Management*, 94, 102872. 10.1016/j.ijhm.2021.10287233897084

Kapila, U. (2003). *"Fiscal Reforms in India: Policy Measures and Development", Indian Economy since Independence*. Academic Foundation Publication.

Kaplan, A., & Haenlein, M. (2019). Siri, Siri, in my hand: Who's the fairest in the land? On the interpretations, illustrations, and implications of artificial intelligence. *Business Horizons*, 62(1), 15–25. 10.1016/j.bushor.2018.08.004

Kargas, A., & Tsokos, A. (2020). Employer branding implementation and human resource management in Greek telecommunication industry. *Administrative Sciences*, 10(1), 17. 10.3390/admsci10010017

Kashyap, B., Sachdeva, V., Shirahatti, A., Singh, G., Arya, A., Jagatheesan, S., & Kumar, C. (2024). A Novel Approach for Human Behaviour Prediction Using Deep Learning Algorithms. *International Journal of Intelligent Systems and Applications in Engineering*, 12(1), 793–801. https://www.scopus.com/inward/record.uri?eid=2-s2.0-85182487249&partnerID=40&md5=be67f71a2ee0cecdb48ded1d5f681e50

Kaur, H., & Singh, T. (2021). Book review: "consumer happiness: Multiple perspectives", by tanusree Dutta and Manas Kumar Mandal (eds.). *Journal of Consumer Policy, 44*(4), 585–591. 10.1007/s10603-021-09494-0

Kaur, P., Sharma, S., Kaur, J., & Sharma, S. K. (2015). Using social media for employer branding and talent management: An experiential study. *IUP Journal of Brand Management*, 12(2), 7.

Keller, K. L. (1993). Conceptualizing, measuring, and managing customer-based brand equity. *Journal of Marketing*, 57(1), 1–22. 10.1177/002224299305700101

Keller, K. L. (1998). *Strategic Brand Management. Building, Measuring and Managing Brand Equity*. Prentice Hall.

Keller, K. L., & Lehmann, D. R. (2006). Brands and branding: Research findings and future priorities. *Marketing Science*, 25(6), 740–759. 10.1287/mksc.1050.0153

Khan, M. S., Mahapatra, S. S., & Sreekumar, N. A. (2009). Service quality evaluation in internet banking: An empirical study in India. *International Journal Indian Culture and Business Management*, 2(1), 30–46. 10.1504/IJICBM.2009.021596

Khosravi, H., Shum, S. B., Chen, G., Conati, C., Tsai, Y. S., Kay, J., & Gašević, D. (2022). Explainable artificial intelligence in education. *Computers and Education: Artificial Intelligence*, 3, 100074.

Kiecker, P., & Cowles, D. L. (2001). Interpersonal communication and personal influence on the internet: A framework for examining online word-of-mouth. *Internet Applications in Euromarketing*, 11(2), 71–88.

Compilation of References

Kim, J. (2021). Advertising in the metaverse: Research agenda. *Journal of Interactive Advertising*, 21(3), 141–144. 10.1080/15252019.2021.2001273

Kim, J., Lee, H., & Cho, Y. H. (2022). Learning design to support student-AI collaboration: Perspectives of leading teachers for AI in education. *Education and Information Technologies*, 27(5), 6069–6104. 10.1007/s10639-021-10831-6

Kim, J., Ryu, S., & Park, N. (2022). Privacy-enhanced data Deduplication computational intelligence technique for secure healthcare applications. *Computers, Materials & Continua*, 70(2), 4169–4184. 10.32604/cmc.2022.019277

Kimpakorn, N., & Dimmitt, N. (2007). Employer branding: The perspective of hotel management in the Thai luxury hotel industry. *Australasian Marketing Journal*, 15(3), 49.

Kim, Y., & Legendre, T. S. (2023). The effects of employer branding on value congruence and brand love. *Journal of Hospitality & Tourism Research (Washington, D.C.)*, 47(6), 962–987. 10.1177/10963480211062779

Kingchang, T., Chatwattana, P., & Wannapiroon, P. (2024). Artificial intelligence chatbot platform: AI chatbot platform for educational recommendations in higher education. *International Journal of Information and Education Technology (IJIET)*, 14(1), 34–41. 10.18178/ijiet.2024.14.1.2021

Kiong, L.V. (2021). *DeFi, NFT and GameFi made easy: a beginner's guide to understanding and investing in DeFi, NFT and GameFi projects.* Independently published.

Kirkpatrick, K. (2020). Tracking shoppers. *Communications of the ACM*, 63(2), 19–21. 10.1145/3374876

Kodaş, B., & Kodaş, D. (2021). Demarketing as a potential solution to overtourism problems in tourism destinations. In *Overtourism as Destination Risk* (pp. 111–127). Emerald Publishing Limited. 10.1108/978-1-83909-706-520211009

Koedinger, K. R., & Corbett, A. T. (2012). Cognitive tutors: Technology bringing learning science to the classroom. [). Academic Press.]. *Psychology of Learning and Motivation*, 57, 1–55.

Koedinger, K. R., & Corbett, A. T. (2012). Cognitive tutors: Technology bringing learning science to the classroom. In *Handbook of educational theories* (pp. 399–416). Routledge.

Kopalle, P. K., Gangwar, M., Kaplan, A., Ramachandran, D., Reinartz, W., & Rindfleisch, A. (2022). Examining artificial intelligence (AI) technologies in marketing via a global lens: Current trends and future research opportunities. *International Journal of Research in Marketing*, 39(2), 522–540. 10.1016/j.ijresmar.2021.11.002

Kotler (2016). Marketing Management, 15th Edition New Jersey: Pearson Prentice Hall, Inc.

Kotler, P., & Keller, K. L. (2006). *Marketing Management*. Pearson Prentice Hall.

Kozinets, R. V., de Valck, K., Wojnicki, A. C., & Wilner, S. J. S. (2010). Networked narratives: Understanding word-of-mouth marketing in online communities. *Journal of Marketing*, 74(2), 71–89. 10.1509/jm.74.2.71

Kreutzer, R. T. (2018). *Praxisorientiertes Online-Marketing*. Springer. 10.1007/978-3-658-17912-0

Krittanawong, C., Zhang, H., Wang, Z., Aydar, M., & Kitai, T. (2017). Artificial intelligence in precision cardiovascular medicine. *Journal of the American College of Cardiology*, 69(21), 2657–2664. 10.1016/j.jacc.2017.03.57128545640

Kronemann, B., Kizgin, H., Rana, N., & K. Dwivedi, Y. (2023). How AI encourages consumers to share their secrets? The role of anthropomorphism, personalisation, and privacy concerns and avenues for future research. *Spanish Journal of Marketing-ESIC*, 27(1), 3–19. 10.1108/SJME-10-2022-0213

Kshetri, N. (2022). Web 3.0 and the metaverse shaping organizations' brand and product strategies. *IT Professional*, 24(2), 11–15. 10.1109/MITP.2022.3157206

Kumar, K. P., Baskaran, P., & Thulasisingh, A. (2022). *Artificial intelligence in healthcare analytics. Applications of Artificial Intelligence and Machine Learning in Healthcare*. 10.36647/AAIMLH/2022.01.B1.Ch011

Kumar, A., Mani, V., Jain, V., Gupta, H., & Venkatesh, V. (2023). Managing healthcare supply chain through artificial intelligence (AI): A study of critical success factors. *Computers & Industrial Engineering*, 175, 108815. 10.1016/j.cie.2022.10881536405396

Kumar, D., & Suthar, N. (2024). Ethical and legal challenges of AI in marketing: An exploration of solutions. *Journal of Information. Communication and Ethics in Society*, 22(1), 124–144. 10.1108/JICES-05-2023-0068

Kumar, R., & Sharma, V. (2023). The AI revolution: Financial services in the age of intelligent machines. In *Leveraging AI and Emotional Intelligence in Contemporary Business Organizations* (pp. 287–305). IGI Global. 10.4018/979-8-3693-1902-4.ch017

Kumar, V., Ashraf, A. R., & Nadeem, W. (2024). AI-powered marketing: What, where, and how? *International Journal of Information Management*, 102783. Advance online publication. 10.1016/j.ijinfomgt.2024.102783

Kushwaha, B. P., Singh, R. K., & Tyagi, V. (2021). Investigating privacy paradox: Consumer data privacy behavioural intention and disclosure behaviour. *Academy of Marketing Studies Journal*, 25(1), 1–10.

Kuzlu, M., Xiao, Z., Sarp, S., Catak, F. O., Gurler, N., & Guler, O. (2023). The Rise of Generative Artificial Intelligence in Healthcare. *12th Mediterranean Conference on Embedded Computing, MECO 2023*. IEEE. 10.1109/MECO58584.2023.10155107

Lagioia, F., Jabłonowska, A., Liepina, R., & Drazewski, K. (2022). AI in search of unfairness in consumer contracts: The terms of service landscape. *Journal of Consumer Policy*, 45(3), 481–536. 10.1007/s10603-022-09520-9

Laitamaki, J., Hechavarría, L. T., Tada, M., Liu, S., Setyady, N., Vatcharasoontorn, N., & Zheng, F. (2016). Sustainable tourism development frameworks and best practices: Implications for the Cuban tourism industry. *Managing Global Transitions*, 14(1), 7.

Lansing, P., & Vries, P. D. (2007). Sustainable tourism: Ethical alternative or marketing ploy? *Journal of Business Ethics*, 72(1), 77–85. 10.1007/s10551-006-9157-7

Laranjo, L., Dunn, A. G., Tong, H. L., Kocaballi, A. B., Chen, J., Bashir, R., Surian, D., Gallego, B., Magrabi, F., Lau, A. Y. S., & Coiera, E. (2018). Conversational agents in healthcare: A systematic review. *Journal of the American Medical Informatics Association : JAMIA*, 25(9), 1248–1258. 10.1093/jamia/ocy07230010941

Latham, A., & Goltz, S. (2019). A survey of the general public's views on the ethics of using AI in education. In I. S., M. E., O. A., M. B., H. P., & L. R. (Eds.), *Lecture Notes in Computer Science (including subseries Lecture Notes in Artificial Intelligence and Lecture Notes in Bioinformatics)*, (pp. 194–206). Springer Verlag. 10.1007/978-3-030-23204-7_17

Lazarus, M. D., Truong, M., Douglas, P., & Selwyn, N. (2022). Artificial intelligence and clinical anatomical education: Promises and perils. *Anatomical Sciences Education*, 17(2), 249–262. 10.1002/ase.222136030525

Lee, H.K., Park, S., & Lee, Y. (2022). *A proposal of virtual museum metaverse content for the mz generation*.

Lee, D., Cutler, B. D., & Burns, J. (2004). The marketing and demarketing of tobacco products to low-income African-Americans. *Health Marketing Quarterly*, 22(2), 51–68. 10.1300/J026v22n02_0415914374

Lee, H. S., & Lee, J. (2021). Applying artificial intelligence in physical education and future perspectives. *Sustainability (Basel)*, 13(1), 351. 10.3390/su13010351

Compilation of References

Lee, J., & Wang, L. (2018). The Influence of Artificial Intelligence on Creativity in Education: A Review. *Educational Psychology Review*, 24(3), 387–401.

Lee, M. K. O., Cheung, C. M. K., Lim, K. H., & Sia, C. L. (2006). Understanding customer knowledge sharing in web-based discussion boards: An exploratory study. *Internet Research*, 16(3), 289–303. 10.1108/10662240610673709

Lewis, R. C., & Chambers, R. E. (2000). *Marketing Leadership in Hospitality. Foundations and Practices* (Vol. III). Wiley.

Lieto, A., Bhatt, M., Oltramari, A., & Vernon, D. (2017). Artificial Intelligence and Cognition. *Proceedings of the 4th International Workshop on Artificial Intelligence and Cognition co-located with the Joint Multi-Conference on Human-Level Artificial Intelligence (HLAI 2016)*. Technical University of Aachen.

Li, J., Dada, A., Puladi, B., Kleesiek, J., & Egger, J. (2024). ChatGPT in healthcare: A taxonomy and systematic review. *Computer Methods and Programs in Biomedicine*, 245, 108013. 10.1016/j.cmpb.2024.10801338262126

Limbu, Y. B., Wolf, M., & Lunsford, D. L. (2011). Consumers' perception of online ethics and its effect on satisfaction and loyalty. *Journal of Research in Interactive Marketing*, 5(1), 71–89. 10.1108/17505931111121534

Limna, P., Kraiwanit, T., Siripipattanakul, S., Limna, P., Kraiwanit, T., & Siripipattanakul, S. (2023). The relationship between cyber security knowledge, awareness and behavioural choice protection among mobile banking users in Thailand. *International Journal of Computing Sciences Research*, 7, 1133–1151.

Lim, W. M., Gupta, S., Aggarwal, A., Paul, J., & Sadhna, P. (2021). How do digital natives perceive and react toward online advertising? Implications for SMEs. *Journal of Strategic Marketing*, 1–35. 10.1080/0965254X.2021.1941204

Lin, P., Abney, K., & Bekey, G. A. (2012). *Robot ethics : the ethical and social implications of robotics*. 386.

Lipton, Z. C., Kale, D. C., Elkan, C., & Wetzel, R. (2015). *Learning to diagnose with LSTM recurrent neural networks*. arXiv preprint arXiv:1511.03677.

Li, S. (2000). The development of a hybrid intelligent system for developing marketing strategy. *Decision Support Systems*, 27(4), 395–409. 10.1016/S0167-9236(99)00061-5

Litvin, S. W., Goldsmith, R. E., & Pan, B. (2008). Electronic word-of-mouth in hospitality and tourism management. *Tourism Management*, 29(3), 458–468. 10.1016/j.tourman.2007.05.011

Liu, J., & Liu, S. (2023). *The application of ChatGPT in nursing education*.

Liu, R., Gupta, S., & Patel, P. (2023). The Application of the Principles of Responsible AI on Social Media Marketing for Digital Health. *Information Systems Frontiers*, 25(6), 2275–2299. 10.1007/s10796-021-10191-z34539226

Liu, Y., Vrontis, D., Visser, M., Stokes, P., Smith, S., Moore, N., Thrassou, A., & Ashta, A. (2021). Talent management and the HR function in cross-cultural mergers and acquisitions: The role and impact of bi-cultural identity. *Human Resource Management Review*, 31(3), 100744. 10.1016/j.hrmr.2020.100744

Li, Z., Qi, H., Zhang, S., & Ding, J. (2024). Enhancement of students' cognitive ability in civics informational education in colleges and universities in the era of artificial intelligence. *Applied Mathematics and Nonlinear Sciences*, 9(1), 20240671. 10.2478/amns-2024-0671

Lobschat, L., Mueller, B., Eggers, F., Brandimarte, L., Diefenbach, S., Kroschke, M., & Wirtz, J. (2021). Corporate digital responsibility. *Journal of Business Research*, 122, 875–888. 10.1016/j.jbusres.2019.10.006

Loh, H. W., Ooi, C. P., Seoni, S., Barua, P. D., Molinari, F., & Acharya, U. R. (2022). Application of explainable artificial intelligence for healthcare: A systematic review of the last decade (2011–2022). *Computer Methods and Programs in Biomedicine*, 226, 107161. 10.1016/j.cmpb.2022.10716136228495

Lu, J., & Nepal, S. K. (2009). Sustainable tourism research: An analysis of papers published in the Journal of Sustainable Tourism. *Journal of Sustainable Tourism*, 17(1), 5–16. 10.1080/09669580802582480

Lukitosari, V., Simanjuntak, T. F., & Utomo, D. B. (2020). A game-theoretic model of marketing strategy using consumer segmentation. *Journal of Physics: Conference Series*, 1490(1), 012026. 10.1088/1742-6596/1490/1/012026

Lu, W., Wang, J., Chen, Y., Qin, X., Xu, R., Dimitriadis, D., & Qin, T. (2024). Personalized federated learning with adaptive Batchnorm for healthcare. *IEEE Transactions on Big Data*, 1–1. 10.1109/TBDATA.2022.3177197

MacInnis, D. J., Morwitz, V. G., Botti, S., Hoffman, D. L., Kozinets, R. V., Lehmann, D. R., Lynch, J. G.Jr, & Pechmann, C. (2020). Creating boundary-breaking, marketing-relevant consumer research. *Journal of Marketing*, 84(2), 1–23. 10.1177/0022242919889876

Madichie, N. O. (2013). 13 "Unintentional Demarketing" In Higher Education. *Demarketing*, 45.

Maglaras, L. (2022). Artificial Intelligence: Practical and Ethical Challenges. In *Studies in Computational Intelligence, 1025*. Springer Science and Business Media Deutschland GmbH. 10.1007/978-3-030-96630-0_3

Majmundar, A., Cornelis, E., & Moran, M. B. (2019). Examining the vulnerability of ambivalent young adults to e-cigarette messages. *Health Marketing Quarterly*, 37(1), 73–88. 10.1080/07359683.2019.168011931880235

Maksymyuk, T., Gazda, J., Bugar, G., Gazda, V., Liyanage, M., & Dohler, M. (2022). Blockchain-empowered service management for the decentralized metaverse of things. *IEEE Access : Practical Innovations, Open Solutions*, 10(Sep), 99025–99037. 10.1109/ACCESS.2022.3205739

Malhotra, N. K. (1999). *Marketing Research: An Applied Orientation* (3rd ed.). Prentice Hall.

Malik, S., & Khera, S. N. (2014). New generation–great expectations: Exploring the work attributes of Gen Y. *Global Journal of Finance and Management*, 6(5), 433–438.

Mandal, P. C. (2023). Public Policy and Ethics in Marketing Research for Organizations: Concerns, Strategies, and Initiatives. [IJPSS]. *International Journal of Public Sociology and Sociotherapy*, 3(1), 1–12.

Markiewicz, T., & Zheng, J. (2018). *Getting Started with Artificial Intelligence. A Practical Guide to Building Enterprise Applications*. O'Reilly.

Matei, M., & Done, I. (2013). The social responsibility: Conceptual interferences and motivational factors specific to corporations. In *Sustainable Technologies, Policies, and Constraints in the Green Economy* (pp. 204–218). IGI Global. 10.4018/978-1-4666-4098-6.ch011

Mayzlin, D. (2006). Promotional chat on the internet. *Marketing Science*, 25(2), 155–163. 10.1287/mksc.1050.0137

Mazur, N. (2023). CHALLENGES AND PROSPECTS OF DIGITAL MARKETING IN THE AGE OF ARTIFICIAL INTELLIGENCE. *Grail of Science*, (26), 75–77.

McAlister, A. R., Alhabash, S., & Yang, J. (2024). Artificial intelligence and ChatGPT: Exploring Current and potential future roles in marketing education. *Journal of Marketing Communications*, 30(2), 166–187. 10.1080/13527266.2023.2289034

McStay, A. (2020). Emotional AI, soft biometrics and the surveillance of emotional life: An unusual consensus on privacy. *Big Data & Society*, 7(1). Advance online publication. 10.1177/2053951720904386

Medsker, G. J., Williams, L. J., & Holahan, P. J. (1994). A review of current practices for evaluating causal models in organizational behavior and human resources management research. *Journal of Management*, 20(2), 439–464. 10.1177/014920639402000207

Compilation of References

Miao, H., & Ahn, H. (2023). Impact of ChatGPT on interdisciplinary nursing education and research. *Asian/Pacific Island Nursing Journal*, 7(1), e48136. 10.2196/4813637093625

Milan, A., Sahu, R., & Sandhu, J. K. (2023). Impact of AI on Social Marketing and its Usage in Social Media: A Review Analysis. *Proceedings of the International Conference on Circuit Power and Computing Technologies, ICCPCT 2023*, (pp. 1749–1754). IEEE. 10.1109/ICCPCT58313.2023.10245676

Misra, K., Schwartz, E. M., & Abernethy, J. (2019). Dynamic online pricing with incomplete information using multi-armed bandit experiments. *Marketing Science*, 38(2), 226–252. 10.1287/mksc.2018.1129

Mitra, G., & Mitra, G. (2019, December 17). *What Led to Uber Eats' Failure in India? Here Are Insides from the Probable Uber Eats-Zomato Meger!* Express Computer. https://www.expresscomputer.in/news/uber-eats-failure-india/44393/

Mittal, A., Aggarwal, A., & Mittal, R. (2020). Predicting university students' adoption of mobile news applications: The role of perceived hedonic value and news motivation. [IJESMA]. *International Journal of E-Services and Mobile Applications*, 12(4), 42–59. 10.4018/IJESMA.2020100103

Mittal, A., Mantri, A., Tandon, U., & Dwivedi, Y. K. (2022). A unified perspective on the adoption of online teaching in higher education during the COVID-19 pandemic. [Top of Form]. *Information Discovery and Delivery*, 50(2), 117–132. 10.1108/IDD-09-2020-0114

Mogaji, E., Soetan, T. O., & Kieu, T. A. (2021). The implications of artificial intelligence on the digital marketing of financial services to vulnerable customers. *Australasian Marketing Journal*, 29(3), 235–242. 10.1016/j.ausmj.2020.05.003

Mogavi, R. H., Deng, C., Kim, J. J., Zhou, P., Kwon, Y. D., Metwally, A. H. S., & Hui, P. (2023). *Exploring user perspectives on ChatGPT: Applications, perceptions, and implications for ai-integrated education*. arXiv preprint arXiv:2305.13114.

Mohd Rahim, N. I., & Iahad, A., N., Yusof, A. F., & A. Al-Sharafi, M. (2022). AI-based chatbots adoption model for higher-education institutions: A hybrid PLS-SEM-Neural network modelling approach. *Sustainability*, 14(19), 12726. 10.3390/su141912726

Moher, D., Liberati, A., Tetzlaff, J., & Altman, D. G. (2009). Preferred reporting items for systematic reviews and meta-analyses: The PRISMA statement. *Annals of Internal Medicine*, 151(4), 264–269. 10.7326/0003-4819-151-4-200908180-0013519622511

Moher, D., Shamseer, L., Clarke, M., Ghersi, D., Liberati, A., Petticrew, M., Shekelle, P., & Stewart, L. A. (2015). Preferred reporting items for systematic review and meta-analysis protocols (PRISMA-P) 2015 statement. *Systematic Reviews*, 4(1), 1. 10.1186/2046-4053-4-125554246

Molina-Collado, A., Santos-Vijande, M. L., Gómez-Rico, M., & Madera, J. M. (2022). Sustainability in hospitality and tourism: A review of key research topics from 1994 to 2020. *International Journal of Contemporary Hospitality Management*, 34(8), 3029–3064. 10.1108/IJCHM-10-2021-1305

Monteiro, S. (2023). Gaming faces: Diagnostic scanning in social media and the legacy of racist face analysis. *Information Communication and Society*, 26(8), 1601–1617. 10.1080/1369118X.2021.2020867

Morrison, D. (2018). Ethical implications of datafication in education. *Learning, Media and Technology*, 43(4), 369–382.

Mura, M., Longo, M., Micheli, P., & Bolzani, D. (2018). The evolution of sustainability measurement research. *International Journal of Management Reviews*, 20(3), 661–695. 10.1111/ijmr.12179

Murthy, A., Mamoria, P., Kumar, R., Shrivastava, S., & Thomas, S. K. (n.d.). *Artificial intelligence and machine learning in marketing: A review of recent advances and future trends*. Eurchembull.com. https://www.eurchembull.com/uploads/paper/13a7ffd5fb16e0a1329d76392bf913cf.pdf

Muzammal, M., Qu, Q., & Nasrulin, B. (2019). Renovating blockchain with distributed databases: An open source system. *Future Generation Computer Systems*, 90(Jan), 105–117. 10.1016/j.future.2018.07.042

Nakamoto, S. (2008). Bitcoin: a peer-to-peer electronic cash system. Bitcoin. htt ps://bitcoin.org/bitcoin.pdf.

Nalbant, K. G., & Aydin, S. (2023). Development and transformation in digital marketing and branding with artificial intelligence and digital technologies dynamics in the Metaverse universe. *Journal of Metaverse*, 3(1), 9–18.

Nalini, M., Radhakrishnan, D. P., Yogi, G., Santhiya, S., & Harivardhini, V. (2021). Impact of artificial intelligence (AI) on marketing. *International Journal of Aquatic Science*, 12(2), 3159–3167.

Nancy, A. A., Ravindran, D., Raj Vincent, P. M., Srinivasan, K., & Gutierrez Reina, D. (2022). IoT-cloud-Based smart healthcare monitoring system for heart disease prediction via deep learning. *Electronics (Basel)*, 11(15), 2292. 10.3390/electronics11152292

Naseer, A., Naseer, H., Ahmad, A., Maynard, S. B., & Siddiqui, A. M. (2023). Moving towards agile cybersecurity incident response: A case study exploring the enabling role of big data analytics-embedded dynamic capabilities. *Computers & Security*, 135, 103525.

Nayyar, V. (2018). 'My Mind Starts Craving'-Impact of Resealable Packages on the Consumption Behavior of Indian Consumers. *Indian Journal of Marketing*, 48(11), 56–63. 10.17010/ijom/2018/v48/i11/137986

Nayyar, V. (2022). Reviewing the impact of digital migration on the consumer buying journey with robust measurement of PLS-SEM and R Studio. *Systems Research and Behavioral Science*, 39(3), 542–556. 10.1002/sres.2857

Nayyar, V. (2023). The role of marketing analytics in the ethical consumption of online consumers. *Total Quality Management & Business Excellence*, 34(7-8), 1015–1031. 10.1080/14783363.2022.2139676

Nayyar, V., & Batra, R. (2020). Does online media self-regulate consumption behavior of INDIAN youth? *International Review on Public and Nonprofit Marketing*, 17(3), 277–288. 10.1007/s12208-020-00248-1

Nayyar, V., Sugiat, M., Singla, B., Rojhe, K. C., & Sharma, S. (2023, August). Influence of Technology in Measuring the Purchase Intention of Indian Consumer. In *2023 International Conference on Digital Business and Technology Management (ICONDBTM)* (pp. 1-6). IEEE. 10.1109/ICONDBTM59210.2023.10327147

Ng, I. C. L., & Wakenshaw, S. Y. L. (2017). The internet-of-things: Review and research directions. *International Journal of Research in Marketing*, 34(1), 3–21. 10.1016/j.ijresmar.2016.11.003

Nguyen, D. C., Pham, Q. V., Pathirana, P. N., Ding, M., Seneviratne, A., Lin, Z., Dobre, O., & Hwang, W. J. (2022). Federated learning for smart healthcare: A survey. *ACM Computing Surveys*, 55(3), 1–37. 10.1145/3501296

Nunan, D., & Di Domenico, M. (2019). Older consumers, digital marketing, and public policy: A review and research agenda. *Journal of Public Policy & Marketing*, 38(4), 469–483.

Nurfadila, S. (2020). The Impact of Influencers in Consumer Decision-Making: The Fashion Industry. *IDJ*, 1(1), 1–14. 10.19184/ijl.v1i1.19146

Nuseir, T., M., Basheer, M. F., & Aljumah, A. (2020). Antecedents of entrepreneurial intentions in smart city of Neom Saudi Arabia: Does the entrepreneurial education on artificial intelligence matter? *Cogent Business & Management*, 7(1), 1825041. 10.1080/23311975.2020.1825041

Nuss, T., Chen, Y. J. M., Scully, M., Hickey, K., Martin, J., & Morley, B. (2023). Australian adults' attitudes towards government actions to protect children from digital marketing of unhealthy food and drink products. *Health Promotion Journal of Australia*.37286359

Compilation of References

Nye, B. D., Graesser, A. C., & Hu, X. (2014). AutoTutor and family: A review of 17 years of natural language tutoring. *International Journal of Artificial Intelligence in Education*, 24(4), 427–469. 10.1007/s40593-014-0029-5

Obermeyer, Z., & Emanuel, E. J. (2016). Predicting the future—Big data, machine learning, and clinical medicine. *The New England Journal of Medicine*, 375(13), 1216–1219. 10.1056/NEJMp160618127682033

OECD. (2019). *Education in the digital age: Making the case for an ethical, responsible, and inclusive digital future.* OECD Publishing.

Ogbuke, N. J., Yusuf, Y. Y., Dharma, K., & Mercangoz, B. A. (2022). Big data supply chain analytics: Ethical, privacy and security challenges posed to business, industries and society. *Production Planning and Control*, 33(2-3), 123–137.

Okazaki, S., Eisend, M., Plangger, K., de Ruyter, K., & Grewal, D. (2020). Understanding the strategic consequences of customer privacy concerns: A meta-analytic review. *Journal of Retailing*, 96(4), 458–473. 10.1016/j.jretai.2020.05.007

Omdia-Tractica. (2020). *Artificial intelligence Software Market to Reach $126.0 Billion in Annual Worldwide Revenue by 2025.* Omdia. https://tractica.omdia.com/newsroom/press-releases/artificial-intelligence-software-market-toreach-126-0-billion-in-annual-worldwide-revenue-by-2025

Online, E. T. (2023, April 25). AI and Privacy: The privacy concerns surrounding AI, its potential impact on personal data. *Economic Times.* https://economictimes.indiatimes.com/news/how-to/ai-and-privacy-the-privacy-concerns-surrounding-ai-its-potential-impact-on-personal-data/articleshow/99738234.cms

Onorato, A. (2022, May 3). *Report: Consumers open to AI in marketing, but privacy concerns remain. Cdp.com - Leading CDP Industry Resource for Marketing & Sales - News, Analysis and Thought Leadership Content on the CDP Industry.* CDP. https://cdp.com/articles/report-consumers-open-to-ai-in-marketing-but-privacy-concerns-remain/

Oo, K. Z. (2019). Design and implementation of electronic payment gateway for secure online payment system. *Int. J. Trend Sci. Res. Dev*, 3, 1329–1334.

Osgood, R. (2016). The future of democracy: blockchain voting. *COMP116: Inf. Secur.* Tufts. https://www.cs.tufts.edu/comp/116/archive/fall2016/rosgood.pdf

Page, M. J., McKenzie, J. E., Bossuyt, P. M., Boutron, I., Hoffmann, T. C., Mulrow, C. D., & Moher, D. (2021). The PRISMA 2020 statement: An updated guideline for reporting systematic reviews. *BMJ (Clinical Research Ed.)*, 372(71).33782057

Panagopoulou, F., Parpoula, C., & Karpouzis, K. (2023). *Legal and ethical considerations regarding the use of ChatGPT in education.* arXiv preprint arXiv:2306.10037. 10.31235/osf.io/c5hf3

Pandey, N., Nayal, P., & Rathore, A. S. (2020). Digital marketing for B2B organizations: Structured literature review and future research directions. *Journal of Business and Industrial Marketing*, 35(7), 1191–1204.

Pantano, E., Pizzi, G., Scarpi, D., & Dennis, C. (2020). Competing during a pandemic? Retailers' ups and downs during the COVID-19 outbreak. *Journal of Business Research*, 116, 209–213. 10.1016/j.jbusres.2020.05.03632501307

Pappalardo, J. K. (2022). Economics of consumer protection: Contributions and challenges in estimating consumer injury and evaluating consumer protection policy. *Journal of Consumer Policy*, 45(2), 201–238. 10.1007/s10603-021-09482-4

Parasuraman, A., Zeithaml, V. A., & Berry, L. L. (1985). A conceptual model of service quality and its implications for future research. *Journal of Marketing*, 49(64), 41–50. 10.2307/1251430

Pardos, Z. A., & Heffernan, N. T. (2010). Modeling individualization in a Bayesian Networks implementation of knowledge tracing. In *Proceedings of the 3rd International Conference on Educational Data Mining* (pp. 61-70). Springer. 10.1007/978-3-642-13470-8_24

Park, S. M., & Kim, Y. G. (2022). A metaverse: Taxonomy, components, applications, and open challenges. *IEEE Access : Practical Innovations, Open Solutions*, 10, 4209–4251. 10.1109/ACCESS.2021.3140175

Paschen, J., Kietzmann, J., & Kietzmann, T. C. (2019). Artificial intelligence (AI) and its implications for market knowledge in B2B marketing. *Journal of Business and Industrial Marketing*, 34(7), 1410–1479. 10.1108/JBIM-10-2018-0295

Pascual, J. M., & de Uribe Gil, C. E. (2023). Renewing Ethics in Public Relations: A Case Study. *Revista Espanola de la Transparencia*, 18, 406–425. 10.51915/ret.263

Pathak, A., & Sharma, S. D. (2022, December). Applications of Artificial Intelligence (AI) in Marketing Management. In *2022 5th International Conference on Contemporary Computing and Informatics (IC3I)* (pp. 1738-1745). IEEE.

Patra, G., Mukhopadhyay, I., & Dash, C. K. (2019). Digital employer branding for enabling gen Y in the ITeS sector in eastern India. *Prabandhan Indian J. Manag.*, 12(3), 38–49. 10.17010/pijom/2019/v12i3/142339

Paulo, R. (2019). The impact of e-service quality and customer satisfaction on customer behavior in online shopping. *Heliyon*, 5(10), 1–14. 10.1016/j.heliyon.2019.e0269031720459

Peattie, K., Peattie, S., & Newcombe, R. (2016). Unintended consequences in demarketing antisocial behaviour: Project Bernie. *Journal of Marketing Management*, 32(17-18), 1588–1618. 10.1080/0267257X.2016.1244556

Perry, V. G., Martin, K., & Schnare, A. (2023). Algorithms for All: Can AI in the Mortgage Market Expand Access to Homeownership? *AI*, 4(4), 888–903. 10.3390/ai4040045

Piech, C., Huang, J., Chen, Z., Do, C., Ng, A., & Koller, D. (2015). Tuned models of peer assessment in MOOCs. In *Proceedings of the 28th International Conference on Neural Information Processing Systems* (pp. 1-9). IEEE.

Pires, P. B., Santos, J. D., Pereira, I. V., & Torres, A. I. (Eds.). (2023). *Confronting Security and Privacy Challenges in Digital Marketing*. IGI Global.

Pitardi, D., & Marriott, H. R. (2021). Alexa, she's not human but… Unveiling the drivers of consumers' trust in voice-based artificial intelligence. *Psychology and Marketing*, 38(4), 626–642. 10.1002/mar.21457

Pitardi, V., Wirtz, J., Paluch, S., & Kunz, W. H. (2022). Service robots, agency and embarrassing service encounters. *Journal of Service Management*, 33(2), 389–414. 10.1108/JOSM-12-2020-0435

Pittz, T. G., Benson, P. G., Intindola, M., & Kalargiros, M. (2017). Opportunity or Opportunism? In advance: An Examination of International Recruitment via Employer and Nation Branding Strategies. *Business & Professional Ethics Journal*, 36(2), 157–176. 10.5840/bpej201742655

Potgieter, A., & Doubell, M. (2020). The Influence of Employer branding and Employees' personal branding on Corporate Branding and Corporate Reputation. *African Journal of Business & Economic Research*, 15(2), 109–135. 10.31920/1750-4562/2020/v15n2a6

Power, B. (2017). How Harley-Davidson used artificial intelligence to increase New York sales leads by 2,930%. *Harvard Business Review*.https://hbr.org/2017/05/howharley-davidson-used-predictive-analytics-to-increase-new-yorksales-leads-by-2930

PricewaterhouseCoopers. *Sizing the prize*. PwC. https://www.pwc.com/gx/en/issues/data-and-analytics/publications/artificial-intelligence-study.html

Priyanka, A. L., Harihararao, M., Prasanna, M., & Deepika, Y. (2023). A Study on Artificial Intelligence in Marketing. *International Journal For Multidisciplinary Research*, 5(3), 3789. 10.36948/ijfmr.2023.v05i03.3789

Puntoni, S., Reczek, R. W., Giesler, M., & Botti, S. (2021). Consumers and artificial intelligence: An experiential perspective. *Journal of Marketing*, 85(1), 131–151. 10.1177/0022242920953847

Qi, R., Feng, C., & Liu, Z. (2017). *Blockchain-powered internet of things, e-governance and e-democracy. E-Democracy for Smart Cities. Advances in 21st Century Human Settlements.* Springer.

Quach, S., Thaichon, P., Martin, K. D., Weaven, S., & Palmatier, R. W. (2022). Digital technologies: Tensions in privacy and data. *Journal of the Academy of Marketing Science*, 50(6), 1299–1323. 10.1007/s11747-022-00845-y35281634

Rajkomar, A., Oren, E., Chen, K., Dai, A. M., Hajaj, N., Hardt, M., Liu, P. J., Liu, X., Marcus, J., Sun, M., Sundberg, P., Yee, H., Zhang, K., Zhang, Y., Flores, G., Duggan, G. E., Irvine, J., Le, Q., Litsch, K., & Dean, J. (2018). Scalable and accurate deep learning with electronic health records. *NPJ Digital Medicine*, 1(1), 1–10. 10.1038/s41746-018-0029-131304302

Rangaswamy, A., Moch, N., Felten, C., van Bruggen, G., Wieringa, J. E., & Wirtz, J. (2020). The role of marketing in digital business platforms. *Journal of Interactive Marketing*, 51(Aug), 72–90. 10.1016/j.intmar.2020.04.006

Rauturier, S. (2023) What is Sustainable Digital Marketing? Solene Rauturier – Mindful Digital Marketing. https://www.solenerauturier.com/blog/sustainable-digital-marketing

Ray, A., Ray, S., Daniel, M. S., & Kumar, B. (2021). Change in attitudes and perceptions of undergraduate health profession students towards inter-professional education following an educational experience in post-natal care. *medical journal armed forces india*, 77, S173-S179.

Raza, A., Tran, K. P., Koehl, L., & Li, S. (2022). Designing ECG monitoring healthcare system with federated transfer learning and explainable AI. *Knowledge-Based Systems*, 236, 107763. 10.1016/j.knosys.2021.107763

Rehman, A., Abbas, S., Khan, M. A., Ghazal, T. M., Adnan, K. M., & Mosavi, A. (2022). A secure healthcare 5.0 system based on blockchain technology entangled with federated learning technique. https://doi.org/10.31219/osf.io/gvkqc

Reich, B. J., & Soule, C. A. A. (2016). Green demarketing in advertisements: Comparing "buy green" and "buy less" appeals in product and institutional advertising contexts. *Journal of Advertising*, 45(4), 441–458. 10.1080/00913367.2016.1214649

Ribeiro, R. P., & Gavronski, I. (2021). Sustainable Management of Human Resources and Stakeholder Theory: A Review. *Revista De Gestão Social E Ambiental*, 15, e02729. 10.24857/rgsa.v15.2729

Rodgers, W., & Nguyen, T. (2022). Advertising benefits from ethical artificial intelligence algorithmic purchase decision pathways. *Journal of Business Ethics*, 178(4), 1043–1061.

Rodrigues, D., & Martinez, L. F. (2020). The influence of digital marketing on recruitment effectiveness: A qualitative study. *European Journal of Management Studies*, 25(1), 23–44.

Roll, I., & Wylie, R. (2016). Evolution and revolution in artificial intelligence in education. *International Journal of Artificial Intelligence in Education*, 26(2), 582–599. 10.1007/s40593-016-0110-3

Romain. (2007). The Ethics of Online Retailing: A Scale Development and Validation from the Consumers. *Perspective. Journal of Business Ethics*, 72(2), 131-148.

Rowley, J. (2001). Remodelling marketing communications in an internet environment. *Internet Research*, 11(3), 203–212. 10.1108/10662240110397017

Rudolph, T. (2023). War of the chatbots: Bard, Bing chat, ChatGPT, Ernie and beyond. The new AI gold rush and its impact on higher education. *1*, 6(1). 10.37074/jalt.2023.6.1.23

Ruggeri, F., Lagioia, F., Lippi, M., & Torroni, P. (2021). Detecting and explaining unfairness in consumer contracts through memory networks. *Artificial Intelligence and Law*, 30(1), 59–92. 10.1007/s10506-021-09288-2

Ruiz (2005). Relationship Outcomes of Perceived Ethical Sales Behavior: The Customer's Perspective. *Journal of Business Research, 8*(4), 439–445.

S., Y., A., H., P.K., A., & H., K. (Eds.). (2023). 2nd International Conference on Mechanical and Energy Technologies, ICMET 2021. *Smart Innovation, Systems and Technologies, 290*. https://www.scopus.com/inward/record.uri?eid=2-s2.0-85134330558&partnerID=40&md5=2bc4dbd7343017a23de838fad58f769a

Sabry, F., Eltaras, T., Labda, W., Alzoubi, K., & Malluhi, Q. (2022). Machine learning for healthcare wearable devices: The big picture. *Journal of Healthcare Engineering*, 2022, 1–25. 10.1155/2022/465392335480146

Saeed, S. (2019). Digital Business adoption and customer segmentation: An exploratory study of expatriate community in Saudi Arabia. *ICIC Express Letters*, 13(2), 133–139.

Saeed, S. (2023). A customer-centric view of E-commerce security and privacy. *Applied Sciences (Basel, Switzerland)*, 13(2), 1020.

Saeed, S. (2023). Digital Workplaces and Information Security Behavior of Business Employees: An Empirical Study of Saudi Arabia. *Sustainability*, 15(7), 6019.

Saeed, S., Altamimi, S. A., Alkayyal, N. A., Alshehri, E., & Alabbad, D. A. (2023). Digital transformation and cybersecurity challenges for businesses resilience: Issues and recommendations. *Sensors (Basel)*, 23(15), 6666.37571451

Saeed, S., Pipek, V., Rohde, M., Reuter, C., De Carvalho, A. F. P., & Wulf, V. (2019). Nomadic Knowledge Sharing Practices and Challenges: Findings From a Long-Term Case Study. *IEEE Access : Practical Innovations, Open Solutions*, 7, 63564–63577.

Saeed, S., Suayyid, S. A., Al-Ghamdi, M. S., Al-Muhaisen, H., & Almuhaideb, A. M. (2023). A Systematic Literature Review on Cyber Threat Intelligence for Organizational Cybersecurity Resilience. *Sensors (Basel)*, 23(16), 7273.37631808

Saeed, S., Wahab, F., Cheema, S. A., & Ashraf, S. (2013). Role of usability in e-government and e-commerce portals: An empirical study of Pakistan. *Life Science Journal*, 10(1), 8–13.

Salem, M. Z. Y. (2013). Factors affecting the demarketing of breastmilk substitutes in Palestine. *Breastfeeding Medicine*, 8(3), 302–311. 10.1089/bfm.2012.012023586626

Salem, M., El-Agha, A., & Qasem, E. (2022, March). Demarketing of Cigarette Smoking in the West Bank, Palestine. In *International Conference on Business and Technology* (pp. 1095-1104). Cham: Springer International Publishing.

Saluja, S., Kulshrestha, D., & Sharma, S. (2023). *Cases on the Resurgence of Emerging Businesses*. 1–316.

Saluja, S., Kulshrestha, D., Sharma, S. (2023). *Cases on the Resurgence of Emerging Businesses*.

Saluja, S. (2024). Identity theft fraud- major loophole for FinTech industry in India. *Journal of Financial Crime*, 31(1), 146–157. 10.1108/JFC-08-2022-0211

Saluja, S., Aggarwal, A., & Mittal, A. (2022). Understanding the fraud theories and advancing with integrity model. *Journal of Financial Crime*, 29(4), 1318–1328. 10.1108/JFC-07-2021-0163

Santos, V., Simão, P., Reis, I., Sampaio, M. C., Martinho, F., & Sousa, B. (2023). Ethics and Sustainability in Hospitality Employer Branding. *Administrative Sciences*, 13(9), 202. 10.3390/admsci13090202

Compilation of References

Santos, V., Sousa, M. J., Costa, C., & Au-Yong-Oliveira, M. (2021). Tourism towards sustainability and innovation: A systematic literature review. *Sustainability (Basel)*, 13(20), 11440. 10.3390/su132011440

Saraswat, D., Bhattacharya, P., Verma, A., Prasad, V. K., Tanwar, S., Sharma, G., Bokoro, P. N., & Sharma, R. (2022). Explainable AI for healthcare 5.0: Opportunities and challenges. *IEEE Access : Practical Innovations, Open Solutions*, 10, 84486–84517. 10.1109/ACCESS.2022.3197671

Sari, A. E. (2023, June 25). *AI in marketing: How chatbots are revolutionizing customer interaction*. Linkedin.com. https://www.linkedin.com/pulse/ai-marketing-how-chatbots-revolutionizing-customer-interaction-sari

Sarwar, S., Imran, M., & Hussain, S. (2020). The role of artificial intelligence in achieving sustainable development goals: A review. *Sustainable Development*, 28(1), 146–158.

Sathya (2017). A Study on Digital Marketing and its Impact. *International Journal of Science and Research, 6*(2), 866-868. ISSN: 2319-7064.

Saura, J. R. (2021). Using data sciences in digital marketing: Framework, methods, and performance metrics. *Journal of Innovation & Knowledge*, 6(2), 92–102.

Saura, J. R., Palacios-Marqués, D., & Ribeiro-Soriano, D. (2023). Digital marketing in SMEs via data-driven strategies: Reviewing the current state of research. *Journal of Small Business Management*, 61(3), 1278–1313.

Schlette, D., Caselli, M., & Pernul, G. (2021). A comparative study on cyber threat intelligence: The security incident response perspective. *IEEE Communications Surveys and Tutorials*, 23(4), 2525–2556.

Schneider, M. J., Jagpal, S., Gupta, S., Li, S., & Yu, Y. (2017). Protecting customer privacy when marketing with second-party data. *International Journal of Research in Marketing*, 34(3), 593–603. 10.1016/j.ijresmar.2017.02.003

Senecal, S., & Nantel, J. (2004). The influence of online product recommendations on consumers' online choices. *Journal of Retailing*, 80(2), 159–169. 10.1016/j.jretai.2004.04.001

Sen, S., & Lerman, D. (2007). Why are you telling me this? An examination into negative consumer reviews on the web. *Journal of Interactive Marketing*, 21(4), 76–94. 10.1002/dir.20090

Sen, T., & Rao, R. K. (2000). *State Fiscal Studies*. NIPFP Study for World Bank.

Shahid, M. Z., & Li, G. (2019). Impact of artificial intelligence in marketing: A perspective of marketing professionals of Pakistan. *Global Journal of Management and Business Research*, 19(2), 27–33.

Shah, V. (2020). Breaking Language Barriers in Education: The Role of AI-Powered Language Translation and Transcription Technologies. *International Journal of Educational Technology in Higher Education*, 17(1), 1–15.

Sharma, A. K., & Sharma, R. (2023). Considerations in artificial intelligence-based marketing: An ethical perspective. *Applied Marketing Analytics, 9*(2), 162–172. https://www.scopus.com/inward/record.uri?eid=2-s2.0-85184230627&partnerID=40&md5=1de1ed003a445b409d307f81cd3915f2

Sharma, D., & Bikshandi, B. (2020). Artificial empathy – An artificial intelligence challenge. *Artificial Intelligence*, 321–326. 10.4324/9780429317415-19

Sharma, G., & Baoku, L. (2012). E-Marketing on Online Social Networks and Ethical Issues. *International Journal of Online Marketing*, 2(4), 1–14. 10.4018/ijom.2012100101

Sharma, G., & Lijuan, W. (2015). The effects of online service quality of e-commerce Websites on user satisfaction. *The Electronic Library*, 33(3), 468–485. 10.1108/EL-10-2013-0193

Shen, H., Han, Y., Zhang, Z., & Zeng, Z. (2011). Notice of Retraction: Marketing strategies for Chinese public legal services companies. *2011 2nd International Conference on Artificial Intelligence, Management Science and Electronic Commerce, AIMSEC 2011 - Proceedings*, 3105–3108. 10.1109/AIMSEC.2011.6011125

Shukla, P. (2010). Impact of interpersonal influences, brand origin and brand image on luxury purchase intentions: Measuring interfunctional interactions and a cross-national comparison. *Journal of World Business*, 46(2), 242–252. 10.1016/j.jwb.2010.11.002

Shveta, G. (2022). Review of Haryana State Spending Strategies and Growth Prospects. *International Journal of Research and Analytical Reviews, 9*(4), 663-672.

Sidlauskiene, J., Joye, Y., & Auruskeviciene, V. (2023). AI-based chatbots in conversational commerce and their effects on product and price perceptions. *Electronic Markets*, 33(1), 24. 10.1007/s12525-023-00633-837252674

Siemens, G., & Gasevic, D. (2012). Guest editorial-learning and knowledge analytics. *Journal of Educational Technology & Society*, 15(3), 1–2.

Silva, V., & Reis, F. (2018). *Capital Humano - Temas para uma boa gestão das organizações*. Edições Sílabo.

Singh, A., & Singh, A. (2023). *The Impact of Social Marketing on SMEs in India: A Theoretical Perspective*. Strengthening SME Performance Through Social Media Adoption and Usage. 10.4018/978-1-6684-5770-2.ch013

Singh, C., Dash, M. K., Sahu, R., & Kumar, A. (2023). Artificial intelligence in customer retention: A bibliometric analysis and future research framework. *Kybernetes*. 10.1108/K-02-2023-0245

Singla. (2017). Role of Ethics in Digital Marketing. *Imperial Journal of Interdisciplinary Research, 3*(7), 371-375.

Smith, D., Menon, S., & Sivakumar, K. (2005). Online peer and editorial recommendations, trust, and choice in virtual markets. *Journal of Interactive Marketing*, 19(3), 15–37. 10.1002/dir.20041

Smith, K. (2020). The Impact of AI on Education: Perspectives from Teachers and Academics. *The Journal of Educational Research*, 45(1), 55–67.

Smith, R. E., & Vogt, C. A. (1995). The effect of integrating advertising and negative word-of-mouth communications on message processing and response. *Journal of Consumer Psychology*, 4(2), 133–151. 10.1207/s15327663jcp0402_03

Soleymanian, M., Weinberg, C. B., & Zhu, T. (2019). Sensor data and behavioral tracking: Does usage-based auto insurance benefit drivers? *Marketing Science*, 38(1), 21–43. 10.1287/mksc.2018.1126

Statista - The Statistics Portal. (n.d.). Statista. https://www.statista.com

Stauss, B. (1997). Global word of mouth: Service bashing on the internet is a thorny issue. *Marketing Management*, 6(3), 28–30.

Stauss, B. (2000). Using new media for customer interaction: a challenge for relationship marketing. In Hennig-Thurau, T., & Hansen, U. (Eds.), *Relationship Marketing* (pp. 233–253). Springer. 10.1007/978-3-662-09745-8_13

Stoeckli, E., Dremel, C., & Uebernickel, F. (2018). Exploring characteristics and transformational capabilities of insurtech innovations to understand insurance value creation in a digital world. *Electronic Markets*, 28(3), 287–305. 10.1007/s12525-018-0304-7

Streamlyn Academy. (2023, September 29). *A Comprehensive Uber Eats Case Study-2023*. Streamlyn Academy. https://streamlynacademy.com/blog/uber-eats-case-study/Tyagi, J. V. A. G. (2022, June 29). *The curious case of Uber India's Rs 721 Cr profit jump in FY20*. Entrackr. https://entrackr.com/2021/04/the-curious-case-of-uber-indias-rs-721-cr-profit-jump-in-fy20/

Subramani, M. R., & Rajagopalan, B. (2003). Knowledge-sharing and influence in online social networks via viral marketing. *Communications of the ACM*, 46(12), 300–307. 10.1145/953460.953514

Su, J., & Yang, W. (2023). AI literacy curriculum and its relation to children's perceptions of robots and attitudes towards engineering and science: An intervention study in early childhood education. *Journal of Computer Assisted Learning*, 40(1), 241–253. 10.1111/jcal.12867

Su, J., & Zhong, Y. (2022). Artificial intelligence (AI) in early childhood education: Curriculum design and future directions. *Computers and Education: Artificial Intelligence*, 3, 100072. 10.1016/j.caeai.2022.100072

Sun, X., Zhang, X., & Xia, Z. (2021). Artificial intelligence and security. In: *Proceedings of ICAIS: International Conference on Artificial Intelligence and Security*. Research Gate.

Sundaram, D. S., Mitra, K., & Webster, C. (1998). Word-of-mouth communications: A motivational analysis. *Advances in Consumer Research. Association for Consumer Research (U. S.)*, 25, 527–531.

Sundqvist, B., & Ohanisian, J. (2023). *Utilization of AI in Digital Marketing: An empirical study of Artificial Intelligence and the impact of effectiveness, ethics and regulations.*

Surovková, J., Haluzová, S., Strunga, M., Urban, R., Lifková, M., & Thurzo, A. (2023). The New Role of the Dental Assistant and Nurse in the Age of Advanced Artificial Intelligence in Telehealth Orthodontic Care with Dental Monitoring: Preliminary Report. *Applied Sciences (Basel, Switzerland)*, 13(8), 5212. 10.3390/app13085212

Sutton, D. (2018). How AI helped one retailer reach new customers. *Harvard Business Review*. https://hbr.org/2018/05/howai-helped-one-retailer-reach-new-customers

Sweeney, J. C., Soutar, G. N., & Mazzarol, T. (2008). Factors influencing word of mouth effectiveness: Receiver perspectives. *European Journal of Marketing*, 42(3/4), 344–364. 10.1108/03090560810852977

Tang, C. (2023). *Innovation of ideological and political education based on artificial intelligence technology with wireless network*. ICST Transactions on Scalable Information Systems. 10.4108/eetsis.3829

Tariq, E., Alshurideh, M., Akour, I., & Al-Hawary, S. (2022). The effect of digital marketing capabilities on organizational ambidexterity of the information technology sector. *International Journal of Data and Network Science*, 6(2), 401–408.

Tatlow-Golden, M., & Garde, A. (2020). Digital food marketing to children: Exploitation, surveillance and rights violations. *Global Food Security*, 27, 100423.

Taweewattanakunanon, R., & Darawong, C. (2022). The influence of employer branding in luxury hotels in Thailand and its effect on employee job satisfaction, loyalty, and intention to recommend. *Journal of Human Resources in Hospitality & Tourism*, 21(4), 501–523. 10.1080/15332845.2022.2106612

Technology Review Insights, M. I. T. (2020). *The global AI agenda: North America*. MIT Technology Review. mittrinsights.s3.amazonaws.com/AIagenda2020/NAAIagenda.pdf

Teng, H., Tian, W., & Wang, H. (2022). Applications of the decentralized finance (DeFi) on the ethereum. In: *Proceedings of IEEE Asia-Pacific Conference on Image Processing, Electronics and Computers (IPEC)*. IEEE. 10.1109/IPEC54454.2022.9777543

Thomas, I. (2021). Planning for a cookie-less future: How browser and mobile privacy changes will impact marketing, targeting and analytics. *Applied marketing analytics*, 7(1), 6-16.

Thrun, S., & Pratt, L. (2012). Learning to Speak: AI tutors for language learning. *AI Magazine*, 33(3), 63–64.

Topol, E. J. (2019). High-performance medicine: The convergence of human and artificial intelligence. *Nature Medicine*, 25(1), 44–56. 10.1038/s41591-018-0300-730617339

Triantafillidou, E., & Tsiaras, S. (2018). Exploring entrepreneurship, innovation and tourism development from a sustainable perspective: Evidence from Greece. *J. Int. Bus. Ent. Dev.*, 11(1), 53–64. 10.1504/JIBED.2018.090020

Tripathi, S., & Verma, S. (2018). Social media, an emerging platform for relationship building: A study of engagement with nongovernment organizations in India. *International Journal of Nonprofit and Voluntary Sector Marketing*, 23(1), e1589. 10.1002/nvsm.1589

Troise, C., & Tani, M. (2021). Exploring entrepreneurial characteristics, motivations and behaviours in equity crowdfunding: Some evidence from Italy. *Management Decision*, 59(5), 995–1024. 10.1108/MD-10-2019-1431

Trusov, M., Bucklin, R. E., & Pauwels, K. (2009). Effects of word-of-mouth versus traditional marketing: Findings from an internet social networking site. *Journal of Marketing*, 73(5), 90–102. 10.1509/jmkg.73.5.90

Tucker, A., Wang, Z., Rotalinti, Y., & Myles, P. (2020). Generating high-fidelity synthetic patient data for assessing machine learning healthcare software. *npj. Digital Medicine*, 3(1), 147. 10.1038/s41746-020-00353-933299100

Tyagi, S., & Rathore, R. (2023). Unveiling the Dynamic Journey from Data Insights to Action in Data Science. *2023 IEEE International Conference on Research Methodologies in Knowledge Management, Artificial Intelligence and Telecommunication Engineering, RMKMATE 2023*. IEEE. 10.1109/RMKMATE59243.2023.10369698

UNESCO. (2020). *Steering AI and advanced ICTs for knowledge societies: A rights, openness, access, and multistakeholder perspective*. UNESCO.

VanLehn, K. (2011). The relative effectiveness of human tutoring, intelligent tutoring systems, and other tutoring systems. *Educational Psychologist*, 46(4), 197–221. 10.1080/00461520.2011.611369

Veloso, C. M., Walter, C. E., Sousa, B., Au-Yong-Oliveira, M., Santos, V., & Valeri, M. (2021). Academic tourism and transport services: Student perceptions from a social responsibility perspective. *Sustainability (Basel)*, 13(16), 8794. 10.3390/su13168794

Venkatesh, V., Morris, M. G., Davis, G. B., & Davis, F. D. (2003). User Acceptance of Information Technology: Toward a Unified View. *Management Information Systems Quarterly*, 27(3), 425–478. 10.2307/30036540

Veríssimo, D., Vieira, S., Monteiro, D., Hancock, J., & Nuno, A. (2020). Audience research as a cornerstone of demand management interventions for illegal wildlife products: Demarketing sea turtle meat and eggs. *Conservation Science and Practice*, 2(3), e164. 10.1111/csp2.164

Verma, S. (2014). Online customer engagement through blogs in India. *Journal of Internet Commerce*, 13(3-4), 282–301. 10.1080/15332861.2014.961347

Verma, S., Sharma, R., Deb, S., & Maitra, D. (2021). Artificial intelligence in marketing: Systematic review and future research direction. *International Journal of Information Management Data Insights*, 1(1), 100002. 10.1016/j.jjimei.2020.100002

Verma, S., & Yadav, N. (2021). Past, present, and future of electronic word of mouth (EWOM). *Journal of Interactive Marketing*, 53, 111–128. 10.1016/j.intmar.2020.07.001

Vesselinov, R., & Grego, J. (2012). *Duolingo effectiveness study*. Duolingo Inc.

Vlačić, B., Corbo, L., Silva, S. C., & Dabić, M. (2021). The evolving role of artificial intelligence in marketing: A review and research agenda. *Journal of Business Research*, 128, 187–203. 10.1016/j.jbusres.2021.01.055

Compilation of References

Volkmar, G., Fischer, P. M., & Reinecke, S. (2022). Artificial Intelligence and Machine Learning: Exploring drivers, barriers, and future developments in marketing management. *Journal of Business Research*, 149, 599–614. 10.1016/j.jbusres.2022.04.007

Wach, B. A., Wehner, M. C., Weißenberger, B. E., & Kabst, R. (2020). United we stand : HR and line managers' shared views on HR strategic integration. *European Management Journal*. 10.1016/j.emj.2020.09.012

Wache, C., Möller, J., Mafael, A., Daumke, V., Fetahi, B., & Melcher, N. (2021, June). Do Not Buy our Product: Consumers' Responses towards Green-Demarketing Ad Messages: An Abstract. In *Academy of Marketing Science Annual Conference-World Marketing Congress* (pp. 111-112). Cham: Springer International Publishing.

Wang, C. (2011). Analyses of underlying causes on the abnormal marketing ethics of Chinese enterprises. *2011 2nd International Conference on Artificial Intelligence, Management Science and Electronic Commerce, AIMSEC 2011 - Proceedings*. IEEE. 10.1109/AIMSEC.2011.6010191

Wang, C. H., & Juo, W. J. Sustainable environmental performance: The mediating role of green reputation in the choice of green marketing or green demarketing. *Corporate Social Responsibility and Environmental Management*.

Wang, C. J. (2014). Do ethical and sustainable practices matter? Effects of corporate citizenship on business performance in the hospitality industry. *International Journal of Contemporary Hospitality Management*, 26(6), 930–947. 10.1108/IJCHM-01-2013-0001

Wang, C., Zhang, J., Lassi, N., & Zhang, X. (2022). Privacy protection in using artificial intelligence for healthcare: Chinese regulation in comparative perspective. *Health Care*, 10(10), 1878. 10.3390/healthcare1010187836292325

Wang, F., Qin, R., Wang, X., & Hu, B. (2022). Metasocieties in metaverse: Metaeconomics and metamanagement for metaenterprises and metacities. *IEEE Transactions on Computational Social Systems*, 9(1), 2–7. 10.1109/TCSS.2022.3145165

Wang, G., Badal, A., Jia, X., Maltz, J. S., Mueller, K., Myers, K. J., Niu, C., Vannier, M., Yan, P., Yu, Z., & Zeng, R. (2022). Development of metaverse for intelligent healthcare. *Nature Machine Intelligence*, 4(11), 922–929. 10.1038/s42256-022-00549-636935774

Wang, S., Ding, W., Li, J., Yuan, Y., Ouyang, L., & Wang, F.-Y. (2019). Decentralized autonomous organizations: Concept, model, and applications. *IEEE Transactions on Computational Social Systems*, 6(5), 870–878. 10.1109/TCSS.2019.2938190

Wang, X., Lin, X., & Shao, B. (2022). How does artificial intelligence create business agility? Evidence from chatbots. *International Journal of Information Management*, 66(102535), 102535. 10.1016/j.ijinfomgt.2022.102535

Wang, X., & Yang, Z. (2010). The effect of brand credibility on consumers' brand purchase intention in emerging economies: The moderating role of brand awareness and brand image. *Journal of Global Marketing*, 23(3), 177–188. 10.1080/08911762.2010.487419

Wardat, Y., Tashtoush, M., Alali, R., & Saleh, S. (2024). Artificial intelligence in education: Mathematics teachers' perspectives, practices and challenges. *Iraqi Journal For Computer Science and Mathematics*, 5(1), 60–77. 10.52866/ijcsm.2024.05.01.004

Webster, F. E.Jr, & Keller, K. L. (2004). A roadmap for branding in industrial markets. *Journal of Brand Management*, 11(5), 388–402. 10.1057/palgrave.bm.2540184

Weinberger, M. G., & Dillon, W. R. (1980). The effect of unfavourable product rating information. *Advances in Consumer Research. Association for Consumer Research (U. S.)*, 7(1), 528–532.

Westbrook, R. A. (1987). Product/consumption-based affective responses and post purchase process. *JMR, Journal of Marketing Research*, 24(3), 258–270. 10.1177/002224378702400302

Winecoff, A. A., & Watkins, E. A. (2022). Artificial concepts of artificial intelligence: Institutional compliance and resistance in ai startups. *AIES 2022 - Proceedings of the 2022 AAAI/ACM Conference on AI, Ethics, and Society*. ACM. 10.1145/3514094.3534138

Winegar, A. G., & Sunstein, C. R. (2019). How much is data privacy worth? A preliminary investigation. *Journal of Consumer Policy*, 42, 425–440.

Woolf, B. P. (2009). *Building intelligent interactive tutors*. Morgan Kaufmann Publishers Inc.

Woolf, B. P. (2010). *Building intelligent interactive tutors: Student-centered strategies for revolutionizing e-learning*. Morgan Kaufmann.

Wu, P. C. S., Yeh, G. Y. Y., & Hsiao, C. R. (2011). The effect of store image and service quality on brand image and purchase intention for private label brands. *Australasian Marketing Journal*, 19(1), 30–39. 10.1016/j.ausmj.2010.11.001

Wu, Y., Huang, H., Wu, N., Wang, Y., Bhuiyan, M. Z. A., & Wang, T. (2020). An incentive-based protection and recovery strategy for secure big data in social networks. *Information Sciences*, 508, 79–91.

Xia, L., & Bechwati, N. N. (2008). Word of mouth: The role of cognitive personalization in online consumer reviews. *Journal of Interactive Advertising*, 9(1), 108–128. 10.1080/15252019.2008.10722143

Yadav, M. (2023, December 3). *UberEats Business Model: How Does Uber Eats Make Money?* ValueAppz - Blog. https://www.valueappz.com/blog/ubereats-business-model-uber-eats-make-money

Yang, Q., Yuan, Y., Sun, J., & Cai, K. (2011). Semantic P2P-based learning resources personalized recommendation system design. *2011 Third Pacific-Asia Conference on Circuits, Communications and System (PACCS)*. IEEE. 10.1109/PACCS.2011.5990360

Yang, G., Pang, Z., Jamal Deen, M., Dong, M., Zhang, Y., Lovell, N., & Rahmani, A. M. (2020). Homecare robotic systems for healthcare 4.0: Visions and enabling technologies. *IEEE Journal of Biomedical and Health Informatics*, 24(9), 2535–2549. 10.1109/JBHI.2020.299052932340971

Yang, W. (2022). Artificial intelligence education for young children: Why, what, and how in curriculum design and implementation. *Computers and Education: Artificial Intelligence*, 3, 100061. 10.1016/j.caeai.2022.100061

Yang, Z., Schaninger, C. M., & Laroche, M. (2013). Demarketing teen tobacco and alcohol use: Negative peer influence and longitudinal roles of parenting and self-esteem. *Journal of Business Research*, 66(4), 559–567. 10.1016/j.jbusres.2012.01.004

Yawised, K., Apasrawirote, D., & Boonparn, C. (2022). From traditional business shifted towards transformation: The emerging business opportunities and challenges in 'metaverse'era. *INCBAA*, 162, 175.

Yeung, S. C., Lee, W. L., Yue, Y., & Hui, S. C. (2014). Educational data mining: A survey and a data mining-based analysis of recent works. *Expert Systems with Applications*, 41(4), 1432–1462. 10.1016/j.eswa.2013.08.042

Yi, J. (2023). Design and development of personalized education information management system based on artificial intelligence. *Applied Mathematics and Nonlinear Sciences*, 9(1), 20230633. 10.2478/amns.2023.2.00633

Yoo, B., & Donthu, N. (2001). Developing and validating a multidimensional consumer-based brand equity scale. *Journal of Business Research*, 52(1), 1–14. 10.1016/S0148-2963(99)00098-3

Zeithaml, V., Berry, L. L., & Parasuraman, A. (1996). The behavioral consequences of service quality. *Journal of Marketing*, 60(2), 31–46. 10.1177/002224299606000203

Compilation of References

Zetzsche, D. A., Arner, D. W., & Buckley, R. P. (2020). Decentralized finance (DeFi). *J. Fin. Regul.*, 6(Sep), 172–203. 10.1093/jfr/fjaa010

Zhang, B., Ying, L., Khan, M. A., Ali, M., Barykin, S., & Jahanzeb, A. (2023). Sustainable digital marketing: Factors of adoption of m-technologies by older adults in the Chinese market. *Sustainability*, 15(3), 1972.

Zhang, C., & Liu, Z., B.R., A., & A, H. (. (2024). Synergizing language learning: Smalltalk AI in industry 4.0 and education 4.0. *PeerJ. Computer Science*, 10, e1843. 10.7717/peerj-cs.184338435575

Zhang, J., Hassandoust, F., & Williams, J. E. (2020). Online customer trust in the context of the general data protection regulation (GDPR). *Pacific Asia Journal of the Association for Information Systems*, 12(1), 4.

Zhang, R., & Tran, T. (2009). Helping e-commerce consumers make good purchase decisions: a user reviews-based approach. In Babin, G., Kropf, P., & Weiss, M. (Eds.), *E-technologies: Innovation in an Open World* (pp. 1–11). Springer. 10.1007/978-3-642-01187-0_1

Zhou, L., Dai, L., & Zhang, D. (2007). Online shopping acceptance model-a critical survey of consumer factors in online shopping. *Journal of Electronic Commerce Research*, 8(1), 1–41.

Zhu, F., & Zhang, X. (2010). Impact of online consumer reviews on sales: The moderating role of product and consumer characteristics. *Journal of Marketing*, 74(2), 133–148. 10.1509/jm.74.2.133

About the Contributors

Shefali Saluja is a Ph.D. in Corporate Governance from Chitkara University, Punjab, India in 2021. Post Graduate from Chitkara University, Punjab, India with 10 years of experience in business management education and expertise in finance and ethics. She has 4 years of working experience in Ernst & Young Pvt Ltd prior joining academics. She has published almost 14 research papers/articles in highly indexed Scopus journals in the areas of corporate governance, sustainability, E-learning & other areas. She is a member of several management associations such as Association of Certified Fraud Examiner (CFE) and International Association of academic plus corporate (IAAC) society. She serves as business consultant to several higher education institutions and small enterprises like MSMEs in Cirebon, Indonesia. Dr. Shefali has received Woman Trailblazer Award in 2022 for her work in Community service towards financial inclusion of rural sector in Punjab, India and various appreciation awards from the international universities. She has filed 2 patents and 5 copyrights in diverse areas. Her current job position includes various teaching and administrative related responsibilities in Chitkara university. Dr Shefali was also invited in many teaching opportunities internationally for teaching a module on "Failing corporates" at Emden University, Germany. She was also invited by Telkom University, Indonesia and Providence University Taiwan to deliver sessions on "Fraud Investigation". She has also delivered a module on "Business in Asia" to the students of Mondragon University, Spain. She has successfully presented research papers in national and international conferences. She is also handling Micro finance and Social Activities with United Nations. The activities are also live on YouTube. She has won best paper awards in the field of corporate governance. Her interests include volunteer work/community involvement at social NGOs in India like Khalsa Aid, AIESEC and Sunshine Youth club.

Varun Nayyar is an academian and motivational speaker. Result oriented, proactive working professional with 15 years of experience, delivered 50+ Guest Lectures in the field of Education and Industry

Kuldeep Rojhe is Dean Academics - CCCE, Chitkara University, Punjab Former Dean Faculty of Management Sciences, Shoolini University. Doctoral in consumer behavior with specialization in customer complaining behavior, have coordinated business schools, developed curriculums, skill development programs & played crucial roles in education management. Led students acquisition, selections, regulatory compliance, industry- academia tie-ups, international collaboration & internship programs, and have developed key skills in higher education management & development. Actively associated with sponsored research projects & consultancy, have publications in National & International journals of repute, edited books and delivered several invited talks at leading forums. Contribution to IPR comprises of one patent granted, two patents filed and ten copyrights registered.

Sandhir Sharma is Ph.D. in Strategic Management with nearly 22 years of experience in higher education and 5 years in Telecom industry. With more than 53 research papers to his credit published in various journals and conferences at national & international level, Dr. Sharma has developed his core expertise in the area of Strategy formulation. Currently, he is serving as Dean, Chitkara Business School & visiting faculty to Binus University, Indonesia, Kedge Business School, France and University of Applied Sciences, Osnabruck, Germany. He is widely travelled all across the globe and an active member of various management associations and University bodies. He is serving as consultant to various SME organizations in the area of strategy formulation. He is Major Guide to 8 Ph.D. Scholars from Academia and Industry. As of now, eight of his students have already completed their Ph.D. successfully in the fields of Neuromarketing| Consumers| Foods| Organic Foods, Work Engagement, Brands |Brands Personality| Brand love, Television |Broadcasting| Digital Television and Green Marketing| Consumer Behaviour. He has filed 14 patents in the fields of Health sciences, life sciences, social sciences, technology, and industrial products.

Abdullah M. Almuhaideb received the B.S. degree (Hons.) in computer information systems from King Faisal University, Saudi Arabia, in 2003, and the M.S. (Hons.) and Ph.D. degrees in network security from Monash University, Melbourne, Australia, in 2007 and 2013, respectively. He is currently an Associate Professor in information security, a Supervisor with the Saudi Aramco Cybersecurity Chair, and the Dean of the College of Computer Science and Information Technology, at Imam Abdulrahman Bin Faisal University, Saudi Arabia. He received several honors, including the Imam Abdulrahman Bin Faisal University President's Award for the highest research publications at the college level and sixth place on the university's list of distinguished researchers for the year 2021. He has published two patents and more than 50 scientific articles in peer-reviewed international journals and premier ACM/IEEE/Springer conferences. His research interests include mobile security, ubiquitous wireless access, authentication, and identification.

About the Contributors

Gurwinder Singh Badal is an Assistant Professor at the Faculty of Economics, Chitkara University, Punjab, India. He completed his Ph.D. in Economics from Punjabi University Patiala on the topic 'Rural-Urban Migration and Changing Pattern of Urban Labor Market: A Study of Punjab'. His research interests include Labor Economics, Development Economics, Urban Planning, and Migration Studies. Before joining Chitkara University, Dr. Badal worked as a Postdoctoral Fellow at Punjabi University Patiala, sponsored by the Indian Council of Social Science Research, studying the impact of COVID-19 on internal migrants in Punjab. Dr. Badal has over a decade of research and teaching experience. He has coordinated workshops, a national colloquium participated in numerous seminars and conferences, and worked as a research associate in various research projects funded by agencies like UGC and ICSSR. His skills include statistical software like STATA, R, and EViews. With a strong academic background and research acumen, Dr. Badal continues to make significant contributions to the fields of migration studies and labor economics.

Ajay Chandel is working as an Assistant Professor at Mittal School of Business, Lovely Professional University, Punjab. He has 12 years of teaching experience. He has 12 years of teaching and research experience. He has published papers in SCOPUS, WOS and UGC listed Journals in areas like Social Media marketing, E-Commerce and Consumer Behaviour. He has published cases on SMEs and Social Entrepreneurship in The Case Centre, UK. He is also a reviewer of The Case Journal, Emerald Group Publishing and International Journal of Business and Globalisation, Inderscience. He has authored and developed MOOCs on Tourism and Hospitality Marketing under Epg-Pathshala- A gateway to all Post Graduate courses (an UGC-MHRD project under its National Mission on Education Through ICT (NME-ICT).

Praveen Chowdary is an MBA student at Mittal School of Business, Lovely Professional University. A budding research, he is working on research publications that revolve around sustainability and SDGs. He is curious to study the role of technology in achieving SDGs.

Krishan Gopal works as an Associate Professor at Mittal School of Business (MHRD NIRF India Rank 34; ACBSP USA, Accredited), Lovely Professional University, Phagwara, Punjab (India). He received his Ph.D degree from Lovely Professional University Punjab in 2020. His interest in teaching and research includes Business Research Methods, Strategic Management, and Consumer Behaviour. Dr. Krishan Gopal has published 13 research papers in refereed national and international journals, 12 book chapters and cases, edited one book, attended various national and international seminars and acted as a resource person in a refresher course on mixed research methods. He has written 4 chapters of "Tourism and Hospitality Marketing," available on "e-PG-Pathshala,"- a Project of UGC (MHRD).

Shveta Gupta is B.A. (Hons.), M.A. (Economics), M.Phil. (Economics), B. Ed., HTET qualified, Ph.D (Economics). She started her career in Teaching in 2006 from Indira Gandhi Mahila Mahavidyalaya, Kaithal. She has also served at R.K.S.D.(P.G.) College, Kaithal for more than 14 years, having more than 17 years of teaching experience. So far, she has authored a book, designed 5 patents, received 1 utility patent, registered 7 copyrights, published various papers in Scopus and UGC Care listed journals. She has attended more than 15 FDPs, 15 Workshops and 37 National and International Conferences/ Seminars/ Webinars at International and National levels. She is also a Member of INDIAN ECONOMIC ASSOCIATION. Recently, actively completed Two Refresher Course on "Advanced Research Methodology Tools and Techniques" and "MOOCS" from Ramanujan College, University of Delhi. She has been Organising Secretary of G20 University Connect Program, Two-Week Workshop on Econometric Research, National Colloquium on Union Budget 2024 (Pre Budget-Expectations) and various Industrial visits and Study Tour including National Institute of Securities Market, Mumbai. Appointed and Served as Staff Secretary for three consecutive years. She has been the Head of Advisory Committee, Women Cell, Career Counselling Cell, Tour Organising Committee etc. Also acted as Stage Coordinator in various events.

Priya Jindal is currently working as an Associate Professor at Chitkara Business School, Chitkara University, Punjab, India and holds a master degree in commerce and economics. She earned her doctorate in management. She has contributed more than 17 years in teaching. She supervised four Ph.D. research scholars and two M.Phil candidates. There are numerous research papers to her credit in leading journals among them seven research paper has been published in Scopus Indexed Journal. Her areas of research included Banking, Finance and insurance. She has filed more than 21 patents and two copyrights. She is the editor of three books under IGI Global and Nova Science publications and the books got indexed in Scopus.

Shalini Kumari is a Scholar in the Department of Computer Science and Engineering at Chitkara University Institute of Engineering and Technology. She has an experience of 2 years in teaching and research. Her area of interest includes AIML, Marketing, Cloud, Data Analytics.

Neha Mishra holds Ph.D. Degree in Business Management and working as Assistant Professor in Chitkara Business School at Chitkara University, India.

Annumeet Nagra is a postgraduate in MCOM, did Bachelor in education and Ph.d too. She has more than 10 years of experience in teaching and has worked in reputed colleges of Jalandhar. Presently, she is working at GNA University, Phagwara as an assistant professor at GNA Business School. She has many research papers to her credit published in various reputed national, international, Scopus indexed and UGC-Care journals. She has also attended many workshops and FDPs to enhance specialization and skill required in her field.

About the Contributors

Anurag Pahuja is currently working as a Professor at Mittal School of Business, Lovely Professional University, Phagwara. She is acting as the Chief Editor of International Journal of Business Ethics in Developing Economies. With a rich experience of more than 24 years in academics, her contribution in the field of Academics has been recognized and awarded the Certificate of Excellence for "Faculty for Exemplary Research in Corporate Governance and Financial Management" during 2nd Intelligentsia Summit (Education Excellence Awards-2016) organized jointly by The Education Post and CIAC-Goal along with CIHF on August 22, 2016 at India International Centre, New Delhi.

Chander Prabha is a Professor in the Department of Computer Science and Engineering at Chitkara University Institute of Engineering and Technology, Chitkara University, Punjab, India. She had done her Ph.D. from M.M. University in Computer Science Engineering in 2017 and her Masters in Engineering from Punjab Engineering College (2004), PEC, Chandigarh, India. A total of 19+ Years of Academic / Research Experience with more than 40+ Publications in various National, International Conferences, and International Journals. She has published many book chapters in CRC Press. She is the Guest Editor Journal of Artificial Intelligence and Internet of Things, Near East University, Turkey. Also, she is a reviewer of many international conferences and Journals of repute. Many online certifications are also there in her credit. She is a Lifetime member of educational societies like ISTE, IAENG, SCIEI, IIRJC, IACSIT etc. Her areas of interest are wireless and mobile networks' architectures, protocols, performance evaluations, Machine learning, data analytics, and Law.

Anju Rohilla is an Assistant Professor at the Department of Business Studies, P.I.E.T, Panipat. She has 5 years of teaching experience. She has done a Ph.D. (Management) from Bhagat Phool Singh MahilaVishwavidyala, Khanpur Kalan, Sonipat. She has done MBA from Guru Jambeshwar University of Science and Technology in Hisar. Her area of interest is on banking fraud. She has delivered ten research presentations at the national conference and published several research papers in national and international journals. She has delivered the workshops on case study analysis.

Saqib Saeed is an Associate Professor with the Department of Computer Information Systems, Imam Abdulrahman Bin Faisal University, Dammam, Saudi Arabia. He received the B.Sc. degree (Hons.) in computer science from International Islamic University Islamabad, Pakistan, in 2001, the M.Sc. degree in software technology from the Stuttgart Technology University of Applied Sciences, Germany, in 2003, and the Ph.D. degree in information systems from the University of Siegen, Germany, in 2012. He is also a Certified Software Quality Engineer from the American Society of Quality. His research interests include human-centered computing, data visualization and analytics, software engineering, information systems management, and digital business transformation. He is also an Associate Editor of IEEE Access and International Journal of Public Administration in the Digital Age, besides being member of the advisory boards of several international journals.

Vasco Santos has a PhD in Business Sciences with specialization in Marketing, Fernando Pesoa University, Porto - Portugal. PhD in Tourism, Seville University, Seville - Spain. Habilitation in Management, Europeia University, Lisbon - Portugal. MSc in Marketing and Tourism Promotion and BA in Hospitality Management. Coordinator Professor of Management, Marketing and Tourism at ISLA Santarém. Coordinator of Master Degree in Business Management, at ISLA Santarém. Coordinator of the Degree in Commercial Management. Researcher in GOVCOPP (Research Unit on Governance, Competitiveness and Public Policies), at Aveiro University, Aveiro, Portugal. Researcher in CiTUR – Center for Tourism Research, Development and Innovation. Author of scientific papers and book chapters. Research areas: marketing, innovation, digital, sustainability, wine tourism, employer branding.

Kavya Shabu is a seasoned professional specializing in Business Analytics and Research Methodology, and holds a notable UGC NET JRF qualification. Accomplishments include the successful completion of an extensive research period at the University of Kerala, where they delved into the realm of "Green Financing: The Role of Banking Industry in Kerala." And publishing of articles in reputed journals. The expertise spans in sustainability, climate finance, and the digitalization of banking and financial technologies.

Anjali Sharma, Ph.D., is an Assistant Professor at Chitkara University, specializing in Corporate Governance with a focus on detecting and preventing corporate frauds. With a total of 12 years of experience, including 4 years at Ernst & Young Pvt Ltd and 8 years at Chitkara University, she brings a wealth of expertise to both academia and industry. She holds an MBA in financial markets from Chitkara University and a degree in Economics Honours from Punjab University.

Jaswinder Pal Singh is a researcher at Department of Library and Information Science, Punjabi University, Patiala, India and currently working as a University Librarian at Chitkara University, Punjab - India. He possesses a comprehensive 18-year tenure within the library field, accumulating extensive expertise and proficiency in various aspects of library management, including cataloging, information retrieval, collection development, and patron services. Throughout this substantial duration, he has demonstrated a deep commitment to fostering an enriching environment for patrons, leveraging his wealth of experience to enhance library operations and meet the diverse needs of users. His areas of research include Media and Information Literacy, Knowledge Sharing, Information retrieval, Knowledge Management in Libraries, Collections Development.

About the Contributors

Bruno Barbosa Sousa is Adjunct Professor of Marketing at Polytechnic Institute of Cávado and Ave (IPCA), Portugal and PhD in Marketing and Strategy in Universidade do Minho, Portugal. Head of Masters Program - Tourism Management and Marketing Tourism (IPCA); CiTUR – Center for Tourism Research, Development and Innovation and UNIAG research member. He has published in the Journal of Enterprising Communities, Tourism Management Perspectives, Current Issues in Tourism, Journal of Organizational Change Management, World Review of Entrepreneurship, Management and Sust. Development, among others. Orcid ID: 0000-0002-8588-2422

Index

A

Artificial Intelligence 11, 12, 14, 15, 19, 24, 25, 27, 42, 53, 55, 56, 57, 59, 60, 61, 62, 64, 65, 67, 69, 70, 72, 73, 79, 80, 84, 85, 86, 87, 125, 126, 127, 128, 129, 130, 131, 132, 133, 135, 137, 138, 139, 140, 141, 142, 143, 144, 145, 147, 148, 149, 151, 152, 154, 155, 156, 157, 158, 159, 161, 162, 163, 165, 166, 167, 169, 170, 171, 172, 173, 174, 175, 176, 177, 179, 186, 187, 188, 189, 190, 191, 192, 194, 195, 197, 198, 199, 200, 201, 202, 203, 204, 206, 208, 210, 211, 212, 213, 214, 215, 216, 217, 218, 219, 220, 221, 222, 223, 225, 227, 228, 237, 239, 240

B

Bibliographic coupling 156, 158, 160, 164, 165, 170, 172, 205, 206, 208, 217
Bibliometric Analysis 29, 158, 159, 173, 174, 203, 205, 206, 207, 219
Brand Image 4, 108, 109, 110, 111, 112, 113, 114, 116, 117, 118, 119, 120, 121, 123, 124
BusiFi 46, 47

C

Chatbots 11, 12, 14, 15, 16, 17, 18, 20, 21, 22, 23, 24, 25, 60, 61, 130, 131, 134, 142, 147, 157, 158, 161, 164, 165, 166, 167, 169, 171, 172, 173, 175, 191, 193, 203, 216, 227, 228
ChatGPT 79, 161, 163, 165, 166, 169, 170, 171, 173, 174, 175, 202, 212, 213, 218, 220, 227, 228, 239, 240
Co-citation analysis 156, 160, 161, 164, 172, 205, 206, 208, 211, 217
Consumer Behaviour 14, 26, 132, 136
Contraction Marketing 29
co-occurrence 156, 158, 160, 168, 172, 205, 206, 208, 215, 217
Cryptocurrency 44
cybersecurity 19, 82, 85, 86, 87, 214

D

data security 19, 22, 53, 56, 57, 68, 71, 143, 169, 187, 188, 196, 224
Demarketing 26, 27, 28, 29, 33, 36, 37, 38, 39, 40

digital era 42, 125, 138, 192, 200
Digital Marketing 11, 12, 13, 14, 15, 19, 20, 21, 22, 24, 71, 72, 73, 74, 77, 78, 79, 80, 81, 82, 83, 84, 85, 86, 87, 200, 203, 241, 242, 243, 244, 245, 246, 247, 248, 250, 251, 252, 253, 255

E

E-Commerce 18, 19, 56, 57, 62, 69, 85, 86, 87, 122, 124, 128, 131, 134, 197, 242, 255
Ethical Considerations 77, 141, 144, 149, 164, 165, 169, 186, 188, 189, 191, 196, 201, 218, 225, 226, 229, 237, 240, 245, 252
Ethics 1, 2, 3, 5, 6, 7, 9, 10, 24, 62, 65, 69, 73, 83, 84, 85, 86, 87, 140, 156, 161, 165, 167, 169, 171, 172, 174, 186, 187, 188, 189, 190, 191, 192, 194, 197, 198, 200, 201, 202, 203, 204, 241, 242, 244, 245, 247, 248, 252, 254, 255
e-WOM 108, 109, 110, 112, 113, 114, 116, 118, 119

F

FanFi 46
fiscal deficits 177, 178, 179
Food Delivery 89, 90, 91, 92, 96, 97, 100, 101, 102

G

GemeFi 46
Generative AI 158, 165, 167, 169, 171, 172, 173
government revenue 177

H

Healthcare 57, 58, 83, 135, 144, 169, 190, 191, 201, 202, 205, 206, 207, 208, 210, 211, 212, 213, 214, 215, 216, 217, 218, 219, 220, 221, 222, 227, 228
Hospitality 1, 2, 3, 4, 5, 8, 9, 10, 123, 126

I

IndFi 47
Industrial 4.0 125, 132

L

Learning Experience 140, 141, 143, 144, 146, 147, 148, 150, 151, 152, 153, 224

M

Market Expansion 90, 93

MediaFi 47, 48
MetaAd 48

N

Natural Language Processing 11, 12, 15, 22, 23, 57, 61, 80, 127, 140, 142, 143, 144, 170, 192, 198, 213, 218, 224, 233, 236

P

Personalized Learning 141, 142, 143, 146, 150, 151, 152, 157, 169, 226, 230, 232, 233, 234, 235, 237
personalized services 125, 126, 127, 132
Psychological perspectives 226, 230
public debt 177, 178, 182, 183
Purchase Intentions 108, 109, 114, 119, 121, 123

R

RegFi 47

S

Smart Contracts 44, 46, 47, 48, 197
sustainable digital marketing 71, 72, 73, 81, 82, 83, 85, 86, 87

T

Thematic analysis 164
Tourism 1, 2, 3, 5, 7, 8, 9, 10, 26, 27, 29, 32, 33, 35, 36, 38, 39, 123
Truthful Branding 241, 247

U

Uber Eats 89, 90, 91, 92, 93, 94, 95, 96, 97, 98, 99, 100, 101, 102
UNESCO 189, 190, 197, 229, 236, 237, 240

V

Violation of copyright 244

Publishing Tomorrow's Research Today

Uncover Current Insights and Future Trends in
Business & Management
with IGI Global's Cutting-Edge Recommended Books

Print Only, E-Book Only, or Print + E-Book.
Order direct through IGI Global's Online Bookstore at **www.igi-global.com** or through your preferred provider.

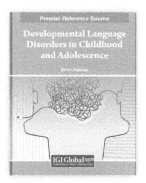

ISBN: 9798369306444
© 2023; 436 pp.
List Price: US$ **230**

ISBN: 9798369300084
© 2023; 358 pp.
List Price: US$ **250**

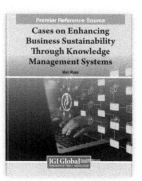

ISBN: 9781668458594
© 2023; 366 pp.
List Price: US$ **240**

ISBN: 9781668486344
© 2023; 256 pp.
List Price: US$ **280**

ISBN: 9781668493243
© 2024; 318 pp.
List Price: US$ **250**

ISBN: 9798369304181
© 2023; 415 pp.
List Price: US$ **250**

Do you want to stay current on the latest research trends, product announcements, news, and special offers?
Join IGI Global's mailing list to receive customized recommendations, exclusive discounts, and more.
Sign up at: **www.igi-global.com/newsletters**.

Scan the QR Code here to view more related titles in Business & Management.

www.igi-global.com | Sign up at www.igi-global.com/newsletters | facebook.com/igiglobal | twitter.com/igiglobal | linkedin.com/igiglobal

Ensure Quality Research is Introduced to the Academic Community

Become a Reviewer for IGI Global Authored Book Projects

 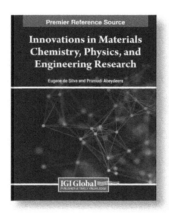 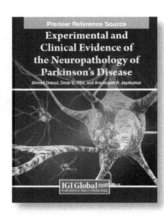 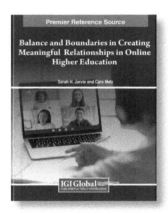

The overall success of an authored book project is dependent on quality and timely manuscript evaluations.

Applications and Inquiries may be sent to:
development@igi-global.com

Applicants must have a doctorate (or equivalent degree) as well as publishing, research, and reviewing experience. Authored Book Evaluators are appointed for one-year terms and are expected to complete at least three evaluations per term. Upon successful completion of this term, evaluators can be considered for an additional term.

If you have a colleague that may be interested in this opportunity, we encourage you to share this information with them.

IGI Global's Open Access Journal Program

Publishing Tomorrow's Research Today

Including Nearly 200 Peer-Reviewed, Gold (Full) Open Access Journals across IGI Global's Three Academic Subject Areas: Business & Management; Scientific, Technical, and Medical (STM); and Education

Consider Submitting Your Manuscript to One of These Nearly 200 Open Access Journals for to Increase Their Discoverability & Citation Impact

Web of Science Impact Factor 6.5	Web of Science Impact Factor 4.7	Web of Science Impact Factor 3.2	Web of Science Impact Factor 2.6

JOURNAL OF
Organizational and End User Computing

JOURNAL OF
Global Information Management

INTERNATIONAL JOURNAL ON
Semantic Web and Information Systems

JOURNAL OF
Database Management

Choosing IGI Global's Open Access Journal Program Can Greatly Increase the Reach of Your Research

Higher Usage
Open access papers are 2-3 times more likely to be read than non-open access papers.

Higher Download Rates
Open access papers benefit from 89% higher download rates than non-open access papers.

Higher Citation Rates
Open access papers are 47% more likely to be cited than non-open access papers.

Submitting an article to a journal offers an invaluable opportunity for you to share your work with the broader academic community, fostering knowledge dissemination and constructive feedback.

Submit an Article and Browse the IGI Global Call for Papers Pages

We can work with you to find the journal most well-suited for your next research manuscript. For open access publishing support, contact: journaleditor@igi-global.com

Recommended Titles from our e-Book Collection

Innovation Capabilities and Entrepreneurial Opportunities of Smart Working
ISBN: 9781799887973

Advanced Applications of Generative AI and Natural Language Processing Models
ISBN: 9798369305027

Using Influencer Marketing as a Digital Business Strategy
ISBN: 9798369305515

Human-Centered Approaches in Industry 5.0
ISBN: 9798369326473

Modeling and Monitoring Extreme Hydrometeorological Events
ISBN: 9781668487716

Data-Driven Intelligent Business Sustainability
ISBN: 9798369300497

Information Logistics for Organizational Empowerment and Effective Supply Chain Management
ISBN: 9798369301593

Data Envelopment Analysis (DEA) Methods for Maximizing Efficiency
ISBN: 9798369302552

Request More Information, or Recommend the IGI Global e-Book Collection to Your Institution's Librarian

For More Information or to Request a Free Trial, Contact IGI Global's e-Collections Team: eresources@igi-global.com | 1-866-342-6657 ext. 100 | 717-533-8845 ext. 100

Are You Ready to Publish Your Research?

IGI Global offers book authorship and editorship opportunities across three major subject areas, including Business, STM, and Education.

Benefits of Publishing with IGI Global:

- Free one-on-one editorial and promotional support.
- Expedited publishing timelines that can take your book from start to finish in less than one (1) year.
- Choose from a variety of formats, including Edited and Authored References, Handbooks of Research, Encyclopedias, and Research Insights.
- Utilize IGI Global's eEditorial Discovery® submission system in support of conducting the submission and double-blind peer review process.
- IGI Global maintains a strict adherence to ethical practices due in part to our full membership with the Committee on Publication Ethics (COPE).
- Indexing potential in prestigious indices such as Scopus®, Web of Science™, PsycINFO®, and ERIC – Education Resources Information Center.
- Ability to connect your ORCID iD to your IGI Global publications.
- Earn honorariums and royalties on your full book publications as well as complimentary content and exclusive discounts.

Learn More at: www.igi-global.com/publish
or Contact IGI Global's Aquisitions Team at: acquisition@igi-global.com

Milton Keynes UK
Ingram Content Group UK Ltd.
UKHW051602021224
3319UKWH00046B/1473